PANAMA

By Nicholas Gill

FROMMER'S STAR RATINGS SYSTEM

Every hotel, restaurant, and attraction listed in this guide has been ranked for quality and value. Here's what the stars mean:

 ★ Recommended
★★ Highly Recommended
★★★ A must! Don't miss!

AN IMPORTANT NOTE

The world is a dynamic place. Hotels change ownership, restaurants hike their prices, museums alter their opening hours, and busses and trains change their routings. And all of this can occur in the several months after our authors have visited, inspected, and written about, these hotels, restaurants, museums and transportation services. Though we have made valiant efforts to keep all our information fresh and up-to-date, some few changes can inevitably occur in the periods before a revised edition of this guidebook is published. So please bear with us if a tiny number of the details in this book have changed. Please also note that we have no responsibility or liability for any inaccuracy or errors or omissions, or for inconvenience, loss, damage, or expenses suffered by anyone as a result of assertions in this guide.

CONTENTS

Panama City's Casco Viejo or Old Town

THE BEST OF PANAMA

F or such a thin squiggle of land, Panama offers travelers a surprisingly diverse selection of landscapes, cultures, and experiences.

In Panama City alone, modern skyscrapers contrast with 18th-century architecture, and a 10-minute cab ride from downtown puts you deep into rainforest teeming with wildlife. From the cool, fertile highlands in the Chiriquí region to the thick lowland jungle and white-sand beaches of Panama's tropical islands, this tiny nation packs fun and adventure into a small package. In addition, Panama boasts a rich history and a melting pot of cultures, including seven indigenous groups, many of whom maintain their customs today. Best of all, the country is gloriously free of tourists. But get here soon—Panama is far too attractive to stay a secret for long.

PANAMA'S best AUTHENTIC EXPERIENCES

o **Eating Ceviche at the Mercado de Mariscos** (Panama City): Have a taste of the rich waters off the country's Pacific coastline with a sample of ceviche, finely diced and marinated fish and/or shellfish, from a Styrofoam cup sold at one of the many carts in Panama City's most famous market. If the tall glass jars and piles of just-caught seafood on ice is a bit too raw an experience for you, step outside to the slightly more formal market stalls with full menus of seafood dishes. See p. 79.

o **Walking Through a Coffee Plantation on the Barú Volcano** (Chiriquí Highlands): The rugged, 3,505m (11,500-ft.) Barú volcano, the highest point in the country, is the centerpiece of **Volcán Barú National Park** and a "bioclimatic island." It's home to a wild, dense rainforest packed with bamboo gardens and towering trees dripping with vines and sprouting bromeliads and orchids from its trunks and branches. Near Boquete, the slopes of the volcano are home to some of the most prized coffee plantations in the world. See p. 169.

o **Exploring the Canal Zone** (near Panama City): Seeing the modern marvel of engineering that is the canal will show you how

A freighter passes through the locks at the Panama Canal.

powerful a force human beings are on this planet. Fittingly, this manmade wonder is enveloped in some of the most pristine wilderness in Central America. See p. 92.

o **Visiting Emberá Villages by Dugout Canoe** (Chagres River, near Panama City): This adventure trip through the jungle-choked Chagres River by motorized dugout canoe to an Emberá Indian village feels worlds away from Panama City. Along the way, guides keep an eye out for wildlife such as monkeys and birds. The Emberá's rustic villages, handicrafts, and temporary *jagua*-stain "tattoos" fascinate kids and adults alike. See p. 99.

o **Living like the Kuna Yala** (Comarca Kuna Yala): This tropical paradise, with more than 350 idyllic islands and islets ringed in white sand, coral gardens, and mangrove swamps, is often populated with not much more than slender coconut palms and a few thatch-roofed huts of the Kuna indigenous community. Along the coast, some of Panama's wildest jungle can be explored on hikes arranged by local tour guides, but most visitors come just to soak in the warm breezes and cool turquoise waters. See p. 213.

o **Whale-Watching in the Gulf of Chiriquí** (Western Panama): The deep waters and sheltered bays and islets in the Gulf of Chiriquí and Coiba National Park attract whales from both the northern and southern hemispheres to mate and calf. Your best chance of seeing humpback, fin, or pilot whales are between the months of August and November, when they come so close they can sometimes be seen from the shore. See p. 180.

o **Watching the Diablos and Congos Dance** (Portobelo): This folkloric dance is performed by the descendants of the *cimarrones,* the runaway slaves who fiercely fought for their freedom during the Spanish colonial period, in this port where the Afro-Panamanian legacy runs deep. The routines feature lively drum beats, colorful and often outrageous costumes, lavish masks, chants, and songs. They are performed during the Carnaval period, though **Casa Congo** (© **202-0880**) in Portobelo can set up performances for groups during the rest of the year. See p. 110.

Crowds celebrating Carnaval in Las Tablas.

o **Experience Carnaval in Las Tablas** (Panama City): Although Panama City's Carnaval is more of a typical metropolitan party, this colonial town in the Azuero Peninsula holds a more traditional festival. The atmosphere is enlivened by an intense rivalry between "high street" and "low street," with each side vying to have the most creative costumes and floats. See p. 143.

PANAMA'S best HOTELS

With a landscape defined by beaches, mountains, jungles, islands, and urban areas, Panama has one of the most diverse sets of accommodations of any country. In Panama City, glass towers and boutique hotels dominate, though a drive just outside the city reveals a world of rainforest ecolodges, thatched beach huts, bird-watching resorts, and coffee haciendas.

The skyscraper-studded face of Panama City.

Over-water bungalows at Punta Caracol.

o **Canopy Lodge & Canopy Tower** (El Valle de Antón & Soberanía National Park): Birders flock to these two ecolodges (just 25 minutes from Panama City, but worlds away in ambiance) for their location in habitats friendly to a wide range of species. The **Canopy Tower,** a remodeled military radar station in thick jungle, is a cross between a stylish B&B and a scientific research center. The **Canopy Lodge** is more luxurious, with a minimalist design that blends into the forested surroundings. Outstanding birding guides, a well-stocked library, day trips, and chats are a part of the stay. See p. 102 and p. 132.

o **American Trade Hotel** (Panama City): U.S.–based Ace Hotels' first foray into the region is this beautifully restored 1917 Casco Viejo building. Rooms are styled with reclaimed wood furniture and paneled walls. A terrace pool, restaurant, and jazz club on property make it oh so hard to leave. See p. 70.

o **Tranquilo Bay** (Bocas del Toro): Embraced by lush jungle and fronted by a thicket of mangroves, this resort, a haven for adventurers, is the most upscale lodging option in Bocas del Toro. The idea here is to provide activities that go where no other tour operator goes, including river kayaking on the mainland, snorkeling in remote areas, jungle hikes, and visits to remote beaches. The simply designed cabins offer plush interiors with high-quality beds and spacious bathrooms. See p. 206.

o **Punta Caracol** (Bocas del Toro): It may not be the most upscale lodging option on Bocas del Toro, but its seclusion and romantic ambience make Punta Caracol a great choice for honeymooners willing to rough it a bit. The property consists of nine well-designed, two-story bungalows. Guests can jump right into the water (literally at your feet) for a bit of snorkeling or rent a kayak for a couple of hours. See p. 198.

o **El Otro Lado** (Portobelo): This all-inclusive design hotel, reached only by boat across Portobelo harbor, is one of the most unexpected luxury accommodations in the country. The posh casitas are filled with luxe amenities and local artwork, while outside the property is a wonderland of mosaic

The interior of San Francisco de La Montaña Church in Varaguas Province.

tiles, lush green jungle, and a network of water features that range from an infinity pool to canals. See p. 111.

o **La Loma Jungle Lodge** (Bocas del Toro): No other lodge (and chocolate farm) envelops you more in nature than this one—it's like playing Tarzan and Jane. Sleeping in an open-air, thatched-roof bungalow is not for everyone, but the cabins are stylish, and two sit high in the forest canopy, with sweeping views. The lodge has guided nature and cultural visits with Ngöbe-Buglé Indians, organic meals, and an on-site butterfly farm. See p. 205.

o **Finca Lérida** (Boquete): In Panama, the best place to escape the heat of the coast is in the highlands of the west, particularly around the coffee-growing town of Boquete. Every room at this cushy, Swiss-style mountain lodge features a balcony and hammock. Gastronomy is a key feature, with a restaurant from a renowned Spanish chef and estate-grown coffee that has been exported since the 1920s. See p. 171.

o **Gamboa Rainforest Resort** (Gamboa): It's billed as an ecoresort, but the Gamboa is more of a "destination megaresort" appealing equally to travelers seeking communion with nature as to those who just want to be surrounded by nature while kicking back at the pool. Guided nature tours include jungle boat cruises, an aerial tram ride through the rainforest, and a minizoo of reptile, butterfly, and marine species. It also has a full-service spa. See p. 102.

PANAMA'S best RESTAURANTS

o **Manolo Caracol** (Panama City): The city's original farm-to-table restaurant features an adventurous daily menu that embraces in-season products and

Intímo restaurant.

Azuero Peninsula seafood. Sit back in the colonial, artsy ambience and wait for a "surprise" of 12 courses to be ushered to your table. See p. 76.

o **Maito** (Panama City): The best restaurant in the country. Chef Mario Castrellón's flagship has helped usher in a new wave of modern Panamanian cuisine, propelling the country's restaurant scene into the international spotlight. Expect innovative tasting menus that rival anything you might find in Peru or Mexico. See p. 73.

o **Donde Jose?** (Panama City): The hardest table to get in Panama City is this barely noticeable, ultra-chic 16-seat restaurant on a Casco Viejo corner. Chef Jose Olmedo Carles has just two seatings a night, 5 days a week, for elegant tasting menus (paired with wine and cocktails) that explore rare Panamanian ingredients. See p. 75.

o **Intimo** (Panama City): Chef-owner Carlos Chombolin Alba turned a long-vacant ranch-style house in the San Francisco neighborhood into the city's most surreal dining experience. Out in the back a small farm supplies much of the produce for a roster of adventurous dishes. The cocktail program is probably the best in town. See p. 73.

o **Madrigal** (Panama City): When Michelin-starred Spanish chef Andrés Madrigal opened this sleek Casco Viejo restaurant a few years ago, it

Monuments and churches adorn Panama City's Old Town.

caught everyone off guard. What caught everyone even *more* off guard? His love of Panamanian ingredients. See p. 75.

o **Mansa** (Buenaventura): This laid-back coastal Panamanian restaurant with Mediterranean touches is worth the drive out to the beach. Wood-fired pizzas, octopus, and possibly the best curried red snapper in the history of the world are all on the menu. See p. 128.

- **Hotel Panamonte Restaurant** (Boquete): This sanctuary of gourmet cuisine is located within the clapboard walls of the oldest hotel in Boquete. The food is inventive and consistently good, and service is attentive and courteous. You can bypass the more formal dining area for a comfy seat in the fireside bar and still order off the main menu. See p. 175.

A Kuna woman stands in front of hanging molas, traditional fabrics made by her tribe.

- **Receta Michilá** (Isla Carenero, Bocas del Toro): Perhaps no restaurant in Panama tells the story of its cuisine better than this laidback, tasting-menu-only restaurant with a handful of tables beside a hostal. After years working in top Parisian restaurants, Chef Joseph Archibold opted to start a restaurant rescuing the recipes (and utilizing the local produce) of his birthplace of Bocas. He literally opened in the same kitchen that his parents once operated as a seafood restaurant. See p. 201.

- **Restaurante Cuatro** (David): David is probably the last place you would expect to find a contemporary restaurant with one of Panama's most skilled chefs. Yet here it is, in an old house in the Doleguita neighborhood. Luis Mendizábal's creative menus showcase the regional ingredients of Chiriquí, which has some the richest farmland, forests, and seas in all of Panama. See p. 154.

PANAMA'S best BEACHES

In spite of the hundreds of kilometers of coastline on both the Caribbean Sea and Pacific Ocean, Panama's beaches (with a few exceptions) are less than noteworthy. To find glorious tropical beaches, you'll need to visit Panama's islands. You'll have plenty to choose from: More than 1,000 are located on the Pacific side and a little more than half that number on the Caribbean. *A word*

San Blas Island in Comarca Kuna Yala.

of caution: Panama is renowned for its riptides. No matter how refreshing the water looks, analyze conditions, stay out of choppy water, or head to a beach known for calm water.

Panama's basilisk lizard.

o **Comarca Kuna Yala (San Blas Archipelago):** This is *the* premier beach destination in Panama, with over 350 islands scattered off the Caribbean Coast that offer picture-postcard beaches with powdery white sand, coral reef, piercing turquoise water, and clusters of swaying palm trees. The colorful Kuna indigenous population administers this province, and their fascinating culture is another good reason to visit. Sorry, scuba diving is prohibited, and lodging is mostly Robinson Crusoe rustic, but all you'll want to do here anyway is swim, sun, and swing in a hammock. See p. 213.

o **Isla Bastimentos National Marine Park, Bocas del Toro:** Cayos Zapatillas, or the "Slippers Islands" (so-called because they resemble footprints), not only fulfill the beach lover's fantasy with their soft sand backed by a tangle of jungle; they are also surrounded by a rich display of coral that attracts hordes of fish, providing good snorkeling. The park's main island, Isla Bastimentos, offers terrific beaches with clean sand and blue water, such as **Red Frog Beach, Wizard Beach,** and **Playa Larga,** which can be reached by a short walk or hike, or by boat during the calm-water season (Aug–Oct). See p. 203.

o **Las Perlas Archipelago:** Despite this Pacific archipelago's proximity to Panama City, its topnotch snorkeling, white-sand beaches, and calm-water swimming conditions, the Pearl Islands are a relatively unsung beach destination, perfect for families with young children. Outside of holidays and the hardcore summer, you won't find crowds here, even on weekends. It's also drier here during the rainy season. **Isla Contadora** offers lodging and day trips for fabulous snorkeling and visits to uninhabited beaches, and **Isla San José** has a luxury lodge, **Hacienda San José.** See p. 115.

Panama Viejo ruins in Panama City.

- **Playa Los Destiladores & Playa Venado, Azuero Peninsula:** Of the multitude of beaches lining the coast of the Azuero Peninsula, these two are the cleanest and the most attractive. Given the deforestation in the area, however, they are less "tropical" than other Panamanian beaches. Currents will occasionally churn up the water at Playa Destiladores, but a protected cove at Playa Venado means it's calm enough for a toddler, and farther east crashing waves have converted the beach into a surfing hotspot. A major bonus here: the nearby picturesque town of Pedasí. See p. 145 and p. 147.
- **Boca Chica Beaches, Chiriquí:** In the Chiriquí lowlands, Boca Chica feels a world (and century) removed from the rest of Panama. Although the beaches themselves aren't the most beautiful, the area's utter seclusion make it a worthy off-the-beaten path destination. See p. 177.
- **Santa Clara & Farallón, Pacific Coast:** These two are the most appealing beaches along the Pacific Coast, and the best for swimming. Better yet, they lie within a 2-hour drive of Panama City, so if you don't plan to go to one of Panama's better beaches, they're worth the drive. Be warned, however, that swimming conditions can be treacherous thanks to large waves and strong riptides. See p. 126 and p. 127.

PANAMA'S best ACTIVE ADVENTURES

- **White-Water Rafting & Kayaking the Chiriquí and Chiriquí Viejo Rivers:** Depending on which section you raft, these two rivers produce serious white water ranging from technical Class III to Class V, some portions of which are so difficult they've been named "Fear" and "Get Out If You Can."

Dancers at an Emberá village.

There are plenty of tamer floats on Class II rivers, such as the Esti, for families and beginners. Virtual solitude, beautiful views, and lush surroundings are part of the tour, too. See p. 168.

o **Surfing Bocas del Toro:** There are plenty of surfing hot spots along the Pacific Coast, especially at Santa Catalina, but Bocas is where surfers find everything from beginner-friendly waves to monster, Hawaii-style waves that reach more than 6m (20 ft.). What's special about Bocas, too, is that the water is clear blue, allowing you to see the reef as you race over it, and it has lots of lodging options, restaurants, and thumping nightlife, unlike in Santa Catalina. Another

The Rainforest Discovery Center.

perk is that the Caribbean tides fluctuate only .9m (3 ft.), whereas the Pacific's fluctuate five times that amount. The waves here are powerful beach breaks, and long, barreling reef point breaks. See p. 194.

o **Diving Around Isla Coiba:** This national park only recently opened to the traveling public—a notorious penal colony that closed here in 2004 kept tourists away, and now the park's virgin waters rate as *the* best diving site in Panama. Isla Coiba is often described as the Galápagos Islands of Panama, and although the snorkeling is outstanding, diving gets you close to pelagics such as white-tipped sharks, sailfish, turtles, manta rays, dolphins, and so much more. Coiba is home to one of the largest coral reefs in the Pacific Coast of the Americas. See p. 182.

o **Trekking the Camino Real:** Centuries before the Panama Canal, the Spanish built an 80km (50-mile) cobblestone path to transport looted gold from the Pacific to galleons waiting in the Caribbean Sea. You can trace their path, much of which still exists in stone, in about 3 days, beginning with a canoe ride up the Chagres River, an overnight in an Emberá Indian Village, and a tramp through earthy jungle full of birds and wildlife to Nombre de Dios, near Portobelo. See chapter 7.

o **Reeling in a Billfish off the Pacific Coast:** Panama's Pacific Coast is legendary for sport fishing, and anglers can battle monster species such as marlin, sailfish, and tuna in the Gulf of Chiriquí and the Gulf of Panama. Near Piñas Bay, the **Tropic Star Lodge** has broken more International Game and Fish Association world records than anywhere else on the planet. See "Fishing" in chapter 5.

- **Kayaking in the Kuna Yala Comarca:** Considering that diving is prohibited in the Kuna Yala, kayaking fills the "sports void," offering travelers a way to intimately explore the mangrove swamps and the undeveloped beauty of the tiny islands this region is famous for. Along the way, kayakers stop at traditional Kuna communities for cultural tours, land-based hiking, and snorkeling. See p. 214.
- **The Panama Rainforest Discovery Center** (near Panama City): A truly amazing experience, the Rainforest Discovery Center has a 40m (130-ft.) observation tower overlooking the dense rainforest canopy on the edge of Soberanía National Park on Pipeline Road, a world-renowned bird-watching hotspot. But you don't have to be a bird-watcher to enjoy the center; you're bound to see plenty of monkeys, butterflies, sloths, and tropical flora—and there's nothing like being high above the rainforest. See p. 101.

PANAMA'S best BIRD-WATCHING

- **Looking for Some 500 Species of Birds Along Pipeline Road in Soberanía National Park:** This is the "celebrity" bird-watching trail for the immense number of species found here. In fact, for several years Pipeline Road has set the world record for 24-hour bird counts. Even non-birders can't help getting caught up in the action with so many colorful show birds fluttering about, such as motmots, trogons, toucans, antbirds, colorful tanagers, and flycatchers. See p. 95.
- **Catching Sight of the Resplendent Quetzal in the Cloud Forests of the Chiriquí Highlands:** Revered by the Aztecs and the Mayans, the iridescent green resplendent quetzal is widely considered to be the most beautiful bird in the Americas. From December to May, the best place to see one is in the cloud forests of **Volcán Barú National Park,** but if you want a near-guarantee, head to **Finca Lérida** (p. 171) in Boquete and have them book a guide—they're the best in the quetzal-spotting business.

- **Being Taken Aback by the Size of the Harpy Eagle in Punta Patiño Nature Reserve:** Panama's national bird is one of the largest eagles in the world, with a wingspan that can reach more than 1.8m (6 ft.). You can't help being struck by this creature's size, though now that

The stunning, and rare, resplendent quetzal.

they're endangered, they're not the easiest birds to spot. Head to Punta Patiño, and your chances soar. See p. 222.

The strawberry poison frog.

o **Grabbing a Cab to View 200+ Species in the Metropolitan Park:** Panama City's Metropolitan Park is the only protected tropical forest found within the city limits of a major urban area in the Americas—a 10-minute cab ride and you're there, checking out orange-billed sparrows, green honeycreepers, rufous-and-white wrens, and thrush tanagers, among more than 200 other species. Head to the top of the Cerro Mono Titi hilltop to view canopy birds, and enjoy a spectacular vista of the city. See p. 61.

o **Discovering Trogons, Blue Cotingas, and Chestnut-Mandibled Toucans on the Little-Known Achiote Road:** The Atlantic Coast village of Achiote, about a 1½-hour drive from Panama City, is quietly revered as a bird-watching mecca by those in the know. Fluttering around Achiote are orange-chinned parakeets, barbets, and flocks of swallow-tailed kites. See p. 106.

o **Delving into the World of Bird-Watching at the Canopy Lodge or Canopy Tower:** These two lodges live and breathe bird-watching, with day trips, viewing platforms, expert guides, and a fully stocked bird-watcher's library. See p. 102 and 132.

A young woman enjoys Pelicano Beach in the San Blas Islands.

SUGGESTED PANAMA ITINERARIES

P anama is home to a staggering array of natural land-scapes, each beautiful in its own way, and each offering attractions and excursions that appeal to different kinds of people. Scuba-diving fanatics or anglers seeking to reel in boatloads of billfish, for example, might plan their entire journey to Panama around their sport. Multisport resorts have been popping up around the country, too, providing guests with a home base and roster of activities as varied as kayaking, hiking, scuba diving, and mountain biking. These range from pricey, boutique-style lodges boasting "rustic elegance" to destination megaresorts, with 300 or more guest rooms.

Whatever your passion or desire, Panama has it all: a thriving metropolis; endless stretches of pristine, hyperdiverse rainforest; legendary sport fishing; scuba diving in the Caribbean and Pacific (even diving both oceans in 1 day, if you wish); white-water rafting and trekking through rugged mountain highlands; cultural encounters with one of the country's seven indigenous groups; a round of golf on a world-class course; a river cruise on a dugout canoe; or boating the Panama Canal. Of course, there are also plenty of relaxing spots for travelers who just want to kick back on a chaise longue or spend their afternoons strolling along the beach.

The itineraries in this chapter are specific blueprints for memorable vacations that can be adhered to explicitly or modified according to your desires and likes—or even expanded if you're lucky enough to have an extended vacation.

PANAMA IN 1 WEEK

Given Panama's compact size and the short flights that quickly connect you to other destinations, travelers can pack a lot into a week here—but the timing is tight. This itinerary includes a 2-day visit to Bocas del Toro, but you might opt instead to spend 2 nights in Boca Chica near David, visit Isla Coiba the first day (a long day trip, but

Panama in 1 & 2 Weeks

COSTA
RICA

Boca del Drago
Beach

Bluff Beach

CARIBBEAN SEA

Bocas Town ⑤

Red Frog Beach

BOCAS
DEL TORO

⑦

⑥
⑩
⑨

La Amistad
International
Park

Laguna de
Chiriquí

Golfo de
los Mosquitos

COLÓN

Volcán Barú
Nat'l Park ⑬ ∘ Boquete
Volcán ∘ ④⑫

COMARCA
NGÖBE-BUGLÉ

∘ Buabidí

Omar Torrijos
Nat'l Park

El Valle
de Antón

CHIRIQUÍ

David ∘ Chiriquí
③⑪

∘ Chiriquí

Penonomé ∘

COCLÉ

∘ Puerto
Armuelles

Boca
Chica

VERAGUAS

Santiago

Golfo de Chiriquí
Nat'l Marine Park

Chitré ∘

Islas Ladrones ∘

Golfo de
Chiriquí

HERRERA

Las Tablas ∘

Península
de Azuero

LOS
SANTOS

Coiba
Nat'l
Park

Santa
Catalina

Isla de
Coiba

Isla Jicarón

Cerro Hoya
Nat'l Park

PACIFIC OCEAN

worth it), and then head out to the Gulf of Chiriquí National Marine Park the next day for sport fishing or lounging on the beach at an uninhabited island.

Day 1: Getting to Know the City

Arrive and get settled in **Panama City.** If your flight arrives early, visit **Panama Viejo** (p. 54) to get your historical bearings and then head across town for a walking tour of **Casco Viejo** (p. 56). Travelers with little time will want to head straight to Casco Viejo to explore, before catching an Uber or taxi to the San Francisco neighborhood to dine at **Humo** (p. 73), where Panamanian flavors meet American BBQ.

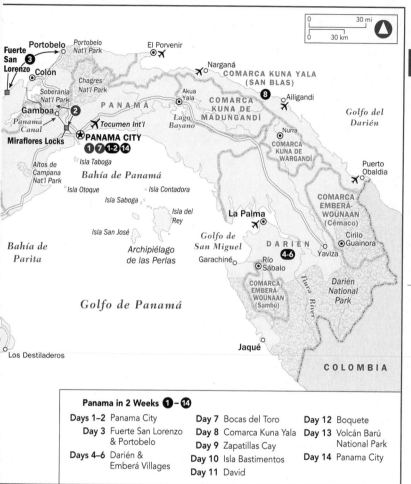

Day 2: Getting Deep in the Jungle

One of Panama's top parks for birding, hiking, and just immersing yourself in the earthy, steamy environs of thick rainforest is only 45 minutes from Panama City: **Soberanía National Park** (p. 95). Leave early and bring your binoculars to view hundreds of birds on a walk or mountain-bike ride along **Pipeline Road;** join a **jungle cruise** to see monkeys, crocodiles, and transiting ships on the Panama Canal (p. 98); or ride a dugout canoe up the **Chagres River** to visit an Emberá village (p. 99). In the afternoon, pay a visit to the country's star attraction, the **Panama Canal,** at the **Miraflores Locks** (p. 90), where you can have lunch and tour the visitor center. Head back to Panama City and cool off with a stroll or bike ride along the **Amador Causeway.**

Days 3 & 4: To the Highlands

Fly to David and grab a taxi or rent a car for the 45-minute drive to **Boquete.** Settle into your hotel and spend the afternoon getting to know the town on foot or by bike, visiting the public gardens and other sights. Another option is to dive into an adventurous afternoon activity such as a canopy ride on the **Boquete Tree Trek** (p. 169) or a low-key booked visit to the **Kotowa coffee farm** (p. 170). The following day, hike the **Quetzal Trail** (p. 159) or spend the day **rafting** on a Class II to Class V river. You can also book a bird-watching tour that includes **Finca Lérida** (p. 171) and **Volcán Barú National Park** (p. 166).

Days 5 & 6: From the Highlands to the Lowlands

Catch an early-morning flight from David to **Bocas del Toro,** and settle in to a hotel in **Bocas Town,** on Isla Colón. Preplan an afternoon tour with your hotel or an outfitter to visit **Swan's Cay** and **Boca del Drago** beach (p. 190), or rent a bicycle and pedal out to **Bluff Beach.** Or take a water taxi over to Isla Bastimentos and then walk the 10 minutes to beautiful **Red Frog Beach** (p. 204). The next day, head out with **Starfleet Scuba** (p. 193), which can put together a snorkeling or diving trip to the region's top underwater playgrounds and a cruise through mangrove swamps.

Day 7: Leaving Bocas del Toro

Spend the morning wandering around town and soaking up the Caribbean vibe, architecture, and culture. Bocas has quite a few **souvenir shops** where you can pick up gifts before your flight back to Panama City.

PANAMA IN 2 WEEKS

Travelers with 2 weeks will be able to see all of Panama's highlights without feeling as if they're on a tight schedule. This itinerary gives travelers the option of visiting the funky, laid-back region of **Bocas del Toro** or experiencing the rustic, indigenous culture of the **Comarca Kuna Yala** and its gorgeous islands—two very different destinations that appeal to different kinds of people.

Days 1 & 2: Panama City & Environs

Follow **Days 1** and **2** in the above "Panama in 1 Week" itinerary, but skip the Emberá village trip because you'll visit one in the Darién.

Day 3: Pirates, Ruins & Gold

Ride the **train** (p. 92) along the historical trans-isthmus route to Colón, but skip the city and head out to visit the ruins of **Fuerte San Lorenzo** and **Portobelo** to learn about pirate raids and the historic gold trade (p. 106 and p. 107). Dine on fresh seafood while gazing out over the sea at Los Cañones, near Portobelo. Drive across the canal and visit the **Gatún Locks** and **Gatún Dam** (p. 105). You can even plan a 1-day Caribbean **scuba-diving** adventure from Panama City, with a tour around Portobelo, by calling Panama Divers (p. 110).

Days 4–6: Wild Darién & Emberá Villages

Join **Ancon Expeditions** for its "Coastal Darién Explorer" itinerary, which offers a taste of Central America's last great wilderness area (p. 223). You'll get there by small plane to La Palma and fill the next 3 days with activities such as traveling the **Tuira River** by dugout canoe as you search for dolphins and birds, visiting an **Emberá indigenous village,** and trekking through dense and diverse tropical forest. Nights are spent in their simple but comfortable lodge overlooking the Pacific Ocean.

Day 7: Off to the Islands

On this day you'll board an early flight from La Palma to **Panama City.** The next destination is the **Caribbean,** and here travelers have two options: Visit **Bocas del Toro** (p. 183) or the **Comarca Kuna Yala** (p. 208) and its gorgeous islands. Travelers to Bocas del Toro can grab a flight out on the same day (Day 7), and lodge anywhere of their choosing. Travelers to the Comarca will need a 6:30am flight out the next day (Day 8). If the Comarca is your choice, do a little souvenir shopping and catch the Panama City sights you missed on your first days there.

Days 8–10: Caribbean Fun

Now for a little fun in the Caribbean sun. Stay in one of the Comarca's all-inclusive lodges such as **Sapibenega.** Visit traditional **Kuna villages,** and spend the rest of your days swimming, snorkeling, or just swaying in a hammock. In Bocas, organize a scuba-diving and/or snorkeling trip to **Crawl Cay** (p. 204) or **Zapatilla Cay** (p. 192). Hike through jungle on **Isla Bastimentos** and end at a long, empty beach. Visit the **Bahía Honda bat caves** (p. 204). You can also **sea kayak** or take a **surf lesson.** Or just take it easy; you deserve it.

Days 11–14: To the Highlands

Fly from Bocas to **David,** or from the Comarca to Panama City, and then to David. Grab a taxi or rent a car for the 45-minute drive to **Boquete.** Settle into your hotel and spend the afternoon getting to know the town by foot or bike, visiting the public gardens and other sights. Aside from the region's trademark coffee tours at farms like **Kotowa** (p. 170), you'll be able to hike through cloud forest on the **Quetzal Trail** (p. 166), bird-watch at **Finca Lérida** (p. 171), zip through the trees on a canopy ride with **Boquete Tree Trek** (p. 169), or spend the day **rafting** on a Class II to Class V river. You can even see both oceans, clouds willing, from the summit of **Volcán Barú National Park** (p. 166) or plan a **sport-fishing** trip leaving from Boca Chica on the Pacific Coast. The final day you'll head back to Panama City from David.

2 FOODIE PANAMA IN 5 DAYS

A surprise to many, Panama is home to one of the most exciting gastronomy scenes anywhere in Latin America. Panama City in particular boasts a vibrant street-food scene and hip farm-to-table restaurants, while elsewhere in the country the food focuses on Panama's diverse regional produce. Coffee stands out too, with the Geisha varietal being one of the world's most prized.

Day 1: Panama City Markets & Street Food

Get an early start at the **Mercado de Mariscos** (p. 79), as artisanal fishing boats are unloading their catch from up and down the coast, turning the market into a frenzy of activity. Snack on a cup of ceviche or cocktail de camarones from one of the stalls as you watch the scene unfold. Stroll to nearby Casco Viejo to elite coffee roaster **Café Unido** (p. 74), where you can taste a pour-over cup of Geisha, considered to be one of the world's finest coffees. For lunch, taxi over to **Sabores del Chorrillo** (p. 78), an outdoor food court serving some of the finest Afro-Panamanian cuisine in the city. For dinner, check out farm-to-table restaurant **Intimo** (p. 73), followed by a craft beer session at **Istmo Brew Pub** (p. 86).

Day 2: David to Volcán

Grab a morning flight from Panama City to David, where you'll pick up a rental car and drive to **Cuatro** (p. 154), a fine-dining restaurant where Chef Luis Mendizábal's food will serve as your introduction to Chiriquí ingredients such as pixbae (a tropical fruit) and otoe (a root vegetable). Drive into the mountains to **Volcán,** where organic farms and coffee plantations thrive in the rich organic soil. Have dinner at **Cerro Brujo Gourmet** (p. 158), renowned for regional dishes.

Day 3: Coffee Boquete

Spend the day driving between coffee plantations in the region, particularly the ones near the town of Boquete. Check in to **Finca Lérida** (p. 171), a boutique hotel with an excellent restaurant on a coffee estate. Later stop by **Finca Hartmann** and **Finca La Milagrosa** (p. 157 and p. 170) for coffee tours, being sure to taste the different Panamanian varietals, such as Caturra, Typica, and the prized Geisha.

Day 4: Boquete to Panama City

Spend the morning visiting any other coffee farms you might have missed, or alternatively go bird-watching or have a treatment at Haven Spa. In the

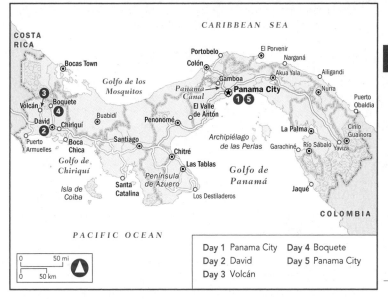

afternoon, fly back to Panama City in time for an exclusive tasting menu at **Donde Jose?** (p. 75) in Casco Viejo. Finish the night with jazz and cocktails at **Danilo's** (p. 85) inside the American Trade Hotel.

Day 5: Fine Dining in the City

Save the best for last. For your final lunch before your flight, go to **Maito** (p. 73), widely considered the best restaurant in Panama. Transfer to Tocumen Airport for your flight home.

PACIFIC COAST ADVENTURES

Panama's Pacific can hold its own against adventure-travel heavyweights like Costa Rica, giving you the opportunity to spend a lot of time on, in, or beside the water. Tailor this itinerary to your interests: If you're a sport fisherman, you can arrange a fishing charter in the Chiriquí Gulf; divers and snorkelers can head out for an underwater adventure from Boca Chica, near David. Less active beachgoers might prefer some extra days on the Pearl Islands.

Day 1: Arrive in Panama City

Arrive and get settled in Panama City. If your flight arrives early enough, head to the **Miraflores Locks** (p. 90) at the Panama Canal, tour the museum, and have lunch here while watching massive tankers pass through the locks. In the late afternoon, tour and photograph the

Pacific Coast Adventures

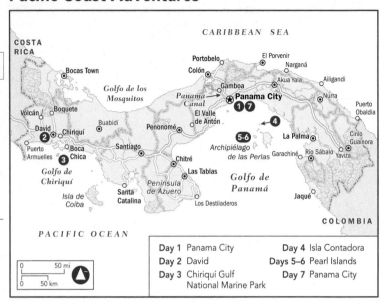

CARIBBEAN SEA

COSTA RICA

Bocas Town

Golfo de los Mosquitos

Volcán   Boquete

David   Chiriquí

Puerto   Boca
Armuelles   Chica

Golfo de Chiriquí

Isla de Coiba

Santa Catalina

Buabidí

Santiago

Península de Azuero

Portobelo   El Porvenir
                      Narganá
Colón   Akua Yala   Ailigandi
Gamboa
Panama Canal   Panama City   Nurra
El Valle   Puerto
de Antón   Obaldia
Penonomé   Cirilo
                      Guainora
                 La Palma
Archipiélago   Garachiné   Río Sábalo
de las Perlas   Yaviza
Chitré
Las Tablas   Golfo de
                 Panamá
                 Jaqué
Los Destiladeros

COLOMBIA

PACIFIC OCEAN

0   50 mi
0   50 km

Day 1 Panama City   **Day 4** Isla Contadora
Day 2 David   **Days 5–6** Pearl Islands
Day 3 Chiriquí Gulf   **Day 7** Panama City
National Marine Park

picturesque streets of **Casco Viejo** (p. 56), planning your stroll late enough so that you end at **Donde Jose?** (p. 75) for an elegant tasting menu experience.

Day 2: Explore the Underwater World

Grab an early-morning flight from Panama City to David, and then drive a little over an hour to the Pacific Coast and the tiny fishing community of Boca Chica, where you can set off for a scuba-diving or snorkeling adventure around the idyllic waters and rocky outcrops of the **Chiriquí Gulf National Marine Park** (p. 177). Keep an eye out for white-tipped sharks. Have lunch on a deserted island ringed with white sand and turquoise water.

Day 3: Fishing or Whales

Set out early and charter a boat to go **sport fishing** in the Chiriquí Gulf, unique for the sheer variety and sizes of fish. You could spend a week fishing off the Islas Ladrones, Islas Secas, Islas Contreras, and Coiba, though you'll have to get your fill of black marlin and bluefin in just a day. If fishing isn't your thing, sign up for a **whale-watching excursion.**

Day 4: Descent to the Beach

In the morning, transfer back to Panama City for an afternoon flight to the Pearl Islands from Albrook Airport. Settle into your hotel or B&B on

Isla Contadora or book an all-inclusive stay at the upscale **Hacienda del Mar** (p. 120) on Isla San José. On Contadora, kids get a kick out of renting an ATV or golf cart to zip around the island.

Days 5 & 6: Sun & Fun in the Pacific Ocean

Your first or second day, book an all-day tour to sail around the idyllic Pearl Islands for the outstanding **snorkeling** and **fishing.** Teens can join a day class to learn the basics of **scuba diving.** For young kids, book a ride in a **glass-bottom boat** to view the underwater world without getting wet. Spend your other day lounging on one of the island's dozen beaches, especially on the calm-water **Playa Larga Beach** (p. 117), a beautiful, quiet strip of sand backed by coconut palms, or **Playa Galeón,** where you can rent snorkel equipment or jet skis.

Day 7: Flight to Panama City

Depending on your departing flight home, leave early or in the afternoon to make your connection. Remember that Albrook Airport is 45 minutes to 1 hour from Tocumen, so plan accordingly.

PANAMA FOR FAMILIES IN 9 DAYS

Panama is a mixed bag as a kid-friendly destination. A share of B&Bs, luxury resorts, and boutique hotels do not accept children under 10 to 12 years of age, and discounts for children are rare. Also, few hotels outside of destination resorts offer activities specifically tailored to kids and teens—though it is easy to book day excursions like snorkeling, jungle treks, or rafting trips, all of which are kid pleasers.

Day 1: Arrival in Panama City

Head to the **Gamboa Rainforest Resort** (p. 102), near the Panama Canal, a 45-minute to 1-hour drive from the Tocumen International Airport. Gamboa has a games center, tours, a butterfly farm, and an aerial tram. If you want to stay in Panama City, book your family at the **Country Inn & Suites—Panama Canal** (p. 70), an oceanfront hotel with a bike path and pool conveniently located near the Amador Causeway and the Frank Gehry–designed **Biomuseo** (p. 63).

Day 2: Jungle Cruises & the Canal Zone

Join an early-morning **jungle cruise** on Lake Gatún to visit "Monkey Island" (p. 98) and view other wildlife such as crocodiles, capybaras, and sloths. Along the route, you'll motor past huge tankers transiting the canal. Alternatively, ride a dugout canoe up the jungle-shrouded **Chagres River** to visit an Emberá indigenous community and get painted with *jagua* juice. At the Gamboa, take a **bike ride** to Pipeline Road in the

Panama for Families in 9 Days

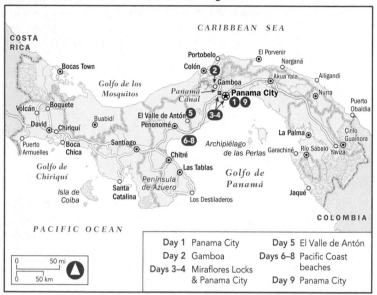

Day 1	Panama City	**Day 5**	El Valle de Antón
Day 2	Gamboa	**Days 6–8**	Pacific Coast
Days 3–4	Miraflores Locks		beaches
	& Panama City	**Day 9**	Panama City

afternoon, or visit the resort's serpentarium and butterfly exhibits, and take a ride on their aerial tram. In Panama City, pedal a bike ride along the **Causeway** and stop at the **Punta Culebra Marine Exhibition Center** (p. 63).

Days 3–5: From Lowlands to Highlands

Visit the harpy eagle exhibition and see tapirs, ocelots, jaguars, and more at the **Summit Gardens Park & Zoo** (p. 101). Afterward, stop at the Panama Canal's **Miraflores Locks** (p. 90), tour the visitor center, and have an early lunch at the restaurant looking out over ships transiting the locks. After lunch, transfer to El Valle de Anton, 2 hours from the city, and stay at the **Los Mandarinos Boutique Hotel & Spa** (p. 133). Relax, bike ride, or let the kids go to the pool or for some horseback riding while you have a massage. The following day, book a ride on the **Canopy Adventure** (p. 130) for a thrilling zipline ride through the forest. Later, families can organize an easygoing horseback ride, bike ride on country lanes, walk to a waterfall, or explore the amphibian exhibit and minizoo at **El Nispero** (p. 131). Spend your last day wandering through the **handicrafts fair** for souvenirs and gifts to take home.

Days 6–8: Descent to the Beach

Drive along the Pacific Coast on the Pan American Highway, stopping for a snack at **Quesos Chela** (p. 124). After about 2 hours, you'll come to **Buenaventura**, a sprawling beachfront residential complex anchored by a hotel, the **JW Marriott Panama Beach & Golf Resort** (p. 127), where you will be staying. Spend the next few days within the complex, visiting the zoo, kicking it lazily by the pool at the El Faro Beach Club or in the sand, and eating at the many restaurants, like **Mansa** (p. 128), a coastal Panamanian restaurant and pizzeria from Panama City chef Mario Castrellón. Utilize the resort's kids club, giving parents the chance to hit up the golf course or spa.

Day 9: Drive to Panama City

Drive back to Panama City to catch your flight home.

PANAMA CITY & THE CARIBBEAN IN 1 WEEK

Panama City is a vibrant metropolis whose proximity to two national parks, the famous canal, and its environs makes it an ideal base for travelers seeking to pack in a lot of adventure and sightseeing, but who'd like to finish the day with gourmet dining, comfortable accommodations, and city nightlife.

Day 1: Explore the Capital

Get your historical bearings at **Panama Viejo** (p. 54) and learn about the country in the handsome visitor center. Browse the extensive handicrafts market here. Head to **Riesen** (p. 77) for lunch, and then walk it off with a tour around the picturesque neighborhood of **Casco Viejo.** Buy a *raspado* (snow cone) at the **Plaza Francia** and enjoy the sea breeze. Check with your hotel for live music and other nighttime events, or drop by a casino at the **Sheraton Panama Hotel & Convention Center** (p. 84) or the **Veneto Hotel** (p. 69).

Day 2: Drive to Colón

Rent a car and drive towards the opposite coast, making a pit stop at the **Miraflores Locks** (p. 90) to watch the ships passing through the canal. Continue on to Colón, stopping to see the Caribbean entrance to the canal at the Gatún Locks and finally checking into the **Meliá** (p. 107), set in the notorious former Escuela de las Americas.

Days 3–4: Portobelo

Drive along the coast to Portobelo, where you can get picked up at a pier and taken across the bay to **El Otro Lado** (p. 111), or you can stay at a smaller hotel in town. Spend the next days kayaking along the mangroves and taking boat trips to remote, jungle-clad beaches. In town, browse for art at **Casa Congo** (p. 110) and watch a **Diablos y Congos dance performance.**

Panama City & the Caribbean in 1 Week

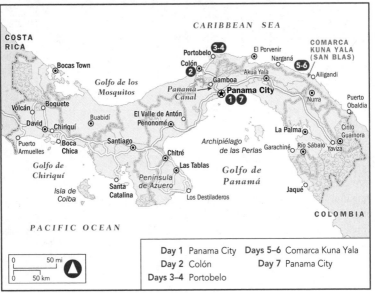

CARIBBEAN SEA

COSTA
RICA

Bocas Town

Golfo de los
Mosquitos

Portobelo **3-4**
Colón
2

El Porvenir
Narganá

Akuá Yala

Gamboa

COMARCA
KUNA YALA
(SAN BLAS)
5-6 Ailigandí

Panamá
Canal

★ **Panama City**
1 7

Nurra

Puerto
Obaldía

Volcán
David
Boquete
Chiriquí

Buabidí

El Valle de Antón
Penonomé

La Palma

Cirilo
Guaínora

Puerto
Armuelles
Boca
Chica

Santiago

Archipiélago
de las Perlas

Garachiné
Río Sábalo
Yaviza

Chitré

Golfo de
Chiriquí

Las Tablas

Golfo de
Panamá

Isla de
Coiba

Santa
Catalina

Península
de Azuero

Los Destiladeros

Jaqué

COLOMBIA

PACIFIC OCEAN

| 0 | 50 mi |
| 0 | 50 km |

Day 1 Panama City	**Days 5–6** Comarca Kuna Yala
Day 2 Colón	**Day 7** Panama City
Days 3–4 Portobelo	

Days 5–7: Comarca Kuna Yala

Drive back to Panama City and catch a flight to **San Blas,** where you'll spend your remaining days on the beach snorkeling, lying in a hammock, and eating grilled fish and lobster. Alternatively, you can stay the night in Panama City and continue on to San Blas the next morning by car or just take a day trip to San Blas, as long as you have an SUV (p. 211).

PANAMA IN CONTEXT

For many years, Panama remained off the radar of international travelers and investors, but those days have come to an end—Panama has come into its own. Panama now receives about 2 million visitors a year, quite impressive for a tiny country of just under 4 million people. Panama has undergone a major boom since the mid-2000s, with new retirement communities, restaurants, and hotels breaking ground practically every week. Prices and speculation have appeared to stabilize, though it's still very much a country on the rise. Escaping much of the tourism boom all too familiar to Costa Rica, likely because of the Noriega years, Panama is proudly making a name for itself as a must-see destination in Latin America.

Rapidly emerging from Costa Rica's shadow, Panama's geography is similar to that of its neighbor to the north, including pristine rainforests, attractive beaches, mountain villages, and, as an added bonus, a vibrant, cosmopolitan city many compare to Miami. Traveling isn't as dirt-cheap as it was a decade ago, but Panama is still less expensive than Costa Rica.

Panama claims a history rich with Spanish conquistadores and colonists, pirates, gold miners and adventurers, canal engineering, international trade, and mass immigration from countries as close as Jamaica and as far away as China. The pastiche of European and African cultures blended with the country's seven indigenous groups has had a tangible effect on Panama's architecture, cuisine, language, and folklore. And now that the dust has long settled after the infamous Noriega era, political stability has taken hold and offers hope for the country's future.

Given Panama's compact size and diversity, visitors here can take part in wildly different experiences without having to travel very far. The growing expat and retirement community, as well as the large number of Chinese, Colombian, and Venezuelan immigrants, make Panama a fascinating country to visit. This chapter will help you understand a little more about Panama's history, people, and culture.

PANAMA TODAY

Panama has almost 4 million residents, and more than a third of them live in Panama City, Colón, and David, the country's three largest cities. The remaining population is concentrated mostly in small towns and villages in central Panama and the Azuero Peninsula. Officially, roughly 70% of the population is *mestizo,* or a mix of Amerindians and Caucasians; 14% are of African descent; 10% are white and other immigrant races; and 6% Amerindian. About 30% of the population is under the age of 14.

Panama is home to seven indigenous groups that have, to differing degrees, held onto their culture and languages, despite foreign influences and modern advancements. Ethnic tribes such as the **Kuna,** who live along the central Caribbean coast, form a semiautonomous and insular society that has hardly changed over the last century. However, the eastern Kuna community, near the Darién, has adapted to modern society, wearing Western clothing and practicing few native traditions. The **Ngöbe-Buglé** are two tribes that are culturally similar and collectively referred to as Guaymí. Ngöbe-Buglés live in the highlands of western Panama and eastern Costa Rica and are the country's largest indigenous group; many travel nomadically and make their living in coffee production. Eastern Panama is home to two indigenous groups, the **Emberá** and the **Wounaan**—several Emberá communities are close enough to Panama City to be visited for the day. Tiny populations of **Teribe** (also called Naso) and **Bri Bri** live scattered around mainland Bocas del Toro.

People of African descent first came to Panama as slaves of the Spanish during the 16th century, and many escaped into Darién Province where they settled and became known as *cimarrones.* In and around Portobelo and the eastern Caribbean coast, they call themselves **Congos.** During the 19th century, jobs in canal building and banana plantations lured immigrants from Jamaica, Barbados, and Colombia, who settled along the western Caribbean coast and are commonly referred to as **Afro-Caribbeans** or *creoles.*

One thing you'll find about Panamanians is that they are warm and outgoing people who are eager to help strangers. Panamanians no longer indulge in afternoon siestas, but things still move at a languid pace. Given this and the country's nascent tourism infrastructure, even well-respected tour companies and other tourism establishments can't always be relied upon for punctuality. If you are an impatient person, or in a hurry, you will not fare well in Panama—so *relax.* You're on vacation, right?

Panama has a dollarized economy whose major natural resources are its rainforests, beaches, and oceans, making this country an irresistible draw for tourism. Panama's principal source of income is derived from the services sector, including the Panama Canal, the Colón Free Trade Zone, banking, and flagship registry among other "export" services, all of which account for about three-quarters of the country's GDP. The withdrawal of U.S. canal workers and military personnel in 2000 had a devastating effect on Panama City's local economy, but a growth explosion in the construction sector is currently underway thanks to juicy tax incentives, and glitzy skyscrapers seem to shoot up overnight along the city's shoreline. Panama has very effectively sold itself as a retirement haven, with its low cost of living and inexpensive land, and many of those who were just passing through are now putting down stakes in gated communities or taking on new roles as hotel or restaurant owners. For many years, foreign investors lured by get-rich-quick schemes were snapping up property in a real-estate boom that had many locals grumbling about the soaring value of land; this has slowed down a bit in the last couple of years, but prices have remained high for a relatively poor population.

On the legislative side, the Panamanian government has reformed its tax structure, opened its borders to free trade with key nations like the U.S., and implemented a social security overhaul. Yet money laundering, political corruption, and cocaine transshipment continue to be problems, as is widespread unemployment, with indigenous groups and Colón residents faring the worst. As the nation grows economically, the split between the rich and the poor widens. Today, about 37% of the population is under the poverty level and lacks adequate housing, access to medical care, and proper nutrition.

The current president of Panama, Juan Carlos Varela, a member of the right-leaning Panameñista Party, is the scion of one of Panama's richest families and owner of a namesake rum distillery. Varela has a degree in engineering from the Georgia Institute of Technology in Atlanta and has promised to shake out corruption in the government.

In 2007, a $5.3-billion expansion of the Panama Canal got underway, a move that caused much controversy, but that ultimately promises to keep the canal relevant. Worldwide tankers have grown too big to fit in the canal, and those ships that can fit must line up for hours to cross. As the project winds down, the country is exploring another $16-billion expansion that would allow the canal to handle the world's largest ships, which can carry up to 20,000 containers. If it happens, work could be ongoing for the next 15 or 20 years.

LOOKING BACK AT PANAMA

Early History

Little is known about the ancient cultures that inhabited Panama before the arrival of the Spanish. The pre-Columbian cultures in this region did not build large cities or develop an advanced culture like the Mayans or the Incas did, and much of what was left behind has been stolen by looters or engulfed in jungle. We know that the most advanced cultures came from Central Panama, such as the Monagrillo (2500–1700 B.C.), who were one of the first pre-Columbian societies in the Americas to produce ceramics. Excavation of sites such as Conte, near Natá, have unearthed elaborate burial pits with *huacas* (ceremonial figurines) and jewelry, which demonstrates an early introduction to metallurgy during the first century, as well as trade with Colombia and even Mexico. What little remains of Panama's prized artifacts can be viewed at the **Museo Antropológico Reina Torres de Araúz** in Panama City.

Panama at a Glance

Spain Conquers Panama

The first of many Spanish explorers to reach Panama was Rodrigo de Basti-das, who sailed from Venezuela along Panama's Caribbean coast in 1501 in search of gold. His first mate was Vasco Nuñez de Balboa, who would return later and seal his fate as one of Panama's most important historical figures. A year later, Christopher Columbus, on his fourth and final voyage to the New World, sailed into Bocas del Toro and stopped at various points along the isthmus, one of which he named Puerto Bello, now known as Portobelo. Esti-mates vary, but historians believe that between 1 and 2 million indigenous people were in Panama at that time. Groups such as the Kuna, the Chocó, and the Guaymí lived in small communities and were highly skilled in pottery making, stonecutting, and metallurgy. Because they frequently wore gold ornaments, Spanish explorers during the following years would be further convinced of the existence of fabled El Dorado, the city of gold. Columbus attempted to establish a colony, Santa María de Belen, near Río Belen, but was forced out after a raid by local Indians.

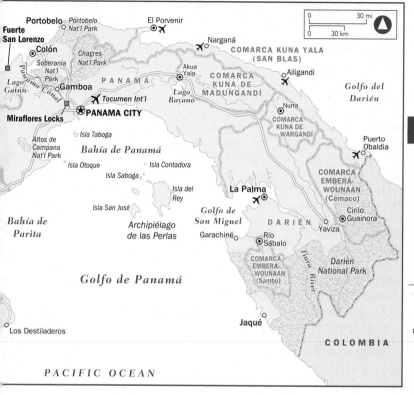

Meanwhile, Balboa had settled in the Dominican Republic but had racked up huge debts. In 1510, he escaped his creditors by hiding out as a stowaway on a boat bound for Panama. In the years since Columbus's failed attempt, many other Spaniards had tried to colonize the coast but were thwarted by disease and indigenous raids. Balboa suggested settling at Antigua de Darién, where he became a tough but successful administrator who both subjugated Indians as well as befriended conquered tribes. Having listened to stories by Indians about another sea, Balboa set out in 1513 with Francisco Pizarro and a band of Indian slaves and hacked his way through perilous jungle for 25 days until he arrived at the Pacific Coast, where he claimed the sea and all its shores for the king of Spain. Balboa was later beheaded by a jealous new governor, Pedro Arias de Avila (Pedrarias the Cruel), on a trumped-up charge of treason.

In 1519, Pedrarias settled a fishing village called Panama, which meant "plenty of fish" in the local language, and resettled Nombre de Dios on the Atlantic to create a passageway for transporting Peruvian gold and riches from the Pacific to Spanish galleons in the Caribbean Sea. The trail was called the Camino Real, or Royal Trail, but later a faster and easier route was established, called the Camino de las Cruces. The land portion of this trail was two-thirds shorter and met with the Chagres River, which could be sailed out to the Caribbean Sea. This trail can be walked today, and portions of the stone-inlaid path still exist.

With Incan gold nearly exhausted, the Spanish turned their interests to the immense supply of silver found in Peruvian mines, and in 1537 they held their first trading fair, which would grow into one of the most important fairs in the world. With so much wealth changing hands on the isthmus, pirate attacks became increasingly common, and ports like Nombre de Dios declined in importance after having been raided by the English pirate Sir Francis Drake twice in 1572 and 1573. Portobelo was refortified and became the main port of trade. Panama City, on the other side of the isthmus, flourished with trade profits and was considered one of the wealthiest cities in the Americas.

By the mid-17th century, dwindling supplies of silver and gold from the Peruvian mines and ongoing pirate attacks precipitated a severe decline in the amount of precious metals being transported to Spain. In 1671, the notorious Welsh buccaneer Henry Morgan sailed up the Chagres River, crossed the isthmus, and overpowered Panama City, sacking the city and leaving it in flames. Those who escaped the attack rebuilt Panama City 2 years later at what is now known as Casco Viejo.

Spain finally abandoned the isthmus crossing and Portobelo after the city was attacked by the British admiral Edward Vernon, and returned to sailing around Cape Horn to reach Peru.

Independence from Spain & the Gold Rush

Spain granted independence to its Central America colonies in 1821, and Panama was absorbed into "Gran Colombia," a union led by liberator Simón Bolívar that included Colombia, Venezuela, and Ecuador. Panama attempted to split from Colombia three times during the 19th century, but wouldn't be successful until the U.S.–backed attempt in 1903.

Having been a colonial backwater since the pullout of the Spanish in the late 17th century, Panama was restored to prosperity from 1848 to 1869 during the height of the California Gold Rush. Given that crossing the U.S. from the Atlantic to the Pacific was a long, arduous journey by wagon and prone to Indian attacks and other pitfalls, gold seekers chose to sail to Panama, cross the Las Cruces trail, and sail on to California. In 1855, an American group of financiers built the Panama Railroad, greatly reducing the travel time between coasts. In 20 years, a total of 600,000 people crossed the isthmus, and both Colón and Panama City benefitted enormously from the business earned in hotels, restaurants, and other services.

The Panama Canal

The history of the canal dates back to 1539, when King Charles I of Spain dispatched a survey team to study the feasibility of a canal, but the team deemed such a pursuit impossible. The first real attempt at construction of a canal was begun in 1880 by the French, led by Ferdinand de Lesseps, the charismatic architect of the Suez Canal. De Lesseps had been convinced that a sea-level canal was the only option. Once workers broke ground, however, engineers soon saw the impracticality of a sea-level canal but were unable to convince the stubborn de Lesseps, and for years rumors flew, financial debts mounted, and nearly 20,000 workers perished before the endeavor collapsed. Few had anticipated the enormous challenge presented by the Panamanian jungle, with its mucky swamps, torrential downpours, landslides, floods, and, most debilitating of all, mosquito-borne diseases such as malaria and yellow fever.

Meanwhile, Panama was embroiled in political strife and a nonstop pursuit to separate itself from Colombia. Following the French failure with the canal, the U.S. expressed interest in taking over construction but was rebuffed by the Colombian government. In response, the U.S. backed a growing independence movement in Panama that declared its separation from Colombia on November 3, 1903. The U.S. officially recognized Panama and sent its battleships to protect the new nation from Colombian troops, who turned back home after a few days.

A French canal engineer on the de Lesseps project, Philippe Bunau-Varilla, a major shareholder of the abandoned canal project, had been grudgingly given negotiating-envoy status by the Panamanian government for the new U.S.–built canal. His controversial Hay-Bunau-Varilla Treaty gave the U.S. overly generous rights that included the use, occupation, and sovereign control of a 16km-wide (10-mile) swath of land across the isthmus, and was entitled to annex more land if necessary to operate the canal. The U.S. would also be allowed to intervene in Panama's affairs.

The French had excavated ⅖ of the canal, built hospitals, and left behind machinery and the operating railway, as well as a sizeable workforce of Afro-Caribbeans. For the next 10 years, the U.S., having essentially eradicated tropical disease, pulled off what seemed impossible in terms of engineering: carving out a path through the Continental Divide, constructing an elevated canal system, and making the largest man-made lake in the world.

The 20th Century to the Present

A stormy political climate ensued in Panama for the following decades, with frequent changes of administration. Presidents and other political figures were typically *rabiblancos,* or wealthy, white elites loathed by the generally poor and dark-skinned public. One especially controversial character in the political scene was Arnulfo Arias, a racist yet populist, one-time sympathizer of the fascist movement who would be voted into and thrown out of the presidency three times. Increasingly, Panamanians were discontented with the U.S. presence and, in particular, its control of the canal. In 1964, several U.S. high-school students in the Canal Zone raised the American flag at their school, igniting protests by Panamanian college students. The protests culminated in

A feast **OF LANGUAGES**

Spanish is the official language of Panama, but other languages are spoken in pockets around the country. The country's seven indigenous groups speak a variety of dialects of Wounaan, Teribe, Emberá, Kuna, and Ngöbe-Buglé (Guaymí)—the most common are the latter two, the dialects of the largest indigenous communities in Panama. In the Bocas del Toro region, descendants of Jamaican immigrants who came to work on banana plantations speak what's known as "Guari Guari," alternatively spelled "Wari Wari." It is also sometimes referred to as Creole English, but the language is really patois English blended with Spanish and Guaymí (Ngöbe-Buglé) words. Native English speakers often have a difficult time understanding Guari

Guari. A good place to hear Guari Guari is at Old Bank on Isla Bastimentos.

San Miguel Creole French, spoken by immigrants from St. Lucía who arrived on the island in the 19th century, is a dying language that's rarely heard in Panama any longer. On the other hand, Chinese immigrants, many of whom work as merchants running corner stores and small markets called *chinos*, continue to speak their native tongue. Adding to this linguistical mélange is Arabic, spoken by immigrants from the Middle East. There is also a growing English-speaking expat community in Panama City, Boquete, Bocas del Toro, and el Valle de Anton, and English is now a requirement in all public schools, meaning more and more Panamanians are bilingual.

the deaths of more than two dozen Panamanians, an event that is now called "Día de los Mártires," or Martyrs Day.

By 1974, the U.S. had begun to consider transferring the canal to Panama. Arias was once again voted into power, and after strong-arming the National Guard, he was deposed in a military coup led by Omar Torrijos Herrera, a National Guard colonel. Torrijos was an authoritarian leader but a champion of the poor who espoused land redistribution and social programs—a "dictatorship with a heart," as he called it. His most popular achievement came in 1977, with the signing of a treaty with then-president Jimmy Carter that relinquished control of the canal to Panama on December 31, 1999. Also part of the treaty was the closing of U.S. military bases and the U.S. right to intervene only if it perceived a threat against the security of the canal. On July 31, 1981, Torrijos died in a plane accident.

By 1983, the National Guard, now renamed the Panamanian Defense Forces (PDF), was firmly controlled by Colonel Manuel Antonio Noriega and continued to dominate political and everyday life in Panama. Noriega created the so-called Dignity Battalions that aimed to stifle citizen dissent through force and terrorize anyone who opposed the PDF. For the next 6 years, Noriega kept the Panamanian public in a state of virtual fear, running the country through presidents he had placed in power via rigged elections, killing and torturing his opponents, and involving himself in drug trafficking.

The U.S. imposed tough economic sanctions on Panama that included freezing government assets in U.S. banks and withholding canal fees, spurring widespread protests against Noriega across Panama City. In 1989, a fresh set of presidential elections pitted the Noriega-picked candidate against Guillermo Endara. When Endara won, Noriega annulled the election amid widespread claims by foreign observers of fraud on the part of the Noriega regime.

With Panama veering out of control, the U.S. began sending troops to bases in the Canal Zone. On December 20, 1989, the U.S. launched Operation Just Cause, led by 25,000 soldiers who pounded the city for 6 days, leaving anywhere from 500 to 7,000 dead, depending on whom you asked. Noriega fled and hid in the offices of the Vatican *nuncio,* where he asked for asylum. He later surrendered and was flown to the U.S., where he was tried, charged, and sentenced to 40 years in prison, which was later reduced. In 2010, he was extradited to France, where he was charged with money-laundering, and then sent to Panama a year later, where he is serving a 20-year sentence.

In the wake of Noriega's extradition, Guillermo Endara was sworn in as president, where he presided over a country racked by instability. In 1994, a former Torrijos associate, Ernesto Pérez Balladares, was sworn in as president. Balladares instituted sweeping economic reforms and worked to rebuild Panama's relationship with the U.S., which still had control of the canal. The same year, the constitution was changed to ban the U.S. military in Panama.

Balladares was followed by Mireya Moscoso in 1999, the ex-wife of Arias and Panama's first female president. During her 5 years in power, her approval ratings dropped to less than 30%; she was generally viewed as grossly incompetent and prone to cronyism and corruption. Moscoso also oversaw the much-anticipated handover of the canal.

Despite decades of protest against the U.S. presence, in the end many Panamanians expressed ambivalence about the pullout when faced with the economic impact on businesses and the loss of jobs. Still, the handover has defied everyone's expectations, and the canal is run today as well, if not better, than before.

After a successful run from 2009 to 2014, billionaire ex-banker Ricardo Martinelli was displaced by Panama's current president, Juan Carlos Varela. Martinelli, despite helping Panama transition into the robust economy that it is today, has since been accused of alleged phone-tapping and corruption scandals. Varela has promised to help fight against corruption and poverty as Martinelli lives exiled in Miami, literally holed up in the luxury condo in which the film *Scarface* was filmed.

THE REGIONS IN BRIEF

PANAMA CITY, THE CANAL & SURROUNDINGS   Beyond the urban streets of Panama City, the Canal Zone is characterized by a species-rich, dense tropical rainforest, hundreds of rivers, mangrove swamps, the Pacific Ocean coastline, and Las Perlas Archipelago in the Gulf of Panama. Thanks to the Panama Canal and its reliance on the local watershed, the rainforest in this area is protected as a series of national parks and reserves (Chagres, Soberanía, Sherman, and Camino de Cruces, for example). Visitors to Panama City are often surprised at how quickly they can reach these parks and surround themselves in steamy jungle and view a dazzling array of both North and South American birds and other wildlife. Near the city, the shore consists mostly of mudflats; visitors seeking beaches must head to the islands or drive about 1 hour southwest (see chapter 8).

CENTRAL PANAMA   Considered the country's cultural heartland, Central Panama in this book covers Panama City beaches, the Coclé Province, and the Azuero Peninsula. In Coclé, city dwellers flock to popular El Valle de Antón, a verdant mountain hideaway located in the crater of an extinct volcano (1,173m/3,850 ft. at its highest peak). The area is blessed with a mild climate that is a welcome respite from the humid lowlands. Southwest of the city, the Pacific Coast is another popular weekend getaway for its beaches and a few all-inclusive resorts. Farther southwest, the Azuero Peninsula has been largely deforested, but it is still a popular destination for its traditional festivals, handicrafts, and Spanish villages whose architecture dates back to the medieval era. The beaches along the peninsula are blissfully uncrowded any time of year.

BOCAS DEL TORO ARCHIPELAGO   In the northwest corner of the country, near the border with Costa Rica, Bocas del Toro is one of the more popular and easily accessed Caribbean destinations, with a wide variety of hotels and amenities. The region is characterized by an eclectic mix of indigenous groups, Spanish descendants, Afro-Caribbeans, and, more recently, American expats; it is also one of the wettest areas of Panama. Outside of brief dry seasons in September/October and February/March, the rain is constant, so bring an umbrella or waterproof gear. Although the area has a few beautiful beaches, it also has dangerous riptides; visitors come more to scuba dive, snorkel, boat, see wildlife, or just soak in the bohemian vibe of Bocas Town, the capital city.

THE WESTERN HIGHLANDS & GULF OF CHIRIQUÍ   The Western Highlands—so-called for the region's location and its Cordillera Central range—is a veritable paradise of fertile peaks and valleys, crystal-clear rivers, mild temperatures, and fresh air. The region is undergoing a palpable growth spurt as hundreds of North Americans continue to buy second and retirement homes here, so expect to hear a lot of English. The region centers around the skirt of Volcán Barú, a dormant volcano capped by a moist cloud forest. Farther south are the humid lowlands, the capital city (David), and the wondrous coast and islands of the Gulf of Chiriquí. This is Panama's up-and-coming beach/ocean destination, with its highlight being Coiba National Park, comprised of some of the world's most diverse and pristine islands for scuba diving and snorkeling.

THE DARIÉN   The easternmost region of Panama is known as the Darién Province, a swath of impenetrable rainforest and swampland that is undeveloped save for a handful of tiny villages and indigenous settlements. It is Panama's wildest region and the most difficult to reach: This is the famous "missing link" of the Pan American Highway, which runs from Alaska to

Puerto Montt, Chile. The interior of the Darién can be reached only by foot, boat, or small plane—and herein lies the allure of adventure for travelers. Within the province lies Darién National Park, most of it inaccessible except for the Cana Research Station, an area revered by birders for the abundance of endemic and "show-bird" species such as macaws and harpy eagles, the largest raptor in the Americas. Along the Pacific shore is the famous Tropic Star Lodge; otherwise, lodging in the Darién is relegated to rustic shelters and tents.

THE COMARCA KUNA YALA (THE SAN BLAS ARCHIPELAGO)

Though commonly referred to as the San Blas Archipelago, this semiautonomous region, or *comarca,* is named for the Kuna Yala, perhaps Panama's most well-known indigenous group. The Kuna are recognized for their tightly knit culture, colorful clothing, and handicrafts such as *mola* tapestries. More than 300 lovely, palm-studded islands in turquoise Caribbean waters make up the archipelago in what is truly an unspoiled paradise. The San Blas is a very popular cruise stop; however, staying on the islands requires a sense of adventure—they can be reached only by small plane or boat. Lodging is largely rustic and alfresco, and there's little in the way of activities other than swimming and swaying in a hammock.

WHEN TO GO

Panama lies between 7 degrees and 9 degrees above the Equator, which places it firmly within the Tropics. Accordingly, average year-round temperatures are a balmy 75°F to 85°F (24°C–29°C), varying only with altitude, from hot and humid in the tropical lowlands to cool in the highlands. The average temperature in the Chiriquí Highlands, for example, is 60°F (16°C), and it is the only area in Panama where you will likely feel cold.

Panama is tropical country, and as such has distinct dry and wet seasons. Generally speaking, December to mid-April are the driest months, while October and November are the wettest. However, cooler mountainous regions such as the Chiriquí Highlands and the Valle de Anton see rain throughout the year, though it's usually limited to a light mist or *barenje* during the dry season. The Caribbean Coast also tends to be wetter than the Pacific, particularly Bocas del Toro, where it can rain anytime of the year. The Darien can be difficult at best in the rainy season, and you'll be hard-pressed to find a company willing to go in the rainiest months, though there are so many bugs during this time that it's unlikely you'd want to go anyway. The Azuero Peninsula is a bit drier than the rest of the country and has been subject to much deforestation. The Kuna Yala Islands represent an interesting topography. Unlike most Panamanian islands, which are heavily forested, the more than 365 Kuna Islands are made up of sand and palm trees, and temperatures are often more comfortable there than other beach destinations, with nights even getting a bit cool.

The Chiriquí Highlands experience a variety of microclimates that can change drastically, sometimes even within a few miles. In Boquete, high winds and a peculiar misting rain called *bajareque* are common from mid-December to mid-February; January sees the occasional thunderstorm, and March to May are the sunniest months.

If you are unable to visit during the dry season, keep in mind that the months April through July are characterized by sunny skies in the morning or afternoon, punctuated by sudden, heavy thunderstorms midday or in early afternoon that are short in duration and can happen every few days.

Average Monthly Temperatures & Rainfall in Panama City

	JAN	FEB	MAR	APR	MAY	JUNE	JULY	AUG	SEPT	OCT	NOV	DEC
Temp. (°F)	82	82	82	82	80	80	81	81	81	80	81	82
Temp. (°C)	28	28	28	28	27	27	27	27	27	27	27	28
Days of Rain	4	2	1	6	15	16	15	15	16	18	18	12

Public Holidays

There is a saying in Panama that the only thing Panamanians take seriously are their holidays—and it's no joke. Nearly every business, including banks, offices, and many stores and restaurants, closes, making even Panama City feel like a ghost town. Official holidays that fall on a Saturday or Sunday are usually observed on Mondays, allowing for a long weekend. Transportation services are also greatly reduced. During holidays, most locals head for the beach or other getaway destinations, so if you plan to travel during this time, book lodging well in advance and make certain you have confirmed reservations.

Panama's most revered holiday is **Carnaval,** the 4 days that precede Ash Wednesday. (Though not officially a holiday, most call in sick to work to recover from Carnaval on Wed.) The largest celebrations take place in Panama City and the Azuero Peninsula, with parades, floats, drinking, costumes, and music. Note that celebrations in Panama City can be a bit raucous and aren't usually as classy as those on the Azuero Peninsula. The first days for upcoming Carnavales are February 6 (2016), February 25 (2017), and February 10 (2018).

Official holidays in Panama include January 1 (New Year's Day), January 9 (Martyr's Day), Good Friday, Easter Sunday, May 1 (Labor Day), August 15 (Founding of Old Panama—observed in Panama City only), October 12 (Hispanic Day), November 2 (All Souls' Day), November 3 (Independence Day), November 4 (Flag Day), November 5 (Colón Day—observed in the city of Colón only), November 10 (First Call for Independence), November 28 (Independence from Spain), December 8 (Mother's Day), and December 25 (Christmas Day).

Panama Calendar of Events & Festivals

Many of the following listings are annual events whose exact dates vary from year to year, and the majority are local festivals. For more details, go to **www.visitpanama.com,** the website for **Autoridad de Turismo Panama (ATP),** the country's official tourism board (or call ✆ **800/962-1526**).

JANUARY

Feria de las Flores y del Café (Flower and Coffee Festival), Boquete. This festival is one of the grandest celebrations of flowers in the world, drawing thousands of people to Boquete for 10 days. Expect lush flower displays, food stands, live music, amusement rides, handicrafts booths, and hotel rooms booked far in advance. Go to http://feriadeboquete.com. Mid-January.

Jazz Festival, Panama City. For one 3-day weekend, Panama City throbs with live jazz performances by outstanding international musicians. Some events are held outdoors and are free; log on to www.panamajazzfestival.com. Mid- to late January.

FEBRUARY

Carnaval (Carnival). Panama's largest yearly celebration (occasionally falling in early March) takes place during the 4 days that precede Ash Wednesday. The largest celebrations are in small towns on the Azuero Peninsula, such as Las Tablas, and Panama City, with parades, music, and dancing. Be prepared to get wet by *mojaderos*, or trucks that spray revelers with water.

MARCH

Semana Santa. During this week (Holy Week), parades, religious processions, and other special events take place across the country. Palm Sunday through Holy Saturday.

Feria Internacional de David. The Chiriquí capital's largest festival (www.feriadedavid.com) draws more than 500 exhibitors from around the world to display industrial products and new technology. During the 10-day fest, the city hosts cultural and folkloric events. Mid-March.

APRIL

Feria de Orquídeas (Orchid Festival), Boquete. It's not as grand as the flower festival, but the Orchid Festival showcases thousands of varieties of these delicate flowers for public viewing. Go to http://feriadeboquete.com. At the fairgrounds late March to early April.

Feria Internacional de Azuero, La Villa de Los Santos. This multiday festival is something akin to a county fair, with animal displays, food stalls, and lots of drinking. Mid-April.

JUNE

Festival Corpus Christi, La Villa de Los Santos. The town explodes with activity for a 2-week religious festival known for its elaborate dances led by men in devil masks. Forty days after Easter.

JULY

Festival Patronales de La Virgen de Santa Librada, Las Tablas. This festival is famous for its **Festival Nacional de la Pollera** on July 22, which showcases the region's most beautiful pollera dresses and elects the "Queen of the Pollera" for that year. July 20 to July 23.

SEPTEMBER

Feria del Mar (Festival of the Sea), Bocas del Toro. This 4-day event features food stands serving local cuisine, handicrafts booths, exhibits by the Smithsonian Institute and ANAM (the park service), folkloric presentations, and dances. Mid-September.

Festival Nacional de la Mejorana, Guararé. This nationally famous folkloric festival features hundreds of dancers, musicians, and singers coming together for a week of events and serious partying. Last week of September.

OCTOBER

Festival del Cristo Negro (Black Christ Festival), Portobelo. Thousands of pilgrims come to pay penance, perform other acts of devotion, and do some reveling at the Iglesia de San Felipe, home to a wooden black Christ effigy that is paraded around town on this day. October 21.

NOVEMBER

Independence Days. Panama celebrates three independence days. November 3 and 4 are Independence Day and Flag Day, and the largest independence celebrations, featuring parades, fireworks, and other entertainment, take place in Panama City and larger cities like David. November 10 is a holiday for the "First Call for Independence," as is November 28, honoring Independence Day from Spain, with regional festivities—but nothing matches November 3 and 4.

Feria de las Tierras Altas, Volcán. This Highlands Festival is a 5-day celebration of agriculture, local arts, and culture. Around the last week of November.

EATING & DRINKING IN PANAMA

Panama is a melting pot of ethnicities, and its cuisine is accordingly influenced by its diverse population. Within Panama City, travelers will find something from every corner of the world, including French, Japanese, Italian, Thai, Middle Eastern, and Chinese food—all of it very good and true to its roots. In regional areas, traditional Panamanian cuisine is an overlapping mix of Afro-Caribbean, indigenous, and Spanish cooking influences incorporating a variety of tropical fruit, vegetables, and herbs. Most Panamanian restaurants are casual—diners, beachfront cafes, and roadside *fondas* (food stands). A large U.S. population has spawned North American cafes and bistros serving burgers and the like, and fast-food chains are plentiful in Panama City.

Meals & Dining Customs

Panamanian cuisine is tasty but can be repetitive, given that every meal is based around coconut rice (rice made with coconut milk) and beans, and fried green plantains called *patacones.* Much Panamanian food is fried—just stop at a *fonda* and see for yourself. Even breakfast is a selection of fried meats and breads. Panamanian food is neither spicy nor heavily seasoned; in fact, salt is often the only seasoning used in many staple dishes.

Dining hours generally follow North American customs, with restaurants opening around 7 or 8am for breakfast, serving lunch from noon to 2pm, and dinner from 7 to 10pm. In smaller towns, you'll find that restaurants close as early as 9pm or sometimes even 8pm.

Note: All Panamanian restaurants and bars are smoke-free, so smokers will have to take it outside.

BREAKFAST   Start your day with a cup of fresh-brewed Panamanian joe. Breakfast menus around the country feature standbys like scrambled eggs, toast, and fruit, but Panamanians like their tortillas, too. These are not Mexican-style tortillas but deep-fried corn batter topped with eggs and cheese, something akin to huevos rancheros. *Hojaldres,* deep-fried bread sprinkled with powdered sugar like a Panamanian doughnut, are another common breakfast staple. Afro-Caribbeans eat meats like pork with their breakfast; if your arteries can handle it, give it a try. A hearty breakfast of "Caribbean porridge," made of rice, beans, and pork, is called *gallo pinto,* or "spotted rooster," and is found in local joints.

APPETIZERS & SNACKS   Ceviche, raw cubes of fish and onion marinated in lemon juice, is a popular dish throughout Latin America. It's usually made with sea bass or with shrimp or octopus. Crunchy cornmeal pastries stuffed with meat are called empanadas—greasy but good when they're fresh and hot. The yuca root, a Panama staple, when fried, substitutes for French fries. Yuca is also used for a *carimañola;* the yuca is mashed, formed into a roll stuffed with meat and boiled eggs, and then deep-fried. Plantains are served in two varieties: *patacones,* or green plantains, cut in rounds, pounded, deep-fried, and salted; or *plátanos maduros,* ripe plantains, broiled or sautéed in oil. Ripe plantains are called *plátanos en tentación* when they are slightly caramelized with sugar and cinnamon. Plantains and *patacones,* along with coconut rice *(arroz con coco)* and beans *(frijoles),* are the standard accompaniment to traditional Panamanian dishes.

MEAT & POULTRY   There is perhaps no dish more emblematic of Panama than the *sancocho,* a chicken stew made with a starchy root called *ñamé* and seasoned with a cilantro-like herb called *culantro.* Sancocho is said to put strength back into your body after a late night out. Meat is commonplace, served as a *bistec* (steak), or in a popular dish called *ropa vieja,* meaning "old clothes" and consisting of shredded beef with a spicy tomato sauce served over rice. Chicken is a staple, too, as is pork. In the Caribbean, some locals still eat turtle soup and turtle eggs, although it is usually kept under wraps thanks to vocal conservation efforts to protect turtles—these are endangered creatures, so please refuse turtle if it is ever offered to you.

SEAFOOD   Panama, which means "abundance of fish," lives up to its name with lots of fresh delicacies from the sea, including *pargo* (red snapper), *corvina* (sea bass), *langostino* (jumbo shrimp), *langosta* (lobster), calamari, *cangrejo* (crab), and *pulpo* (octopus). Traditional Panamanian seafood dishes come four ways: fried, grilled, *al ajillo* (with a spicy garlic sauce), or *a la española* (sautéed with tomatoes and onions). Lobster and jumbo shrimp are expensive because of overfishing and dwindling supplies.

VEGETABLES   Panama's agricultural breadbasket is around the flank of Volcán Barú in the western Highlands; here the volcanic soil and high altitudes encourage year-round growing conditions, and vegetables are readily available. Salads are not hard to come by, but traditional Panamanian fare is typically only served with just a small cabbage salad topped with a slice of tomato. Sometimes you'll see corn or the exotic root vegetables such as the aforementioned yuca and *ñamé.*

FRUIT   Panama has a wealth of tropical fruit, but the most common you'll see (especially at breakfast) are pineapple, papaya, banana, and melon. Other fruit are the *maracuyá,* or passionfruit, which is better as a juice than off the tree; *guanabana,* or soursop; and *guayaba,* or guava.

DESSERTS   *Pastel tres leches,* or "three-milk cake," is made with just that: evaporated, condensed, and regular milk, cooked into a rich, puddinglike cake. Flan is as popular here as it is all over Latin America. Street vendors in Panama City (especially on Av. Balboa or in Casco Viejo) sell *raspados,* or fruit-juice–flavored snow cones. Panamanians like to top the cone off with a dollop of condensed milk.

BEVERAGES   You can't find a more fresh-off-the-tree beverage than a *pipa,* the sweet, clear liquid of an unripe coconut. Roadside vendors hack a hole in the crown of the coconut and pop in a straw, and for about 25¢ you have what some refer to as the "nectar of the gods." It is also said to aid digestion. *Chicha* is the common name for juice, and the variety of fresh fruit juices in Panama make a tasty and refreshing elixir on a hot day. *Chichas* come in a variety of common flavors such as watermelon and pineapple, but there are more exotic *chichas* such as *chicha con arroz y piña,* a beverage made from rice and boiled pineapple skins; *naranjilla,* a tropical fruit whose juice has the taste of apple cider; or *chicha de marañón,* a beverage made from the fruit of a cashew tree. A local favorite in the outskirts of Panama City (mostly sold at roadside stands) is *chicheme,* a corn-based beverage mixed with water, sugar, and cinnamon. Panamanians tout the drink for its nutritional properties.

Panama is known for its high-quality coffee, with Café Durán being the most common brand. Artisanal roasters in Panama City, such as Café Unido and Bajareque, have taken Panamanian coffee to new heights, including selling the ultra-premium Geisha varietal, one of the most expensive coffees in the world and one that grows best in Panama.

BEER, WINE & LIQUOR   When in Panama, do as the locals do and down an icy-cold local beer. Beer is Panama's most popular alcoholic drink, and you'll have a wide variety of national brands to sample, such as Balboa, Atlas, Panamá, Soberana, and Cristal—all light pale lagers, none particularly outstanding, but all tasting divine in a hot, sticky climate. International brands such as Heineken, Corona, and Guinness can be found even in small-town markets, though an emerging craft beer scene has taken the country by storm.

Panama's most famous drink is *seco,* a sugar-cane-distilled alcohol produced in Herrera and commonly served with milk and ice. You won't find *seco* in trendy bars or high-end restaurants; it's consumed mostly in rural communities and cantinas. Also popular in Panama are rum, vodka, and scotch. And you won't want to forget to purchase a couple of bottles of **Abuelo,** Panama's surprisingly tasty rum.

You'll find Chilean, U.S., and Spanish wines on most menus, but the selection is limited, and many restaurants serve red wines cold (something to do with the climate). Wine consumption is on the rise, however, evidenced by the growing number of upscale restaurants that put time and thought into their wine lists and a few wine-specialty stores popping up here and there.

THE LAY OF THE LAND

Panama's Ecosystems

Once covered almost entirely in dense rainforest, Panama has seen irreversible damage from deforestation and development. Natural habitats along the Pacific Coast, for example, are being rapidly replaced by high-rise condominiums and golf courses. The Azuero peninsula continues to be harvested and deforested at an alarming pace, meaning that this region is now much drier than the rest of the country, with its natural landscape permanently altered. Over the last decade or so, however, Panama has taken great strides toward protecting its rich biodiversity, and a government focus on eco-minded tourism means Panama is taking measures to conserve its natural resources. About 22% of the country is protected within 14 national parks.

Panama's **lowland rainforests** are true tropical jungles with sweltering, humid climates and up to 180 inches of rainfall per year. The most impressive lowland rainforests stretch from the vast Darién along the coastal Kuna Yala Comarca to the immediate Panama City surroundings to the Bocas del Toro archipelago.

The Darién, covering nearly 17,000 square miles, is Panama's largest province, and one of its least traveled. Bordering Colombia, it has an exaggerated reputation as a dangerous destination, and it is perhaps this reputation that has allowed the Darién to thrive as one of the last bastions of pristine rainforest in the Americas, save for a few towns and a couple dozen Emberá settlements deep in the forest. Here you'll find primary forests, chemically pure rivers, and intricate ecosystems that have thrived thanks to little to no human contact. Thanks also to the Gatun Lake, the fourth-largest manmade lake in the world, the rainforest surrounding Gatun has remained protected from the onset of development, and jungle river cruises are the perfect way to see monkeys, sloths, caymans, birds, and much more if you're sticking around Panama City. Panama's rainforests remain relatively dry between December and mid-April (Oct and Nov are the rainiest months).

In the Chiriquí Highlands and the Valle de Anton, **cloud forests** are a major attraction, with frequent rain, cloudy days, and cooler temperatures. Because cloud forests are found in generally steep, mountainous terrain, the canopy here is lower and less uniform than in lowland rainforests, providing better chances for viewing elusive fauna. Panama's most impressive mountain park and cloud forest is the **Amistad International Park,** spread between the provinces of Chiriquí and Bocas del Toro and actually sharing a border with Costa Rica. **Volcán Barú National Park** is another well-known destination for wildlife and bird-watching, home to **Volcán Barú,** Panama's only active volcano.

Along the coasts, primarily along the Pacific Coast where river mouths meet the ocean, you will find extensive **mangrove forests** and **swamps.** Mangrove swamps are often havens for water birds: cormorants, frigate birds, pelicans, and herons. The larger birds tend to nest up high in the canopy, while the smaller ones nestle in the underbrush. In the province of **Cocle,** the mangroves are well known as crustacean and salt factories, and are also believed to have medicinal and therapeutic properties. Around the seemingly monotonous tangles of mangrove roots lining the shores of the **Bocas del Toro** islands, you'll find one of the richest and most diverse ecosystems in the country. All sorts of fish and crustaceans live in the brackish tidal waters. Caimans and crocodiles cruise the maze of rivers and unmarked canals, and hundreds of herons, ibises, egrets, and other marsh birds nest and feed along the silted banks.

Isla de Coiba on the Pacific side has drawn comparisons to the Galápagos Islands because of its fascinating ecosystems—in fact, the entire island has been declared a national park.

Flora & Fauna

Panama's incredible geographical diversity and hundreds of ecosystems make this tiny sliver of a country a haven for thousands of species of flora and fauna.

Panama is the land bridge that connects Central and South America, and as such is home to flora and fauna native to both continents. In fact, the tiny country of Panama has more bird species than that of the U.S. and Canada combined, and more species of plants in the Canal Basin than in all of Europe! Bird-watchers have spotted up to 367 bird species on trails such as Pipeline Road and the Achiote Road, and there have even been sightings of the elusive **harpy eagle**.

Panama is home to more than 225 species of mammals. Although it is very unlikely that you will spot a **puma,** you have good odds of catching a glimpse of a **monkey, coatimundi, agouti,** or **sloth.** Panama has more than 940 identified species of resident and migrant birds. Panama's reptile species range from the frightening and justly feared **fer-de-lance pit viper** and the massive **American crocodile** to a wide variety of turtles and lizards. With 2,490km (1,547 miles) of shoreline on both the Pacific and Caribbean coasts, the country's diverse sea life includes **whale sharks, leatherback sea turtles, manatees, bottlenose dolphins,** and **humpback whales**.

Tip: Remember that ecosystems are delicate and it is a privilege to visit wildlife in their native habitat. Do not poke, prod, scare, or antagonize wildlife just to have a better look. It may sound obvious, but I've been on enough wildlife excursions to know there are always people who don't seem to remember that you're in the animals' home, not your own—so show respect. Good advice: Travel with a knowledgeable guide for the best chances of seeing a broad selection of Panama's impressive flora and fauna.

PANAMA IN POPULAR CULTURE: BOOKS, MUSIC & FILMS

For a guide to English-language bookstores in Panama City, see "Fast Facts: Panama City," in chapter 4. For literature concerning the natural habitat of Panama, its forests, birds, insects, and wildlife, head straight to the **Corotu Bookstore** at the Smithsonian in Panama City on Roosevelt Avenue in Ancon (© **212-8000**); you won't find a better selection anywhere. Many of the books listed here can be ordered from a Web-based book dealer such as Amazon.

GENERAL INTEREST & HISTORY *Emperors in the Jungle,* by John Lindsay-Poland (Duke University Press, 2003), digs deep into the history of U.S. military involvement in Panama during the past century. *Panama,* by Kevin Buckley (Touchstone, 1992), is a gripping read by a former *Newsweek* correspondent who vividly describes the events leading to the overthrow of Manuel Noriega. Another probing insight into the failure of U.S. policy that led to the rise of Noriega and the invasion is *The Noriega Mess: The Drugs, the Canal, and Why America Invaded,* by Luis E. Murillo (Video Books, 1995), but prepare yourself for 900 pages.

CULTURE *A People Who Would Not Kneel: Panama, the United States and the San Blas Kuna,* by James Howe (Smithsonian Books, 1998), tells of the powerful resistance by the Kuna Indians to set their own terms against invading Europeans and a Panamanian government intent on flattening their culture and relegating them to inferior social status. *The Art of Being Kuna: Layers and Meaning Among the Kuna of Panama,* by Mari Lynn Salvador (University of Washington Press, 1997), is a beautifully illustrated guide to the arts and culture of the Kuna.

THE PANAMA CANAL *Path Between the Seas: The Creation of the Panama Canal, 1870–1914,* by David McCullough (Simon & Schuster, 1978), brings the epic history of the canal to life with McCullough's meticulously researched book—a whopping 704 pages. *How Wall Street Created a Nation: J.P. Morgan, Teddy Roosevelt, and the Panama Canal,* by Ovidio Díaz Espinoso (Four Walls Eight Windows, 2001), is a page-turning account of the intrigue and back-door dealings between a group of Wall Street bankers and lawyers who paved the way for the construction of the Panama Canal.

FIELD GUIDES *A Guide to the Birds of Panama,* by Robert S. Ridgley and John A. Gwynne, Jr. (Princeton University Press, 1992), is the layman's bible to identifying the many birds you'll see during your visit, including tips on where you're most likely to see them. Most guides and nature lodges have a copy of this book on hand, although it's always smart to have your own. A good all-around book to have is Carrol L. Henderson's *The Field Guide to the Wildlife of Costa Rica* (University of Texas Press, 2002). Although it's a Costa Rican guide, this book is useful in Panama since these two neighboring countries are home to much of the same fauna.

NATURAL HISTORY *Tropical Nature: Life and Death in the Rainforests of Central and South America,* by Adrian Forsyth and Ken Miyata (Touchstone Books, 1987), is a passionate, lucid exploration of the interrelationships of flora and fauna in the tropical rainforest. *The Neotropical Companion,* by John C. Kricher (Princeton University Press, 1999), is tremendously popular with field guides, giving a lively and readable overview of ecological processes at work in the neotropics. Juan Carlos Navarro, the former mayor of Panama City, is the author of a glossy coffee-table book, *Parques Nacionales de Panamá* (Balboa Ediciones, 2001), featuring gorgeous photos of national parks in Panama and the flora and fauna found within.

MUSIC & FILMS **Ruben Blades** may be an international movie star and Panama's former Minister of Tourism, but he found fame as a salsa singer/songwriter. He's made dozens of CDs, but you might want to check out his latest creation, *Tangos* (2014), the Grammy-nominated *Eba Say Ajá* (2011), or *Lo Mejor, Vol. 1 and 2* (2004), his greatest hits over his decades-long career.

The Panama Deception (1992) is an interesting documentary that aims to tell the truth about the 1989 invasion of Panama by the U.S.

The Tailor of Panama (2001) is an excellent spy-thriller starring Pierce Brosnan, Geoffrey Rush, and Jamie Lee Curtis and centers around the transfer of power of the canal from the Americans to the Panamanian people during the post-Noriega years.

PANAMA CITY

Long overshadowed by the Panama Canal, Panama City is not only reinventing itself as the thriving commercial and financial hub of Central America, it is asserting itself as a burgeoning tourist destination. In the last decade, the Panama City skyline has ballooned into a Dubai-like cityscape filled with glitzy glass skyscrapers designed by world-renowned architects. It is one of those rare Latin American capitals that appears to have it all: a relatively high standard of living, a seemingly endless supply of investment from abroad, a surplus of natural beauty, and a rich cultural brew of ethnicities and religions. A sizeable expat presence, as well as a growing Asian community, continues to change the face of Panama City.

Signs of Panama City's reinvention are everywhere. The Amador Causeway, formerly a U.S. military base, is now home to the Biomuseo, a biodiversity museum designed by famed architect Frank Gehry. The once rundown 19th-century buildings of Casco Viejo were long off limits at night but have been revitalized with private and public funds and declared a World Heritage Site by UNESCO. The Casco Viejo is now home to dozens of boutique hotels and hip restaurants. Along the coast, swiftly rising skyscrapers, spurred by an irresistible 20-year tax exemption (and rumors of drug laundering), portend a megalopolis in the making. Although traffic can still be a nightmare, a subway system, the first in Central America, has helped alleviate some of the gridlock. Even the dirty Panama Bay has undergone significant cleanup.

But Panama City's visitors need not venture far from their air-conditioned hotels to immerse themselves in the wild tropical jungle that is characteristic of this region. Even the city's Natural Metropolitan Park is the protected home of more than 200 species of birds, mammals, and reptiles. Dozens of remarkable destinations outside the city limits can be reached in less than 2 hours, meaning travelers can spend the day exploring but head back to the city and be well fed and rested for the next day's adventure. Keep in mind, however, that hard-core nature lovers may be put off by Panama City's chaotic layout, traffic, and noise and will probably just want to use Panama City as a stopover before heading elsewhere.

Panama City is the oldest Spanish settlement on the mainland of the Americas, founded in 1519 by Pedro Arias Dávila (Pedrarias the

Cruel). The settlement was used as a base for stealing Peruvian gold and silver and transporting it back to Spain via a treacherous road that linked Panama City with the Caribbean Sea. The immense wealth that passed across the isthmus proved irresistible to treasure-thirsty pirates and buccaneers, who conducted raids throughout the region during the 16th and 17th centuries. In 1671, the Welsh buccaneer Henry Morgan sacked Panama City, and the settlement burned to the ground. The ruins of **Panama Viejo,** or Old Panama, can be toured today. (See "Exploring Panama City," later in this chapter.)

By 1673, Panama City had been rebuilt in what is now known as Casco Viejo; it was heavily fortified and the city was never taken again. Raids on the Caribbean coast mounted, however, and the Spanish, defeated, returned to sailing around Cape Horn in 1746. Panama declared its independence from Spain in 1821 but declined in importance until the Gold Rush of the mid-19th century when thousands of forty-niners used the isthmus as a shortcut from the East Coast of the U.S. to California. Later, when Panama seceded from Colombia in 1903, Panama City was designated the capital. With the opening of the canal in 1914, Panama City became the most important center of trade and commerce in the Americas.

Panama City's modern history was marred by the rise of strongman dictator Manuel Noriega and by the 1989 U.S.–led invasion to overthrow him, which left hundreds dead, most of whom lived in the poor Chorrillo neighborhood. But today Panama City is one of Latin America's safer cities, and the average tourist should feel perfectly secure walking the city's streets.

ESSENTIALS

Arriving
BY PLANE

All international flights, except some from Costa Rica, land at **Tocumen International Airport** (PTY; http://tocumenpanama.aero; ℂ **238-2700**), located 21km (13 miles) from Panama City. Some flights from Costa Rica to Panama City land at Albrook Airport (see below), and there is direct service from San José to David and Bocas del Toro airports. (See chapters 7 and 8, respectively.)

Inside Tocumen's arrival terminal are **Autoridad de Turismo de Panama (ATP) visitors' kiosks** (one in baggage claim and another through the Customs gate), with information about Panama City and some brochures.

The unit of currency in Panama is the U.S. dollar, so for those coming from the United States there is no need to exchange money. If you are coming from elsewhere, the Tocumen airport has currency exchange booths as well as ATMs.

A **licensed taxi** from Tocumen to Panama City costs $30 to $35, including toll fees. Depending on the traffic and the route, the ride can take as little as 20 minutes and as long as an hour. Many hotels offer free scheduled pickup and drop-off service, or you can arrange transportation for a cheaper price—inquire when booking at your hotel. Another taxi option is **Easy Travel Panama** (www.easytravelpanama.net; ℂ **6617-4122**), which offers high-quality

Panama City

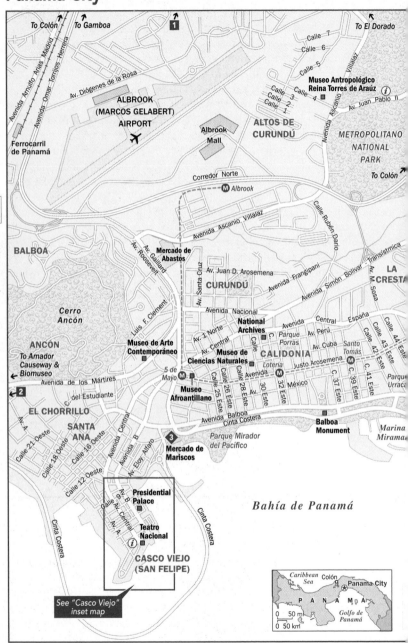

HOTELS ■
Albrook Inn **1**
American Trade Hotel **8**
Bristol Panama **18**
Country Inn & Suites–
  Panama Canal **2**
Hard Rock Hotel Panama
  Megalopolis **26**
Las Clementinas **6**
Luna's Castle Hostel **7**
Panama House B&B **24**

Panama Marriott **19**
Radisson Decapolis **28**
Riande Granada
  Urban Hotel **22**
Tantalo **9**
Torres de Alba **21**
Veneto – A Wyndham
  Grand Hotel **20**
Waldorf Astoria
  Panama **17**

RESTAURANTS ◆
Athanasiou **27**
Bajareque Coffee
  House &
  Roastery **14**
Café Unido **32**
Crave **10**
Donde Jose? **5**
Granclement **12**
Humo **29**
Intimo **30**

La Posta **16**
Las Clementinas **4**
Madrigal **11**
Maito **31**
Manolo Caracol **13**
Market **15**
Palacio Lung Fung **25**
Restaurant Mercado
  del Mariscos **3**
Riesen **23**
Salsipuedes **18**

4

PANAMA CITY | Essentials

vehicles and bilingual drivers and costs just a little bit more than a standard taxi. Rates depend on the itinerary and the number of passengers.

All **rental-car agencies** have desks in the arrival terminal and are open 24 hours a day. See "Getting Around," below, for more information.

Domestic flights, flights to Costa Rica, and charter flights to the 150 or so airstrips located on Panama's islands and remote jungle areas leave from **Marcos A. Gelabert Airport** (PAC), which is more commonly referred to as **Albrook Airport.** Albrook is located northwest of Cerro Ancón (Ancón Hill) off Avenue Omar Torrijos Herrera, near the canal. A taxi costs $5 to $7 to downtown Panama City and takes about 20 minutes without traffic. Rental-car agencies here are generally open from 8am to 6:30pm. Each company offers a key drop-box for customers who need to return a vehicle when rental desks are closed.

Tip: Travelers who arrive at Tocumen Airport and plan to head directly to another destination in Panama via a domestic flight must transfer to Albrook Airport, about a 45-minute drive (or longer during rush hour) from Tocumen. A taxi costs about $40.

BY BUS

If arriving by bus, you'll be dropped off at the Albrook bus terminal near the Albrook airport and shopping center. A taxi to town costs $5 to $7 and takes about 20 minutes without traffic. A taxi to the Gamboa area costs $30 and takes 30 minutes.

BY CAR

Travelers arriving in Panama City by car will do so via the **Pan American Highway** from the west, first crossing the canal on the Puente de las Américas

WHERE THE #@&!%$ IS IT?

Ah, the aggravation of finding an address in Panama City. Just like in the U2 song, this is "Where the Streets Have No Name"—most of the residential streets, anyway. And of the streets that do have an appellation, they are either not signed or are referred to by two or three different names. Some say the reason is that Panama City has never had a postal delivery system. Residents have post office boxes, called *apartados*, which is abbreviated as Apdo, or A.P.

Unbelievably, even taxi drivers are clueless when it comes to city street names beyond major avenues, even if they're labeled on a map. With taxi drivers, it is important to give as much **detailed information** as possible, such as the **cross street** or the **closest major** intersection or, better yet, a **recognizable landmark**—I've found that major hotels are helpful landmarks. Annoyingly, most buildings don't have numbers, so you'll have to rely on landmarks and main streets to get anywhere. Uber cars, where you can plug in the address beforehand, have been a godsend since arriving here in 2014.

If you're nuts enough to drive through Panama City, never do so without a map or an app on your phone. Avenida Balboa runs from Casco Viejo to Panama Viejo and along the coast and is the least-confusing route across town. Also, if you're new to driving in Panama City, it's probably best to practice during off-peak hours; you don't want your initiation to Panama's roads to be rush hour.

(Bridge of the Americas) and arriving in the Balboa district of the city. Follow signs to Avenida Balboa to reach downtown. Drivers headed to Panama City from the west may also use the Puente Centenario (Centennial Bridge), which crosses the canal near Paraíso, and avoid traffic congestion on the Bridge of the Americas. The road that crosses this bridge is also known as Vía Benedicto XVI, named after Pope Benedict XVI.

The Pan American Highway continues east toward Colombia and ends in the Darién Region. It is not possible to reach Colombia by car.

Visitor Information

The **Autoridad de Turismo de Panama (ATP)** has kiosks in both Tocumen and Albrook airports (www.visitpanama.com; ✆ **526-7000** or 526-7100).

City Layout

Panama City lies on the eastern shore of the Panama Canal and is bordered by the Pacific Ocean to the southeast, which can disorient first-time visitors unaccustomed to seeing the sun rise over the Pacific Ocean. Throw in a mesh of looping avenues and streets with two different names, or no name at all, and prepare to feel hopelessly lost during your first few days in Panama City unless you are sticking just to Casco Viejo. Visitors rely on taxis, which are safe and cheap, about $2 to $8 for most locations in the city. Taxis from the city center to the Amador Causeway usually run about $8.

In very general terms, Panama can be divided into **four areas: Old Panama** (the ruins of the first settlement here); **Casco Viejo,** the city center during the late 19th and early 20th centuries; the **former Canal Zone;** and **modern Panama,** with its wide boulevards, glittering skyscrapers, and impoverished slums.

At the southwest end of the city lie the Amador Causeway, Casco Viejo, Cerro Ancón (Ancón Hill), and the former Canal Zone. As a tourist, you'll probably spend most of your time here. From this area, three principal avenues branch out across the city. Avenida Central, which begins in Casco Viejo as a thriving shopping center hawking cheap, imported goods, changes its name to Avenida Central España as it passes through Calidonia, and then becomes Vía España as it runs through the commercial area and financial district of El Cangrejo. Avenida Balboa extends the length of the coast and then forks into Vía Israel, later called Cincuentenario as it heads out to Old Panama. Corredor Sur, a fast-moving toll expressway, connects the city with Tocumen Airport. Avenida Simón Bolivar (also known as Av. 2da. Norte Transístmica) heads north to Colón; however, a toll expressway, called the Corredor Norte, provides a faster route to Colón, eventually connecting with the Transístmica around Chilibre.

There are no beaches in the immediate area of the city—only mudflats. Visitors will need to travel northeast to the Caribbean or southwest to the Pacific beaches, both about a 1- to 1½-hour drive from the city. The following Panama City neighborhoods run from west to east.

NEIGHBORHOODS IN BRIEF

Amador Causeway This manmade peninsula on the south end of town is a popular recreation and dining area with sweeping views of the city skyline and a reliable breeze that is a cool tonic on hot Panamanian days. It is also the site of several condominium and marina developments, as well as the Frank Gehry–designed Biomuseo. Despite its somewhat "manufactured" feel, this is still one of the most pleasant and peaceful areas of the city.

Balboa/Cerro Ancón/Albrook These three quiet residential neighborhoods are located within the former Canal Zone. The domestic airport, Albrook, is here, occupying what once was the U.S. Air Force base, and many young professionals have moved into the "reverted area" for its trademark sturdy wooden houses with wide verandas and lush foliage. Cerro Ancón (Ancón Hill) is the most salient landmark here, offering a 360-degree view of the city and the canal from the lookout point up high. As a tourist, you're unlikely to spend much time in these three neighborhoods.

The neighborhoods El Chorrillo, Santa Ana, and Chinatown, on the eastern side of Cerro Ancón, are dangerous and generally not safe to visit, especially at night.

Calidonia/La Exposición Although the shoreline that fronts these two neighborhoods has been cleaned up and a marina has been built, the interior is still a bit dodgy. Many budget (and downright scary) lodging options are available here, but low-cost lodging can also be found in better neighborhoods like El Cangrejo. Cinta Costera, which hugs the shore, is an excellent place for an afternoon stroll.

Casco Viejo/San Felipe Panama's loveliest neighborhood was once a collection of homes built during the late 1800s and early 1900s, before it became fashionable to live elsewhere in the city. Now revitalized with public and private funds, this historic barrio boasts plenty of impressive old homes and upscale bars and restaurants. Casco Viejo's thorough renovation prompted UNESCO to designate it a World Heritage Site. If you have time to visit just one neighborhood in Panama City, make it this one.

The Coastline: Marbella/Punta Paitilla/ Punta Pacífica Residential towers and shopping malls are the identifying characteristics of this area, where a confluence of Panama's newly moneyed, illegally moneyed, and recently retired residents lives in glitz-and-glass high-rises overlooking the sea. The new Cinta Costera, a boardwalk of sorts on the ocean side of Avenida Balboa, is a popular Friday and Saturday night hangout for Panamanians.

El Cangrejo/Area Bancaria/Bella Vista/ Obarrio These four neighborhoods border each other, but they are so compact they could be considered part of the financial/ business district. Older El Cangrejo has a "lived-in" look and hilly streets that lend this neighborhood charm. Just to the south, the Area Bancaria (Financial District), in addition to El Cangrejo and Obarrio, is where most travelers end up lodging, since it has the highest concentration of hotels, restaurants, shopping, and nightlife.

Panama Viejo On the eastern edge of the city are the ruins of Panama Viejo, the first settlement in Panama, which was later burned to the ground. Many people visit as part of a guided tour, but the area also has a pleasant walking/jogging path along the shore and a self-guided interpretive trail that winds through the ruins.

Getting Around
BY TAXI

Taxis are inexpensive, safe, and plentiful—except when it is raining during rush hour and it seems as if every worker heading to, or leaving, work is trying to flag one down. Quite often, a taxi will stop for another passenger if he or she is headed in your general direction, but the driver will usually deliver you to your destination first. Panama City taxis also have the infuriating habit of refusing to drive you if they don't feel like heading where you're headed, so you may have to hail a few cabs before one agrees to take you. Taxis charge $2 to $7 for most destinations within Panama City, but confirm the price beforehand—the "zones" that taxi drivers use for price reference are vague. Taxis from the city center to the Amador Causeway will run you about $6. Unscrupulous drivers may try to charge you more, especially to and from the Amador Causeway. What I do to prevent overcharging is simply pay the driver without asking how much I owe. I pretty much know that anywhere within El Cangrejo and the Area Bancaria should cost no more than $3; Albrook $5. I figure if the driver thinks you know what you're doing, he's less likely to rip you off.

Tip: Some taxis, usually black cars, work directly for a hotel and charge up to three times the going fare—and they're not going to budge when you contest the fare. These are the taxis that await guests directly at the front door. Simply walk out to the street and flag a taxi down for a cheaper fare. Better yet, order an Uber, which will usually turn up within a few minutes.

ON FOOT

Panama City is not easy to navigate on foot because of its interweaving streets, streets that are not signed, and lack of recognizable landmarks for visitors. Also, many neighborhoods aren't within walking distance of each other. To get around without a fuss, take a cab.

On the other hand, the best (really *only*) way to see **Casco Viejo** is on foot. Walking lets you savor the neighborhood's colonial architecture, visit a museum, and stop for lunch. For a walking tour, see p. 56. The Cinta Costera has a long seafront walkway that starts near Punta Paitilla and ends at the Mercado de Marisco (the fish market). The Calzada de Amador (Amador Causeway) was designed for walking, jogging, and bicycling, with some 6.5km (4 miles) of landscaped pedestrian trails.

BY PUBLIC TRANSPORT

The traveler in Panama City will feel more comfortable getting around by taxi than by bus or Metro, even after the city overhauled its famous "Red Devil" buses for a more modern mass transit system. The first phase of the Metro, Central America's first subway, runs for 13km (8 miles) from the Albrook Mall/International Bus Station and through the city to the neighborhood of Los Andes. Although it's clean, secure, and efficient, the line is limited and not much use for tourists, since most stops are outside of prime areas. You can buy rechargeable Metro fare cards from automated machines in the stations for $2, and additional money is added for the fare ($0.35). The cards can also be used on the MetroBus.

TIPS FOR drivers IN PANAMA CITY

If for some reason you must drive through town, consider the following advice:

o Prepare for abrupt stops when cars turn into or cross your lane, especially on wide avenues such as Balboa. You as a driver should be aggressive in this sense, too, and nose your way into oncoming traffic when making a left turn or merging into traffic—other cars will slow down for you, but this is a maneuver that is best learned from watching other drivers.

o Many streets are unsigned or not named, and often a one-way street is only advertised by the fact that all parked cars face one direction. First-time drivers in Panama City make a lot of U-turns and last-minute decisions, so don't lose patience.

o Keep cool under pressure and don't panic if an unexpected turn takes you into a spooky neighborhood. Have an open map at hand, keep your doors locked, and pull over if you need to find a route to get you headed in the right direction again.

o Crosswalks in Panama City are poorly marked to nonexistent, so most pedestrians jaywalk (or rather run) across the street when the coast is more or less clear. Keep this in mind while driving in Panama City—the last thing you want is to have an unfortunate accident.

o Do not leave anything inside a parked vehicle.

o On some busy streets, a raggedy, self-styled "parking guard" might ask to watch your car. Pay him or her around 50¢. Some parking guards will demand payment of $1 or $2 before you leave your car in neighborhoods such as Casco Viejo or Bella Vista. Just do it. Do you really want to argue with a less than savory-looking character over $1?

BY CAR

You do not need a rental car while visiting just Panama City, considering how economical taxis are. Admittedly, many destinations and attractions lie outside the city; if you're an independent traveler who wants to see the sights beyond the city on your own, pick up your car rental at one of the airport terminals and head straight out of the city on a well-signed thoroughfare. Some road signs are small and easy to miss, so pay attention to every sign on the road; in other places there are no "official" signs for a turnoff, only a sprinkling of commercial signs bearing the town name, which should clue you in to where you are. Travelers who have a basic command of Spanish will have the easiest time asking directions. In any case, bring a good map. If you are renting a car to visit outlying areas such as the canal, Portobelo, or the Panamanian interior, have your rental agency show you in detail the quickest and most efficient route to your destination. See "Tips for Drivers in Panama City," below.

You'll find car-rental kiosks at both the Tocumen and Albrook airports (car-rental agencies at Tocumen are open 24 hr.; Albrook rental agencies are open 8am–6:30pm), and most agencies also have a few locations in town. For contact information for Tocumen Airport car-rental agencies, see "Getting Around" in chapter 11.

[FastFACTS] PANAMA CITY

ATMS ATMs are all over Panama City in banks, hotel lobbies, malls, gas stations, and pharmacies. Many, if not most, are available 24 hours.

Doctors Many Panamanian doctors received their medical degrees in the U.S.; therefore, many speak English. The best hospitals in Panama City are **Centro Médico Paitilla,** at Calle 53 and Avenida Balboa (www.centromedicopaitilla.com; ⟨✆⟩ **265-8800); Clínica Hospital San Fernando,** at Avenida Central España (⟨✆⟩ **305-6300); Hospital Nacional,** at Avenida Cuba between Calle 38 and Calle 39 (⟨✆⟩ **207-8100** or 207-8102); and **Hospital Punta Pacífica,** at Calle 53 in Bella Vista (www.hospitalpunta pacifica.com; ⟨✆⟩ **204-8000).** Punta Pacífica is the most modern hospital in the country and is affiliated with Johns Hopkins University.

Drugstores Called *farmacias* in Spanish, drugstores are plentiful in Panama City. For 24-hour service, visit a branch of **El Rey** supermarket, the most central of which is on Vía España (⟨✆⟩ **223-1243).** Another reliable pharmacy

is **Farmacias Arrocha** (⟨✆⟩ **360-4000),** with locations at Vía España in front of El Panama Hotel, Vía Argentina, and Punta Paitilla. You will probably be able to get most of your medication without a prescription, but bring an empty prescription container just in case; medications often have different names and an official prescription or prescription container can help the pharmacist figure out what medicine you're asking for.

Emergencies For fire, dial ⟨✆⟩ **103;** for police, dial **104;** for an ambulance, dial **Seguro Social** at ⟨✆⟩ **502-2532** or **Cruz Roja** at ⟨✆⟩ **228-2187.**

Express Mail Services Many international courier and express-mail services have offices in Panama City, including **UPS** (⟨✆⟩ **269-9222)** in Obarrio (near El Cangrejo) at Calle 53 E in the Edificio Torre Swiss Bank; **Fed Ex** (⟨✆⟩ **800-1122)** on Calle 3 in Costa del Oeste; and **Mail Boxes Etc.,** a one-stop service with locations on Avenida Balboa in Paitilla in the Marisol Building, no. 1 (⟨✆⟩ **264-7038),** on Vía España next

to Niko's Café in the Financial District (⟨✆⟩ **214-4620),** and in the Multiplaza Mall (⟨✆⟩ **302-4162).**

Internet Nearly every hotel in Panama City has Wi-Fi, usually without a fee.

Post Office Postal service is scarce in Panama City; your best bet is to ask your hotel to mail something for you or try Mail Boxes Etc. (see "Express Mail Services" above). The central post office (Correos y Telégrafos) is open Monday through Friday 8am to 4pm and Saturday 8am to 1pm, and is located on Avenida Central in front of the Mercado de Mariscos (⟨✆⟩ **212-7680).**

Safety As Latin American cities go, Panama City is very safe for foreign travelers who stay out of bad neighborhoods such as Calidonia, Curundú, El Chorrillo, and Santa Ana. Chinatown is dangerous day and night as well. As in any major urban area, use common sense when it comes to safekeeping valuables—for example, don't put your wallet in your back pocket. Money and other valuables are best carried in hard-to-reach places, like deep pockets or a money belt or cross-body purses for women. Keep an eye out for suspicious characters who linger too close or follow too closely. Consider taking money out of ATMs during the day to avoid stepping out from a brightly lit cashpoint into darkness. Scams are not common here; muggings and purse-snatchings happen, but not frequently. Be smart and don't go out late at night by yourself, especially if you've been drinking. If you park a car on the street, do not leave any valuables inside that could attract a thief, even if you park in a guarded parking lot.

EXPLORING PANAMA CITY

Few cities in the Americas can compete with Panama City when it comes to things to see and do. Some travelers spend their entire visit in and around Panama City, touring sights such as the historical ruins of Panama Viejo, walking the enchanting streets of Casco Viejo, visiting Natural Metropolitan Park, or strolling the Amador Causeway. Visitors also head outside the city limits for day excursions such as boating in the canal, bird-watching and trekking in Soberanía National Park, and visiting Emberá Indian villages. Excursions outside the city limits are highlighted in chapter 5, "Around Panama City."

It is recommended that travelers book a city tour; transportation is included, and the experience is enriched by interpretative background provided by a bilingual guide. Half-day city tours include a morning visit to Old Panama and Casco Viejo; full-day tours head to the Miraflores Locks at the canal in the afternoon. **Ancon Expeditions** (www.anconexpeditions.com; ✆ **269-9415**), **Gloria Mendez Tours** (www.viajesgloriamendez.com; ✆ **263-6555**), and **Pesantez Tours** (www.pesantez-tours.com; ✆ **223-5374**) all offer full and half-day tours of Panama City and the surrounding area.

If you want to see Panama City on your own, taxi drivers charge between $20 and $30 per hour. Every hotel has a personal recommendation for a private cab and can arrange the details.

Panama Viejo ★★

Many mistake the Casco Viejo port neighborhood for Panama City's first Spanish settlement. It is actually Panama Viejo, which lies a few minutes northeast of the city center. From the highway, the area looks like the ruins of an ancient Roman city. It was founded by conquistador Pedrarías Dávila in 1519, making it one of the oldest European settlements in the Americas. It was burnt down by pirate Henry Morgan in 1671 and then abandoned, with the capital moving to its present-day location. Sometimes called Panamá la Vieja, the city was where much of the gold raided from the Andes was unloaded before it was hauled across the isthmus on mules to depart on Spain-bound ships. Much of the stone of the city, now a UNESCO World Heritage Site with Casco Viejo, was dismantled for use in building the modern city.

You can still admire the newly restored Plaza Mayor and adjoining bell tower of Panama's original cathedral, as well as collections of walls from

SPANISH-LANGUAGE programs

If you're moving to Panama or plan to stay for an extended time, you'll need to pick up the local lingo. The many language institutes in Panama offering group and private classes tend to vary in quality. If you're limited on time, I recommend working with a private tutor until you decide which school is the best fit for you. The following are some recommended options.

Spanish Panama, Calle 2a Norte, off Vía Argentina (www.spanishpanama.com; © 213-3121), is a Canadian-directed school with certified bilingual professors, offering crash courses or private classes either at the school or in your hotel, residence, or business. A month-long program is also available that includes excursions around town to place yourself in real-life situations where Spanish is necessary. It also offers salsa dance classes, instruction in traditional Panamanian dance, and other cultural talks and activities. The Spanish Panama school has been modernized to include a space three times larger than its previous location, with spacious classrooms overlooking tree-lined and fashionable Vía Argentina. It has a lab and a large city-view terrace and kitchen area. The staff is very friendly and professional. Group lessons start at $260 per week to $790 for 4 weeks. Additionally, it offers varying housing options suitable for all types, from homestays with Panamanian families to discounts at major hotels or furnished apartments.

Spanish Abroad, Inc. (www.spanish abroad.com; © 888/722-7623), is located in the El Dorado neighborhood and offers group (a maximum of four people) and private classes, plus homestays with local Panamanian families. Classes focus on travel and professional Spanish, and specialty courses, such as law, business, and medical Spanish, are also available. Group lessons run from $450 to $780 per week to $1,490 to $3,120 per month. Classes are usually given between 8:30am and 12:30pm Monday through Friday. Cultural activities, homestays, books and learning materials, and two meals a day are included in all prices.

EPA! (www.studyspanishinpanama. com; © 391-4044) offers semi-intensive, intensive, and super-intensive classes, as well as general Spanish and private classes. Located in the Plaza Paitilla shopping center in downtown Panama, classes start at $850 per month for intensive Spanish and $700 per month for semi-intensive Spanish. Check the website for class start dates. EPA! can also hook students up with accommodations options: Homestays range from $95 to $150 per student depending on whether you want a shared or private room, and shared apartments range from $150 to $225 per week.

various convents and palaces. The visitor center displays indigenous pottery that predates the city, artifacts from colonial times, and a model of what the city would have looked like before it was destroyed. Save a few minutes before leaving to browse the small but good handicraft market beside the visitor center. You'll need a half day here at least. Panama Viejo is at Vía Cincuentenario, beside la Estatua Morelos (www.panamaviejo.org; © **226-8915;** admission $6 for Plaza Mayor and visitor center; $4 for tower and ruins; daily 9am–5pm).

Casco Viejo ★★★

No trip to Panama City would be complete without a visit to Casco Viejo, the Old Quarter, also referred to as Casco Antiguo or by its original and formal name, San Felipe. This quintessentially charming neighborhood, with its narrow streets, has turn-of-the-19th-century Spanish-, Italian-, and French-influenced architecture, bougainvillea-filled plazas, and a breezy promenade that juts out into the sea. Visitors often compare Casco Viejo to Havana or Cartagena. The neighborhood's historical importance and antique beauty spurred UNESCO in 1997 to declare it a World Heritage Site. Because Casco Viejo provides such an ideal place to wander around and lose yourself in the splendor of the city streets, I've included a walking tour (see below), with dozens of points of interest; you can really begin and end wherever it suits you.

For the past century, Casco Viejo was nothing more than a rundown neighborhood whose antique mansions were left to rot after wealthy residents moved to other parts of Panama City. With the drop in land value, squatters and low-income families moved in, many of whom continue to live here but are being pushed out by a public and privately funded large-scale gentrification project. Throughout the neighborhood lovingly restored mansions line the streets and are being turned into stylish boutique hotels, trendy restaurants, hipster brewpubs, sleek art galleries, and upscale private residences.

Safety note: In spite of Casco Viejo's renovation projects and the fact that both the mayor's *and* the president's offices are located here, tourists should stay alert and protect themselves from theft. Generally speaking, the peninsula of Casco Viejo, starting at Calle 11 Este and heading east and away from the Santa Ana neighborhood, is safe. There are two principal entryways into Casco Viejo, but both pass through poor ghettos, so always take a **taxi** to get here. Taxis for a trip out of Casco Viejo can usually be found around the Plaza de la Independencia, or if you are dining here, have the restaurant call one for you. The Estación de Policía de Turismo (Tourism Police Station) is on Avenida Central at Calle 3a Este; the office is open 24 hours, and it has an English-speaking attendant from Monday to Friday, 8am to 5pm. Generally, they do a good job of patrolling Casco Viejo and are relatively helpful if you run into any problems.

WALKING TOUR: HISTORIC CASCO VIEJO

START:	**At Plaza Independencia.**
FINISH:	**At Iglesia de San José (a 2-block walk from Plaza Independencia).**
TIME:	**Approximately 1 to 2 hours.**
BEST TIMES:	**The streets are quieter on Sundays, when churches are most active.**
	Some restaurants and museums are closed either Sunday or Monday.

Walking Tour: Historic Casco Viejo

1 Plaza de la Independencia

2 Palacio Presidencial (Presidential Palace)

3 Plaza Bolívar

4 Teatro Nacional (National Theater)

5 Plaza de Francia

6 Iglesia de Santo Domingo & the Museo de Arte Religioso Colonial

7 Casa Góngora

8 Iglesia de la Merced

9 Plaza Herrera

10 Iglesia de San José

1 Plaza de la Independencia

Take a taxi to Plaza de la Independencia and begin your tour. This is where Panama declared its independence from Colombia on November 3, 1903. Several important landmarks are located here, notably the **Catedral Metropolitana (Metropolitan Cathedral),** easily recognizable by its contrasting gray, ashlar-stone facade flanked by two white neoclassical bell towers inlaid with mother-of-pearl. The cathedral took more than 100 years to build and is one of the largest in Central America.

On the south side of the plaza is the must-see **Museo del Canal Interoceánico** (p. 65). The neoclassical building was built in 1875 as the Gran Hotel and converted into Canal Headquarters by the French in 1881; later it was used as offices for the U.S. canal commission. It is considered to be the finest example of French architecture in Casco Viejo.

Next door, on the second floor of the Palacio Municipal, is the **Museo de la Historia de Panamá,** a ho-hum display of exhibits charting the history of the Panamanian republic.

The **Hotel Central,** on the east side of the plaza, was built in 1880 and was once among the most luxurious hotels in the Americas. It sat abandoned for many years, though at press time a new 150-room hotel and spa was being constructed there.

Walk north on Calle 6a Este (from the middle of the plaza toward the city skyline of Panama City) to Avenida Alfaro, and turn right.

2 Palacio Presidencial (Presidential Palace)

Calle 6a Este leads to the Presidential Palace, but you'll have to show your passport (or a copy) to the security guards on the street before they'll let you pass. This is the White House of Panama, the offices of Panama's President Juan Carlos Varela, and a gorgeous Spanish mansion with a Moorish interior patio and fountain (you can't enter, but you can take a peek from the outside). Two African herons—whose Spanish name, *garza,* is the reason the palace is also called the Palacio de las Garzas—glide back and forth across the front patio. The city skyline views from this street are outstanding.

Turn right on Calle 5a Este, head south 1 block, and then turn left on Avenida B. Walk 1 block until you reach Parque Bolívar.

3 Plaza Bolívar

One of Casco Viejo's prettiest spots, Plaza Bolívar and the buildings that surround it have undergone a facelift over the past few years, and there are several cafes here for those who feel like stopping for a coffee or snack. Originally called Plaza de San Francisco, the plaza was renamed in 1883 in honor of Simon Bolívar, widely considered in Latin America to be the hero of independence from Spain. A commemorative monument to Bolívar is in the center of the plaza.

The grand **Palacio Bolívar** (now the offices of the Ministry of Foreign Relations), on the northeast edge of the plaza, was built on the grounds of a former Franciscan monastery that succumbed to various fires. Of interest here is the totally restored **Salón Bolívar ★★** (© **228-9594;** Tues–Sat 9am–4pm, Sun 1–5pm; $2 adults, 50¢ students), site of the famous 1826 congress organized by Bolívar to discuss the unification of Colombia, Mexico, and Central America. The historical importance of this salon prompted UNESCO to declare Casco Viejo a World Heritage Site. During office hours (Mon–Fri 9am–3pm), it is possible to visit the courtyard inside the Palacio and admire the building's lovely architecture and tile work.

Next to the Palacio is the **Iglesia y Convento de San Francisco de Asís (Church and Convent of St. Francis of Assisi),** one of the original structures from Casco Viejo but nearly totally destroyed by fires in 1737 and 1756. Its most recent restoration was in 1998.

Across the plaza, on Avenida B and Calle 4 Este (you'll pass it when arriving at the plaza), is the **Iglesia San Felipe de Neri,** one of the first churches built in Casco Viejo (1684–88). Though damaged by fires, the church has been restored and is worth checking out, at least from the outside. The church apparently opens to the public only twice a year.

Turn left on the south end of the plaza onto Avenida B to visit the:

4 Teatro Nacional (National Theater)

Built between 1905 and 1908 on the grounds of the old Concepción Monastery, the lovely Teatro Nacional hosts theater, classical music, and ballet performances; unfortunately, they do not have a website and their show calendar is available only by calling ✆ **262-3525** or by checking local listings, such as the www.thepanamanews.com.

The theater opened in 1908 with a presentation of Verdi's *Aida,* and it is perhaps best known for the frescoes rendered by Panama's most famous painter, Roberto Lewis. Recent renovations have preserved both the frescoes and the baroque decor (scarlet and gilded tiered balconies and a grand chandelier). The cost to enter and poke around is $1 per person. It's open Monday through Friday 8am to 4pm and sometimes on the weekends (but with no set schedule).

Following Avenida B, behind the National Theater, is the **Ministerio de Gobierno y Justicia,** initially designed as a presidential building and built in a neoclassical design in 1908 in tandem with the National Theater by the Italian architect Genaro Ruggieri.

Continue along Avenida B (the street bends and changes names for 1 block to Calle 2da) until it ends at Avenida Central. Turn left on Avenida Central (Calle 1a) and follow until arriving at the stairs to the Esteban Huertas walkway. Walk up and circle the:

5 Plaza de Francia

The Plaza de Francia (French Plaza) is a Casco Viejo highlight, a historically important site, and a delightful place to stroll around and crunch on a *raspado* (snow cone) from one of the several vendors. There is also a wonderful fresh breeze here.

When you head down Calle 1a, the road turns into an inviting and lovely walkway called **Paseo Esteban Huertas,** which is partially covered by pretty bougainvillea. Originally part of Panama City's defense against pirate attacks, this colonial-era stone promenade and seawall stretches from the Antigo Club Union for several blocks. Abandoned for centuries, *las bóvedas* refers to the chambers and jail cells that form part of the structure. These vaults were restored in the 1980s and now contain several posh shops and cafés. Sidewalk vendors, including Kuna Yala women selling *molas,* are everywhere here.

The **Instituto Nacional de Cultura** occasionally holds art exhibits and special events in two of the restored chambers. From this vantage point you can see the Bridge of the Americas and ships lining up for their turn to enter the canal.

Continue along the walkway and down to the French Plaza. Originally the main plaza (Plaza de Armas) of Panama City, it is now a commemorative monument to the failed French canal effort.

6 Iglesia de Santo Domingo & Museo de Arte Religioso Colonial

Only ruins remain of Iglesia de Santo Domingo, built in 1678 but victim of several fires, including one in 1781, from which time it was never fully rebuilt. The church kept its fame, however, through the building's unusual supporting arch made of stone, which survived the fire. The arch, called Arco Chato, was unusual in that it was long and not very arching, seemingly defying gravity. It's the centerpiece of what is now an event and cultural space. When U.S. senators debated whether to build a canal in Panama or Nicaragua, they took the arch's longevity to mean that little earthquake activity made Panama a safer place to build. Next to the ruin site is the **Museo de Arte Religioso Colonial.**

Continue 1 more block to Calle 4ta, turn right, and walk 1 block to Avenida Central. Here on the east corner is:

7 Casa Góngora

This structure is the best-preserved example of a Spanish colonial home in Casco Viejo. The house, built in 1760 by a wealthy merchant, was renovated with city funds, and much of its original woodwork, including ceiling beams, has been maintained. The Casa is also home to the **Centro Cultural Casa Góngora** (© **393-6243**), a cultural center for local artists, with occasional live jazz music, folkloric presentations, fashion shows, and changing art exhibitions. Drop by to see what's happening or check out the newspaper's calendar listings for shows.

Head up Avenida Central, crossing the Plaza de la Independencia (where you started). Continue on to Calle 9a to:

8 Iglesia de la Merced

Built in 1680, this church was transferred, stone by stone, from its Panama Viejo site. The facade is still an excellent example of one of Casco Viejo's oldest buildings.

Walk south down Calle 9a until you come to:

9 Plaza Herrera

The lively Plaza Herrera is dedicated to General Tomás Herrera in honor of his battle for independence when Panama was still part of Colombia. Park benches here are good for people-watching or just for resting. It's become the heartbeat of Casco gentrification, being the setting for the American Trade Hotel and several other upscale ventures.

Walk 1 block east on Avenida A to Calle 8a. You'll come to:

10 Iglesia de San José

Your last stop is at the most famous of Casco Viejo's churches, the Iglesia de San José, and its baroque golden altar. The story goes that when pirate Henry Morgan raided Panama Viejo, a priest had the altar painted black to hide it from looters, later moving the altar to Casco Viejo. However, studies place the altar's stylistic details to the 18th century, casting doubt on this legend. It's a gorgeous work of art nevertheless and worth a stop. From here, you can head back to Plaza Independencia by walking 1 more block east on Avenida A, turning left on Calle 7, and walking 1 block.

Cerro Ancón ★★

This conspicuous forested hill rising 200m (650 ft.) above the city is another "reverted" property from the canal days that is now open to the public. The hill is bordered in the north by Heights and Culebra streets, and avenidas Arías and de los Mártires in the south. At the entrance to the office of the environmental organization ANCON at Calle Quarry Heights, a winding, pedestrian-only road provides for a brisk uphill walk to a **lookout point ★★★**, with 360-degree views of the city center, Casco Viejo, and the canal. The hill is home to tiny Geoffrey's tamarins, *ñeques* (agoutis), and migratory birds. The **Museo de Arte Contemporáneo** is here (see "Museums," below).

Panama Canal Murals ★ The effort to create a water passage across the isthmus of Panama is one of mankind's greatest achievements, and these vibrant murals powerfully depict the process. The four murals were done by William B. Van Ingen, a painter from New York who also did murals for the Library of Congress in Washington and the U.S. Mint in Philadelphia. The first depicts the excavation of the Gaillard Cut, the second shows the construction of the Gatún Dam, the third the construction of the Gatún Locks, and the last is an impressive depiction of the building of the Miraflores Locks.

The murals are located high on a grassy slope in the **Canal Administration Building** (© 272-7602), built by the U.S. in 1914, and it houses the offices of the Autoridad del Canal de Panamá (Panama Canal Authority). At the bottom of the slope is the formidable Goethals Monument, dedicated to the chief canal engineer, George W. Goethals, who initiated construction of the Canal Building. Entering the building, visitors are taken aback by the beauty of the glass cupola, the focal point of the lobby. The cupola is encircled with the handsome murals that narrate the heroism and relentless struggle to build the canal. Visitors may visit only this wing of the building, and admission is free.

To put the Canal Zone in perspective, head out to the back of the building, facing the Goethals Monument. The flagpole here once displayed ensigns from both Panama and the United States, but today the only flag proudly flapping in the wind is Panamanian. There is a broad view of the Balboa neighborhood and the Bridge of the Americas beyond it. This area was a residential zone for American canal employees before the handover. Today the buildings have been converted into residences for Panamanians, most of whom have no connection to the canal.

You may wish to visit the Canal Building before heading up to the top of Cerro Ancón because the road (via Quarry Heights) leads up from here.

Parque Natural Metropolitano ★

The Natural Metropolitan Park is one of the only protected tropical forests within the city limits of a major urban area in the Americas. In just a 5- to

10-minute taxi ride, you can delve into the earthy environs of thick jungle with a surprising array of fauna, more than 200 species of birds, and 40 species of mammals. Expect to see mostly birds and the occasional blue Morpho butterfly fluttering by. The park, roughly 265 hectares (655 acres), is located on the northern edge of Panama City, hemmed in by a few rather busy roads, including the noisy Corredor Norte, which runs along the eastern flank of the park. The park is overseen by the Smithsonian Tropical Research Institute, which carries out scientific studies here, and by the city, which maintains an administration center with maps, educational exhibits, and a bookstore. If you're planning to visit any regional national parks such as Soberanía, skip this attraction; if your visit to the country is limited to Panama City, this park is worth a visit.

Three short trails give visitors a chance to get out and stretch their legs. **Los Momótides** trail is the shortest (30 min.) and the best choice for young children and visitors in a hurry. It begins at the administration center, but you must cross busy Avenida Juan Pablo II, so be careful. **Mono Tití Road** heads up to Cedro Hill and a lookout point with sweeping views of the city; alert hikers occasionally catch sight of Geoffrey's tamarins, a pint-size primate, along this trail. The most difficult trail, and the longest at 2 hours round-trip, is **Cienequita Trail,** which begins just up the road from the center. It is possible to connect with Mono Tití Road after reaching the lookout point. If you'd prefer something more adventurous, **Ancon Expeditions** recently launched its "Metropolitan Nature Park and Smithsonian Rainforest Canopy Crane" tour, perfect for nature lovers and bird-watchers alike, especially if you won't be venturing far from the city. The tour consists of a 50-minute ride on the Smithsonian's 42m-high (138-ft.) research crane, plus 2 hours of nature observation along Parque Metropolitano Natural's hiking trails. The guided tour is limited to groups of four, costs $140 per person, and includes transportation to and from any hotel in Panama City, plus an English-speaking guide.

The park (www.parquemetropolitano.org; ✆ **232-5516** or 232-5552) is open daily from 6am to 6pm; the visitor center is open Monday to Friday 6:30am to 4:30pm and Saturday 8am to 1pm. Adult entrance is $4 per person, children $2. Trail maps are also available for a small fee.

Calzada de Amador (Amador Causeway) ★★

The Amador Causeway is a series of four small islands—Naos, Culebra, Perico, and Flamenco—connected by a road and pedestrian walkway that projects out into the Panama Bay, offering spectacular views of the glittering city skyline and a consistent breeze. The islands, once the haunt of pirates, were connected in the early 1900s with rock and dirt excavated from the Culebra Cut in the Panama Canal to form a breakwater for a protective harbor for ships waiting to enter the canal, and to prevent the buildup of sediment. Later, the United States militarized the promontory and fortified it with ordnance for protection during the two world wars. The causeway remained off-limits to Panamanians until 1999, when the canal handover opened this prime spot of real estate, much to the delight of walkers, joggers, bike riders, and diners. There is nothing like strolling along the causeway early in the morning with the sun rising over the Pacific and casting its pastel hues on the glittering high-rises of downtown Panama City. The causeway is packed on Sundays. Numerous large-scale tourism and real-estate projects have been recently completed or are in the works here, such as the Frank Gehry–designed **Biomuseo,** a **marina,** a **convention center,** and the **Smithsonian's Punta Culebra Nature Center.**

Punta Culebra Nature Center (PCNC) ★ MUSEUM Set out on the tiny islet of Naos near the very end of the Amador Causeway, this is part of the Smithsonian's Tropical Research Institute and a kid-friendly, open-air museum dedicated to the interpretation and conservation of the coast. It has turtle and shark pools, as well as a "touching pool" where children can get up close and personal with sea cucumbers and starfish. There are also white mangroves, tropical aquariums with native species, and a nature trail that winds through the dry forest. Strategically set on the site of a former U.S. defense base, the nature center has a lookout point with sweeping views of the entrance to the canal. The opening of the Biomuseum nearby has caused attendance to fall; you'll likely have this place all to yourself. Bring sunscreen—you'll be outside quite a bit—and plan to spend a few hours here. Note that the Nature Center is closed from April through late December.

> ### Biking Along the Causeway
>
> Although downtown Panama City's chaotic, potholed streets don't exactly lend themselves to biking, the Amador Causeway and the surrounding residential neighborhoods are a perfect spot to spend a couple hours burning off those *patacones* (fried green plantains) and *yucca fritas.* Most shops along the causeway rent bicycles and "family bikes" for up to four people. Rates range from $3 per hour for a standard bike to $18 per hour for a four-person cart.

Isla Naos, Amador Causeway. www.stri.si.edu/english/visit_us/culebra/index.php. ℂ **212-8793.** Admission $2 adults, 50¢ kids 11 and under, $1 seniors. Late Dec–Mar, daily 10am–6pm; call ahead to confirm. Closed Apr–late Dec.

Museums

Museums across Panama are underfunded and poorly staffed, and the story here in the capital isn't any different just because it's a metropolitan city. Volunteers and nonprofit organizations are the ones who keep the museums hanging in there, sometimes only by a thread. Aside from the recommendations below, most museums in Panama City are worth visiting only if you happen to already be in the neighborhood.

Keep in mind that museums are closed on Monday and hours often change, so it's wise to call ahead and verify.

Biomuseo ★★★ MUSEUM Nature and architecture meet at Frank Gehry's first Latin American project, Biomuseo, a natural diversity museum on the Amador Causeway, not far from the entrance to the Panama Canal. The $90-million project, which took a decade to get off the ground, is highlighted by a vibrant shell of vivid red, orange, green, blue, and yellow plates. As you might expect, it is nothing like any natural history museum you have ever seen. Designed with the help of scientists from the Smithsonian Institution and the University of Panama, the site includes eight different galleries. The aim is to educate through interactive experiences rather than more traditional static displays. In the Panarama gallery, for example, three levels of screens make visitors feel as if they are actually in the jungle. In the Human Footprint gallery, 3 million years of Panama Isthmus wildlife is displayed through sculptures. Through two different aquariums you'll learn the difference between marine life on Panama's Pacific and Caribbean coasts. You could literally spend days here and never get bored, though a few hours will probably suffice. A great on-site café serves Panamanian foods. An outdoor biodiversity park, still under construction, will serve as a living extension to the museum.

Amador Causeway. www.biomuseopanama.org. © **314-0097.** $22 adults; $11 students/children 18 and under. Mon, Wed–Fri 10am–4pm; Sat–Sun 10am–5pm.

Museo Afroantillano (Afro-Antillian Museum) ★ MUSEUM This
small museum housed in the 1910-era Iglesia de la Misión Cristiana pays tribute to the more than 30,000 West Indians who represented 85% of all foreign laborers during the building of railroads and later the canal. Afro-Antillians were relegated to the most menial and treacherous of all work, and many lost their lives in the process. Within the museum are reconstructed examples of their poor living quarters, as well as old photos and other antiques from the early 1900s. It takes about 20 minutes to see everything, which is good because the neighborhood here is awfully sketchy and doesn't induce you to linger or wander around. Take a cab directly to and from here.

Calle 24 Oeste and Av. Justo Arosemena (Av. 3 Sur). www.samaap.org. © **501-4131.** Admission $1 adults, 25¢ children. Tues–Sat 9:30am–3:30pm. Closed holidays. Museum occasionally closes early; call ahead to verify hours.

Museo Antropológico Reina Torres de Araúz ★ MUSEUM Infa-
mously robbed in 2003 (thieves hauled off some 300 pre-Columbian gold artifacts, since recovered), Panama's premier anthropological museum, the MARTA, has subsequently regained much of the reputation it lost. With more than 15,000 pre-Columbian pieces on display in its new location in the Altos de Curund, the museum is dedicated to Panama's pioneering anthropologist, Reina Torres de Araúz. On display are artifacts from the Barriles tribe, the earliest residents of Panama, and a collection of golden *huacas,* the tiny ceremonial figures that were buried with indigenous nobility. There are also more modern *pollera* dresses and antique household items from early settlers on display. The modern space features lots of glass, sharp lines, and open terraces filled with tropical plants. Temporary exhibitions are usually quite good,

attracting large school groups and tours midweek. A half day here should be more than enough.

Av. Juan Pablo II. www.inac.gob.pa/museos/72-museo-m-a-r-t-a. © **501-4731.** Admission $2.50. Tues–Sun 9am–4pm.

Museo de Arte Contemporaneo (MAC) ★ MUSEUM   Better and better each year, Panama's only contemporary art museum near Cerro Ancón is worth a stop if you are in the area. The primary focus in the well-maintained, gallery-like space is a small group of Panamanian artists, both established and up and coming. Panamanian painter Brooke Alfaro is one such artist worth checking out. The museum also displays the work of artists from around Latin America, most of them not widely known. The permanent collection is comprised of mostly watercolor and oil paintings. Surprisingly spacious, the institution acts much like a cultural center, with frequent events like film screenings and art classes for children and rotating temporary exhibitions, including a recent Japanese anime series. Allot an hour or two to explore the entire museum.

Av. Martyrs at Calle San Blas. www.macpanama.org. © **262-8012.** Admission $5 adults, $1.50 children. Tues–Sun 10am–5pm.

Museo de Ciencias Naturales ★ MUSEUM   Open since 1975, the permanent exhibition of the Museum of Natural Sciences is oriented toward kids and teens. It hasn't really been updated much since opening, with local stuffed animals in glass-enclosed displays of their "natural habitat," large plaster renditions of prehistoric sloths and mastodons, cardboard representations, and so forth. There is also a reptile and insect display of specimens found in Panama and a library.

Av. Cuba btw. Calle 29 and Calle 30. © **225-0645.** Admission $1 adults, 75¢ seniors, 25¢ children. Daily 9am–4pm. Closed holidays.

Museo del Canal Interoceánico de Panamá ★★★ MUSEUM   Set in a building that was once the Gran Hotel and later the French canal headquarters, this museum is a prime stop for Panama City visitors. The history of the isthmus of Panama is covered from pre-Columbian times to the arrival of the Spanish and up through the long and storied construction of the canal. The museum contains important historical documents and artifacts, such as the 1977 Carter-Torrijos treaty, a register of the U.S. Senate votes approving the canal, and the famed Nicaraguan stamp of an erupting volcano that was sent to deter said senators from choosing Nicaragua for the construction. You'll need at least a few hours to see all the interactive exhibits, but you'll gain a thorough understanding of why the canal is arguably the physical center of all world trade. Displays are in both Spanish and English, and bilingual tours are available from on-site guides.

Av. Central at Plaza de la Catedral. www.museodelcanal.com. © **211-1649.** Admission $2. Tues–Sun 9am–5pm.

WHERE TO STAY

Panama City is relatively small when compared with other major Latin American cities, but a chaotic city layout means you'll probably have to take a cab ride to get to most tourist destinations, unless you stay in Casco Viejo. Most hotels are concentrated in **El Cangrejo, Obarrio,** and the **Area Bancaria (Financial District),** home to banking institutions, commercial services, and shopping malls. For charm, you can't beat the cobblestone streets and renovated antique homes in **Casco Viejo,** now filled with atmospheric boutique hotels, though some edges of the barrio are still a bit seedy at night.

Elsewhere, excellent hotels are scattered about the city in the **Marbella/Coastal** area, on the slope of leafy **Cerro Ancón,** and near the **Amador Causeway** (specific information about these neighborhoods can be found in each lodging description). If cities aren't for you, you may want to consider staying in the comparatively quiet **Ancón** or **Amador** neighborhoods. **La Exposición** and **Calidonia** are home to mostly anonymous, divey hotels that seem better suited for a criminal hiding out from the feds than for a tourist seeing the sights.

Tip: All hotels recommended in this chapter have **free parking** and at least one computer with an **Internet connection.** And if you're in town on a weekend, be sure to ask about weekend discount rates. Hotels in Panama City fill up during the week and empty out a bit on the weekends, and hotels are sometimes willing to negotiate weekend rates. Note that you'll probably get better rates when booking online than calling in person.

El Cangrejo/Area Bancaria (Financial District)
EXPENSIVE
The Bristol Panama ★★ Centrally located in Panama City's financial district, the Bristol feels more like a large boutique hotel than the big

---

Push-Buttons & the Pit Stop

Rent-by-the-hour hotels in Latin America are ubiquitous and largely patronized by young adults who still live with their parents, as well as by those carrying on the usual clandestine affairs. In Panama they're called "push-buttons." To admit to having patronized a push-button carries far less stigma in Panama than it would in the U.S., but still, no one wants to be caught *in flagrante delicto,* and therein lies the origin of the name. Push-buttons are commonly found on the outskirts of towns and are clearly identifiable by cheesy names like "Lagoon of Love." Without getting out of the vehicle, a driver/client pushes an intercom button, and the gate opens. Each room has its own enclosed parking area and private entrance, and a small sliding partition that opens to the hallway means you can pay or order drinks without having to see or talk with anyone. Push-buttons come with all the romantic bells and whistles: heart-shaped tubs, mirrored ceilings, minibars—the works. To leave, the process is reversed; only the intercom button and exit area are called the "pit stop"—as the gate opens, the driver revs his engine, hits the gas, and quickly races to get out and avoid being seen.

business-traveler–oriented properties nearby. Much of the decor in the carpeted guest rooms is quite conservative, with mahogany furnishings and custom fabric themes of gold or gray. Double-paned windows keep the noise outside, while mostly marble bathrooms with potted orchids and soaking tubs keep the feel swanky. The ground floor, though small, has more local flavor, with paintings and sculptures from leading regional artists, and the playful decor includes a ceiling of Panama hats and handpainted clay tiles. The cozy bar has a vast rum selection. Coquita Arias de Calvo's restaurant, **Salsipuedes,** is one of the best in town.

Aquilino de la Guardia at Obarrio. www.thebristol.com. ☏ **265-7844.** $229 double; $409 junior suite. **Amenities:** Restaurant; bar; outdoor pool; gym; concierge; room service; free Wi-Fi.

Hard Rock Hotel Panama Megalopolis ★

The massive Hard Rock became part of the ever-growing Multicentro mall and entertainment complex in 2013. The additional 1,500 rooms—that's right, 1,500—have single-handedly altered the city's hotel landscape. With seven bars and four restaurants, the atmosphere is loud and brash, as befits a 24/7 party atmosphere. Even the infinity pool and its bar stay open to 1am on the weekends. Rock 'n' roll amenities include a 10-song downloadable playlist given at check-in, and Fender Stratocasters delivered to rooms with headphones and an amp. Rooms are decorated like a Def Leppard concert, accented in bright purples and reds. They're actually quite comfortable, and the minibar is well stocked for afterparties. Opt for an oceanview balcony if you can.

Av. Balboa at the Multicentro Mall. www.hrhpanamamegapolis.com. ☏ **380-1111;** or 888-890-5057 toll-free from the U.S. $199 double; $219–$309 suite. **Amenities:** 4 restaurants; 7 bars; outdoor pool; gym; spa; concierge; salon; room service; free Wi-Fi.

Panama Marriott ★

Although overshadowed by the arrival of more luxurious brands with more interesting amenities, the Panama Marriott is still an excellent hotel. The 20-floor behemoth, with its 18 meeting rooms, is a favorite among business travelers. Tourists will appreciate the seriously rich set of amenities, like the huge bouquets of fresh flowers in the lobby, high-tech fitness center, and large spa. Standard rooms, which keep the traditional decorating scheme of most Marriott hotels, are spacious and have a couch and large bathroom; executive rooms are basically the same but give you entree into the private lounge on the 19th floor. The inhouse casino and nightclub attract a local crowd on the weekends.

Calle 52 at Ricardo Arias. www.marriot.com. ☏ **210-9100** or 800/228-9290 toll-free from the U.S. or Canada. $220 double; $270 executive; $350 executive suite. **Amenities:** 3 restaurants; bar; outdoor pool; gym; spa; concierge; room service; free Wi-Fi.

Waldorf Astoria Panama ★★

The storied Waldorf brand's first foray into Latin America is this stately, 36-floor glass tower in the heart of Panama City's thriving entertainment district. High ceilings and off-white marble touched with splashes of gold, bronze, and silver bring a sophistication Panama City has yet to see in the flashier Trump Ocean Club or Casco Viejo boutique hotels. Check-in takes place in a palatial ground-floor lobby, which comes complete with a Peacock Alley lounge like the one in New York. For many visitors, the next stop is the 7th-floor terrace, which is anchored by a pool and Jacuzzi that stare out toward the Bay of Panama (a few apartment buildings obscure much of the ocean view). The rooms are just as plush as the New York original, with 600-thread-count sheets, Ferragamo bath products, and pillow menus. Aside from the pool bar, with its excellent Panamanian-style mojitos, the hotel has two fine restaurants, one a casual international bistro and the other a sushi spot.

Calle 47 at Uruguay. www.waldorfastoriapanama.com. ℂ **294-8000.** $159–$289 double. **Amenities:** 2 restaurants; bar; outdoor pool; gym; concierge; room service; free Wi-Fi.

MODERATE

Radisson Decapolis ★★   Steps across an elevated walkway from the Multicentro Mall and Majestic Casino, this sleek glass-and-brushed-steel tower attracts a young, wealthy crowd. Edgy design elements throughout—a metal Easter Island moai in the restaurant, Kuna Indian mola textiles, and tiger-striped hardwoods—keep this feeling far from the average chain hotel. Rooms look out of blue-tinted windows at neighboring skyscrapers and feature oversized photos of indigenous art. The rooms are comfortable and decorated in white and pastel hues, with the occasional splash of leopard print. The hotel's martini and sushi bar brings in the local fashionistas spilling over from the 20 or so restaurants next door at the mall. The small, heated outdoor swimming pool has cozy lounge chairs and is great for some solitude. Little extras like 3-hour express laundry, a home-away cellular service that will forward your messages to you, and the **Aqua Spa,** one of the most complete in the city, are bonuses.

Multicentro Mall, Av. Balboa. www.radisson.com. ℂ **215-5000** or 888/201-1718 in the U.S. $144 double standard; $164 executive double; $209 executive suite. **Amenities:** Restaurant; bar; outdoor pool; gym; concierge; meeting facilities; room service; free Wi-Fi.

Riande Granada Urban Hotel ★★   Formerly the Riande Continental, this under-the-radar hotel recently underwent a massive renovation that has transformed it from an average business hotel to a spectacular high-design one. As soon as you hit the lobby, you enter a Phillipe Starck–like world of glitzy metallics, ambient lighting, multitextured surfaces, and strikingly colored Victorian armchairs. The decorators didn't shy away from pushing boundaries in the rooms either, adding a zebra-print chair or splashy art above the bed, with design that varies from room to room. Outside, an inviting pool is fringed by palms. The building itself blocks out much of the sun, although the huge terrace, also used for special events, isn't as shaded. **Restaurant Solo,** entered through an archway made of two giant faces, goes well beyond typical hotel fare, serving Panamanian fusion dishes that can compete with some of the city's top restaurants. Unbelievable online price breaks make this one of the best-value hotels in the city.

Calle Eusebio A. Morales. www.riandehoteles.com. ✆ **204-4444.** $114 double; $140 suite. Rates include breakfast buffet. **Amenities:** Restaurant; bar; outdoor pool; gym; concierge; room service; free Wi-Fi.

Torres de Alba ★ This modern tower in the heart of El Cangrejo feels rather sterile, though for the price you won't find anything better in the neighborhood. The hotel was designed for long-term business travelers, with a kitchenette and a washer/dryer in every room. The pink marble floors, green walls, and board-like beds don't scream comfort, though they're exceptionally clean. There's a pleasant rooftop patio and pool, a decent-sized workout room, and a nice-enough terrace and bar. Seniors can ask about promotional rates.

49 B. Oeste. www.torresdealba.com.pa. ✆ **269-7770.** $90 double; $140 suite. **Amenities:** Restaurant; bar; outdoor pool; gym; concierge; Wi-Fi (free).

Veneto—A Wyndham Grand Hotel ★ Las Vegas is the first impression one gets from Veneto. With its purple tones, Sin City–style signage, glittering lights, and full-scale casino, this is not your traditional Panamanian hotel. This isn't some second-rate Strip dive either, but rather a full-on entertainment complex. The mezzanine-level casino is somewhat seedy, though it has more than 40 tables and 600 slot machines, plus nightly live entertainment. The rooms are surprisingly conservative, with marble-lined bathrooms and fine linens. On the seventh floor you can hide away from the non-overnight guests in the gym, the reasonably priced spa, or the resort-like swimming pool. When it's time to mingle, head to the **V Lounge,** which overlooks the entire casino. Dining options include a New York–style steakhouse, a sushi bar, and an Italian restaurant.

Via Veneto and Av Eusabio Morales. www.venetopanama.com. ✆ **340-8888** or 877/531-2034 in the U.S. $180 double; $255 suite. **Amenities:** 4 restaurants; 2 bars; outdoor pool; gym; spa; casino; concierge; room service; free Wi-Fi.

INEXPENSIVE

Panama House B&B ★ Formerly known as La Casa del Carmen, this cheery guesthouse is ideal for budget travelers who want something a bit more grownup than a hostel. The simple tile-floored rooms vary in size—one has bunk beds and sleeps four, while another is more of a suite with a kitchen. All are kept clean, painted in bright colors, and lightened up with artwork found in local markets. Cheaper rates are available for those willing to share a bathroom. The location is good, in a residential area 1 block from Vía España and a short cab ride to El Cangrejo. A plant-filled patio with hammocks and lounge chairs beside the breakfast area is a fine place to bring a book or tell travel tales.

Calle 1a #32, btw. Vía Porras and Vía Brasil. www.panamahousebb.com. ✆ **263-4366.** $60.50 double with private bathroom. Rates include breakfast. **Amenities:** Free Wi-Fi.

Cerro Ancón/Balboa

MODERATE

Albrook Inn ★ Formerly one of seven U.S. military bases built in 1922 for the defense of the Panama Canal, and afterward a guesthouse for single officials, this converted inn is particularly convenient if you have an early flight at Albrook airport or just need to avoid the rush-hour traffic getting there. It's a leafy yet attractive (not mention rather Americanized) residential area, which allows the property to spread out more than in the city center, adding a resort-style pool and well-maintained gardens full of birds and flowers. The rooms are motel style, opening to the garden, and comfortable though unimpressive.

Calle Las Magnolias No. 14. www.albrookinn.com. ⓒ **315-1789.** 30 units. $77 double; $99 junior suites. **Amenities:** Restaurant/bar; outdoor pool; Jacuzzi; free Wi-Fi.

Country Inn & Suites—Panama Canal ★ The proximity to the Amador Causeway, looking out toward the Miraflores Locks and the Bridge of the Americas, gives this standard chain hotel special consideration. If you want to wake up early and go for a jog or bike ride with water views at every angle, or just kick back by the outdoor pool with no car horns blasting in your ear after a long day at a conference, this cookie-cutter hotel is about as good as getting out of the city. The tiled-floor rooms are decidedly average in terms of decor, though they make up for it with terraces and kitchenettes. Oceanview rooms, an extra $25, are worth it for the views of the bridge lit up at night.

Av. Amador at Av. Pelícano, Balboa. www.panamacanalcountry.com/amador. ⓒ **211-4500** or 800/456-4000 in the U.S. 98 units. $100–$110 deluxe standard; $125–$150 junior suite; $185 master suite. **Amenities:** Restaurant; bar; outdoor pool; tennis courts; gym; spa; bike rentals; children's play area; room service; free Wi-Fi.

Casco Viejo

Although Casco has long been a major tourist draw in Panama City, it was only recently that it became the city's hippest hotel and nightlife zone. What used to be a few budget guesthouses has blossomed into more than a dozen chic design hotels in restored landmark buildings, with many more under construction. If it's big, boxy chain hotels you are looking for, stick to the Financial District, but come to Casco if you prefer small, independent hotels, sometimes with as few as three rooms.

Although Casco Viejo isn't ultra-dangerous, it does get a bit sketchy at night in some corners, so you'll want to take a taxi around here if you're traveling alone or in a small group.

EXPENSIVE

American Trade Hotel ★★★ When trendsetting Oregon-based hotel brand Ace announced they were going to expand internationally, few would have picked Panama City's Casco Viejo neighborhood as one of the first ventures. After the American Trade Hotel opened in late 2013, though, it was easy to see why. Mixing the grandeur and exceptional framework of the Art Nouveau neoclassical American Trade Building with the hip, modern sensibilities of Atelier Ace, this instantly became the most charming hotel in the city. Abandoned since the 1990s, the structure is now stunning, thanks to the help of local design team Conservatorio. There are high ceilings, handpainted clay tiles, rocking chairs, and potted plants. Guest rooms vary in size from big to bigger, all decked out in a sort of Havanesque tropical-chic vibe, with wood floors and furniture that would do Papa Hemingway proud. It also has a jazz bar, a farm-to-table restaurant, a rooftop pool, and a lobby cafe that roasts single-source Panamanian coffee.

Calle 10a Oeste, Plaza Herrera. www.americantradehotel.com. *©* **211-2000.** 50 units. $299–$429 double; $579 suite. **Amenities:** Restaurant; 2 cafés; jazz bar; outdoor pool; concierge; event space; room service; free Wi-Fi.

MODERATE

Las Clementina's ★★★   Built in the 1930s as an apartment building, Las Celmentinas is one of Casco Viejo's most atmospheric boutique hotels. Everything you imagined a Casco hotel could have is here: exposed brick walls, a lush walled garden with twin 50-year-old palm trees, handpainted clay tiles, and furniture made of reclaimed Florida pine from an old U.S. army barracks. Each room has its own personality, infused with antiques and contemporary paintings, plus separate living areas, a balcony, and a kitchenette. The larger chamber room adds a wraparound balcony. Guests are served a free breakfast in the downstairs restaurant, a neighborhood hotspot worth sampling even if you're not a guest.

Las Clementinas Chambers y Av. B. www.lasclementinas.com. *©* **308-6550.** 6 units. $180–$200 double; $280 chamber room. Rates include breakfast. **Amenities:** Restaurant; bar; rooftop terrace; concierge; room service; free Wi-Fi.

Tantalo ★★   Perhaps the most happening hotel in the city, Tantalo has helped usher in a new era in Casco. The property attracts a cool crowd of local hipsters and foreign jet-setters, who now come to the city to soak up culture, rather than just to make a deal. Each of Tantalo's boho-chic rooms has a different theme and is decorated by a different artist. Nocturne, for instance, is an ode to Charles Bukowski, with documentary photography and quotes about night, romance, and darkness. Insulated with old phone books and newspapers, the hotel goes out of its way to be green, including using recycled plastic as potters on a green wall that's watered with reclaimed rainwater from the lounge skylight. The great house restaurant, with two long communal tables, serves eclectic tapas-style dishes. The rooftop bar, **Encima,** occasionally has live music and is one of the best hangouts in Casco.

Calle 8 Este with Av. B. www.tantalohotel.com. *©* **262-4030.** $153–$204 double. Rates include breakfast. **Amenities:** Restaurant; bar; concierge; event space; room service; free Wi-Fi.

INEXPENSIVE

Luna's Castle Hostel ★   This always-popular backpacker hostel in a colonial building decorated with funky contemporary artwork in Casco Viejo will plant you firmly on the gringo trail across Central America. While hanging out on the comfy couches in the house's "chill rooms" (there are three friendly communal spaces) or over mojitos at the popular bar, you can find other long-term travelers—or a sailboat to Colombia. Some of the less expensive dorm rooms lack A/C, so be sure to specify when reserving. It can get loud here, so if you're looking for a quiet night's sleep, this probably isn't the best place.

Calle 9a 3-28. www.lunascastlehostel.com. © **262-1540.** $30 double; $15 dorm bed with A/C. Rates include pancake breakfast. **Amenities:** Restaurant; bar; tour desk; free Wi-Fi.

WHERE TO EAT

Like any port city worth its salt, Panama City has a gastronomic scene influenced by a melting pot of immigrants from around the world and by its regional neighbors Colombia, Mexico, and Peru. Foodies will be overjoyed by what's on offer in this metropolitan city: Chinese food ranked by gourmets as some of the best on this side of the Pacific, fine European cuisine, Middle Eastern eateries, Argentine steakhouses, English-style pubs, and, of course, Panamanian restaurants influenced by Afro-Caribbeans, indigenous groups, and Spanish descendants.

Although traditional Panamanian food is tasty, a lot of it is fried—especially breakfast items like empanadas, *hojaldras* (fried bread), and tortillas—and most main courses are accompanied by a rice-beans-plantain combo that can become repetitive. In Panama City, however, the vibrant and varied culinary scene rivals that of any major Latin American metropolis. It's full of modern Panamanian spots, hipster-filled gastropubs, artisanal coffee roasteries, upscale burger shops, and gourmet food trucks.

Restaurant reviews here are divided by individual neighborhoods. The El Cangrejo district represents the area northwest of Vía España. The Financial District southeast of Vía España is included with the area "Bella Vista," which is south of Vía España and also referred to as Calle Uruguay (or Calle 48 Este, just to make it more confusing).

Note: All Panamanian restaurants and bars are smoke-free, so smokers will have to take it outside. Restaurants come and go in Panama with relative frequency, so you may want to call ahead to make sure newer restaurants are still open. Also,

Grocery & Specialty Stores

The supermarket chain **El Rey** is Panama's largest, and most branches are open 24 hours a day. You can find national products plus a large selection of imported brands from the U.S. The most convenient location is on Vía España, near the Continental Riande; there is another in the Albrook area on Avenida Omar Torrijos on the way to Gamboa. The premier wine store **Felipe Motta,** in Marbella on Calle 53 (© **302-5555**), is the most complete in Central America, and their prices are reasonable.

restaurants tend to come in and out of fashion quickly, so a place that was hopping a year ago may be empty most weeknights now.

San Francisco
MODERATE

Humo ★★ BBQ/PANAMANIAN   Humo could be called the world's first Panamanian barbecue restaurant. Mario Castrellón, who owns nearby Maito, has combined American-style Southern barbecue with local ingredients to stunning results. The two-level space in a wooden house definitely has an Austin-like vibe going for it, with reclaimed wood tables and butcher charts on the walls. Most dishes center around the grill, from smoked and grilled queso fresco to wood-smoked beef brisket to what many call the best burgers in town. There's a fine craft beer and whiskey list, too.

Calle 70 Este, just past Av. 5a Sur. www.humopanama.com. ✆ **203-7313.** Main courses $9–$25. Mon–Sat noon–10:30pm.

Intimo ★★★ PANAMANIAN   There's an energy at Intimo, set in a funky and refurbished ranch-style house, unlike any other restaurant in town. More than just serving good food and great cocktails, these guys are having big fun. Whether you order the tasting menu or a la carte, Chef Carlos Chombolin Alba's approach to Panamanian flavors rarely misses its mark. There's no set menu; rather the dishes are market based and change sometimes daily. Out in the back of the restaurant is a small farm supplying more and more of the restaurant's produce.

Calle 70 Este, just past Av. 5a Sur. www.intimorestaurante.com. ✆ **388-1365.** Main courses $15–$25. Tues–Thurs 6:30–11pm; Fri–Sat 6:30pm–midnight.

Maito ★★★ PANAMANIAN/CONTEMPORARY   Though it feels more laidback than some of Panama City's classic fine-dining restaurants, the food coming out of this kitchen is the most innovative and exciting in the city, if not the entire country. Maito is set in a Canal-style house with stone floors and generous patio seating. It has its own organic garden, the harvest of which is incorporated into the menu. The kitchen infuses elements from the cuisine of the country's many ethnicities, ranging from Chinese to indigenous groups to the Afro-Panamanian fare of the Caribbean Coast. The menu changes often, though expect to find plates like farm-raised octopus with a honey glaze or short ribs with coconut aioli, representative of the new class of future-forward Panamanian food that's being invented here. Spanish-trained Chef Mario Castrellón and his team form the foodie core of Panama City, and their elaborate tasting menus are not to be missed. (There are a la carte options as well.)

End of Calle 50, just past Cincuentenario. www.maitopanama.com. ✆ **391-4657.** Main courses $16–$31. Mon–Fri noon–3pm and 7–10:30pm; Sat 7–10:30pm.

INEXPENSIVE
Athanasiou ★ GREEK   The senses are overwhelmed by the sweet smell of baked goods at this classy Greek pastry shop and cafe on a busy road in the San Francisco neighborhood. This is a family-operated chain that dates to

1938 and includes locations in Greece, Boston, and now Panama. Athanasiou is a temple to sweet, succulent confections, layered with fruits, nuts, and honey. The baklava, pistachio shortbreads, and Kritsinia, bought by weight or in pre-made packages, are as authentic as what's sold in Greece. There's a small and often-filled seating area with table service. Different soups are sold each day, and there is also a full coffee bar.

Vía Porras, Plaza Ledakon. www.athanasioupastry.net. ☎ **203-1010.** Pastries $2–$7. Daily 7am–10pm.

Café Unido ★★ CAFE   If you had to pick one cafe in Panama to drink Panamanian coffee at, it would be this one. This artisanal coffee-roasting company is to Panama what Blue Bottle or Stumptown is to the United States. The specialty is Geisha, a varietal grown in the rich volcanic soils of Boquete that has become one of the most expensive coffees in the world. Besides sourcing its beans from top Panamanian growers like Hacienda La Esmeralda, Café Unido invests a considerable amount of capital in helping other producers expand. The cafe has a decent menu with pastries, breakfast sandwiches, burgers, and other goodies, as well as a market area, so you can pick up Geisha for a fraction of the price you would pay in the states. Additional locations around town include a cafe in the American Trade Hotel.

Calle 79 Este at Av. 5 Sur, Edificio La Mare. www.cafeunido.com. ☎ **399-2408.** Snacks $3–$12. Mon–Sat 7:30am–9pm; Sun 9am–8pm.

Bella Vista/Area Bancaria (Financial District)
MODERATE

La Posta ★ ITALIAN   The flagship of a mini-empire of restaurants from David Henesy and Carolina Rodriguez, La Posta has been attracting the jet set since it opened in 2005. Evoking 1950s Havana with its wicker ceiling fans, patterned tile floors, tropical foliage, and plantation-style architecture, this is perhaps Panama City's finest restaurant interior. A coastal Italian menu from the American-trained chef is elegant but not in the least bit pretentious, dishing out octopus carpaccio, yellowfin tuna ceviche with capers, and seafood risottos. Thin-crust pizzas from a wood-fired oven are also quite delicious. La Posta is one of those places where you can come and linger for hours with wine and good company.

Calle 49 at Calle Uruguay. www.lapostapanama.com. ☎ **269-1076.** Main courses $9.75–$16, pizzas $6.50–$9. Daily noon–3pm and 7–10:30pm.

Market ★ STEAKHOUSE   It's often crowded at Market, Panama City's premier American-style steakhouse and burger bar. As with owner David Henesy's sibling spot La Posta, the space is beautifully designed (zebra-print floors, polished concrete, walls lined with bottles of Chianti). For all that, Market stays in touch with the casual diner. Meat, obviously, is the signature element, be it New York strip or grass-fed Angus from the Chiriquí highlands, or the dozen different sandwiches and burgers. Mouth-watering sides include bacon mac 'n' cheese and portobello hash. Surprisingly, the salad selection here is superb as well. *Note:* Make sure you have the right address. The current location is 1 block from the original.

Corner of Calle Urugay and Calle 48. www.marketpanama.com. © **264-9401.** Main courses $9–$45. Mon–Fri noon–2:30pm and 6:30–11pm; Sat 11:30am–midnight; and Sun 11:30am–8pm.

Casco Viejo
EXPENSIVE
Donde Jose? ★★★ MODERN PANAMANIAN Despite being named after a no-frills *fonda* (a rustic food stall), Donde Jose? might be the most sophisticated restaurant in the history of Panama City. The elegant corner space has just 16 seats, most of them at a long bar overlooking a piece of the kitchen area. Chef Jose Olmedo Carles searches the country for native Panamanian ingredients, many of them wild and foraged for personally, which form the backbone of his intimate tasting menus. The drink pairings include not just wine, but cocktails and local beers. With only two seatings a night, reservations here are essential and should be made weeks, if not months, in advance.

Av. Central at Calle 11. www.dondejose.com. © **262-1682.** Tasting menu $80. Tues–Sat 7pm and 9pm seatings.

MODERATE
Crave ★ GASTROPUB As his more formal restaurant inside a nearby boutique hotel was being built, Chef Luis Young opened this one-room gastropub to much applause. Many of the dishes feature Asian flavors, such as chicharrones dusted with togarishi or Korean BBQ chicken wings. There's also a decent craft beer selection, and the weekend brunches are among the best in town, serving dishes like shrimp and grits.

Calle José de Obaldía, between Calle 8a and 9a. © **209-0094.** Main courses $10–$18. Mon, Wed–Fri 11:30am–3pm and 5:30–11pm; Sat 12:30–11pm; Sun 11am–4pm.

Las Clementinas ★★ INTERNATIONAL This intimate restaurant, carved out of a meticulously restored colonial building that also houses the Las Clementinas boutique hotel, is one of Casco's most stylish. The bar area is exceptionally lovely, though I still prefer the patios, if the temperature allows it. One outdoor space is lined with towering palm trees, and the other is a secret garden beside the old city wall that was hidden from view for decades. The kitchen turns out excellent versions of classic international comfort foods with touches of Panama. There's *gaucho,* a Caribbean-style seafood risotto, and a seabass burger with ginger and Sriracha aioli, as well as various fried snacks. The weekend prix-fixe brunch ($29.50) comes with an appetizer, main course, and two Bloody Marys or mimosas, and is quite popular.

Calle 11 at Av. B. www.lasclementinas.com. © **228-7617.** Main courses $11–$22. Tues–Sat 7am–11pm; Sun 7am–4pm.

Madrigal ★★★ SPANISH/CONTEMPORARY After helming some of Madrid's most renowned restaurants (Balzac, Alboroque), Michelin-starred

Spanish chef Andres Madrigal moved to Panama. In mid-2013 he opened this sleek two-level restaurant in a beautifully renovated building in the Casco Viejo. The restaurant features impossibly pretty waitresses and original stone walls adorned with contemporary artwork. The excitable chef, who has fallen deeply and madly in love with his new country, primarily uses Panamanian ingredients, more than 90%, in a unique style that blends modern Spanish and Mediterranean. The wine list is excellently chosen and reasonably priced. Tasting menus are also available.

Av. A at Calle 5ta Oeste. www.andresmadrigal.com. © **211-1956.** Main courses $18–$32. Tues–Sat 7–11pm.

Manolo Caracol ★★★ PANAMANIAN Until 2015 there had never been an a la carte menu at Manolo Caracol, only a prix-fixe set lunch or an elaborate 10-course dinner. Ten years ago, while other chefs were touting their imported ingredients, Spanish owner Manuel Madueño championed what was local. He has been years ahead of the game at times. Now he's left his Casco kitchen in the hands of Guatamalan chef Andres Morataya while he works on some of his farms in the Azuero Peninsula. The day's menu might change on a whim, depending on whatever high-quality ingredients Madueño sends to the city for the simple yet original Caribbean-inspired dishes. The colonial building housing the restaurant has an all-around pleasant and cozy atmosphere, adorned with religious art and local handicrafts. Free classical music performances take place in the restaurant a few nights a week.

Av. Central and Calle 3ra. www.manolocaracol.net. © **228-4640.** Fixed-price lunch $15, fixed-price dinner $30. Mon–Sat noon–3pm and 7–10:30pm.

INEXPENSIVE

Bajareque Coffee House & Roastery ★ CAFE Though Panama doesn't grow nearly as much coffee as Costa Rica or neighboring Colombia, it does have some exceptional beans, particularly those from the Boquete area. This small roastery and cafe in a narrow colonial building is the Panama City home of the region's Elida Estate coffee farm, which produces the award-winning Geisha coffee, one of the most prized and expensive coffees in the world (and not cheap here either). You can buy beans, just sample a cup, or opt for more standard Panamanian coffees. They also serve very average light meals and fresh-baked croissants and pastries.

Calle 1a Oeste. www.bajarequecoffee.com. © **6157-1590.** Coffee $3–$6. Daily 8am–7pm.

Granclement ★★ ICE CREAM Cool down in this stylish one-room, French-style ice cream shop, with checkered tile floors and stone walls, while doing the rounds in Casco Viejo. First absorb the air-conditioning, and then savor one of the artisan-style ice creams and sorbets. Flavors range from the obligatory vanilla and chocolate to less common picks like lavender, basil, or rum raisin. The highest-quality ingredients are used, resulting in full-flavored and wildly refreshing treats.

Av. Central at Calle 3. www.granclement.com. © **208-0737.** Ice cream $2.50–$4. Mon–Sat 11:30am–8pm; Sun 12:30–8pm.

El Cangrejo/Area Bancaria (Financial District)

MODERATE

Riesen ★★ PANAMANIAN/INTERNATIONAL Chef Hernan Correa Riesen opened this small, casual, farm-to-table restaurant in a nondescript space in El Cangrejo with prize money from the annual food festival, Panama Gastronomica. He also had some help from his mother and grandmother, who can be seen at the restaurant taking orders. Relying on a tight network of local farmers and fishermen, Riesen serves very simple but creative fare. Start with a *hojadre,* a sort of sweetened flatbread topped with pulled pork and cilantro cream; then move on to larger plates like achiote-spiced handmade tagliatelle with artisanal chorizo. The interior is modern and comfortable, with white walls, dangling bulbs, and black leather seats and benches.

Calle D Casa 16. ℂ **264-0473.** Main courses $9–$19. Wed–Mon 6–10pm.

Salsipuedes ★ PANAMANIAN/CONTEMPORARY In 2012, local celebrity chef Cuquita Arias de Calvo reworked her space in the posh Bristol boutique hotel into Salsipuedes, which quickly made a name for itself. Decorated with handpainted clay tiles, contemporary photography, and plenty of flowers, the restaurant takes in the best of Panama. The atmosphere is low-key and works for a range of ages. The menu is a combination of contemporary regional dishes and modern takes on Panamanian ingredients, such as coconut rice with pigeon peas, chorizo flavored with curry, or veal jerky smoked in nance tree wood with julienned green plantains. Don't miss the superb desserts, which include tastings of different flavors of arroz con leche.

Inside the Hotel Bristol, Aquilino de la Guardia at Obarrio. www.facebook.com/salsipuedespanama or www.thebristol.com/en/restaurant. ℂ **264-0000.** Main courses $15–$26. Daily 6am–10:30pm.

INEXPENSIVE

Palacio Lung Fung ★★ CHINESE This busy, out-of-the-way dim sum palace might offer the most classic Panama City restaurant experience. It's best at breakfast, as is the Cantonese way, though you can stick around for lunch or dinner to find no-frills Chinese-Panamanian classics like chow mein, which is served in Panama with shredded carrots, cabbage, and pork or chicken. More than 40 varieties of dim sum are pushed around on carts, from which diners choose what they want as it passes. Even if you over-order, it is difficult to spend a lot of money here. The interior covers two floors in traditional style, looking like any glossy oversized Chinese restaurant in the world.

Vía Simón Bolívar (Transístmica) and Calle 62 C. Oeste. ℂ **260-4011.** Main courses $3.75–$11, dim sum 50¢–$2. Daily breakfast 6am–noon; daily lunch and dinner noon–1am.

Caledonia

INEXPENSIVE

Restaurant Mercado del Mariscos ★ SEAFOOD The freshest seafood in Panama City is without a doubt at the Mercado del Marisco (Fish Market), where a fleet of more than a thousand small fishing boats from

MARKET fare

o **Sabores del Chorrillo** (Cinta Costera III): Right beside Maracana Stadium, this clean and organized 11-stall food court serves the mostly Afro-Panamanian food of the gritty Chorrillo neighborhood. Most of the stalls offer fried red snapper in curry sauce with *patacones* (fried green plantains). Order and then eat on the ocean-facing patio.

o **Mercado de Mariscos** (Calle 15 Este): This bustling seafood market at the entrance to Casco Viejo is an obligatory tourist stop, so you might as well grab a snack while you're there. Don't be put off by the ceviches served in Styrofoam cups; they're actually quite good. A handful of outside stalls offers full menus of classic Panamanian seafood as well.

o **Cuara y Cuara** (Av. Cuba, in front of the Alcadía): This string of 12 *fondas*, or rustic food stalls, have some of the best no-frills traditional Panamanian dishes in town. Each one has a specialty, such as fried chicken, *patacones*, or *torrejitas* (Cuban toast).

villages all along Panama's Pacific Coast unload their catch. Although some visitors may be frightened off by the sheer number of ceviche vendors inside and along the outer rim of the market, the second level is slightly more formal (there are tables and chairs) and has a larger menu. The Peruvian owner upstairs adds several dishes from his country, like Peruvian-style ceviches and *jalea* (battered and fried seafood), though plenty of straight Panamanian plates are served, too, including grilled seabass with *patacones* and seafood stews. Come before 1pm or after 2pm because this place gets packed during the lunch hour.

Fish Market, Av. Balboa. ℭ **212-3898.** Main courses $3–$8.50. Daily 11am–7pm.

SHOPPING

You'll hear a lot of talk about duty-free shopping in Panama, but it is exaggerated. Really, the only place you can duty-free shop is at the plethora of stores at the Tocumen Airport. Shopping complexes such as the **Flamingo Center** on the Amador Causeway limit duty-free purchases to cruisers landing at their port. Even the duty-free zone in Colón is overrated, as most wholesalers do not sell to independent travelers. The major shopping malls here offer excellent quality and feature national and international brands, though prices are comparable to those in the United States. A principal shopping avenue is **Vía España,** where both high- and low-end shops vie for business, as well as grocery stores and pharmacies. Designer stores are located around Calle 53 in Marbella and in the nearby World Trade Center's Centro de Comercio. Also try Plaza Paitilla in the Paitilla neighborhood. You'll find electronics shops around Vía Estronga in the Financial District.

WILDLIFE contraband: DON'T DESTROY WHAT YOU'VE COME SEEKING

International laws prohibit the trade of endangered plants or animals, or products made from endangered wildlife. Yet many travelers to Panama who purchase such goods rarely realize that what they are doing is illegal, nor do they understand the consequences of their purchase. Illegal trade destroys the very wildlife and habitat that travelers come here to enjoy. You could also set yourself up for a heavy fine from law-enforcement officials upon your return. To help with wildlife conservation, ask yourself, Do I know what this product is made of? Do I know where this product came from? Do I need a special permit to bring this product home?

The World Wildlife Fund's trade-monitoring network, TRAFFIC, and the U.S. Fish & Wildlife Service have a series of "Buyer Beware" brochures, including one aimed at travelers in the Caribbean, that you can download from their site at **www.worldwildlife.org/buyerbeware**. When in Panama, avoid purchasing:

o Products made from turtle shell (including jewelry)
o Leather products made from reptile skins
o Live birds, including parrots, macaws, and toucans
o Live monkeys
o Certain coral products
o Orchids (except those grown commercially)

Modern Shopping Malls

Globalization and the rising demand for high-quality products have shifted the shopping scene to spacious megamalls housing international brands, cinemas, and a food court. **Multiplaza Pacific** (© 302-5380), in the city center on Via Israel Panama, offers the most in terms of selection and quality, though the **Multicentro** (www.multicentropanama.com.pa; © 208-2500), across from the Hard Rock, is just as nice and far more convenient; plus it also has a cinema. The most expensive shopping destination in town, however, is **Soho Mall** (http://sohopanama.com.pa; © 264-3000), at Calle 50 between calles 54 and 56, with 120 stores from major international luxury retailers like Gucci, Chanel, and Louis Vuitton. **Albrook Mall** (© 303-6333) is an air-conditioned shrine to low-cost outlet shopping, but you'll have to do a lot of digging around to find a gem. Because it is next to the bus terminal, it is busy with families who arrive from the interior of Panama, ready to shop. (Albrook Mall also has a cinema.) **Metro Mall,** located on Avenida Domingo Diaz at Via Tocumen, is located near the airport. You'll find designer and non-designer shops here, and because the mall always seems to be empty, most stores usually have 20%- to 75%-off sales.

Markets

The **Mercado de Mariscos** ★★★, on Avenida Balboa and Calle 15 Este, is distribution headquarters for fresh seafood pulled from the Pacific and Caribbean. It's a vibrant market with lots of action as fishmongers shout while they deftly fillet corvina, tuna, octopus, and more. You can dine here at the market restaurant, though several food stands sell seafood snacks like ceviche.

Artesanía, or indigenous handicrafts, are the number-one buy here in Panama (with the exception of real estate). *Molas,* the reversed appliqué panels made by Kuna Indian women, rank high on the popularity list for souvenirs and gifts, either sewn onto a beach bag, as a shirt, or sold individually for you to frame or stitch onto anything you'd like (pillowcases are an ideally sized canvas). Other popular handicrafts, such as *tagua* nuts or vegetable ivory carved into tiny figurines, Ngöbe-Buglé dresses, and Emberá Indian baskets and masks, can be found at the following markets. These markets do not have phones, and all are open daily with the general hours of 8 or 9am to 5 or 6pm (until about 2pm Sun).

For the more adventurous traveler seeking an "authentic" shopping experience, you can't beat **Avenida Central** ★, a pedestrian street and market that stretches from where Justo Arosemena meets Vía España to the Santa Ana Plaza near Casco Viejo. It's a scrappy, rundown neighborhood, with cheap stores, outdoor fruit and vegetable markets, and a bustling fusion of ethnic groups shopping for a bargain. Visually, it's the most colorful neighborhood in town. Apart from $1-and-under kinds of shops, vendors lining the streets hawk clothing, accessories, plastic gizmos, and knickknacks. Shopkeepers like to blare music or announce their deals through megaphones to pull buyers in. It's a slice of everyday Panama, but it's also street theater and people-watching as fascinating as catching sight of Kuna Indian women lining up at McDonald's. Don't wander too far off Avenida Central, and keep an eye on your personal belongings. This area is patrolled by police and is generally safe during the day.

Kuna women have **handicraft stands** throughout Casco Viejo with many vendors concentrated on Paseo Esteban Huertas. Though it's not an official market, you can find plenty of high-quality *molas* and handicrafts in Casco Viejo.

Panama Hats: Not Very Panamanian, After All

Despite the name, Panama hats did not originate in Panama, but in Ecuador, and were traditionally made by the Ecuadorian indigenous group from the Manabí Province using fibers from the *toquilla* palm. The hat was first popularized by Ferdinand de Lesseps during the French canal effort and later during the canal building by the U.S., when thousands were imported from Ecuador and given to workers for protection from the blistering tropical sun. Hence, the name "Panama hat" stuck. The hat became fashionable not only in the U.S., but also among the English haberdashery and European royalty. Really, you'd have the best luck ordering a high-quality hat over the Internet from a reputable importer, though Panama does its own version called the *sombrero pintado* in the Penonomé region. But if you must buy your Panama hat in Panama, you'll find a range of hats at the stands at Plaza Cinco de Mayo.

ART GALLERIES

Panama City is by no means an art city, but things are starting to change, with new galleries popping up, particularly in the Casco Viejo neighborhood. The following art galleries showcase Panamanian contemporary artists and other well-known Latin American artists. Check **www.thepanamanews.com** and its calendar listing for upcoming shows and special events. **Galería Arteconsult,** located at Gran Plaza Calle Andrés Mójica at Calle 50 in San Francisco (www.arteconsultgaleria.com; ✆ **270-3436**), displays modern paintings, photography, glasswork, and sculptures by local and regional artists. **Galería y Enmarcado Habitante** (✆ **264-6470**), at Calle 47 and Uruguay, has a small collection and worth a stop only if you're in the Bella Vista neighborhood; it also offers framing. The store is located in the Balboa Plaza on Avenida Balboa at Calle Anastacio Ruiz. **Diablo Ross Gallery,** Av. A y Calle 7 (www.diablorosso.com; ✆ **257-7674**), is a cutting-edge gallery in Casco Viejo showcasing the works of emerging artists. New shows open every month.

BOOKSTORES

El Hombre de la Mancha ★ (www.hombredelamancha.com; ✆ **302-3761**) is an excellent bookstore cafe with a selection of English-language literature, guidebooks, and the best Panama City map in town. It has several locations around town, including stores in the Multiplaza and Albrook malls. The Smithsonian's small but excellent **Corotu Bookstore,** at the Earl S. Tupper Research and Conference Center on Roosevelt Avenue in Ancón (www.stri.org; ✆ **212-8029;** Mon–Fri 10am–4:30pm), offers a comprehensive collection of books about Panama's flora, fauna, history, and culture, including large-format photo books, maps, and gifts.

DESIGN

For contemporary homewares, modern Panamanian artwork, kitchen supplies, books, brainy toys for children, independent jewelry, and all sorts of upscale knickknacks, try **Nina Concept Store** (Calle 54 Este at Av. Arango; www.ninaconceptstore.com; ✆ **390-5671**), a two-level store in Obarrio. They also have a juice bar and cafe, which on the weekends serves a killer brunch.

HANDICRAFTS

The widest selection of handicrafts in Panama City can be found at one of several markets (see above). Otherwise, an outstanding selection of *molas* can be found at **Flory Saltzman Molas,** located at Via Espana and Via Veneto (www.florymola.com; ✆ **223-6963**). Flory also sells bedspreads made of sewn-together molas, but the laborious work required for such an extensive, intricate piece of work means you'll pay top dollar. **Galeria Latina** (✆ **314-1985**), at Calle 5ta and Avenida A in Casco Viejo, sells upscale handicrafts made by indigenous groups from around Panama, such as the Kuna Yala, Embera, and Wounaan. Look for baskets, wood carvings, molas, and a number of other authentic handmade items.

The **Gran Morrison** variety/department store chain is located in three locations: at Vía España and Calle 51 Este (www.granmorrison.com; ✆ **202-0029** or 202-0030), El Dorado (℗ **202-0038**), and the Marriott Hotel (℗ **210-9215**); it offers a selection of handicrafts. In Casco Viejo, about a dozen stores sell indigenous crafts and other Panama-themed souvenirs. **Galería de Arte Indígena,** 844 Calle 1a (℗ **228-9557;** daily 9am–8pm), sells high-quality indigenous arts and crafts, and features folkloric dancing on Friday and Saturday nights from 6 to 8pm. Down the road from the Galería, on Calle 1era in Casco Viejo, is the shop **La Ronda** (℗ **211-1001;** daily 9am–7pm), with an outstanding selection of high-quality arts and crafts, hats, and paintings. Shops can be found at the **Mi Pueblito** cultural center (see "Cerro Ancón," under "Exploring Panama City," earlier in this chapter), but the selection is better elsewhere.

JEWELRY

During the centuries before the arrival of the Spanish, indigenous groups produced decorative gold pieces called *huacas,* which they laid to rest with the dead to protect their souls in the afterlife. The word comes from the Incas, meaning something that is revered, such as an ancestor or god. Spurred by the theft of *huacas* from the national anthropology museum, an American living in Panama during the 1970s set up **Reprosa** (http://treasuresofpanama.com) with locations on Avenida Samuel Lewis and Calle 54 in Obarrio (℗ **269-0457**); Edificio Art Deco at Avenida A in Casco Viejo (℗ **228-4913**); and Costa del Este in Parque Industrial (℗ **271-0033**). Reprosa makes elaborate and stunning jewelry casts using the "lost wax" process of the ancient indigenous groups. If you're searching for a one-of-a-kind luxury gift for someone special, come here. Reprosa has several more demure collections that include orchids, treasures from the sea, and so forth.

Reprosa also offers a popular factory tour to demonstrate the casting and assembly process. The factory can be found just off the Costa del Este exit near Panama Vieja, and just after turning left on the first street next to the Felipe Motta shop. English-language tours cost $10 per person and must be booked at least 1 day in advance; call ℗ **271-0033**.

NIGHTLIFE

You don't have to experience 5 days of Carnaval to know that Panamanians are party-loving people. When the sun goes down, Panama City lights up with a vibrant scene that caters to all ages, interests, and levels of stamina. Nightspots are concentrated in a few neighborhoods, such as Bella Vista (also called Calle Uruguay), the Amador Causeway, Marbella (Calle 53 Este), Casco Viejo, and the new "Zona Viva," located a couple miles before the Amador Causeway. Underground dance clubs pop up across town like mushrooms and can be best found by asking your concierge or checking out the Weekend supplement in Thursday's *La Prensa* newspaper. *La Prensa* has a daily section called Vivir +, which lists nightly events, but in Spanish only. Also try the calendar at **www.thepanamanews.com**.

Visitors should be aware that Panamanians are more open-minded about sex than Americans. **Prostitution** is legal in Panama, and therefore it is common to see prostitutes not just on seedier streets and in brothels, but in the nicer parts of town such as El Cangrejo. They're also often at hotel lobby bars and casinos, or employed by one of the many "anything goes" massage parlors around town. If you're a foreign-looking guy or group of guys, women may approach you, but for the most part, prostitutes tend to sit by themselves or groups and wait for men to approach. Government authorities demand a weekly health check for all prostitutes, among other regulations, but cases of AIDS and other sexually transmitted diseases are swiftly multiplying in Panama, so be sure to be safe 100% of the time.

The Performing Arts
THEATER, BALLET & CLASSICAL MUSIC
Theater tickets can be purchased by calling the theater directly or at the bookstore **El Hombre de la Mancha** (see "Bookstores" on p. 81). All theater productions are in Spanish, with the exception of the **Ancón Theater Guild** (www.anconguild.com; ℭ **212-0060;** admission $15). The well-respected guild has been around for more than a half-century, first opening its doors in Colón to provide entertainment to U.S. troops during World War II. The guild normally produces contemporary dramas and comedy with a mix of native English speakers and Panamanian actors trained in English-language schools. Most performances begin at 8pm.

Classical music productions, plays, and ballet take place at Panama City's turn-of-the-20th-century **National Theater,** on Avenida B in Casco Viejo (see "Walking Tour: Historic Casco Viejo," p. 56), but shows are infrequent. The best Spanish-language theater productions can be found at **Teatro la Quadra,** on Calle D in El Cangrejo (www.teatrolaquadra.com; ℭ **214-3695;** tickets average $10). This cultural center was founded to promote and develop the art of theater in Panama, and it receives acclaim for its nightly performances of well-known plays and children's theater. **Teatro ABA** at Avenida Simon Bolívar (Transístmica), near Avenida de los Periodistas in front of the Riba Smith supermarket (www.teatroaba.com; ℭ **260-6316;** tickets cost an average of $10), produces half its own shows and rents out its 200-person theater to independent groups; productions are mostly comedy, drama, and well-established plays. Check www.prensa.com for theater listings here. The historic **Teatro Anita Villalaz** (ℭ **501-5020;** tickets average $15), on Plaza Francia in Casco Viejo, is administered by the National Cultural Institute (INAC); the intimate theater is home to folkloric productions, concerts, and plays, some of which are produced by the University of Panama students.

NIGHTLIFE
Panama City's nightlife scene has become more diversified in recent years, moving beyond giant nightclubs to intimate lounges and craft beer bars. Still, differentiating between a bar and a nightclub can be difficult these days in Panama City because so many bars have live DJ music, occasional live music, and maybe even a small dance floor and chill-out lounge. The clubs listed

below open at 10pm but don't really get going until midnight or later; during the first hours of operation, however, nightclubs typically offer drink specials. Ladies' night specials are a bargain for women, giving them free drinks and entry. Otherwise, expect to pay between $7 and $10 for a cover charge, or more if there is live music. Nightclub partyers tend to dress smartly for the occasion, so don your slinkiest or sharpest outfit or risk being refused entry (or just feeling out of place). To reel people in before the late crowd, these bars offer happy hours from 10pm to midnight, and even free drinks (usually for women).

For folkloric presentations in a less trendy environment, try **Las Tinajas,** Calle 51 at Calle 22 (*ⓒ* **269-3840**), or **Al Tambor a la Alegría,** Brisas de Amador (*ⓒ* **314-3380**).

Gambling is legal in Panama, and virtually every major hotel in the city has an adjoining casino. You'll find slot machines, video poker, gaming tables, sports betting, and special shows and parties. The hottest casino at the moment is at the **Veneto Hotel & Casino.** The Veneto has a sophisticated gaming area and often hosts over-the-top parties such as E! Entertainment's *Wild On.* It has a sushi bar, too. The **Marriott's Fiesta Casino** is popular with foreigners and expats, thanks to its convenient central location. The **Sheraton Hotel & Convention Center** hotel has a large, elegant casino, but its out-of-the-way location means it's really only visited by guests. The bar here, though, is popular with young Panamanians.

Alta Bar ★ DANCE CLUB   This flashy two-level dance club attracts the moneyed partyers of its upscale 'hood. You'll need to order bottle service to snag one of the tables surrounding the large and often crowded neon-lit dance floor. Climb up to the mezzanine for the perfect view of the high-energy dancers below, or just sidestep to the more relaxed outdoor deck to catch your breath. Entrance is always free, though I recommend you reserve a spot in line online first. There are happy hours and drink specials every night.

Calle 48, at Calle Uruguay. www.altabarpanama.com. *ⓒ* **390-2582**. Free admission. Tues–Sat 5pm–3am.

Barlovento Café & Terraza ★★ BAR   More laidback and less of a pickup scene than the rooftop at Encima above the Tantalo hotel, this second-floor terrace is Panama City all grown up. Rather than grinding your way across the bar, settle in the comfortable lounge area, a cross between Goa and South Beach with its colorful cushions and white umbrellas. A menu of tasty small plates is highlighted by ceviche and sliders. On most nights there is live jazz, acoustic music, or DJs, as well as screenings of big fights or soccer games. A daily happy hour from 5 to 10pm offers two-for-one margaritas.

Av. Central at Calle 10. *ⓒ* **6613-4345**. Drinks $3–$10. Tues–Sat 5pm–2am.

Bling ★ DANCE CLUB   Among the many nightlife offerings in the humongous Hard Rock Megapolis, Bling is the most exclusive. This velvet-rope dance club is modeled after flashy clubs in Las Vegas, bringing in top DJs that pump up the house beats for the local ballers and silicon beauties. Justin Bieber even partied here when he was in town on tour. Amid the neon lights and glitzy bar are exclusive VIP areas. Reserve a table and order bottle service to get a guaranteed in; otherwise, it's to the back of the line. Covers vary by night.

Av. Balboa at the Multicentro Mall. www.hrhpanamamegapolis.com. ✆ **380-1111.** Cover varies. Mon–Sat 9pm–3am.

Casa Jaguar ★★ BAR   You'll need to wait in line and head up the stairs beside the Teatro Amador to enter this hip, often-crowded Casco nightspot. The place gets especially crowded with 20- and 30-somethings on the weekends and then stays that way until the sun rises. Nightly drink specials, bottle service, DJs, and a menu of snacks are an added bonus.

Av. Séptima Centra, Casco Viejo. ✆ **6866-8483.** Tues–Wed 6pm–2am; Thurs–Sat 6pm–4am.

Danilo's Jazz Club ★★★ JAZZ CLUB   A collaboration between the Panamanian, Grammy-winning jazz pianist and composer Danilo Perez and the ultra-cool American Trade Hotel, Danilo's Jazz Club has become the focal point of the jazz scene in Panama. The intimate 50-seat club, with its painted clay tile floors and red curtains, attracts top local and international performers. Tickets average around $15, though many performances are free.

Plaza Herrera, American Trade Hotel, Casco Viejo. ✆ **211-2000.** Wed–Sat 7pm–midnight; Sun 3–10pm.

DiVino Enoteca ★ WINE BAR   This newish wine bar is riding the wave of Casco sophistication, attracting an upscale crowd of wine drinkers. It's always mellow here. The interior has a semi-industrial vibe, with exposed air ducts and a crafty bar area designed from wooden wine crates. Cozy couches make it feel more lounge-like. The lists of wines by the glass and by the bottle are extensive, and the vintages pair well with the house's Italian-inflected tapas. The bar hosts frequent tastings, both promotional and educational, and live music is occasionally on tap.

Av. A at Calle 4. ✆ **6867-0132.** Free admission. Daily 6pm–midnight.

Encima ★★ BAR   The rooftop bar at the impossibly trendy Tantalo Hotel has been one of the most happening nightspots in Casco Viejo since it opened in 2012. The large deck, strewn with dangling Edison bulbs, is anchored by a big rectangular bar with seating all around it. It's a primo spot to sip on a mojito and watch the world turn. The view of the modern skyline on one side and Casco's centuries of history on the other is incredible. Most nights feature live music, film screenings, or theme parties. The downstairs lounge, with its two-story green wall and art gallery, is also quite lively.

Calle 8 Este with Av. B. www.tantalohotel.com. ✆ **262-4030.** Free admission. Tues–Thurs 7pm–midnight; Fri–Sat noon–2am.

Habana Panama ★ DANCE CLUB   This sexy salsa club is Panama's center of Latin dance. A throwback to Cuba in the 1950s, it boasts high ceilings, a long wooden bar, and a huge stage where sultry dancers and crooners perform backed by tall red velvet drapes. Visitors sip on one of the many flavors of mojitos, snack on Caribbean food, and watch the orchestra perform from snug tables. More confident patrons can join the hardcore *salseros* on the dance floor. Perch yourself on the second-floor balcony for the best view.

Calle Eloy Alfaro and Calle 12 Este, San Felipe. © **212-0152.** Cover $10 for men on most nights; women free. Thurs–Sat 8pm–4am.

Istmo Brew Pub ★★ BAR & PUB   When it opened in 2005, Istmo was well ahead of its time. Now Panama City's first microbrewery is at the fore-front of the city's growing craft beer scene, which has its own annual festival. Istmo has four decent artisanal beers on tap at any given time, as well as another 20 or so varieties from around the world in bottle form. The crowd here is a nice mix of tourists, expats, and locals all looking for a fun night out. The interior feels like a rustic English pub, with wooden beer barrels behind the bar. Of the two levels of seating, the patio is particularly pleasant in the evenings after the sun has gone down. A small menu of grilled meats and sandwiches provides sustenance.

Av. Eusebio A. Morales and Via Veneto. © **265-5077.** Pints $4. Mon–Wed 4–11:45pm, Thurs–Sat 4pm–2am; Sun 4:30–11:45pm.

La Buat ★★ MUSIC VENUE   This electronic music club is helping open up the once dangerous farthest reaches of Casco Viejo. Situated on the water-front inside an old stone building that looks a little bit like a pirate fort, top DJs from Panama and elsewhere in the region help attract a sexy, mixed crowd of well-to-do hipsters, where everyone is young and fabulous. Some nights there's even live music. The outdoor bar and taqueria, **Tacos La Neta,** is worth coming for on its own. It's run by the team from the fine-dining restaurant Maito.

Calle O, San Felipe, Casco Viejo. www.labuatpanama.com. © **228-6532.** Tues–Sat 5pm–late.

La Rana Dorada ★ BREWPUB   Named after the Panamanian golden frog, this brewpub on the edge of Casco Viejo has quickly blossomed into a major player on Panama's craft beer scene. A second pub has opened at Vía Argentina and Calle Arturo Motta in El Cangrejo, and the same folks also operate their own food truck. This location has four beers on tap, each brewed in large tanks that are separated by a glass wall from the main saloon-like bar area. My favorites are the porter and pale ale. A large patio has nice views of the bay and gets crowded most nights. The decent menu offers pizzas and pub grub.

Av. Eloy Alfaro at Calle 11 Este. www.laranadorada.com. © **212-2680.** Pints $4. Daily noon–2am.

Los Del Patio ★ COFFEEHOUSE   It's hard to define exactly what Los Del Patio is exactly, but that's art, right? The first floor acts as a funky gallery space, dedicated to emerging local and regional artists, while the second floor is more of an open cultural center for workshops and lectures. The cafe and bar, in the very bohemian interior patio, is where the passing visitor is most

PANAMA CITY | Nightlife

likely to end up. The venue can be absolutely dead or slammed with hipsters depending on the night. Live performances, held here often, are much more tranquil experiences than checking out resident DJs in Casco's other nightspots.

Calle 3, btw. Av. Central and Av. B. www.losdelpatio.org. ✆ **6680-8875.** Free admission. Daily 5pm–1am.

Relic ★★ BAR   In the basement of the century-old mansion that also houses the Luna's Castle hostel, Relic is not your typical expat and backpacker hangout—though expect dreadlocks, plenty of beer, and under-30s. The bar starts in a stone cellar attached to historic city walls dating back hundreds of years before spilling out onto an ivy-covered beer garden/patio. DJs spin tunes from Thursday through Saturday; other nights are considerably more chilled out. The friendly crowd is made up of a mix of travelers and locals. If you're a solo traveler, this is a good spot to mingle and meet fellow sojourners.

Calle 9a 3-28 C. www.relicbar.com. ✆ **262-1540.** Free admission. Mon–Wed 8:30pm–2am, Thurs–Sat 8:30pm–3am.

AROUND PANAMA CITY

This chapter's focus is on a sizeable region around Panama City, including the **Panama Canal,** the **Canal Zone,** the **Central Caribbean Coast** (including Colón and its surroundings), and the **Gulf of Panama.** At first glance, it seems like a lot of ground to cover, but these destinations can be reached by a short drive, a puddle-jump flight, or a boat ride from the city, and some attractions are even close enough to visit by taxi. With its high level of services and amenities, Panama City is an ideal base from which to explore this region, and many travelers, especially those with limited time, plan their entire trips around this area, owing to its surprisingly diverse range of attractions.

5

EXPLORING THE REGION A trip to Panama wouldn't be the same without visiting one of the engineering marvels of the world, the **Panama Canal.** There are several ways to do this: at the viewing platform in Miraflores, on a jungle cruise or partial canal transit, or at the Gatún Locks near Colón.

Along the Canal Zone corridor, the national park **Soberanía** puts you in a thick rainforest teeming with birds and wildlife, and you can visit an Emberá Indian village nearby or raft the Chagres River. Near Colón, **Portobelo** pays homage to the Spanish colonial era with its forts and ruins, as well as **Fort San Lorenzo,** on the canal's western side. Around the area, a couple of cool ecolodges and resorts offer accommodations in natural surroundings yet are still close to Panama City—a tantalizing option for travelers deciding where to stay.

This chapter also covers the **Archipiélago de las Perlas (Pearl Islands)** and **Isla Taboga,** which are located in the Pacific, off the coast of Panama City. Even if your travels don't take you too far from the city, you can visit everything from popular beaches to mountain villages to idyllic islands, all within a 2-hour drive, thanks to Panama's incredible geographical diversity.

THE PANAMA CANAL

77km (48 miles) long from Panama City to Colón

The construction of the Panama Canal was one of the grandest engineering feats in the history of the world, an epic tale of ingenuity and courage, but marked by episodes of tragedy. When it was finally completed in 1914, the canal cut travel distances by more than half for ships that previously had had to round South America's Cape Horn. Today the canal is one of the world's most traveled waterways, annually handling around 14,000 ships that represent 5% of global trade.

The history of the canal dates back to the 16th century, when Vasco Núñez de Balboa discovered that Panama was just a narrow strip of land separating the Caribbean from the Pacific. In 1539, King Charles I of Spain dispatched a survey team to study the feasibility of building a waterway connecting the two oceans, but the team deemed such a pursuit impossible.

The first real attempt to construct a canal was begun by the French in 1880, led by Ferdinand de Lesseps, the charismatic architect of the Suez Canal. The Gallic endeavor failed miserably, however, as few had anticipated the enormous challenges presented by the Panamanian jungle, with its mucky swamps, torrential downpours, landslides, floods, and, most debilitating of all, mosquito-borne diseases such as malaria and yellow fever. In the end, more than 20,000 perished.

In 1903, the United States bought out the French and backed Panama in its secession from Colombia in exchange for control of the Canal Zone. For the next 10 years, the U.S., having essentially eradicated tropical disease, pulled off what seemed impossible in terms of engineering: It carved out a 14km (9-mile) path through the Continental Divide and constructed an elevated canal system and a series of locks to lift ships from sea level up to 26m (85 ft.) at Lake Gatún. The lake, created after construction crews dammed the Chagres River near the Gatún Locks, was at the time the largest man-made lake in the world.

In 1977, U.S. President Jimmy Carter and President Omar Torrijos of Panama signed a treaty that would relinquish control of the canal to the Panamanians on December 31, 1999. It was a controversial move because most Americans did not believe that Panama was up to the task—but those concerns have proved to have been unfounded. As an autonomous corporation, the Panama Canal Authority has reduced safety problems and improved maintenance and productivity to the point where the canal basically runs itself.

5

AROUND PANAMA CITY

The Panama Canal

It takes between 6 and 8 hours to transit the entire canal. There are three locks, the **Miraflores, Pedro Miguel,** and **Gatún,** whose maximum size is 320m (1,050 ft.) in length and 34m (112 ft.) in width. Ships built to fit through these locks are referred to as **Panamax** ships, which set the size standard until the 1990s, with the building of post-Panamax ships (mostly oil tankers) that are up to 49m (161 ft.) wide. Since 2007, the Panama Canal Authority, seeking to avoid becoming obsolete, has been working on two multibillion-dollar three-chamber locks, which will allow for wider ships and double capacity by 2025.

Seeing the Panama Canal in Action

For information about visiting the canal at the Gatún Locks, see "Colón," later in this chapter. There is no viewing area at the Pedro Miguel Locks.

MIRAFLORES LOCKS ★★★

The best land-based platform from which to see the Panama Canal at work is at the **Miraflores Visitors Center** (www.visitcanaldepanama.com; © **276-8325**), located about a 15-minute drive from the heart of the city. The center is an absorbing attraction for both kids and adults, with four floors of exhibitions and interactive displays—and a theater—providing information about the canal's history and its impact on world trade, plus explanations of how the region's natural environment is crucial to the function of the canal. Ships can also be viewed from an observation deck. In fact, it's probably Panama's best museum. *Tip:* You'll have better luck catching sight of enormous Panamax ships in the afternoon around 11am or around 3pm. I recommend calling the Visitors Center ahead of time to find out what time these large ships are expected to cross.

As you view ships in the locks, a monologue (in Spanish and English) piped through a loudspeaker indicates what a ship is carrying, where it is registered, where it is going, and how much it paid; the speaker is cheerleader-like and tends to qualify the experience by saying such things as, "Can you *believe* they spent $200,000 to transit the canal, man?" The center also has a snack bar and gift shop. It's open daily from 9am to 5pm (the ticket office closes at 4:15pm). Admission to the center's exhibitions and observation terrace is $15 for adults, $10 for children and students with ID, and free for children 4 and under. It includes entrance to a 3D movie and the museum too.

The **Atlantic & Pacific Co. Restaurant** ★ (daily 11:30am–10:30pm; buffet $42) is best visited more for its extremely unique location than the overpriced food. Here you can dine while watching colossal ships transit the locks just 30m (100 ft.) away. It's a popular place to eat, so arrive early or make a reservation, and try to get a table as close to the railing as possible. At night, the locks are well lit and provide clear views of the ships.

GETTING THERE & DEPARTING   City tours of Panama usually include a 2-hour stop at Miraflores, or you can take a taxi for $35 to $40 round-trip for a 45-minute to 1-hour visit. Agree on a price with the driver beforehand. If you are on an airport layover, you can even take a 4-hour round-trip tour from Tocumen Airport with **Amber Moon Cab** (www.ambermooncab.com; ☏ **6664-0171**) for $80. For buses, see "Getting There & Departing," below, under "Gamboa & The Canal Zone."

TRANSITING THE PANAMA CANAL ★★★

Visitors to Panama who are not part of a long-haul cruise can still transit the canal by boat on a journey from Panama City to Colón, or they can do a partial transit from Gamboa to the Pacific or vice versa. Beyond the thrill of transiting locks is the opportunity to get close to colossal Panamax-size ships en route from one ocean to the other. Partial tours are by far the most popular because they pass through the Pedro Miguel and Miraflores locks and sail under the grand span of the Bridge of the Americas, which is enough for most visitors. Transiting a lock can take up to 2 hours, which can grow tiresome on full-transit journeys. In fact, unless you're an engineer or transiting the canal has been a lifelong dream, you'll probably get bored on a full-transit tour, so opt for a partial transit journey or bring a good book; at least you'll be able to say you crossed the Panama Canal. The companies below are all reputable and offer excellent transit tours of the canal. *Tip:* If you book a canal transit through the **Gamboa Rainforest Resort** (www.gamboaresort.com or www.gamboatours.com), you will pay more than reserving directly with a company.

Panama Marine Adventures (www.pmatours.net; ☏ **226-8917**) offers partial canal transit with a shuttle leaving from the Flamenco Resort and Marina on the Amador Causeway at 10am and going to their *Pacific Queen,* docked at Gamboa. Trips leave every Saturday year-round, and every Thursday and Friday from January to April. The company offers full transit of the canal one Saturday every month (check the website for dates), leaving at 7:30am, first passing through the Miraflores locks, and finishing at the Gatún locks; the company provides transportation by vehicle back to Panama City. Partial transit, which lasts 4 to 5 hours depending on traffic, costs $105 for adults and $95 for kids 11 and under; full transit costs $195 for adults and $105 for kids 11 and under; it lasts 8 to 9 hours. The price includes all transportation, a bilingual guide, and lunch and soft drinks. The *Pacific Queen* has a capacity of 300 passengers.

Canal & Bay Tours ★★★ (www.canalandbaytours.com; ☏ **209-2009** or 209-2010) is a pioneer in canal tourism, offering transit aboard one of two boats, the refurbished *Isla Morada,* a wooden boat with a capacity of 100 guests, or the *Fantasía del Mar,* a steel boat with a capacity of 500 passengers. The company offers partial-day transit of the canal the first Saturday of every month; prices are $150 for adults, $95 for children 11 and under (check website for occasional online specials). Canal & Bay also has partial transit (you pick) the third Tuesday of every month from January to April. Tours leave at 7:30am from the Flamenco Marina, docking in Gamboa or Gatún, depending on the tour.

Ancon Expeditions (www.anconexpeditions.com; ☏ **269-9415**) also offers full and partial transits of the canal. Ancon offers early-morning hotel pickup to the Port of Balboa, where you'll board a passenger ferry. Partial transits cost $195 for adults and $105 for children under 12. Partial transits depart three to four times each week January through March, plus every Saturday year-round. After transiting, a bus will take you back to your hotel. **Margo Tours** (www.margotours.com; ✆ **264-8888**) also offers partial and complete canal transits. Partial transits cost $150 and leave every Saturday from La Playita de Amador on the Causeway. Complimentary hotel pickup is available.

THE PANAMA CANAL RAILWAY ★★

The **Panama Canal Railway** (www.panarail.com; ✆ **317-6070**) is the most picturesque mode of travel between Panama City and Colón. It gives passengers a chance to relive the experience of the California Gold Rush. The railway was first built in 1855 to meet the demands of forty-niners seeking quick passage from the East Coast of the U.S. to the West. It later was rebuilt along more or less the same lines to transport workers and equipment during the building and maintenance of the canal. The train was relaunched in 2001 and features executive and tourist service and renovated coaches modeled after their 19th-century counterparts, with carpeted floors, wood paneling, and blinds. The trains have air-conditioning, as well as open-air viewing platforms. The journey lasts about an hour and borders the canal, racing through lush rainforest, past canal locks, and along slender causeways across Gatún Lake. Round-trip fare is $50 adults, $30 children; one-way fare is $25 adults, $15 children, and $17.50 seniors. The Corozal Train Station in Panama City is located in Albrook and is a $4-to-$6 taxi ride from anywhere in Panama City. The trip takes 1 hour.

See "Tour Operators," below, for organized trips that include a ride on the train. The major issue for do-it-yourself travelers is departure times. From Panama City, the train leaves at 7:15am, with the return trip leaving Colón at 5:15pm—meaning round-trip travelers need to hire a taxi at the Colón station to get to attractions like Portobelo, which can be expensive. Killing an afternoon in the city of **Colón** (p. 102) can be a bit drab, so consider riding the train one-way at the beginning or end of a journey to or from the Caribbean (in other words, after staying at the Meliá Panamá Canal or at a Portobelo hotel). Cruisers docking in Colón are offered this journey, but the ships charter an entire train for their passengers.

GAMBOA & THE CANAL ZONE

Gamboa is 20km (12 miles) from the Miraflores Locks

This is one of the most exciting natural areas to explore in Panama, if not in the Americas, and most of it is less than an hour's drive from the city. North America meets South America here in a confluence of hyperdiversity; accordingly, the bird-watching is epic and easy to access in places like Soberanía National Park. The area has a birder's ecolodge, a recreational park and zoo, spots for white-water rafting, and opportunities to visit with Emberá Indian

The Canal Zone

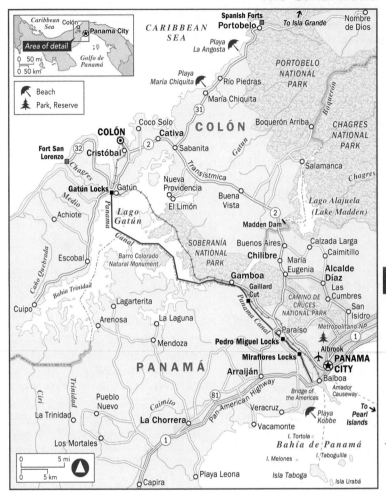

tribes. Gamboa, formerly an American Canal Zone residential area for workers in the canal's dredging division, is also the name for a full-scale resort here. It sits on the shore of Gatún Lake, home to the Smithsonian's Barro Colorado Nature Monument, where visitors can learn about the rich biodiversity of this area. Travelers either lodge here or simply visit the region's highlights by tour, taxi, or rental vehicle.

Essentials

GETTING THERE & DEPARTING By Taxi or Tour The **Gamboa Rainforest Resort and Canopy Tower** (www.gamboaresort.com) offers transportation to and from its property. Nearly every visitor to the Canal Zone is part of a planned tour with a guide, or visitors can hire a taxi for a full- or half-day tour for around $20 to $30 an hour, depending on the number of passengers and the deal you're able to strike with your driver. The road to Gamboa ends at that town and is about a 40-minute drive from the Cerro Ancón/Balboa area of Panama City.

If you're not taking part in an organized tour of the Canal Zone and Gamboa and would like to visit the area on your own, you can expect to pay $85 to $100 one-way to Colón from Panama City, $150 to $200 round-trip (including waiting time); $30 one-way to Gamboa, $55 round-trip; and $80 to $125 one-way to Portobelo, $120 to $160 round-trip. From Colón to Portobelo, expect to pay about $65 one-way and $100 round-trip. With the price of car rentals being so cheap and roads good, you are much better off with your own set of wheels.

BY BUS   Buses headed to Gamboa leave from the **SACA station** at the Palacio Legislativo at Plaza Cinco de Mayo, near Avenida Central, not from the main terminal in Albrook. The cost is $1 adults, 5¢ children. This bus drops passengers off at stops along the Gaillard Highway and Gamboa Road, including at the Miraflores Locks. However, the stop for Miraflores is an 8- to 10-minute walk from the visitor center. Buses leave weekdays at 5, 5:45, 6:30, 8, and 10am, noon, 1, 2, 3, 4:30, 6:30, 8, and 10:30pm; on Saturday and Sunday at 6, 7, 8, and 10am, noon, 2, 4:30, 6:30, 8, and 10:30pm. Keep in mind that you'll need to wait in the 90-degree weather for the return.

BY CAR   To get to Gamboa and the Canal Zone, head out of Panama City toward Albrook to the Gaillard Highway, which runs along the canal and passes the Miraflores Locks. The road continues on past the Pedro Miguel locks and the Summit Golf Course until it forks at the ANAM ranger station just after you pass under a railway bridge. To get to Gamboa, the Gamboa Resort, Barro Colorado Island, the Canopy Tower, El Charco Trail, or Pipeline Road, take a left here on Gamboa Road. To get to the Camino de Cruces trail, continue straight on a lovely, jungle-fringed road that cuts through Soberanía National Park and eventually connects with the road to Colón. The sign for the Cruces trail is clearly marked at an off-road picnic site.

What to See & Do

Travelers to the Canal Zone have two options: Visit on **day excursions** and lodge in Panama City, where you'll be closer to shops and services, or base yourself at one of the **resorts** or **hostels** highlighted below and take part in the in-house tours. (If a resort or hostel doesn't offer the tour themselves, it can book an outside tour for you.)

TOUR OPERATORS   It makes sense to hire a guide or join a day tour, especially if you don't have your own car; things are far apart in the Canal Zone, making getting around without a car nearly impossible. Transportation, a bilingual nature guide, equipment (if necessary), and often lunch are included in the price, and it may be cheaper and more efficient than trying to see all the area's attractions on your own.

For contact information about the **tour companies** mentioned here, see "Panama Canal Tour Operators," below. Be sure to check tour companies' websites for detailed excursion information, recently added tours, and updated prices.

SOBERANÍA NATIONAL PARK ★★★

Soberanía National Park comprises 19,425 hectares (48,000 acres) of undulating, pristine tropical rainforest on the eastern shore of the Panama Canal. It is undoubtedly Panama's most important national park in terms of tourism and economics: Not only is Soberanía one of the most accessible, species-rich parks in the Americas, it is also part of the watershed that provides hundreds of millions of gallons of water to keep the Panama Canal in operation and the cogs of international commerce greased and moving. The park is just 40 minutes from Panama City, but it feels worlds away.

Wildlife from North and South America, including migratory birds, meet here in Soberanía, creating a diverse natural wonderland. The park has 105 species of mammals and a staggering number of bird species—525 at last count. There are jaguars, collared peccaries, and night monkeys, too, but you're more likely to catch sight of a coatimundi, a three-toed sloth, or a diminutive tamarin monkey. Bring binoculars even if you're not an avid birder.

There are several ways to see the park. ANAM, the park ranger service, has several excellent hiking trails for day excursions that range from easy to difficult. The park also has a full-scale resort, a birder's ecolodge, a recreational park and zoo, and the Pipeline Road, a site revered for its abundant diversity of birds. Open daily from 6am to 5pm, Soberanía National Park costs $5 per person to enter (free for kids 11 and under). Paying is tricky; they ask that you stop at the ranger station to pay because there isn't anyone to collect money at the trail head—but it's unlikely that every visitor does this. Play it safe, though, and stop to pay; the pass permits you to use any trails within the space of a day.

The park can be accessed by rental vehicle, taxi, or joining a tour. If you take a taxi, plan a time for the driver to pick you up or have the driver wait. For more information, call the park's office at ☎ **232-4192.** The park office is open from 7am to 7pm daily, but if no one is inside, check around out back.

HIKING & BIRD-WATCHING TRAILS   Sendero El Plantación (Plantation Trail), located at the turnoff for the Canopy Tower lodge on the road to Gamboa, is a moderate, 6.4m (4-mile) trail that ends at the intersection for the Camino de Cruces trail. This is not a loop trail, so hikers will either need to return via the same trail or, with a little preplanning, arrange to be dropped off at the Camino de Cruces trail on the road to Colón, hike northwest and connect with the Plantation Trail, and finish near the Canopy Tower, or vice versa (see info on Camino de Cruces, below). The Plantation Trail follows a road built in the 1910s by La Cascadas Plantation, the largest in the old Canal Zone during that period, producing cacao, coffee, and rubber. Alert hikers will

PANAMA CANAL tour OPERATORS

Dozens of tour operators offer a variety of activities centered on the canal, from full and partial transits to fishing on Gatún Lake and wildlife-watching in the surrounding jungle. Here is a sampling of recommended companies:

- **Ancon Expeditions** (www.anconexpeditions.com; ☎ **269-9415**): Ancon offers full and partial transits of the canal from the Port of Balboa, where it has a passenger ferry. Ancon also offers rainforest boat trips on Gatún Lake, Emberá village visits, and hikes and bird-watching trips along Pipeline Road.

- **Canal & Bay Tours** (www.canalandbaytours.com; ☎ **209-2009** or 209-2010): One of the original canal boat operators, Canal & Bay have two boats, the refurbished wooden *Isla Morada*, with a capacity of 100, or the steel *Fantasía del Mar*, with room for 500 passengers.

- **Jungle Land Explorers** (www.junglelandpanama.com; ☎ **209-5657**): In addition to offering a motorboat tour of Gatún Lake and a stop at their anchored, double-decker floating lodge, Jungle Land provides kayaking trips across the canal and even *Survivor*-style corporate retreats.

- **Panama Canal Fishing** (www.panamacanalfishing.com; ☎ **315-1905**): Run by Panamanian-American Richard Cahill, Panama Canal Fishing has a 5.5m (18-ft.) boat with a 115-horsepower motor for fishing for peacock bass on Gatún Lake, as well as the Bayano River.

- The **Panama Canal Railway** (www.panarail.com; ☎ **317-6070**): This railway runs between Panama City and Colón, flanking the canal. It's a good alternative to driving between the two cities, giving you a chance to view the canal from a different angle.

- **Panama Marine Adventures** (www.pmatours.net; ☎ **226-8917**): For partial canal transit, this group offers a shuttle leaving from the Flamenco Resort and Marina on the Amador Causeway at 10am and going to its boat, *Pacific Queen*, docked at Gamboa.

- **Panama Pete Adventures** (www.panamapeteadventures.com; ☎ **888/726-6222**): This long-running, reliable operator offers standard Panama Canal and nature tours, including combination boat and bus tours along the canal, as well as bird-watching, hiking, and Emberá village day tours.

spot remnants of these crops, especially the cacao plant. This trail is popular with bird-watchers, but mammals such as tamarins are frequently seen, too.

Continuing on the road to Gamboa, and to the right, is the trail head for **Sendero Charco (Pond Trail),** an ultra-easy, 20-minute loop that follows the Sardinilla River. The trail gives even the most reluctant walkers a brilliant opportunity to immerse themselves in thick tropical rainforest.

A little more than a mile past the bridge and turnoff to Gamboa Resort is **Camino de Oleoducto,** better known as **Pipeline Road,** the celebrity trail for bird-watching in Panama, renowned worldwide as a record-setting site for 24-hour bird counts. Even non-birders can't help getting caught up in the action with so many colorful show birds fluttering about, such as motmots, trogons, toucans, antbirds, a rainbow of tanagers, and flycatchers. Bird-watching starts at the crack of dawn, when the avian world is at its busiest, so try to make it here at least before 9am, if not earlier. In spite of the name, Pipeline Road is not drivable. More than half the bird-watchers who visit here walk only a mile or so, but if you like to hike or mountain bike (see below), push on because the chances of spotting rare birds and wildlife increase the farther you go. To get here by vehicle, pass the Gamboa Resort turnoff and continue until you reach a fork. Turn left here onto a gravel road and continue until you see the Pipeline Road sign.

Soberanía's other prime attraction is historic **Camino de Cruces (Las Cruces Trail).** Before the railway and the canal existed, the only path from the Caribbean to the Pacific was the Chagres River to what's now called Venta de Cruces, followed by a treacherous walk along Las Cruces Trail. The Spanish used this route during the 16th century to transport looted treasure to the Caribbean and onward to Spain. In some areas, the cobblestone remains of the trail still exist or have been restored, and can be seen even if you walk just 10 or 20 minutes from the picnic area and trail head off Madden Road.

The trail is moderate to difficult and is about 9.7km (6 miles) to its terminus at Venta de Cruces. From here, a local boat can pick you up and drop you off at the Gamboa Resort, but you'll need a guide (a tour operator or your hotel can arrange this for you). Also, hikers may lose their way because the trail becomes somewhat indecipherable the closer you get to Venta las Cruces, another reason to have a guide. Backpackers can camp along the trail but must pay a $5 fee at the park ranger station beforehand.

If this trail really piques your interest, check out Ancon Expeditions' 8-day "Camino Real Trek," which gives travelers a taste of what it was like to cross the isthmus by foot during the Gold Rush era, and it includes tent lodging in the rainforest and at an Emberá Indian village. **Ancon Expeditions, Advantage Panama,** and **Panama Pete Adventures** (see contact information for all in "Panama Canal Tour Operators," above) all offer bird-watching, hiking, and Emberá village day tours, as does **Adventures Panama Canal** (✆ **6636-4647**).

The second alternative is to hike the trail and turn into the Plantation Trail, which finishes near Canopy Tower and the road to Gamboa. This hike takes around 5 hours to complete and is a moderately difficult trek. To get to the trail head, continue straight at the fork in the road to Gamboa on what's known as Madden Road (but not signed as such). The road presents a lovely drive through the park along a road flanked with towering rainforest canopy. About 6km (3¾ miles) past the fork there are covered picnic tables and the trail head.

MOUNTAIN BIKING The tour company **Adventures in Panama** (www. adventurespanama.com; ✆ **800/614-7214** in U.S., 6679-4404 in Panama) offers a unique half-day mountain-bike trip on Pipeline Road, leaving Panama City at 8am and returning at 1:30pm (cost averages $110 per person and includes transportation, equipment, and a box lunch). The bike terrain is sand,

Gamboa & the Canal Zone

pavement, packed dirt, and mud and is classified as moderate to difficult. Your group can bike up to 29km (18 miles) round-trip or less depending on your appetite for riding. The minimum age for this bike trip is 12 years old.

LAGO GATUN

Engineers understood that the only feasible way to build the Panama Canal was to employ a system of locks to lift ships up and over higher altitudes on the isthmus. Central to this was the creation of Gatún Lake. The lake was formed in 1913 with the completion of the Gatún Dam, which stanched the powerful Chagres River—a tremendous feat considering that Gatún Dam and Gatún Lake were the largest earth dam and largest manmade lake of their time. The lake flooded roughly 425 sq. km (164 sq. miles), an area slightly larger than Detroit, creating islands out of hilltops and submerging entire forests and villages.

The thick rainforest that cloaks the shoreline provides water for Gatún Lake, which in turn provides water for the canal locks, and therefore the Canal Authority is keen to keep deforestation at bay. This is good news for eco-travelers—wildlife sightings are common. Ships traverse 38km (24 miles) across the lake from the Gatún Locks to the Gaillard Cut, and travelers can take part in this experience with a **partial canal transit** (see "Transiting the Panama Canal," earlier) or take a **jungle cruise** (see below) on the lake. **Fishing** is also an option (see below), or you can visit **Barro Colorado Island** (see "Learn About the Rainforest with the Smithsonian Institute," below). Getting on the lake provides a more intimate view of the canal than a visit to the Miraflores Locks does.

JUNGLE CRUISES ★★★   Half-day jungle cruises in Lake Gatún are mini-adventures that are as fun for kids as they are for adults, and are dependable ways to catch sight of monkeys such as white-faced capuchins, howler monkeys, and Geoffrey's tamarins up-close and in their natural habitat. Expect to see sloths, crocodiles, caimans, turtles, and even *capybaras,* the world's largest rodents. The boat ride also allows passengers to get unusually close to monster tankers and ships transiting the canal. The **Gamboa Rainforest Resort** (www.gamboaresort.com) offers a jungle cruise as part of its in-house excursions; others leave from the Gamboa pier and provide land transportation to and from Panama City. Guides provide passengers with an entertaining account of the history of the canal, the mechanisms that operate the canal, and fun anecdotes, while ducking in and out of island passageways searching for birds and wildlife. **Ancon Expeditions** (p. 104) has the best guides and service, not to mention the most experience in the area. Their Panama Canal Rainforest Boat Adventure leaves early from Panama City and returns in the midafternoon; the cost is $110 adults, $65 kids 12 and under, which includes lunch, naturalist guides, and all transportation. **Advantage Panama** (www.advantagepanama.com; ✆ **221-4123**) also offers a rainforest land and water tour, including a stroll through Soberanía National Park before boarding their aquatic vessel. The tour lasts about 6 hours and includes drinks and snacks, costing $87 per person.

Gamboa & the Canal Zone   AROUND PANAMA CITY

Jungle Land Explorers (p. 96), part of Panama City Tours, offers an interesting motorboat tour of Gatún Lake and a stop at its anchored, double-decker floating lodge, where guests have lunch and kick back in the middle of the jungle; kayaking and fishing are also options. Jungle Land has a library with educational videos and books, too. The tour leaves from La Represa dock on the west side of the canal; however, round-trip transportation from Panama City is included, leaving at 8am and returning at 4:30pm. Tours cost $115 adults and $65 kids 12 and under. Call ahead for tour days and availability.

FISHING ★★★   Gatún Lake is packed with peacock bass, and all you need to do is just casually throw a line in and you'll easily snag one, sometimes within minutes. Fishermen tell stories of catching not dozens but hundreds of peacock bass and tarpon, which also reside here. Like a jungle cruise, you will get relatively close to ships on the canal and enjoy wild surroundings. **Panama Canal Fishing** (www.panamacanalfishing.com; ✆ **315-1905**) has a 5.5m (18-ft.) Fun Deck with a 115-horsepower motor, live bait box, and fishing rods. The cost is $495 a day for two people, plus $65 for each additional angler, with lures, rods, snacks, and beer included. It also recently began offering ocean boats for inshore fishing. The operation is run by Richard Cahill, a Panamanian-American who knows the lake inside and out. Rich also has fishing trips for snook and tarpon in the Bayano River ($850 all-inclusive), located about 1½ hours from Panama City. **Gamboa Tours** (www. gamboatours.com) at the Gamboa Rainforest Resort charters private fishing excursions as well.

RÍO CHAGRES & EMBERÁ VILLAGES

The Chagres River flows from the San Blas Cordillera down into Gatún Lake near Gamboa—on the other side of the lake, the river is blocked by the Gatún Dam, which created its namesake lake. Travelers visit this river for two reasons: **cultural tours of Emberá Indian villages** or intermediate-level **whitewater rafting.** Along the way, jungle-draped riverbanks teem with birds, animals, and fluttering butterflies, providing an exciting sense of adventure.

EMBERÁ INDIANS VILLAGE TOUR ★★   Emberá Indians are native to the Darién Province, but many groups have resettled here on the banks of the Chagres River. For the most part, they continue to live life much as they have for centuries, traveling by dugout canoe, wearing nothing more than a skirt or sheath, and sleeping under thatched-roof huts. To earn income, the Emberá villages Parara Puru, Emberá Puru, and Emberá Drua, which are close to the mouth of the Chagres River, have opened to tourism, allowing visitors to share in their culture and see how they live. In the true sense, the villages are not pristine examples of Emberá life, but the chance to travel by dugout canoe, interact with this fascinating culture and, yes, buy a few of their intricately woven baskets and other handicrafts is an informative and delightful experience. For a few bucks, you can have a traditional "tattoo" with *jagua* vegetable dye on a part of your body (kids love this), but keep in mind that it takes 10 to 14 days for it to fade away! Part of the tour includes a typical Emberá

Gamboa & the Canal Zone

LEARN ABOUT THE rainforest WITH THE SMITHSONIAN INSTITUTE

The **Barro Colorado Nature Monument** ★★★ is home to one of the most important—and oldest—biological research stations in the world, administered by the Smithsonian Tropical Research Institute (STRI). It contains more than 5,261 hectares (13,000 acres) of land, including five surrounding mainland peninsulas, but the spotlight is on Barro Colorado Island in Gatún Lake, a short boat ride away from Gamboa. The forested island, the largest in the lake, was once a hill called West Hill. It became a 16-sq.-km (6-sq.-mile) island after the surrounding area was flooded during the creation of Gatún Lake. The island is essentially a capsule of biodiversity that provides an opportunity for scientists to monitor population changes and test diversity theories about the rainforest without having their studies encroached upon by loggers, developers, poachers, or farmers. Each year, between 200 and 400 international scientists visit Barro Colorado, making this one of the most well-studied forests in the world. Scientists have discovered more than 1,200 plants, 120 mammals, and innumerable insects on the island, but really the chances of your spotting wildlife here are the same as at any rainforest in Panama (but count on seeing howler monkeys).

What's unique here is that the average layman can visit the island and see what's going on in the world of tropical science. It's an outstanding tour—part

boat ride, part hike, part learning experience—and the price includes a delicious buffet lunch and access to the visitor center and Espavé bookstore. The only downside to the tour is that it is expensive ($80 adults, $50 students) and nonrefundable—don't even think about showing up late for the boat ride or you'll be left behind. Reservations should be made more than 2 weeks in advance, but you can always call and see if there is a last-minute cancellation. If you're short on time or not up to giving tropical rainforests more than a cursory glance, this is probably not the best tour for you.

The tour leaves at 7:15am on Tuesday, Wednesday, and Friday, and 8am on weekends, from STRI's dock, located just past the turnoff to the Gamboa Resort (heading left at the fork and onto a gravel road). The boat ride to the island takes 45 minutes. Once there, a guided tour takes visitors on a 2- to 3-hour hike along a sometimes steep trail through forest, ending at the visitor center for lunch, followed by a Q&A session. At 3:40pm on weekdays and 2:30pm on weekends (a weekday tour is longer), the boat takes visitors back to the pier. Bring proper walking shoes, bug repellent, your passport, and your confirmation letter from STRI, and wear long pants, not shorts. Complete information is available from **STRI** (www.stri.si.edu; ✆ **212-8961**). You can reserve and pay by credit card on the STRI site.

lunch and a folkloric dance show. Bring your swimsuit—tours include a walk to a cascade for a dip in cool water. All Panamanian tour operators offer this Emberá trip, though prices vary. **Ancon Expeditions** (p. 104) charges $130 for the half-day trip, while **Advantage Panama** (p. 98) charges $81. **Margo Tours** (www.margotours.com; ✆ **264-8888**) charges $85.

RAFTING & KAYAKING ★★ The tour company **Aventuras Panama** (www.aventuraspanama.com; ✆ **260-0044**) specializes in what it calls the

"Chagres Challenge," with a hiking and rafting trip down the Class II and III river. It's a long float but technically not difficult, and it starts early, leaving Panama City at 5am by four-wheel-drive (4WD) and going to the village San Cristóbal. From here, you hike for more than an hour to the put-in site on the Chagres. The rafting portion lasts about 5 hours, but included in that is a picnic lunch on the river. Travelers pass by Emberá villages but do not spend much time there. Expect to arrive back in Panama City around 7pm. The cost is $185 per person and includes transportation, breakfast, and lunch, and all equipment. You must be between the ages of 12 and 70 to participate.

SUMMIT GARDENS PARK & ZOO ★★

There's a lot of wildlife in the jungles of Panama, but almost all species shy from the public and are close to impossible to spot in their natural environment. If this is your first trip to Panama or your time is limited here, **Summit Gardens Park & Zoo** is a good introduction to the flora and fauna native to the country. For kids, there are a lot of wide, grassy areas on which to run around, and enough animals on view to delight all ages. It isn't a fancy, state-of-the-art zoo by U.S. standards, but Summit has a wonderful display of "showcase" wildlife, including tapirs, white-faced capuchins and spider monkeys, ocelots, a jaguar, a puma, collared peccaries, and more, some of which have been rescued from unscrupulous wildlife poachers. Without a doubt, the **harpy eagle** takes center stage here with its own interpretive center. The harpy is Panama's national bird and the largest eagle in the world, about half the size of an average human—it really is worth a visit just to see this regal bird.

Summit began as a botanical garden in 1923, created by the U.S. in an effort to reproduce and distribute tropical plants from around the world. It is now home to the world's leading collection of palms, among other exotic species. Because Panama City has few green spaces for a picnic or a chance to let the kids run free, Summit is popular with families on weekends. The zoo costs $5

Rainforest Discovery Center ★★★

The **Rainforest Discovery Center** (www. pipelineroad.org; © **264-6266**) is run by the Fundacíon Avifauna and opened in 2008. The center is home to 3km (1.8 miles) of hiking trails, a visitor center, cafeteria, and tower; the tower overlooks lush rainforest and is a must-do for serious birders, who can expect to see the most species between 6 and 10am. Keep in mind it's 172 steps to the top, so visitors who are less fit may not enjoy this activity. Only 25 people are allowed up the tower at the time and you are pretty much guaranteed to see birds and other wildlife. The center is open daily (except Christmas and New Year's) between 6am and 4pm. Entrance is $20 during the center's regular hours of 10am to 6pm, and $30 during the "premium" hours of 6 to 10am. For an extra-special experience, book a "special night hours" guided tour for $35; night tours require a five-person minimum, and all reservations should be made 48 hours in advance. If you don't have a car, the easiest way to get here is by contracting a cab for a few hours to take you and drop you back off in Panama City.

for adults, $1 for students and teens, free for kids 12 and under. It's open daily from 9am to 3pm. Call ℂ **232-4850** for more information.

Where to Stay & Dine

Lodging and dining options are limited and relatively expensive in the Gamboa area, which is why many people choose to visit as part of a day tour.

Canopy Tower ★★★   When it opened in 1999, this ex–U.S.–military radar station instantly became one of the world's greatest hotels for bird-watchers. The circular tower, topped by a 9m-high (30-ft.) dome, is at the top of Semaphore Hill, giving once-in-a-lifetime views of the lush green of Soberanía National Park and its 400-plus species of birds. Birders gather with binoculars at the 360-degree observation deck to observe the treetops and take in a view that reaches the Panama City skyline. On the top floor there's a comfortable lounge, dining area, and library loaded with nature guides with wraparound windows that allow you to search for birds even in the rain. The functional rooms are on the floors below, and all except the single rooms have private bathrooms. Grab a pair of earplugs from the hallway if you want to sleep in and block out the birdsong in the morning—seriously, it's that intense. Rates include meals and wine with dinner, plus 1 free tour with a 3-night stay. Other tours have an additional fee. There is a 2-night minimum stay.

Road to Gamboa. www.canopytower.com. ℂ **800/616-7451** from the U.S. or 264-5720. 12 units. $129 single; $184–$267 per person double; $209–$303 per person suite. Rates include all meals and wine with dinner, plus 1 free tour with a 3-night stay. **Amenities:** Restaurant; bar; free Wi-Fi.

Gamboa Rainforest Resort ★   This sprawling resort in Soberanía National Park along the shore of the Chagres River is one of the most family-friendly retreats in Panama. Although the immensity of the resort can make you feel two steps removed from the stunning nature around it, it's ideal for those families who are looking for a safer, cozier version of their jungle experience, one with amenities ranging from a full-service spa and riverfront pool to several restaurants. Still, guided tours, jungle boat cruises, aerial tram rides through the rainforest, and mini-zoos make it as easy as possible to get out into the wild. The resort has a variety of rooms, all quite sterile, with tile floors and wicker furniture, plus big balconies with even bigger views of the river or rainforest. Suites add extra living space.

Gamboa. www.gamboaresort.com. ℂ **314-5000.** 166 units. $127–$220 double with garden view; $150–$230 double with river view; $235–$450 1-bedroom and themed suites. **Amenities:** 3 restaurants; 2 bars; outdoor pool; tennis courts; fitness center w/ whirlpool, spa, steam, and massage; bike and kayak rental; concierge; room service; free Wi-Fi.

COLÓN

76km (47 miles) NW of Panama City

Spread across a square peninsula at the mouth of the northern canal gateway is **Colón,** capital of the larger Colón Province, which runs along Panama's central Caribbean Coast. Most residents here are Afro-Caribbean descendants of canal workers who arrived around the turn of the 20th century. In spite of its status as the largest **duty-free zone** in the Americas, with billions in annual sales, its profits do not trickle down to locals, and the city is rife with poverty and crime. A splashy $45-million cruise-ship port, called **Colón 2000,** has also failed to alleviate mass unemployment or improve living conditions. There is not much of interest in the actual city of Colón, and although stories of muggings and purse snatchings have been greatly exaggerated, Colón is definitely not one of Panama's safer cities. A drive through the city streets provokes shock, sadness, or just a very uncomfortable feeling at how impoverished Colón's residents are.

But don't let Colón scare you from visiting some of Panama's most important historical attractions, lying within a 30-minute to 1-hour drive from the city, such as **Portobelo** and **Fort San Lorenzo,** as well as the impressive **Gatún Locks** and **Gatún Dam** (see "The Panama Canal," earlier in this chapter). The translucent Caribbean Sea also beguiles visitors with outstanding **diving** and **snorkeling** opportunities, and the province is home to several oceanfront hotels and resorts that are popular weekend getaways for Panama City residents.

Colón was founded in 1850 during the California Gold Rush. At the time, crossing the United States from coast to coast was dangerous and time-consuming; a far better option was to take a ship to Panama, cross the isthmus via the Panama Railroad, and board a ship for California. Economically, the city flourished with businesses and hotels catering to travelers until 1869, with the completion of the transcontinental railway in the U.S. The arrival of the French, and later the U.S., around the turn of the 20th century, brought new prosperity to the city, and much of the architecture here dates from that era. Most of these buildings today are dilapidated shells of their former glory, the city having fallen on hard times when the focus turned to Panama City.

Essentials
GETTING THERE & DEPARTING
BY BUS The **Colón bus terminal** is located at Calle Terminal and Avenida Bolívar. There is daily service to and from the Albrook Terminal in Panama City, leaving every 20 minutes from 6am to 10pm; the trip is just under 2 hours and costs $3 one-way. Buses headed to Portobelo leave every 15 minutes from 6:30am to 8:45pm; the ride is 1 hour and costs $2. To reach Portobelo from Panama City, it is not necessary to transfer in Colón; instead, take a bus to Sabanitas and transfer to a bus headed to Portobelo (catch the transfer on the corner at the El Rey supermarket in Sabanitas). The fare is $3.

BY TRAIN By far the most picturesque journey to Colón is aboard the **Panama Canal Railway** (see "The Panama Canal Railway" in "The Panama Canal," earlier in this chapter).

BY CAR Driving here can be a little tricky because most streets are not signed. There are two ways to Colón from Panama City: The easiest is via the

Corredor Norte, which connects to the Boyd-Roosevelt Highway, also known as the Transístmica Highway, at Chilibre. The other, more scenic route is to go through Soberanía National Park and then connect to the Boyd-Roosevelt highway—follow the Omar-Torrijos Avenue to the Gaillard Highway toward Gamboa, but continue straight rather than turning left at the park ranger's office and the sign for Gamboa and Summit Gardens.

GETTING AROUND

If you are not part of a tour and do not have a vehicle, a taxi (which fits up to four people) is your best bet. Taxis are not metered—expect a driver to set a flat fee for visits to multiple destinations in the area. The Colón 2000 port has set rates for taxis, and even though you may be hiring one from the bus or train terminal, drivers like to adhere to these general rates for all tourists. I recommend having your hotel call a cab for you rather than taking one off the street. Most taxi drivers speak little English and are not tour guides. Considering this, you might want to stick with a bilingual tour.

GENERAL TOUR OPERATORS   The tour operators listed in "Panama Canal Tour Operators" (earlier in this chapter) can put together custom day and multi-day tours in the central Caribbean region. Typical day tours begin with a ride on the Panama Railroad to Colón and are followed by minivan transportation to the Gatún Locks and Fort San Lorenzo, a historical tour of Portobelo, and finally return ground transportation to Panama City. **Ancon Expeditions** (www.anconexpeditions.com; ℡ **269-9415**) offers a unique, 7-night "Camino Real Tour" following the old Spanish-built cobblestone trail across the isthmus. The tour involves several days of moderate trekking and overnights in tents and hotels.

What to See & Do

Two principal attractions are located in Colón. The **Colón Free Zone** is a walled-in, city-within-a-city located on the southeastern edge of town. Its 1,600 showrooms are for wholesalers and retailers in Central and South America who travel here to buy consumer products at cost. The Free Zone is open to the public, but most showrooms sell to wholesalers only, and others only reluctantly sell to individual tourists. Really, you can't buy anything here that isn't available in an airport duty-free store, and legally any purchase here must be sent by the retailer to the airport for pickup, which is another hassle. To visit, you'll need to sign in and show your passport at the Free Zone office, located at the right of the Free Zone entrance at Calle 13 near Avenida Roosevelt.

Running the length of the city's eastern shore is the modern cruise-ship port, **Colón 2000,** with two restaurants, a grocery store, and a dozen shops selling duty-free electronics, jewelry, and other handicrafts. There's really nothing interesting enough to keep you here, and the port is more of a jumping-off point to explore the area outside Colón. Excursions for cruise ships are provided by the port-owned **Aventuras 2000** tour agency.

Tip: ATMs in the central Caribbean region are scarce. Major hotels and most restaurants accept credit cards, but your best (and safest) bet is to use the ATM inside the grocery store in the Colón 2000 cruise-ship port; there is also an HSBC cash machine at the Gatún Locks, next to the visitor center entrance, or bring enough cash to cover your visit.

Where to Stay

Unless you really have to stay in Colón, you're better off staying outside the city.

New Washington Hotel ★   Although the city also has a newer, more comfortable Radisson, the much more atmospheric New Washington is still the city's grande dame. It was built in 1913 and has been updated continuously for the past century. It's right on the harbor in one of the more secure corners of the city and has gardens that continue to be kept to high standards despite the lack of guests. There's an outdoor pool and a casino, and although rooms are somewhat dreary, the price is a steal.

Calle 2. www.newwashingtonhotel.com. ✆ **441-7133.** 124 units. $65 double; $75 suite. **Amenities:** Restaurant; bar; outdoor pool; casino; disco; room service; free Wi-Fi.

West of Colón
GATÚN LOCKS & DAM ★★★

The Gatún Locks, located at the Caribbean entrance of the canal about 10km (6 miles), or a 20-minute drive, from Colón, are the canal's busiest because there is just one set of locks here instead of the two at Miraflores—meaning you have a better chance of seeing Panamax ships backed up here and waiting their turn to enter the canal. These locks are also the most impressive because they lift ships and tankers up 26m (85 ft.) to the level of Lake Gatún in three steps (taking about 1½ hr. to complete), where they continue for 37km (23 miles) before reaching the Pedro Miguel Locks. The neat thing here is that you can **drive over the canal** at near-water level on your way out to Fort San Lorenzo (see "Colón," above).

The **Gatún Locks Visitors Pavilion** (daily 9am–4pm; free admission), enlarged and renovated during the expansion, has a viewing platform, reached by a long flight of stairs, that offers a high perch for excellent photo opportunities. Apart from a model of the canal and a bilingual brochure, there are no other tourist facilities here. The visitor center is not well signed; to get here, head left just at the canal vehicle bridge until you see a parking lot to your right (pass around traffic if there is a line waiting to cross the canal bridge).

About 2km (1¼ miles) from the Gatún Locks is **Gatún Dam,** a tremendous earthen dam across Chagres River that was, at its completion, the largest in the world and one of the finest engineering achievements in history. The dam was built to create the artificial Lake Gatún, crossed by ships to reach the Pedro Miguel Locks. During the rainy season from April to December, you'll want to visit when the spillway is open, but there are no regular hours, so ask at the visitor center at the Gatún Locks.

The majority of visitors here are on shore excursions from the cruise-ship port at Colón or are staying at the Meliá Panama Canal hotel. If you're coming from Colón or the train station (in Panama City), a round-trip taxi ride will cost between $25 and $35 for an hour, or $45 to $55 for 2 hours (to see both the dam and the locks).

FORT SAN LORENZO & ACHIOTE ROAD ★★

Continuing past the Gatún Locks, the road hugs the edge of the Sherman Forest Reserve until reaching the old U.S. military base Fort Sherman, a part of which was torn down to make way for a new Decameron Resort that never happened. If you're driving your own vehicle, the police guard at the gate may ask to see your passport. Continue for 8.9km (5½ miles) on a paved/unpaved road shrouded in tropical greenery, until the road ends and the view opens onto the Caribbean Sea and the mouth of the Chagres River. The Chagres has been called the "world's most valuable river," for it was here that the Spanish transported staggering quantities of Incan gold, later followed by forty-niners passing through with millions of dollars of mined treasure. Now the river's immense value is derived from the fact that the Chagres provides the necessary water to keep the Panama Canal in operation.

Most intriguing here is **Fort San Lorenzo** (© **226-6602**), a Spanish defensive fort first built in 1595 but subsequently sacked and burned three times and finally rebuilt in 1761—the version you see today. It was later used as a prison and, for a brief period, a campground for forty-niners during the Gold Rush. Fort San Lorenzo is a UNESCO World Heritage Site, and with its well-preserved state—rusty cannons pointed at enemies long gone, walls made of thick coral and rock, and a grassy moat—it's a worthwhile detour. However, if you're short on time and already planning to visit the forts at Portobelo, you might skip San Lorenzo because of the 1½-hour drive from Colón (unless you're a bird-watcher—see below). The fort is open daily from 9am to 4pm, and you must be back out of the police guard station by 6pm. The cost is $3 per person, though there is not always someone there to take it.

The village of **Achiote** lies midway between Piña and Escobal on the Achiote Road, quietly revered as a bird-watching mecca by those in the know—the Audubon Society holds its Atlantic Christmas Bird Count here and has counted up to 390 species in 1 day, including the black-throated trogon, bare-crowned antbirds, white hawks, blue cotingas, and chestnut-mandibled toucans. The area is just now developing as an ecotourism site as a way to support the small local community, and the **Centro El Tucán** (no phone; Mon–Fri 7–10am and 3–7pm) in Achiote has interpretive exhibits. The best way to visit is with a birding guide who can arrange transportation. Try **Ancon Expeditions** (see above) or check the Audubon Society's site, **www.audubonpanama.org**, to see if they have any day trips planned to the area.

WHERE TO STAY & DINE

Marina Hotel at Shelter Bay ★   Located at the Caribbean entrance to the canal, the Marina Hotel is utilized primarily by bird-watchers wanting easy access to Achiote Road and San Lorenzo or yachtsmen anchored at the marina. The rooms have a Caribbean feel, with bright colored paintings and shell-shaped lamps, as well as balconies overlooking the marina or the jungle, which is beyond the parking lot. The remote waterfront setting is rather pleasant and eclectic, and the cast of characters dining at the surprisingly decent restaurant, drinking at the bar, or milling around the docks is always fascinating.

Fort Sherman, Shelter Bay. www.marinahotelatshelterbay.com. © **433-0471.** 11 units. $130–$140 double. Extra person $15. Children 12 and under stay free in parent's room. **Amenities:** Restaurant; bar; pool; gym; store; Wi-Fi (extra fee).

Meliá Panama Canal ★ The three buildings that make up the Meliá have been named the Niña, Pinta, and Santa María in an attempt to make over the notorious military school that spawned Manuel Noriega, the Escuela de las Americas, where it is set. All in all, the chain has done a good job of making use of the landmark architecture and decorations, from the soaring lobby to the Spanish colonial art reproductions. The hotel's focal points are the two resort-style pools, with a swim-up bar. Many guests come here just to lounge around, though there are kayaks for paddling in the lake, a zipline, day excursions to Portobelo and Fort San Lorenzo, and a mediocre casino. The rooms have king-size beds and marble bathrooms, and suites are significantly bigger. Skip the package rates that include meals; they're not worth it.

Gatún Lake, Colón. www.meliapanamacanal.com. © **470-1100** or 877/696-6252 in the U.S. 232 units. $120 double; $150 suite. **Amenities:** Restaurant; piano bar and pool bar; 2 outdoor pools; tennis court; fitness center; massage service; sports equipment and kayak rental; children's activities; concierge; room service; babysitting; free Wi-Fi.

PORTOBELO ★★

99km (62 miles) from Panama City; 43km (27 miles) from Colón

Portobelo is a modest seaside village made of clapboard homes built around and among the ruins of what was one of Spain's richest and liveliest ports from the mid-16th to early 18th century. The village, squeezed tightly between thick jungle and the blue Caribbean Sea, is less than an hour from Colón, and it's a very popular destination on the central Caribbean Coast for day excursions. This historic site was once the scene of the famous Portobelo fairs that took place for 2 centuries, when Spain's plundered gold and silver from South America passed through here. Around Portobelo are well-preserved forts that are splendid examples of 17th- and 18th-century military architecture, as well as a recently restored Customs House. The ruins, along with Fort San Lorenzo (see above), were named World Heritage Sites by UNESCO in 1980.

Portobelo's residents call themselves *congos* and are descendants of African slaves brought here during the Spanish colonial era; they are culturally different from the Afro-Caribbeans in Colón. The *congos* possess a rich folkloric expression that arose from slavery as well as African traditions and religion fused with Catholicism, and which is now best expressed by the

The London–Panama Connection

Portobelo was named "Puerto Bello" (Beautiful Port) by Christopher Columbus on his first visit here in 1502, a name that gradually became known as Portobelo. Known for its grand and lively 3-month-long trade fairs and the hordes of gold and silver that flowed through here, Portobelo was irresistible to pirates. But it's a battle led by British Admiral Edward Vernon in 1739 for which the town is most remembered. Vernon attacked Portobelo during the War of Jenkins' Ear, a 9-year British war against the Spanish, and his victory resulted in the use of "Portobello" as a commemorative name for a well-known farm in what is now the Notting Hill neighborhood of London. The road leading to the farm was called Portobello Road. Today this road is itself internationally famous for its own lively market. Vernon is also associated with the term "grog," which was his moniker and the name his sailors gave to the watered-down rum he served them to stem drunkenness.

colorful costumes and devil masks that they don during festivals such as Carnaval and the famous **Black Christ Festival** on October 21.

Sailors and yachties like to anchor in the calm Portobelo bay, and you'll see lots of boats bobbing in the turquoise sea. There is decent scuba diving and snorkeling around here, too. Portobelo is not exceedingly dangerous, but it is an economically depressed town with rundown homes, a worn-out central plaza, and a good many people hanging around without much to do. If you use common sense and don't flash expensive equipment or money, you shouldn't have any problems.

Essentials

GETTING THERE & DEPARTING   By Car   Drivers from Panama City should take the Corredor Norte, a modern toll road that ends at Chilibre; from here, head right, then turn left on the Transístmica Highway, and drive about 40km (25 miles) to the town of Sabanitas. Keep your eyes open for El Rey supermarket and turn right on the road just past it. Follow the signs for Portobelo, located about 33km (21 miles) from Sabanitas.

By Bus   Buses from Panama City leave from the Albrook Terminal. You'll want a bus to Sabanitas or a bus to Colón that stops in Sabanitas (verify this with the driver; the cost is $3) and to transfer at the El Rey supermarket on the highway for a bus to Portobelo ($2). To get back to Panama City, you'll need to get a bus to Sabanitas, cross the highway, and flag down a bus headed to Panama City. Buses to and from Colón leave every half-hour. Getting here by car or taxi is recommended.

By Taxi   Taxis from Colón to Portobelo average $50 to $55 for a one-way trip.

VISITOR INFORMATION   See "Colón," earlier in this chapter, for tour operators.

What to See & Do

FORT RUINS & THE CUSTOMS HOUSE ★★

If you're a history buff, plan on spending about 2 hours touring the ruins and the Custom House—more if you take a water taxi to the ruins at Fuerte San Fernando across the bay. You'll only need an hour if you plan to just walk around a bit and snap a few photos. Portobelo is tiny enough to see all the sights on foot.

Entering town, the first attraction you'll encounter on your left-hand side is the **Batería Santiago,** a defensive fort built after the famous raid on Portobelo by the British Admiral Edward Vernon in 1739. The fort is remarkably well preserved, with rusty cannons, ramps, and a sentry box. Across the road is a short uphill path to **Casa Fuerte Santiago,** which overlooked the bay and acted as a depository for ammunition.

Farther into town is **Castillo Santiago de la Gloria,** built in 1600 but destroyed after an attack by Henry Morgan, before his famous sacking of Panama City. The fort was rebuilt but attacked again by Vernon; after this, the fort was left in ruins and abandoned. From here, you can take a water taxi at the pier ($3) to **Fuerte San Fernando,** which really isn't much of a fort any longer because much of the fort's stone was taken and used for construction of the canal by the U.S. Leading up from the Castillo is another short, uphill hike to **Mirador el Perú,** a lookout offering a lofty view of the Portobelo bay.

The **Real Aduana de Portobelo (Customs House),** located in front of the *parque* (plaza) in the center of town, is a highlight of Portobelo. This fine old building is the restored version of what was known as the "counting house" during the Spanish colonial days, so-named for the gold and silver that was counted, registered, and distributed here. For a century, a third of all the gold in the world passed through this spot. The Spanish built the Customs House in 1630, but it was damaged in both 1744 (by a cannon) and 1882 (by an earthquake). There is also a small museum here (no phone; daily 8am–4pm). The museum will hold your attention for about 15 minutes—there's really nothing much to see in the main section except a jumbled collection of clipped articles about Portobelo, cannonballs, coin collections, and other items that are not very representative of the Spanish colonial days. You can pick up a free map of Portobelo here, however. The museum has a short informational video, in Spanish and English, for $1 per person. On the second floor is a Spanish-only folkloric display.

The best-preserved fort in town is **Fuerte San Jerónimo,** next to the Customs House. Like the other forts of Portobelo, this one, originally built in 1664, was attacked by Vernon and rebuilt using a more streamlined design.

IGLESIA DE SAN FELIPE ★ & THE BLACK CHRIST

One of the most curious churches in Panama is **Iglesia de San Felipe,** home to the famous "Black Christ" statue and the source of Portobelo's largest yearly festival on October 21. Legend has it that a ship headed to Cartagena, Colombia, left the statue behind in Portobelo either to lighten its load or because the crew believed that the statue was causing them bad luck. Later, Portobelo residents prayed to the statue to spare them from a cholera epidemic—and indeed they were spared. Praying to the statue has become so widespread that every year pilgrims don ornate purple robes and walk to San Felipe Church, sometimes from as far away as Sabanitas and beyond, either to give thanks or pray for something they need in their lives. It's a spectacle, and not always as religious as you might suspect, with music and drinking thrown into the mix. The best way to see this festival is with a guided tour, because parking is impossible and you might need someone to get you out after a long day.

Behind San Felipe Church is **Iglesia de San Juan,** the original hospital of Portobelo that eventually became a church. Now it holds a small **museum** that displays dozens of the purple robes used by pilgrims during the Black Christ Festival. It's open daily from 8:30am to about 3:30pm.

Adventure Activities
SCUBA DIVING & SNORKELING
The waters off Portobelo do not provide divers with the rich diversity of marine life found in places such as Coiba in the Chiriquí Gulf, but diving is one of the main draws to this area beyond touring the ruins in town. One of the most well-respected dive operators, **Panama Divers** (www.panamadivers.com; ✆ 448-2293), has a base at the Octopus Garden Hotel. They offer day trips, multiday trips, and Professional Association of Diving Instructors (PADI) courses. The good news about diving off the Central Caribbean Coast is that it is surprisingly accessible, even if you're lodging in Panama City; the bad news is that visibility is poor when the sea gets churned up (Dec–Feb) or when it rains. On a good day, expect visibility depths of about 40m (131 ft.). Popular dive spots include Drake's Island, with sponges in a rainbow of colors, Buffet Reef, and Iron Castle. Divers can also visit a submerged plane. Panama Divers is a competent, fully licensed, and insured operation with professional guides and travel assistance. Panama Divers includes a tour of the ruins at Portobelo as part of their scuba excursions. For snorkeling, the best place in the area is Playa Blanca, reached by a 20-minute boat ride from the pier.

Scubaportobelo (www.scubapanama.com; ✆ 261-3841), located 4km (2.4 miles) before town, also has dive and snorkel tours of area reefs, starting at $125.

BEACHES & BOAT TOURS
Local boatmen operate at the pier near the Castillo Santiago de la Gloria, ferrying passengers to the empty **Playa Blanca,** located on the coast north of Portobelo. It's one of the best beaches in the area—if you're looking for a little beach time, this is your place. The cost to get here is about $20 to $25. There is a two-person minimum.

CULTURAL ACTIVITIES
La Casa Congo (www.fundacionbp.org; ✆ 202-0111), attached to the B&B of the same name, runs an incredible art gallery that helps local painters and

wood carvers hone their craft for an international clientele. They also arrange visits to a local music school and to see dance performances, all of which they help support. Check before your visit. They also **rent kayaks** for use in the harbor ($20 for 3 hr.).

Where to Stay & Dine

Besides La Casa Congo, most hotels lie outside the very small, compact city center. During the high season (Dec–Apr), restaurants in Portobelo are open according to the times listed in each review, though when tourism is sluggish, they may shut their doors around 5pm. In addition to the places listed below, around the Iglesia de San Felipe several modest restaurants and food stalls serve up delicious Caribbean seafood dishes.

Captain Jack's INTERNATIONAL ★   On the edge of the center of town, up a slight incline, Captain Jack's is an all-around decent option for a meal. It has a little bit of everything, from burgers to Thai curries to pasta, plus cold beer and Bloody Marys. From the second-floor dining area you get a nice view of the town and the harbor. Owner Jack is also an excellent resource on finding sailboats to Colombia.

Calle Genea. www.captainjackpanama.com. © **448-2009.** Reservations not accepted. Main courses $8–$12. Daily noon–8pm.

El Otro Lado ★★★   One of the most unique and luxurious hotels in all of Panama is hidden across Portobelo harbor, reached only by boat. The sprawling property, which includes a maze of canals and a jungle-covered hillside with a small lagoon and waterfall, was the private paradise of the owner for several decades before being opened up to guests. Five colorful casitas designed according to local construction are totally decked out and infused with local artwork and top-of-the-line electronics. I particularly like the Sun House at the end of the property, with its extra terrace and views of the harbor. The staff helps organize kayak and stand-up paddleboarding (SUP) trips into the mangroves, boat trips to uninhabited islands and isolated beaches, hikes into the national park, and cultural activities focused on Afro-Panamanian dance. There's a funky fine-dining restaurant at the center, just beside the infinity pool. The hotel's foundation also runs La Casa Congo in town as well, and much of the artwork and woodwork created at El Otro Lado and used to decorate the property is sold there.

Portobelo Bay. www.elotrolado.com.pa. © **202-0111.** 8 units. $490–$980 casas. **Amenities:** Restaurant; bar; pool; kayaks; Free Wi-Fi.

La Casa Congo ★★   On the second floor above La Casa Congo's mosaic-tile–lined art gallery are four basic yet charming rooms. Afro-Panamanian artwork from the gallery and Ikea-like furniture decorate the rooms, two of which have balconies overlooking the harbor. There are no common areas to speak of, other than a hallway and the amenities on the first floor. It's one of the few good options right in the center of town and their restaurant and bar are two of the more reliable spots for a snack, coffee, or drink at any time of the day.

10 min. before Portobelo. www.fundacionbp.org. © **202-0111.** 4 rooms. $80–$100 double. Rates include breakfast. **Amenities:** Restaurant; art gallery; free Wi-Fi.

Octopus Garden Hotel ★   This more or less dive resort—it's the home base for Panama Divers—is on the road into town, a 10-minute drive away. The rooms, with red-tile floors, are bright and airy but rather unassuming. As expected, divers make up the majority of guests, though non-divers can snorkel, kayak, or go on excursions into town. The on-site restaurant isn't bad either.

10 min. before Portobelo. www.panamadivers.com. © **448-2293.** 8 rooms. $55 double. **Amenities:** Restaurant; free Wi-Fi.

OUTSIDE OF PORTOBELO

Adriana's ★ SEAFOOD   This Afro-Panamanian seafood restaurant is a 25-minute drive outside of Portobelo in La Guaira, just before Isla Grande. It's a rustic open-air restaurant known only by locals, Panama City chefs, and in-the-know area foodies. The restaurant is right on the water, looking out at Isla Grande, and serves traditional dishes such as *ceviche de pulpo* (octopus in coconut milk served with fried plantains) and fried red snapper. If food is the experience you favor, this nondescript little local restaurant is worth the effort to get here.

La Guaira, about 19km (12 miles) from Portobelo. No phone. Main courses $7–$10. No credit cards. Daily noon–7 or 8pm.

ISLA GRANDE

20km (12 miles) from Portobelo; 105km (65 miles) from Panama City

Isla Grande is a Caribbean island getaway frequented by residents of Panama City because of its easy access; it's close enough to get to without flying. A tiny village stretches along the western shore, and there are no roads—residents get around by foot or water taxi. During high season and some weekends, Isla Grande can get very festive, with drinking and loud reggae music; weekdays are often dead. With beach areas on the Pacific Coast improving in recent years, Isla Grande has lost much of its luster.

Essentials

GETTING THERE & DEPARTING **By Car or Taxi**   To get to Isla Grande, you'll want to continue past Portobelo along a pockmarked road for about 20km (12 miles) to **La Guaira,** an impoverished fishing village with two piers, one with boats to Isla Grande. You can park at either dock, but the Isla Grande dock charges a $3-per-day fee. And upon your return, you can count on some slacker or young kid hanging around and asking for $1 or $2 for additional "security"—and they're not nice if you decide not to pay. If you really want to get out of paying this "fee," simply ask how your car looks. Likely, they have no idea.

By Bus   For buses from Colón or Panama City to La Guaira, you'll need to follow the same procedure you would for Portobelo (see "Getting There & Departing" in "Portobelo," earlier), but catch a bus to La Guaira instead of Portobelo when transferring in Sabanitas. You'll be dropped off at a small port from which you'll have to hop a $2 water taxi to Isla Grande.

By Water Taxi   Boat taxis at the public pier charge $2 one-way to Isla Grande. (They'll sometimes charge a $10 minimum if there aren't enough people.) When the sea is rough, you might get a little wet.

Fun in the Water

SCUBA DIVING & SNORKELING

Panama Divers (p. 110), based out of Portobelo, can put together a day excursion from Isla Grande (reservations required).

BEACHES & BOATING

There is no "day tour" center with a roster of excursions and set prices; instead, you'll need to hire a local boatman and negotiate a price. If you're staying on the island, your hotel can organize a boat tour for you with a local, or in a pinch you can find a boat and driver at the main dock near Cabañas Jackson or at the pier in La Guaira. It's best to plan ahead and reserve a time with a local boat, but on slow days you shouldn't have a problem finding a willing captain. You can also try checking the pier at the Hotel Isla Grande or check with the staff there to see if they have boat trips planned.

The best beaches are on the north side of the island or a short boat ride away on uninhabited islands. Day-boat tours usually include a zip through a mangrove swamp and a visit to one of the offshore islands such as **Mamey Island.** The fine white-sand beach here offers good snorkeling opportunities, but you'll need to bring your own gear. This trip can range between $40 and $55, depending on the amount of time you'd like to stay on the beach (in the event that they drop you off and pick you up later).

Where to Stay & Dine

Hotels and cabins on Isla Grande fill during weekends and the high season, from late November to early April. Outside of these dates, it's difficult to find a restaurant that is open. For lodging, there are a few small hotels and hostals, which never seem to stay open very long. One of the more reliable options is **Cabanas La Cholita** (www.hotellacholita.com; ☎ **448-2962;** doubles $77–$98), which offers and offers comfortable, air-conditioned cabins and enjoys an attractive beachfront location.

ISLA TABOGA ★★

19km (12 miles) from Panama City, in the Bay of Panama

Isla Taboga, known as the "Island of Flowers" for its lush bougainvillea, hibiscus, and jasmine, isn't a destination with adventurous offerings; instead, it's a place to escape the streets of Panama City, enjoy the fresh sea breeze, get a little beach time in, and enjoy a lazy lunch. The island is only 19km (12 miles) off the coast, and the ferry ride here provides passengers with a dazzling view of Panama City and ships waiting to transit the canal. The drowsy, charming village here is a nice place to stroll; you'll find a couple of restaurants and hotels, but really this is a very low-key excursion and best as a day trip. If your Panama travel plans include a beach destination such as Bocas or the San Blas Peninsula, skip Isla Taboga. But if you've got a lot of time in Panama City and are looking for a quick excursion, this is a do-it-yourself trip that doesn't require a tour operator or a lot of advanced planning—just show up at the ferry dock and head over.

Isla Taboga is one of the most important historical sites in Panama. The village was founded in 1524, and later conquistador Francisco Pizarro pushed off from here on his way to conquer Peru. During the 17th century, the island became the haunt of pirates in search of treasure, and in the 19th century it was a port for the Pacific Steamship Navigation Company, which brought over hundreds of Irish, whose Anglo-Saxon names can be seen on gravestones here. The United States even used Isla Taboga as a training ground for military practice during World War II. Today the village is home to about 1,000 residents.

Essentials

GETTING THERE & AROUND   Ferry service to Isla Taboga is provided by the ferryboats *Calypso Queen, Calypso King,* and *Calypso Princess* (© **314-1730**), which leave from the Isla Naos pier on the Amador Causeway, next to the Smithsonian's Centro de Exhibiciones. From Panama City to Isla Taboga, the ferry runs Monday, Wednesday, and Friday at 8:30am and 3pm; Tuesday and Thursday at 8:30am only; and Saturday, Sunday, and holidays at 8am, 10:30am, and 4pm. Service from Isla Taboga to Panama City runs Monday, Wednesday, and Friday at 9:30am and 4:30pm; Tuesday and Thursday at 4:30pm; and Saturday, Sunday, and holidays at 9am, 3pm, and 5pm. The cost is $14 adults, $12 seniors, and $12 children 12 and under. Arrive at the pier 1 hour before departure. A cafe is located at the dock.

You get around Isla Taboga primarily on walking paths. It also has a few roads for the three service vehicles on the island (which occasionally double as taxis). Nearly everyone here walks to get anywhere, but a few residents get around by golf cart.

Note: There are no ATMs on Isla Taboga, and few establishments accept credit cards. Be sure to bring enough cash to get you through your stay.

What to See & Do

There's not much to do here other than amble around the little village and snap photos. When you arrive, head left from the pier into the village—the streets are hilly so you'll do a lot of walking up and down. At the town center is **Iglesia San Pedro,** the second-oldest Spanish colonial church in the Western Hemisphere; it's rarely open, however, so you'll probably have to make do admiring the facade. In the plaza, locals meet to chat and play games. If you're okay with walking, continue southeast toward Cerro de las Cruces and continue up a moderate path to a lookout point that offers a sweeping view of the sea and other islands in the area. The west side of the island is the **Taboga Wildlife Refuge,** which protects nesting brown pelicans, but it's mostly off-limits.

Beaches here aren't secluded and can get a little busy on weekends, but they offer soft sand and blue water. The best beach here is **Playa Restinga,** especially past the pier after the end of town when it becomes just a strip of sand with water on both sides. Like all beaches on the island, admission is free; the hotels mentioned below will either rent snorkel gear or put you in touch with someone who does. Playa Honda is the beach that fronts the village.

Where to Stay & Dine

Despite its proximity to Panama City and its popularity as a weekend-getaway destination, Isla Taboga has few good dining and lodging options, another reason many opt for a day trip. It's almost eerily underdeveloped despite the short ferry ride. By far, the best place to stay and dine in town is at **Vereda Tropical Hotel** (www.hotelveredatropical.com; ✆ **250-2154;** doubles $65–$90), overlooking Playa Honda near the pier. The view from the hotel restaurant is stellar, and it serves tasty, international cuisine and refreshing fruit drinks. As an alternative, **Cerrito Tropical** (www.cerritotropicalpanama.com; ✆ **6489-0074;** rooms $65–$270) is a five-room B&B with apartment-style units that include kitchenettes.

ARCHIPIÉLAGO DE LAS PERLAS

64km (40 miles) S of Panama City, in the Pacific Ocean

Historically famous for its pearls and more recently as the island Shangri-La for television's *Survivor* series in 2003 and 2006, the Archipiélago de las Perlas (Pearl Islands) is nevertheless an unsung beach destination that has taken a back seat to places such as Bocas del Toro. Perhaps residents have done a bad job promoting the Pearl Islands as a getaway destination—or perhaps keeping the masses at bay has always been the goal. Whatever the reason, the archipelago is going to get a lot more attention with two high-speed ferries and an 80-room resort and spa that will open on a 3,500-acre private island by posh hotelier Ritz Carlton, part of their ultra-luxury Reserve brand, sometime in 2016.

The archipelago is surprisingly close to Panama City, just 20 minutes by small plane. The rich aquatic life here offers great snorkeling on sunny days—sometimes manta rays and schools of tropical fish can be seen by just popping on a mask and walking out from the beach. The cerulean sea laps at picture-postcard white- and golden-sand beaches backed by a forest canopy. And the big-game sport fishing around the islands is revered by fishers around the world—you're pretty much guaranteed to catch something. Need I say more?

Las Perlas is composed of more than 200 islands and islets, the majority of which are unnamed and uninhabited. The most developed of the islands is **Isla Contadora,** with a full range of amenities, including hotels and B&Bs, restaurants, tour companies, and daily flights. **Isla San José** is privately owned and home to one luxury resort, the Hacienda del Mar, but that's it. There has been chatter of development on **Isla del Rey,** the largest island in the archipelago, though thus far little has happened. Beyond these islands there is nowhere else to stay in the archipelago, though small islands and islets can be visited as part of a day trip.

Tip: Here in the Pearl Islands, the weather is drier than in the rest of Panama, meaning that low season (May–Dec) can be quite enjoyable and cooler, with showers lasting an hour or so rather than the all-day downpours other parts of the country experience. Lodging rates drop during this time, and there will be so few people on Isla Contadora it almost feels deserted.

Isla Contadora ★

Isla Contadora is one of Panama's most underrated vacation destinations; it's a relatively tiny island with a dozen white-sand beaches including Panama's only nude beach, Playa Suecas. The island harbors a reputation as the exclusive playground for the Panamanian elite and international figures such as Christian Dior, Julio Iglesias, and the deposed Shah of Iran, all of whom constructed palatial mansions here during the past 50 years. Isla Contadora once offered only a couple of funky hotels, but now several attractive and affordable B&Bs have opened their doors, providing comfortable lodging and services to more-demanding travelers. Still, those seeking world-class luxury will want to head straight to **Hacienda del Mar** (see "Isla San José," below).

Isla Contadora is so-named because of its historical role as the "counting house," a colonial-era distribution center that recorded and classified pearls before they were shipped to Spain. African slaves were brought to Isla Contadora to harvest pearls, and their descendants still work here, although most cannot afford to live on Isla Contadora and instead live a 10-minute ferry ride away on neighboring Isla Saboga.

The island's center of activity is at the end of the airport runway on the northeastern side of the island; here you'll find public telephones, a few restaurants and bars, grocery stores, and a basic medical clinic (© **250-4209**). (Walk around to the back of the clinic if no one answers the door.) You'll find an Internet cafe next to the dive center across from the airstrip; there's also Internet service inside Restaurant Sagitario. The island has neither a post office nor ATMs (although credit cards are accepted at hotels), so be sure to bring enough cash to cover expenses. And no need to pack your snazziest outfits—the look here is beach casual.

ESSENTIALS
Getting There & Departing
BY PLANE   Air Panama (www.flyairpanama.com; © **316-9000**) offers flights to Isla Contadora daily, departing at approximately 10am, with an extra

5pm flight on Fridays. Their return flights are daily at 10:30am with an extra return flight at 5pm on Friday. Prices are about $80–$100 round-trip, including taxes. When boarding your flight back to Panama City, you'll need to stop by the Air Panama office by the airstrip to confirm your flight and check in. Flight availability and times can change depending on demand; also bear in mind flights rarely leave or arrive on time.

BY BOAT Two high-speed ferry services operate trips between Panama City to Contadora. **Sea Las Perlas** (www.ferrypearlislands.com; ℗ **392-1424**) departs from the Balboa Yacht Club on the Amador Causeway every day at 7:30am, returning at 3:30pm. Prices are $45 each way for adults, $35 for children. Travel time is 1 hour, 40 minutes. It also offers less-frequent service to Viveros and San Miguel. **Ferry Las Perlas** (www.ferrylasperlas.com) departs from the Trump Ocean Club for $57 each way or $95 round-trip, though schedules are less frequent.

Some of the boating and yacht companies mentioned in chapter 11, "Planning Your Trip to Panama," can also offer shared catamaran or sailing excursions to and from the Islas de Perlas. Although some of these are all-inclusive, you can request only pickup and drop-off as well.

Getting Around

Isla Contadora is a compact island, and although most roads are paved, there are few vehicles—and no taxis—on the island. People get around by **walking,** by **bicycle,** or, more popularly, by **golf cart** or **ATV.** Most visitors get a kick out of coasting the island on a cart, searching out the perfect beach or ogling the stately vacation homes that line the streets. Ask your hotel about a multiple-day discount for a golf cart or if they provide drop-off and pickup service around town. If your hotel doesn't have a vehicle for rent, the **Perla Real Inn** (www.perlareal.com; ℗ **250-4095**) has a fleet of **golf carts and ATVs** they rent out for $50 for 24 hours or $20 per hour. **Casa del Sol** (http://panama-isla-contadora.com; ℗ **250-4212**) rents out four-wheel-drive **Kawasaki Mule carts** (which can go down dirt roads that golf carts can't) for $70 to $90 per day, as well as **scooters** for $40 a day. Cheaper still are bike rentals; you can rent a **mountain bike** from Casa del Sol for $15 a day.

WHAT TO SEE & DO

BEACHES The principal activity on Isla Contadora is spending sun-drenched days lounging on the beach, reading a book, and cooling off with a dip in the turquoise sea. No strong riptides and powerful waves take place here so swimming is safe, even for kids. Surfers, however, should look elsewhere. The island has 13 beaches, all perfectly lovely and virtually empty every day except for weekends and holidays.

Panama's sole nude beach, **Playa Suecas (Swedish Beach),** is located on Isla Contadora and can be reached by taking the dirt road at the end of **Playa Larga (Long Beach),** the strip of beach that fronts the abandoned Hotel Contadora Resort. This beach, like its neighbor, **Playa Galeón,** is convenient for its proximity to restaurants and shops. Both beaches are also recommended for snorkeling, and outfitters rent snorkel equipment, jet skis, and other marine toys. There are also a couple of beachfront bars. **Playa Ejecutiva** is a pretty beach on a tiny cove on the north side of the island, and **Playa Cacique** (often referred to as "Playa Hawaii") is another good option for solitude and beautiful tropical surroundings. During the high season, you'll find the fewest people on Playa Suecas.

Beyond the beaches at Isla Contadora, the region is replete with uninhabited islands that offer isolated and heavenly beaches—those seeking to really get away from other people will find this a tantalizing option. There's a substantial economic gap between native islanders and wealthier expats on Contadora, so socially conscious tourists looking for less formal snorkeling or fishing options can support the local economy by hiring one of the local boatmen who hang around Playa Larga, Playa Cacique, or Playa Galeón. Most charge between $30 and $35 an hour and offer island, fishing, and snorkeling tours.

You can visit other islands either by hiring a local boatman or taking part in a half-day or full-day excursion. **Isla Chapera** has a couple of empty beaches surrounded by a rich variety and abundance of marine life and some of the best snorkeling in the area. It's located straight across from Playa Cacique, about a 10-minute boat ride away. A local boatman can take you here in a wooden *cayuco* for about $30 to $35 per hour (if he waits for you), or about $60 if you want drop-off and pickup; the cost depends on the fluctuating price of gas. Bring a picnic lunch and beverages; there are no stores or restaurants here. Local boatmen can be found at the beach at Punta Galeón. For organized excursions and charter-boat rentals, see "Snorkeling," below.

DIVING   **Coral Dreams** (www.coral-dreams.com; © **6536-1776**), at the airport runway, is Isla Contadora's only full-fledged scuba operation, run by a friendly young Argentine couple. Dives take place around the island and never exceed 18m (60 ft.), with visibilities of 4.5 to 9.1m (15–30 ft.) of mostly sponges, some brain and fan coral, and an abundance of marine life. Two-tank dives cost $95 for certified divers. Coral Dreams also offers course instruction, including their intensive "Discover Scuba Diving" course ($120), which lasts 1½ days and is for beginners who are short on time or who just want a taste of the diving experience. They also offer PADI open-water courses ($300) and 3-hour snorkeling excursions ($70 adults, $32 children 6–10). Between July and October they offer whale-watching excursions around the area ($75 adults, $37 children 6–10).

FISHING   The Pearl Islands are legendary for deep-sea fishing. If you want to get out and cast a line for an hour or so, negotiate with local boatmen at Punta Galeón beach; they often have a few beat-up poles lying around and charge lower rates. *Tip:* If you've caught fish but don't have a kitchen, most restaurants will prepare your fish for you and your friends at a negotiated price.

SNORKELING   Isla Contadora offers excellent snorkeling opportunities, with five coral fields encircling the island that attract a wealth of marine life, including schools of tropical fish, white-tipped reef sharks, manta rays, and turtles. From Playa Larga, you can reach one of the best snorkeling spots on the island at **Punta Verde,** located at the southeastern end of the beach. Other prime spots include **Playa Ejecutiva** and **Punta Galeón.**

Coral Dreams (see "Diving," above) rents snorkel gear for $20 a day.

WHERE TO STAY & DINE

A slow-moving (some would say stagnant) tourism economy means many hotel owners are willing to drop their prices on weekdays and during the low season. The price for a weeklong stay or longer can also be negotiated. Restaurants on the island tend to be overpriced. If you want something cheap, try the **minimarket Duty Free**—their simple *comida corriente* costs about $3 to $5.

Contadora Island Inn ★ This cheerful B&B is set in a converted, low-slung house in a quiet residential area. Each room is colorful with modern furniture and its own private sundeck. Among the common areas, a full kitchen and two decks made of native hardwoods surrounded by flowers and palm trees encourage you to venture out of your room. With advanced notice the entire house can be rented out.

Located on the western side of the island. www.contadoraislandinn.com. ℭ **250-4164.** 5 units. $110–$140 double. Rates include breakfast. **Amenities:** Full kitchen (in common area); free Wi-Fi.

Gerald's ★ This laid-back B&B with a rooftop splash pool is conveniently located within a short walk of downtown and two of Contadora's best beaches. The rooms are simple yet airy with high wood-beamed ceilings. The onsite **restaurant** (main courses $15–$25; Mon–Fri 11am–3pm and 6pm–midnight; Sat–Sun 11am–midnight) is the best on the island. The Euro-inflected Panamanian dishes, particularly the catch of the day with a choice of sauce, are above average, but (like everywhere else) overpriced. During busy weekends, it's best to make dinner reservations.

Near the airport. www.island-contadora.com. ℭ **250-4159.** 8 units. $90–$130 double. Rates include breakfast. **Amenities:** Restaurant; pool; golf cart/ATV rentals; free Wi-Fi.

Perla Real Inn ★ This sleek boutique hotel with white stucco walls is the closest thing to a trendy Panama City vibe and crowd that you will find on the island. The property surrounds a small courtyard and lounge area, home to happy hours and welcome drinks plus a popular hot tub. Rooms are comfy, with French doors and private entrances. Suites add kitchens.

Perla also has a beachfront property, **Hotel Playa Cacique,** with similar amenities plus a restaurant and beach bar.

Located on the western side of the island. www.perlareal.com. ℭ **250-4095** or 6513-9064. For reservations, call U.S.-based number at 949/228-8851. 6 units. $127–$160 double; $165–$200 suite. Rates include breakfast. **Amenities:** Bar; Jacuzzi; free Wi-Fi.

Isla San José ★

This private island is quite large at 44 sq. km (17 sq. miles). It is almost totally covered with forest, save for a luxury lodge, an airstrip, and more than 97km

(60 miles) of roads built by the U.S. military when it held training operations and weapons testing from World War II and onward here. Today the owner of the island is the Panamanian George Novey, who is also the owner of Air Panama. The Hacienda del Mar (see below) arranges flights on Air Panama for visitors.

WHERE TO STAY & DINE

Hacienda del Mar ★★   The most upscale property on the islands (at press time), Hacienda del Mar was built predominantly out of the handsome bamboo-like *caña Blanca,* each bungalow boasting ocean views and a balcony/deck with lounge chairs to kick back and admire the island's surroundings. It's an eco-oriented lodge, with no TV or Internet in the rooms. Sport fishermen appreciate the house fleet of boats, there to take you offshore or deep-sea fishing (back at the hotel they'll even cook up the wahoo, amberjack, sailfish, and tuna you catch). For an extra cost, you can choose from a number of guided excursions, including night safaris, ATV tours across the island, kayaking, scuba diving and snorkeling, jet-ski tours, and mountain biking.

Isla San José. www.haciendadelmar.net. (ℰ) **832-5439** or 866/433-5627 in the U.S. 17 units. $187–$350 low season; $375–$700 high season, depending on type of suite. Rates include breakfast. **Amenities:** Restaurant; 2 bars; outdoor pool; fitness center; sauna; sports equipment rental.

CENTRAL PANAMA

I n this guide, Central Panama is defined as the Panamá and Coclé provinces west of Panama City, along with the Herrera and Los Santos provinces that make up the Azuero Peninsula. The Central region includes **El Valle de Antón,** a lovely mountain village located in the center of a volcanic crater; the **Pacific beaches,** with an array of lodging accommodations, from rustic cabins to all-inclusive destination resorts; and the charm of Panama's cultural "heartland," the **Azuero Peninsula,** dotted with colonial villages and home to the liveliest festivals in Panama. What these destinations all have in common is that they are reached by vehicle (or bus) from Panama City, not by plane—unless, of course, you fly to Pedasí at the tip of the peninsula or charter a flight to the rarely used Río Hato Airport. This region begs to be explored by car, however, so consider renting a vehicle, which will give you the freedom to plan your own itinerary and wander at your own pace, stopping off at villages and attractions that interest you and buying gastronomic treats from vendors that line the highway.

The **Interamericana Highway** and the **Carretera Nacional** are modern roads that are easy to drive and do not require any kind of special considerations or a four-wheel-drive. Distance is measured by markers that show the kilometers from Panama City—this is how locals give directions, such as "Turn at kilometer 54." The markers are white and look like oversize dominoes.

PACIFIC BEACHES

Every weekend, hordes of residents from Panama City and the interior head out to the Pacific Coast to frolic on the beaches of the Panamá and Coclé provinces. Until a decade ago, this long stretch of beach was the home of fishermen and humble people who moved here after their villages were flooded with the building of the Panama Canal. But the proximity to Panama City (just 30 min.–2 hr. from downtown) has proved tempting to well-heeled Panamanians and foreign retirees, and now the coast is the haunt of

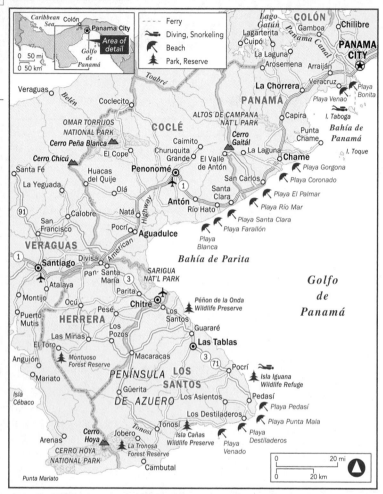

extravagant homes, manicured residential communities, and a few splashy megaresorts. There are several exclusive seaside golf courses—Playa Coronado, Tucan Country Club, and the Buenaventura course—and a couple of surf schools with packages or day lessons. Most coastal destinations in this section see few people outside of weekends, and at some beaches during low season, weekends can be relatively free of crowds.

Note that despite their popularity with weekend city dwellers, the Central Pacific beaches are certainly not Panama's most attractive and are really only worth visiting if you don't have time to reach some of Panama's better beaches or if you're taking part in an all-inclusive vacation at one of the resorts along the coast. The farther you drive from Panama City, the whiter the

El Valle de Antón is characterized by year-round spring weather conditions, and a cooler cloud forest in higher areas; the Pacific beaches are driest from January to March; and, because of deforestation, the Azuero Peninsula is very dry in comparison with the rest of Panama.

sand turns and the bluer the sea. (The iron-rich sands of some of the beaches are blackish.)

The modern, four-lane Interamericana (also called Panamericana) Highway connects Panama City with the coast's beaches, which are listed in this section in descending southwest order: **Playa Bonita, Coronado, Santa Clara,** and **Farallón (Playa Blanca).**

Important note: The Pacific beaches have strong riptides and choppy swimming conditions, so they aren't always the best choice for families.

Essentials

GETTING THERE & DEPARTING

There are two primary exit routes from the city: the Puente de las Américas (Bridge of the Americas), which spans the mouth of the canal; and the newer cable-stayed span bridge Puente Centenario, which crosses the canal at the Gaillard (Culebra) Cut, the section of the canal whose excavation cost the most lives during its construction. Both routes are nearly the same in terms of distance. Do not leave Panama City from 3:30 to 6:30pm, or return between 7 and 9am, when heavy traffic jams can add an extra 30 minutes to an hour to your travel time.

BY CAR I suggest renting a car to get around the Pacific Coast, especially if you don't want to be stuck at your resort or hotel because tours and excursions can be pricey. For the Bridge of the Americas, take Avenida de los Mártires along Cerro Ancón, which connects with the Panamericana and the bridge. For the Puente Centenario, head out past the Miraflores Locks until you see the bridge entrance. The four-lane Interamericana Highway is in good shape, and turnoffs are marked by either a municipal sign or a promotional billboard.

BY BUS OR TAXI Buses leave from the Albrook Terminal. They will drop you off at the turnoff for each beach, where cheap taxis (about $4–$6) wait for the quick ride to the beach. Taxis from the city charge an average of $50 to $70 for transportation to all beaches listed in this section, less if heading to nearby Playa Bonita. Some resorts here provide transportation for guests from the airports or from any hotel in Panama City.

Playa Bonita

The formal name for this area is Playa Kobbe, but with the opening of resorts here it became more commonly referred to as Playa Bonita. This is the closest beach to Panama City. Take the first exit after the Bridge of the Americas and

ROADSIDE gastronomy

Cheap road stops and hole-in-the-wall restaurants that usually go unnoticed by tourists dot the Pacific coast, such as the following culinary gems.

○ **Bollos Chorreranos** (no phone; Fri–Sat 8am–8pm, Sun–Thurs 8am–6pm): This open-air dive is recognizable by the dozens of parked cars of Panamanians out front. It's on the highway outside Chorrera, 35km (22 miles) west of Panama City. Every Panama City resident, it seems, stops here for local specialties that include *tasajo,* out-of-this-world gooey smoked beef; *bollos,* tamale-like corn patties filled with chicken or coconut; *chichas,* fresh juices such as passionfruit and the exotic gua-nabana; and the regionally famous *chicheme,* a thick, sweet beverage made with corn and cinnamon.

○ **Quesos Chela** (no phone; daily 7am–8pm): Farther down the road, at kilometer 57, Quesos Chela offers heavenly light, fresh cheeses, fresh yogurt (even *chicheme* yogurt), soft egg bread, warm beef and chicken empanadas, and *chichas* to wash it all down. Don't miss the fresh roasted cashews sold at the front door—this is what cashews were meant to taste like.

○ **Fresh Fruit & Sweet Treats:** The town of **Chorrera** is known for its juicy pineapple. When pineapple is in season, road vendors often sell three for $1; a little farther past Chorrera, vendors sell fresh mango and papaya. At **Antón,** vendors sell sweet treats such as candies and coconut cakes.

follow the road 6.5km (4 miles) to get there. A taxi from downtown will cost you about $50 one-way or $75 from the international airport.

A LUXURY RESORT

Westin Playa Bonita Resort & Spa ★★ This colossal megaresort, one of the largest hotels in the country, is the most accessible beach vacation near Panama City. The only comparable Pacific beach hotels would be the Playa Blanca and Decameron resorts in Farallón, though those are much farther out. The property is rich with amenities: three infinity edge pools lining the long oceanfront, a spa, a kids' club, 20 meeting and event spaces, and bars and restaurants that range from a casual poolside grill to a glitzy Latin steakhouse. The interior decor is modern and contemporary throughout, with lots of glass and warm woods. Rooms look out over the rainforest or ocean, some with balconies or views of the Bridge of the Americas. Suites add living/dining areas, plus kitchenettes in some. On the 18th floor, Club Rooms feature private balconies and have access to the Westin Executive Club Lounge, where food and drinks are available all day. *Note:* A Dreams resort is in the works next door on the grounds of the former InterContinental resort.

Km 6 Camino a Veracruz. www.starwoodhotels.com. © **304-6600.** 611 units. $221 double; $285 club room; $389 suite. **Amenities:** 6 restaurants; 3 bars; outdoor pools; fitness center w/whirlpool, spa, steam, and sauna; sports equipment rental; kids' activities; room service; babysitting; Wi-Fi ($16/day but free for SPG members booking on Starwood sites).

Playa Coronado

Playa Coronado is the oldest community on the coast and the most developed, with a sprawling residential area and full range of services such as a 24-hour El Rey supermarket, shops, and restaurants. It's located 83km (52 miles) from Panama City, and 3km (1¾ miles) from the highway. The many residential homes here have been around long enough to give off that lived-in feel, unlike other beach areas that are mostly modern condo developments. Both Panamanians and expats like Coronado for its services and for its lengthy beach, though this is certainly not the best beach on the coast—the sand here contains a lot of iron and is dark. A controlled security gate helps keep the crowds at bay—even if you're not registered at a hotel, tell the gate attendant that you are headed to the Coronado Beach Resort so that he'll let you pass.

WHERE TO STAY

BlueBay Coronado Golf & Beach Resort ★ This property has attempted to transition from being simply a golf resort to more of an all-around family resort since BlueBay took over management. Although the resort has less of the stuffy, country-club feel it once had, golf is still the primary reason guests stay here. The beach is far from the rooms and reached by a shuttle, though a large pool area and plenty going on in the core area keep the family occupied, from five restaurants to a gym and spa that can be used at no additional charge. Rooms are airy but lack beach views, and suites can sleep four to six guests. The staff tries their best, and there are nice little touches like cold towels in the lobby, but the resort has a sad, empty feeling during the low season.

Av. Punta Prieta, Coronado. www.bluebayresorts.com. ℂ **264-3164** or 866/465-3207 from the U.S. 104 units. $156 double; $177–$205 suites. **Amenities:** 5 restaurants; 2 bars; Olympic-size pool and kids' pool; tennis courts; fitness center w/sauna, spa whirlpools, and Jacuzzis; bike rental; kids' playground and kids' miniclub w/activities; Wi-Fi.

Dlaaya ★ In the hills, a 10-minute drive above Playa Coronado, this fun, funky little inn makes for a nice escape for a day or two. Chill out in the infinity pool while staring out over the ocean and jungle below as you sip on a mango mojito. The open-concept suites have interiors marked by polished concrete, reclaimed wood accents, and colorful, handcrafted knits and pillowcases. Each unit has a soaking tub and open-air shower, plus a terrace with a daybed. Rates include a three-course made-from-scratch breakfast.

Loma del Guayabo, Las Lajas. www.dlaaya.com. ℂ **6092-0721.** 3 units. $150–$190 double. **Amenities:** Bar; pool; Wi-Fi.

WHERE TO DINE

Caracoles Café ★ INTERNATIONAL In a small strip mall off the Pan-Americana, this cozy eatery is a far better option than most of the overpriced, mediocre beach and hotel restaurants in Playa Coronado. The menu is made up of an assorted mix of international comfort foods such as sliders, Cajun shrimp, banh mi sandwiches, and Guinness Irish stew. There's also a long list of cakes and pies. The menu is probably a little too extensive and some dishes work better than others, though for straightforward food and good service, look no further.

#44 The Village Mall, Layas. www.caracolescafe.com. ✆ **389-5707.** Main courses $9–$15. Mon–Sat 11am–9pm.

AN ELEGANT RESTAURANT IN VISTA MAR
Restaurant Terrazas del Mar ★★ MEDITERRANEAN   Inside the Vista Mar Resort, an oceanfront golf and residential community, this upscale restaurant, which is open to the public, is the most elegant dining experience in the area. Whitewashed walls and Moroccan decor serve as the setting for French chef Pascual Finet's Mediterranean-influenced dishes such as Galician octopus and calamari stuffed with crabmeat. The terraced patio overlooking the Pacific is a more pleasant place to eat when the weather isn't quite so hot. Vista Mar is located at Km 90, 2km (1¼ miles) from the highway turnoff.

Road to Vista Mar. ✆ **345-4077.** Main courses $8–$18. Thurs–Tues 11am–10pm (to 11pm Fri–Sat).

Santa Clara

Santa Clara and its neighbor down the road, Farallón, are home to the nicest beaches in this Pacific coastal area, though even here you won't find any particularly breathtaking beaches; however, the sand is clean and white and the swimming conditions are relatively good. Santa Clara doesn't have much of a town to speak of, consisting mostly of tourist lodgings and residential and weekend homes for urbanites. It's a little farther from Panama City than other beaches mentioned earlier in this chapter, but it's worth the extra effort to get here, especially if you plan on spending the night. The turnoff for Santa Clara is 113km (70 miles) from Panama City; keep your eyes open—it's easy to miss. After turning, the road forks; head left for Las Sirenas, right for Las Veraneras and the public beach.

WHERE TO STAY
Sheraton Bijao Beach Resort ★   Continuing the growing list of major international chains setting up all-inclusives on Panama's Pacific Coast, Sheraton opened this monster resort in 2011. The amenities are the highlight here: three swimming pools, two Jacuzzis, children's pools, tennis courts, and a spa with four treatment rooms and saunas. The restaurants open on a rotating basis and range from Japanese to a standard international grill. The rooms are airy and bright, though not nearly as modern as those at Starwood's other property, the Westin at Playa Bonita, closer to the city. All rooms do come with a balcony or terrace, however.

Santa Clara. www.starwoodhotels.com. ✆ **908-3600.** 293 units. $285 double, all-inclusive. **Amenities:** 5 restaurants; 3 bars; 3 outdoor pools; tennis court; gym; spa; kids' club; free Wi-Fi.

Villa Botero By Casa Mojito ★   In a quiet neighborhood near the Río Hato Airport, this adults-only (unless the entire house is rented) B&B is for those looking for comfort without breaking the bank. The small inn with clay-tile roofs backs on to a charming pool and BBQ that is enticing enough to keep you from making the easy 10-minute walk to the beach at Santa Clara. Each of the three basic, tile-floor rooms faces the pool and comes with better amenities than that at much pricier beach hotels. The owners will cook for guests upon request, and a scrumptious French-style breakfast with home-made croissants is included in the rates.

Santa Clara. www.casamojitopanama.com. ✆ **6012-7074.** 3 units. $130 double. Rates include breakfast. **Amenities:** Pool; BBQ area; free Wi-Fi.

WHERE TO DINE

Restaurante Los Camisones ★★ PANAMANIAN Look for the thatched roof, right off the Interamericana Highway, at kilometer 104, just before hitting Santa Clara from Panama City, to find the laidback, open-air Los Camisones. The Spanish-owned restaurant specializes in seafood, nothing fancy, but nicely prepared and for a good price. The menu includes lots of fried goodies, like breaded oysters or calamari or even alligator, plus Galician octopus sautéed with olive oil and hearty cazuelas. There are steaks and the occasional roasted pig, though the seafood dishes are far superior. This is a popular stop for drivers on the road from Panama City and points west.

Km 104. ✆ **993-3622.** Main courses $8–$22. Mon–Thurs 9:30am–9pm; Fri–Sun 9:30am–11pm.

Farallón

Farallón is more often referred to as Playa Blanca, for the lovely white-sand beach that stretches along the coastal area here. It's mostly known for its gigantic resorts and residential complexes, such as the Decameron and the Buenaventura (see below). It is a hot property for retirement and weekend homes, so it's anyone's guess how this area will look in a decade.

WHERE TO STAY

JW Marriott Panama Golf & Beach Resort ★★ This high-end resort is part of the enormous Buenaventura complex, which includes several residential communities, commercial areas with restaurants and shops, and a Jack Nicklaus–designed golf course that is widely considered the country's best. The JW Marriott is laid out like a Spanish hacienda with courtyards and miniplazas, a vibe that continues into the rooms, with their earthy tones and colonial-style mahogany beds. Each room has a sitting area and a balcony or terrace that overlooks the pool or a courtyard. Although it's not on the beach, it's a short walk or golf cart ride away and has a beautiful, full-service beach club that all guests have access to. The dining options were better before Marriott took over, when the hotel was the Bristol, though thankfully the Buenaventura complex now has plenty of better restaurants to choose from.

Playa Buenaventura. www.marriott.com. ✆ **908-3333.** 114 units. $299–$365 double; $469–$599 suite; $1,659 villa. **Amenities:** 4 restaurants; bar; 3 pools; golf course; fitness room; spa; kids' activities; room service; Wi-Fi ($14/day).

Royal Decameron Beach Resort, Golf, Spa & Casino ★ The Decameron is the all-inclusive resort that travel agents think of when they hear

Going Local: Pipa's Beach Bar

If you're not staying at the aforementioned resorts, or if you are but would like to get out and find a more "local" experience than lining up at a buffet, walk down to Pipa's ★ (✆ **6575-7386**)—it's located between both resorts. (You can also reach the restaurant by driving to the Decameron, turning right, and continuing on for about 2km/1¼ miles.) Pipa's is owned by a laid-back California couple who serve some great seafood, like fresh jumbo shrimp and lobster, in a true-to-fashion beach-bar atmosphere. It's a good place to just hang for the day, and beach chairs are available. At night they'll sometimes fire up a beach bonfire. Pipa's is normally pretty mellow, but get enough patrons filled with booze and the mood can turn festive. It's open daily from 11am to 8 or 9pm.

"all-inclusive" in Panama. This behemoth of a resort is so big (852 rooms) that you need a map to get around—and even if you stay here a week you probably won't have seen it all. More size-appropriate options, such as the Playa Blanca Resort and RIU nearby, are similar and should merit consideration if an all-inclusive is what you are after. This white-hued resort with cerulean-blue awnings has a little bit of everything: seven swimming pools, an 18-hole golf course, casino, spa, and marina. The restaurants are topnotch and the rooms bright and comfortable. The size is a negative at times though, particularly if you are not staying oceanside, since you'll need to walk up and down stairs in the intense heat to reach the beach. Rates include all meals, drinks (alcohol included), nonmotorized watersports equipment, entertainment, kids' activities, and tips. A premium package adds another $20 per person, per night.

Playa Blanca. www.decameron.com. ✆ **993-2255**. 852 units. $292 double. Rates include all meals, drinks (alcohol included), nonmotorized watersports equipment, entertainment, kids' activities, and tips. **Amenities:** 2 buffet restaurants; 6 specialty restaurants; 2 snack bars; 7 bars (1 swim-up); casino; disco; 7 outdoor pools; tennis courts; 18-hole golf course; volleyball; fitness center and spa; watersports equipment; kids' activities; room service; babysitting; free Wi-Fi.

WHERE TO DINE

Mansa ★★★ PANAMANIAN/MEDITERRANEAN   From Panama City star chef Mario Castrellón, this restaurant brings a bit of refined style and service from the capital to the beach. The dining room has hand-painted tile floors and a wood-burning oven in one corner that turns out flawless pizzas with gourmet toppings like lamb bacon. The menu is playful, riffing on Mediterranean dishes like risotto or grilled octopus, and all turns out beautifully. The Chorillo-style red snapper, fried whole and served with shrimp and clams in a coconut curry sauce, is possibly the best thing I have ever eaten in Panama. Outside of the summer, hours can be sporadic during the week.

Hotel Playa Blanca Beach Resort, Rio Hato Coclé, Centro Comercial, Buenaventura. www.playablancaresort.com. ✆ **908-8150**. Main courses $8–$20. Tues–Sat noon–3pm and 6–10:30pm; Sun 10am–3pm and 6–10:30pm.

EL VALLE DE ANTÓN

124km (77 miles) W of Panama City

Nestled in the crater of the world's second-largest extinct volcano, El Valle de Antón—popularly known as El Valle—is a delightful and relaxing destination popular with urbanites escaping the heat and hectic pace of Panama City. It's about 2 hours from the city and is easily reached by rental vehicle or by bus. El Valle is ringed by steep, verdant peaks, and its streets are abloom with flowers and lined with stately weekend homes that open onto well-manicured gardens and lawns. Best of all, El Valle enjoys springtime conditions year-round due to its altitude at 762m (2,500 ft.), with temperatures that vary between 68° and 80°F (20°–27°C).

On Sundays, the main street comes alive when vendors come to town to sell handicrafts, vegetables, and ornamental flowers at the town's famous market, but otherwise El Valle moves at a languid pace, offering low-key activities like bird-watching and bike riding through town. Visitors seeking a little more action can hike through rainforest, race through the forest on a zipline at Canopy Adventure, or go horseback riding high up to a lookout point.

Essentials

GETTING THERE & DEPARTING

BY CAR   The road to El Valle is well maintained and suitable for any kind of vehicle (unlike many destinations in Panama, you won't need a four-wheel-drive). To get there, take the Interamericana Highway west for 98km (61 miles) until you see the turnoff for El Valle. From the Interamericana, it's 28km (17 miles) to El Valle, along a very curvy road. Drive slowly and keep an eye out for people and animals walking on the road, especially at night. The road is quite scenic, and you'll likely want to stop occasionally to snap a photo or two.

BY BUS   Buses leave from the Albrook Terminal near the national airport every 40 minutes to an hour, depending on demand. The trip takes a little less than 2 hours and costs $5 one-way. Buses are surprisingly convenient because drivers will drop you off at your hotel if you let them know ahead of time; otherwise, buses stop at the market on Avenida Principal. There aren't many taxis in El Valle, though, so getting dropped off at your hotel really is the better option, especially at night. Direct buses run from 6am to 6pm, or you can catch a later bus until 9pm and be dropped off at the highway, where you can flag down any bus headed for El Valle.

BY TAXI   A taxi from Panama City costs around $80 to $100 one-way or about $160 round-trip. A taxi to any one of the beaches from El Valle costs around $35 to $45 one-way.

GETTING AROUND

BY TAXI   There are only a handful of taxis in El Valle. If you're lucky, you might be able to flag one down on the main street, though it's usually quicker to have your hotel give one a ring. The cost to travel around El Valle is around $2 to $3.

FAST FACTS

A 24-hour **ATM** is located inside Banco Nacional on Avenida Principal, as well as inside the red supermarket on the main street. The **medical clinic** is located directly behind the Iglesia San José and is open from 7am to 3pm (℃ **983-6112** for 24-hr. emergencies). A large natural-medicine health complex is in the works as well. The **post office** is located adjacent to the police station on Carlos Arosemna Guardia. There is **laundry service** next to the Supercentro NG on Avenida Principal, open daily from 10am to 6pm.

What to See & Do
OUTDOOR ACTIVITIES

BIKING   There's no better way to get around El Valle than by bicycle. The terrain is perfectly flat and mostly paved, with some bumpy side roads that have potholes and rocks. Around the edge of town, a couple of dirt roads head high into the hills if you're looking for more of a workout. Many hotels rent bicycles to their guests, though several businesses on the Avenida Principal rent bikes for approximately $4 per hour, $8 half a day, or $15 full day.

CANOPY ADVENTURE   Sharing an entrance with Chorro El Macho, a 150-foot waterfall on the west side of town, this exhilarating, adrenaline-fueled activity involves zipping from tree to tree while strapped into a harness connected to a pulley on a steel cable. The setting is just behind Canopy Lodge, which owns the **Canopy Adventure** (www.canopytower.com/canopy-adventure; ℃ **264-5720**), a lush, green rainforest filled with wildlife.

The adventure begins with a 30-minute walk to a high platform that is flush with the canopy (the uppermost branches of the forest). A guide gives instructions and demonstrates how the equipment works and how to put on the brakes using a thick leather glove; from here, you let gravity do the work. The full tour includes four "zips," which are connected by platforms that gradually descend from the canopy, allowing you to appreciate tropical vegetation from different vantage points, not to mention ride past the falls. The full tour takes about 1½ hours, although the actual cumulative time you ride is less than 15 minutes. Part of the experience is spending time on the platform to observe wildlife—the reason the canopy opens daily at 8am when the animal world is most active (it closes at 4pm).

The full tour costs $65 per person, and children must be at least 6 years old to participate. It also offers a day-trip package with transportation from Panama City for $180 per person (a minimum of two people). It is recommended that you make a reservation on weekends or during the high season for groups of four or more.

HIKING & BIRD-WATCHING   More than 350 species of birds have been recorded in El Valle, making the lush valley one of the top five spots in Panama for bird-watching. A prime spot here is at **Cerro Gaital National Monument ★★★**, which covers the northern slope of El Valle. This national monument also offers one of the **best hikes** in the area, a 2½-hour, easy-to-moderate loop trail that reaches a lookout point where, weather permitting, you can see the Pacific and Atlantic oceans, and even as far as the Panama Canal. The trail is pretty straightforward, but it's always better with a guide who can point out wildlife and make sure you don't get lost. Cerro Gaital is administered by the ANAM park service, which charges a $5 entrance fee per person.

The second hiking area is a 3-hour, moderate trail at **La India Dormida ★★**, which means "Sleeping Indian Woman" and refers to the outline of the western peaks that locals claim resembles a reclining woman. (Have someone point it out to you—it's hard to make out at first.) This trail is not clearly marked, so it is advisable that you walk it with a guide. There is a swimming hole along the way, so bring your swimsuit.

HORSEBACK RIDING   Riding horseback is one of the best ways to appreciate El Valle's gorgeous mountain views. Most hotels, including Los Mandarinos, can rent horses, though the best independent option is a woman named **Mitzila** (✆ **6646-5813**); who offers horseback riding for $15 per hour (minimum 1 hr.), plus $105 an hour if you want a guide. She has a corral on Calle El Hato near the old Hotel Campestre.

ZOOS & MUSEUMS

Aprovaca Orquídeas ★   Six percent of the world's orchid species can be found in Panama, and more than 1,000 are believed to grow in the Coclé province. The Asociación de Productores de Orquídeas El Valle y Cabuya (APROVACA) is a nonprofit agency that cultivates and conserves endangered local and regional orchids at this nursery. More than 150 species are on display here.

Off Av. Principal near the entrance to town, next to the ANAM office. www.aprovaca. com. ✆ **983-6472.** $2 admission. Daily 8:30am–4:30pm.

El Nispero Zoo ★   The Nispero Zoo never planned to be a zoo; it just happened. The owner, an agronomist who runs a small for-profit nursery here, had a large collection of animals and birds, and over time so many people donated abandoned or sick animals that it just made sense to open a zoo, though conditions at the 2.8-hectare (7-acre) site could be improved. The main reason to come here is for the **Centro de Conservación de Anfibios de El Valle (EVACC),** an amphibian study center sponsored by the Houston, San Antonio, and San Diego zoos. The center studies the bacteria that are wiping out the golden frog and is working to ensure the amphibians' survival. The center has aquariums, exhibits, and a video and reading center.

Turn up Carlos Arosemna Guardia St. and follow signs to El Nispero. ✆ **983-6142.** Admission $5 adults, $2 children 3–12, free for children 2 and under. Daily 7am–5pm.

SPAS

Crater Valley Boutique Hotel & Spa (www.crater-valley.com; ✆ **983-6942**) has a limited-service spa that offers massages, a tiny sauna, and an outdoor whirlpool, and it also has an attractive outdoor pool ringed with hammocks and lounge chairs. Surely, the best spa in the area is at **Los Mandarinos** (see below), which has a thermal circuit (sauna, Turkish bath, biothermal shower, Jacuzzi) and a range of massages and body treatments, including couples packages and chocotherapy. **Cariguana Spa** (www.cariguanaspa.com; © **908-7045**), a holistic health and wellness facility located off Main Street on Calle Los Millionarios, offers a range of massages, scrubs, wraps, and facials.

Shopping
SUNDAY MARKET ★★

El Valle is regionally famous for its Sunday Market, which takes place along the town's main Avenida Principal. It's not a grand bazaar but a colorful and lively event that draws vendors, many of whom are Ngöbe-Buglé and Emberá Indians from around the area who come to hawk traditional clothing, handicrafts, baskets, ceramics, vegetables, orchids, food items, and more. A scaled-down version of the market is open every day—Saturdays are often quite happening. Hours for the market are 8am to 5pm.

Next to the market is the **Tienda Artesanía Don Pepe** (© **983-6425;** daily 8am–6pm), which has an extensive selection of well-made indigenous art and handicrafts from around Panama, plus other trinkets, souvenirs, and maps.

Where to Stay

There is something for every wallet in El Valle, with good budget accommodations, B&Bs, and a few upscale hotels and lodges. Note that some hotels jack up their prices on weekends, even during low season. On the backpacker end, the best option is **Bodhi Hostal and Lounge** (www.bodhihostels.com; © **908-7120**), which offers dorms right in the center of town for $15 per person.

EXPENSIVE

Canopy Lodge ★★★   Part of the Canopy family, which includes Canopy Tower in Soberanía National Park and Canopy Camp in the Darién, Canopy Lodge caters, mostly, to serious bird-watchers. You take your morning coffee on a veranda surrounded by hummingbirds and tanagers. Staff birding guides

---

End of the Golden Era for the Golden Frog?

Animal extinction is normally a result of habitat loss, but El Valle's amphibians are facing a more insidious enemy: *Batrachochytrium dendrobatidis*. It's a fungus that infects an amphibian and blocks the creature's ability to breathe, and it is spreading so quickly across Panama that conservationists from the U.S. have recently collected and relocated hundreds of amphibians in a Noah's Ark–style evacuation to prevent a mass extinction. Central to this tragedy is the **golden frog** (*Atelopus zeteki),* a beloved cultural symbol in Panama not unlike the bald eagle in the U.S. This little frog can be found on T-shirts, posters, and even lottery tickets, and historically it was considered good luck by pre-Columbian cultures. You can see the frog, among other amphibians, at El Nispero Zoo's amphibian center.

lead guests along cloud forest trails and can identify almost every species by hearing even the slightest call. Many guests keep binoculars handy in their rooms, as the stream outside attracts an array of birds. Yes, the bird is the word here. Still the guest rooms, with their whitewashed walls, Kuna *mola* art, and balconies that open on to a sea of green, are some of the best in town. It's a quiet, peaceful lodge built of river rock, wood, and glass. Most stay here on bird-watching packages that include airport transfers, guided tours, and meals. The lodge has a 2-night minimum stay and a free tour with a 3-night stay.

Road to Chorro El Macho. www.canopylodge.com. © **264-5720** or 263-2784. 12 units. $184–$303 per person per night. Rates include all meals and wine with dinner. **Amenities:** Restaurant; bird-watching and other tours; library; no phone in room; free Wi-Fi.

Los Mandarinos Hotel & Spa ★★★   This once small B&B comprised of several adjoining Tuscan-style villas has blossomed into a full-service, upscale resort. It has nearly tripled in size since opening, adding a variety of rooms, half of which open on to the pool area. The hotel has five classes of rooms, with decor and furnishings a wee bit better at each step, such as marble bathrooms in the deluxe rooms, four-poster beds in the suites, and Jacuzzis in the honeymoon rooms. The surrounding facilities go well beyond a simple B&B too, with a full-service spa and two restaurants: an elegant Spanish eatery called **La Tasca de Triana** and **O'Pedros,** serving typical Irish fare.

Calle El Ciclo. www.losmandarinos.com. © **983-6645.** 56 units. $174–$235 double; $258 honeymoon room; $298 suite. Rates include breakfast. **Amenities:** Restaurant; pub; outdoor pool; fitness center w/whirlpool, steam room, and spa; library; room service; babysitting; free Wi-Fi.

MODERATE

The Golden Frog Inn ★★   The Golden Frog Inn proves that a hotel doesn't need to be posh and glamorous to be fantastic. A combination of factors help this relaxed inn stand out: meticulously maintained gardens, beautiful views, and friendly, helpful service from the onsite owners and staff. Each room has some extra pluses. For instance, #1 and #2 share a patio facing the pool, while #3, which can easily sleep a family of four, has a full kitchen and a private veranda with views of La India Dormida. The inn has a great happy hour, usually enjoyed by everyone staying at the resort as the sun goes down. The staff can also help arrange tours and excursions in the Valle de Anton region.

Calle Los Veraneras, El Hato neighborhood. Follow signs from Texaco Station at beginning of El Valle. www.goldenfroginn.com. © **6565-8307.** 6 units. $77–$150 double. Rates include breakfast. No credit cards. **Amenities:** Outdoor pool; kitchen; free Wi-Fi.

Park Eden Bed & Breakfast ★★   You have the impression of stepping into a fairy tale when seeing Park Eden for the first time. Practically hidden amid the tall trees of the forest, the two-story house on almost 1 hectare (2½ acres) of land features colorful wood paneling with white trim. There are stone pathways and patios, not to mention swings and hammocks hanging lazily in the shade. Each unit is unique, though all have private entrances and a comfy, grandmothery feel to them. The two suites add kitchens, while other units have small patios or balconies. Park Eden is popular with bird-watchers and gets lots of return visitors.

Calle Espavé #7. www.parkeden.com. ℭ **983-6167** or 6695-6190. 8 units. $90–$140 double; $260 house for 4. Rates include breakfast. **Amenities:** Bike rentals; tours.

INEXPENSIVE

Anton Valley Hotel ★   If you don't have a car, the Anton Valley Hotel, right on the main road in town, is probably your best bet. Quaint and quiet, though far from fancy, this hotel is well managed and cared for. The rooms are on the smaller side, though a bright coat of paint does wonders. The rooms on the second level are preferred for their balconies with views of the surrounding mountains. A full service restaurant, **Bruschetta,** relocated here from elsewhere in town.

Av. Principal. www.antonvalleyhotel.com. ℭ **983-6097.** 10 units. $83 double; $106–$115 suite. **Amenities:** Restaurant; bike rental; room service; free Wi-Fi.

A TENT CAMP OUTSIDE OF EL VALLE DE ANTÓN

Luxury Camping Altos del Maria ★★   Set in a remote residential complex 20.5km (12.7 miles) east of El Valle de Anton, this cushy tent camp is in the middle of a mountainous secondary forest and reforestation project where no tree was disturbed in its making. The luxury tents are, let's face it, hardly tents. Each is outfitted with a minibar, coffeemaker, and private bathroom with hot-water shower. This isn't roughing it; it's glamping (even *they* call it that). Every tent, either boxy or a round yurt, has a furnished terrace with a view that extends to the Pacific Ocean. You don't even have to walk down to the restaurant to eat. Staff will deliver your meal to your tent. There's plenty to do while you're here, primarily hiking along different trails looking for birds and waterfalls. At night, the staff will point out the different constellations while you roast marshmallows by the fire pit.

20.5km (12.7 miles) east of Valle de Anton, Altos del María. www.luxurycamping panama.net. ℭ **260-4813.** 4 units. $221 double; $281 suite. Rates include 3 daily meals. **Amenities:** Restaurant; tours; free Wi-Fi.

Where to Dine

If you're just looking for a snack, a cup of coffee, or even a to-go sandwich or picnic lunch, stop off at **El Valle Gourmet & Coffee Shop** on the main street (ℭ **6715-5785;** Fri noon–9pm, Sat 9am–10:30pm, and Sun and holidays 9am–6pm). The shop has juices, coffee, imported cheeses and cold cuts, sandwiches, frozen meals, jams, tinned delicacies, and more. For breakfast, you can't beat **Bruschetta,** at the Anton Valley Hotel (www.antonvalleyhotel.com), where $3 or $5 will get you a very tasty traditional American or Panamanian breakfast.

EXPENSIVE

La Casa de Lourdes ★★ INTERNATIONAL   By far the most famous restaurant in El Valle, La Casa de Lourdes is the glamorous Tuscan-style manor house, now a small hotel, of Lourdes Fábrega de Ward, who studied with Martha Stewart and Paul Prudhomme. The dining area is mostly out-doors, beneath a series of arches beside an outdoor pool. The food is very classic, old-school white-tablecloth French and Italian, with the occasional Panamanian ingredient like yucca or tamarindo tossed in. The restaurant gets packed on Saturdays and Sundays, sometimes with day-trippers from Panama City, so be sure to have a reservation during the high season.

Calle El Ciclo. www.lacasadelourdes.com. ✆ **983-6450.** Reservations required on weekends and recommended for all other days. Main courses $8–$20. Wed–Mon 7:30am–9pm (to 10pm Fri–Sat).

INEXPENSIVE

Don Pepe ★ PANAMANIAN   This low-key local spot offers inexpensive homemade food. They have a little bit of everything, from burgers to classic Panamanian dishes to roasted chicken. Service can be slow at times and there's usually a TV blaring the news, but you'll find a local color here that sometimes gets lost in expat-heavy El Valle.

Av. Principal. ✆ **983-6425.** Reservations not accepted. Main courses $4–$10. Mon–Thurs 7am–9pm; Fri–Sun 7am–11pm.

Fruit Shop ★ CAFE/ICE CREAM   Fruit is the key ingredient at this cutesy walk-up stand with a shady patio. The popular family spot serves a rotating list of smoothies, homemade ice creams, and *raspados* (snow cones), using mostly local fruits. You can even order fruit with chocolate fondue. Light breakfast and snacks like empanadas are available throughout the day.

Av. Principal. ✆ **6650-8658.** Snacks $2–$4. Mon–Sat 7am–5pm.

WESTERN COCLÉ PROVINCE & PENONOMÉ

145km (90 miles) W of Panama City

The Coclé Province from Penonomé to Aguadulce is scarcely visited by for-eign tourists. Historical, cultural, and natural attractions are scattered around in such a fashion that renting a vehicle or booking a custom tour is key to exploring the area, unless you're headed straight for Cerro La Vieja outside of Penonomé. Travelers normally visit this area on their way to the Azuero Pen-insula or as a side trip from the Pacific Coast.

The capital of the Coclé Province is **Penonomé,** a town that for a few years during the 17th century was the nation's capital after Panama City had been sacked by the pirate Henry Morgan. Little of the town's colonial history is evident today. The **Mercado de Artesanías** (Mon–Fri 9am–5pm) is located on the Interamericana Highway just before the exit for Penonomé. You'll find a limited selection of mostly Ngöbe-Buglé indigenous handicrafts and cloth-ing. Near the plaza is the small yet interesting **Museo de Penonomé ★** (✆ **997-8490;** Tue–Sun 9am–12:30pm and 1:30–4pm; $1 adults, 25¢ kids) on Calle San Antonio at Parque Rubén Darío Carles in what's left of the San Antonio colonial neighborhood. The museum occupies four adjoining homes and displays colonial religious art, pre-Columbian artifacts, and artifacts from the town's initial stages.

Heading north out of Penonomé, **La Pintada** village (see below) is regionally known for its own handicrafts fair and especially for its locally renowned straw hats and cigar factory.

Getting There & Departing

BY BUS Buses leave every 20 minutes from Panama City's Albrook Terminal to Penonomé; it takes a little over 2 hours and costs $5. You'll be dropped off on the Interamericana Highway on the opposite side of the Hotel Dos Continentes. From there, local buses to La Pintada leave every 20 minutes and cost $1.50. You can also grab a taxi to take you to La Pintada for $4 to $6.

BY CAR The drive to Penonomé takes 2 hours. The exit is clearly signed and is at the Hotel Dos Continentes.

La Pintada

About 20 minutes from Penonomé is the charming, sleepy village of La Pintada, known for its *sombreros pintados,* or "painted hats," made from intricately handwoven black and white fibers of the *bellota* plant. It's a long, arduous task to create this traditional hat, and prices average $75 to $100, twice that amount if bought in Panama City. You'll find a good selection of *sombreros pintados* at the **Mercado de Artesanías La Pintada ★** (Tues–Sun 9am–5pm), as well as *montuño* embroidered shirts, woven rugs, dolls dressed in folkloric dresses such as the pollera, and other regional knickknacks. The market is on the left side of the main road from Penonomé, once you enter La Pintada.

Ancient Burial Grounds

Parque Arqueológico El Caño (El Caño Archaeological Park) displays the excavated burial grounds and artifacts of indigenous groups that inhabited this region from A.D. 500 to 1500. Considering that it is one of the most important archaeological sites in Panama, it's surprising that you don't even need a full hour to take it all in—much of what was found was shipped to the U.S. when an American amateur archaeologist excavated the site in the 1920s. More important, it is estimated that many unearthed burial sites still exist here, yet there is little interpretive information about these or other items.

Nevertheless, if you're in the area, this 8.1-hectare (20-acre) park makes for an interesting stop. It has burial mounds and a burial pit with skeletons still intact; a small museum with pottery, tools, and other artifacts taken from burial sites; and a reproduction of what it's imagined the site originally looked like. Hours are Tuesday to Sunday 9am–noon and 12:30–4pm; admission is $1 adults, 25¢ kids.

To get here, take the exit for El Caño, about 27km (17 miles) west of Penonomé, and continue for 3km (1¾ miles), always keeping to the left until you reach the site. If you don't have a vehicle, you'll need to take a taxi from Natá.

AN ECOLODGE OUTSIDE OF PENONOMÉ

Villa Tavida ★★   On a private reserve filled with thick, green jungle on a hill called Cerro La Vieja, this little-known ecolodge is a diamond in the rough. Bordering the Tavida River, the reserve includes a 58m (190-ft.) waterfall with a natural pool that's a short hike away, plus several different petroglyphs. The property is comprised of 19 spacious rooms divided into thatched-roof cabins, with four rooms to each cabin. Every unit includes a balcony with a hammock. Day visitors can explore the reserve for $5 per person. The lodge is located on the road to Churuquita Grande and Caimito. To get here, turn into Penonomé on the Interamericana Highway, and then turn right (northeast) onto the road to Churuquita and Caimito. The road from Penonomé is paved, but if you come from El Valle, it isn't, and you'll need a 4x4.

Caimito, Coclé Province. www.villatavida.com. ℭ **983-8905** in Panama or 786/206-0219 in the U.S. 18 units. $150 double. Rates include breakfast. **Amenities:** Restaurant; bar; full-service spa w/massage, facials, and thermal baths; no phone in rooms.

Natá

Natá is the oldest village in Panama, founded by the Spanish in 1522 and named after the powerful *cacique* (chieftain) Natá who once ruled this region. Natá is known for its venerable church **Basilica Menor Santiago Apostal de Natá,** which was erected during the same year and is therefore considered to be the oldest surviving church in the Americas. Extensive renovations took place during the 1990s, yet visitors can still appreciate the church's original wooden columns, altars, and artwork. The church is located on the plaza, about a half-mile from the Interamericana Highway. Natá is 180km (112 miles) from Panama City, and 31km (20 miles) from Penonomé.

LA PENINSULA DE AZUERO

From Panama City: Chitré is 250km (155 miles), Las Tablas is 282km (175 miles), and Pedasí is 324km (201 miles)

Entering the Azuero Peninsula past Divisa, you'll feel as if you've gone back in time a hundred years. The Azuero Peninsula is considered the cradle of Panamanian folklore and rural culture, passed down from Spanish colonists who settled here during the 17th and 18th centuries. The region is dotted with terra-cotta-tile-and-gingerbread representations of early Spanish villas, and everything is very, very slowly paced—except when residents join together for the raucous festivities for which this region is famous. Nowhere in Panama is **Carnaval** celebrated with as much gusto as it is here in the Azuero, especially in towns such as Las Tablas and Chitré; and religious festivals honoring saints are livened with fireworks, music, and costumed folkloric dances that are as pagan as they are Catholic. Really, the best time to visit the peninsula is during Carnaval, though you'll want to be sure to book your hotel in advance. The Azuero Peninsula is the birthplace of the *pollera,* widely

FESTIVALS & events IN THE AZUERO PENINSULA

Residents of the Azuero Peninsula seemingly live for festivals, and indeed they are livelier here than anywhere else in the country. The following are the major festivals, but the list is by no means comprehensive. Check the website of the Tourism Authority of Panama (ATP) at **www.visitpanama.com** for information about all the events taking place during your visit.

February: Carnaval kicks off the Friday before Ash Wednesday and continues until the following Tuesday in this nationwide event—and it's at its rowdiest and most colorful here in the Azuero. See "Party On! Carnaval in the Azuero Peninsula" on p. 143.

March/April: Semana Santa's most colorful celebration is in La Villa de Los Santos and Guararé.

Late April: Feria Internacional de Azuero in La Villa de Los Santos. As at a county fair, this features animal displays, food stalls, and drinking.

June: Festival Corpus Christi in La Villa de Los Santos. This village explodes with activity for the 2-week festival known for its elaborate dances led by men in devil masks.

July 20 to July 22: Festival Patronales de La Virgen de Santa Librada in Las Tablas. This festival is famous for its **Festival de la Pollera** on July 22, which showcases the region's most beautiful polleras and elects the year's "Queen of the Pollera."

September 24: Festival Nacional de la Mejorana in Guararé. This nationally famous folkloric festival sees hundreds of dancers, musicians, and singers converging for a week of events and serious partying.

October 19: Fundación del Distrito de Chitré in Chitré. A large festival with parades celebrates the founding of the city.

November 10: Grito de la Villa, or "Cry of Independence," in Villa de Los Santos. Commemorates this national independence holiday with parades and music.

considered to be one of the most beautiful traditional dresses in the world. *Seco*, the sugarcane alcohol and national drink, hails from this region, too. But what makes the Azuero Peninsula special are its people, who have a fondness for greeting strangers, so practice your *"buenos días"* and get ready to smile.

The Azuero Peninsula protrudes south from the Panamanian isthmus into the Pacific Ocean, separating the Gulf of Panama to the east and the Gulf of Chiriquí to the west; most of the peninsula is within the Herrera and Los Santos provinces. It is about 100km (60 miles) wide and 90km (56 miles) long. Sadly, most of the terrain has been completely denuded because of the region's large-scale cattle production. Indeed, a visitor who has just come from the green and lush panorama farther north is in for a surprise here in the Azuero. Some areas, such as Sarigua National Park, have been so thoroughly stripped of vegetation that they are now considered desert. Oddly, most towns sit inland despite the beautiful coastline here—but investors and foreigners are starting to move in, especially near Pedasí and Playa Venado. This pristine coast is seeing drastic changes—and many have been controversial.

So where to go and how to best see this region? You'll notice that destinations or towns in this section seem to include only the highlights, but in most cases there is just one museum or one church to see in each village. Also, decent lodging is scarce here, the reason you won't see much listed outside of Chitré and Pedasí. My advice is to rent a car in Panama City or Chitré and take in the sights at your own pace, stopping from town to town and lodging near Pedasí. This picturesque village has the widest range of lodging and dining options, is close to beaches, and has snorkeling, surfing, and diving, too. If you have a car, you'll also be able to stop at the roadside stands that dot the Carretera Nacional and that sell everything from fresh watermelon to sausages; there are *fondas,* or cheap food stands, too, with fried Panamanian snacks, as well as open-air cantinas that sell three beers for $1.

Commercial flights travel to Pedasí with **Air Panama** (www.airpanama.com) several times per week. Bus service is inexpensive, but you'll need a taxi to get around from the station. It takes more than 4 hours to reach Pedasí by vehicle from Panama City; those with enough time might consider breaking up the trip with a stay in El Valle or on the Pacific Coast.

Parita

About 25km (16 miles) after Divisa is Parita, one of the most charming villages in Panama. It's a very humble place, but the streets are lined with well-preserved examples of Spanish colonial architecture. At the plaza is the **Iglesia de Santo Domingo de Guzmán,** but apart from this there really aren't any attractions here other than city streets to be wandered and photographed. If you're driving along the Azuero Peninsula, make this a quick stop on your itinerary.

Chitré

Chitré is the capital of Herrera Province, and it is the largest town on the Azuero Peninsula, founded in 1848. Many of the streets here ooze charm, yet on the whole Chitré isn't as picturesque as Pedasí. Many of its colonial buildings have been replaced by more utilitarian structures, and the downtown bustles with shops hawking cheap plastic goods and clothing. Chitré does offer plentiful services, including lodging and car rental, and it can be a convenient base for exploring the region, but don't expect 17th-century colonial charm. Visitors during Carnaval will find higher-quality lodging here than in Las Tablas, but this option is better for those with a rental vehicle (don't forget that Chitré is pretty lively, too, during Carnaval). Before arriving at Chitré, you'll pass through the tiny village of La Arena, which is described below in "What to See & Do."

GETTING THERE & DEPARTING
BY PLANE There are no regularly scheduled commercial flights between Panama City and Chitré. To charter a private flight, contact **Air Panama** (© **316-9043**).

BY BUS & TAXI   The **Transportes de Herrera bus terminal,** a $1.50 to $2 taxi ride from the center of town, is located on Calle 19 de Octubre (also called Av. Roberto Ramírez de Diego). The turnoff for this street is next to the Hotel Hong Kong. Buses to and from Panama City cost $9 and run every hour between 6am and 6pm; the trip is 3½ hours. Buses to Las Tablas leave every 15 minutes from 6am to 6:30pm and cost $2. For buses to Pedasí, you'll need a bus to Las Tablas, and then you must transfer to a Pedasí-bound bus. Or you can take a taxi for $30 to $35.

BY CAR   When you arrive at La Arena, just before Chitré, the road forks; take the left road and continue along the Carretera Nacional, which will take you directly into the center of town. If you turn right at the plaza, the road will funnel back into the Carretera Nacional south to La Villa de los Santos. Chitré is 37km (23 miles) from the start of the Carretera Nacional at Divisa, and 252km (157 miles) from Panama City.

For **rental cars** in Chitré, **Thrifty** (www.thrifty.com; ✆ **996-9565**), is on Paseo Enrique Geenzier.

FAST FACTS

There are 24-hour ATMs at HSBC bank on Avenida Herrera, ½ block north from the plaza, and Banco Nacional on Paseo Enrique Greenzier, near the Hotel Versailles. For the **police,** call ✆ **996-4333**.

WHAT TO SEE & DO

There really isn't much to do in the town itself, other than pay a quick visit to the **Museo de Herrera** (✆ **996-0077**; Tues–Sat 9am–4pm; admission $1 at press time) at Calle Manuel María Correa and Avenida Julio Arjona; you'll recognize the whitewashed colonial building—it sticks out from its more modern neighbors. The museum staff has put a lot of effort into providing visitors with a better understanding of the anthropology and ecology of the Herrera Province. There are a few gems here, including pottery dating back to 2500 B.C., and folkloric costumes and polleras.

Take a step into the lovely **Catedral de San Juan Bautista** on the plaza, built at the turn of the 20th century with a bold stone exterior and exposed-wood interior with stained glass and chandeliers.

La Arena

This tiny artisans' village is almost entirely dedicated to pottery making, which began during pre-Columbian times. Most of the vendors who hawk their ceramics along the two principal streets here sell gaily painted pots called *tinajas,* which traditionally were used as all-purpose storage vases but are now primarily decorative. There are also wall hangings, flowerpots, and animal figurines, but the best buy here: **reproductions of terra-cotta-colored pre-Columbian vases** and other such storage vessels. For a good selection, head to the **Mercado de Artesanías** in the large, white building found where the road divides near the center of town (no phone; daily 9am–4:30pm). For traditional, pre-Columbian-influenced pottery, visit **Cerámica Hermanos Calderón** (✆ **910-4076;** daily 7am–5pm), which has been handcrafting beautiful, museum-quality pieces for half a century. The staff are happy to show visitors how the pieces are made, from pottery wheel to the voluminous ovens out back. The workshop is on the right just as you enter town. La Arena is only 2km (1¼ miles) west of Chitré.

WHERE TO STAY & DINE
Cubita Boutique Resort & Spa ★★   A surprising find in Chitré, this beautifully designed resort features architecture inspired by the region's Spanish colonial past. The Cubita is by far Chitré's best hotel, with stately rooms featuring checkered tile floors and heavy, dark wood furnishings. Many rooms open up to a hard-to-resist outdoor pool. Suites are located beside the hotel's chapel and add a separate sitting area with a sofa bed. Surprises are all around, from a small archeological museum with pieces on loan from the Instituto Nacional de Cultura (INAC) to the region's largest spa to a sophisticated modern Panamanian restaurant.

Vía Circunvalación. www.cubitaresort.com. ⓒ **978-0200.** 96 units. $100 double; $185 suite. Breakfast included in rates. **Amenities:** 2 restaurants; bar; outdoor pool; gym; spa; museum; free Wi-Fi.

Gran Hotel Azuero ★   Although it lacks the sense of place that the Cubita provides, the more straightforward Gran Hotel Azuero is still one of Chitré's more reliable and well-rounded hotels. The rooms are cookie-cutter bland with tile floors, one blood-red wall, and tacky gold-framed landscape paintings, though the TVs are LCD and the air-conditioning is strong. Many rooms face the rather large, resort-style pool with a swim-up bar. The hotel has a considerable amount of meeting and event space, so it can fill up in no time for weddings and corporate events.

Paseo Enrique Geenzier. www.hotelazuero.com. ⓒ **970-1000.** 64 units. $75–$80 double; $125-$250 suites. Breakfast included in rates. **Amenities:** Restaurant; bar; outdoor pool; gym; meeting facilities.

La Villa de los Santos

Just 4km (2½ miles) south of Chitré, you'll cross over Río la Villa and into Los Santos Province. A few minutes later, you'll arrive at the colonial town of La Villa de Los Santos, often referred to simply as "Los Santos." This is the site of the famous "Cry of Independence," when Panamanians issued the first

Pollera: The National Dress

The national dress, the *pollera*, from the Azuero Peninsula, is considered to be one of the most beautiful traditional dresses in the world. It consists of a full, gathered skirt over several petticoats, and a flounced top, intricately embroidered with floral designs and trimmed with lace. The pollera is worn during special occasions and would not be complete without *mosquetas* and *tembleques,* or gold and pearl jewelry, as well as hair combs encrusted with pearls. A pollera takes several months to a year to make and can cost thousands of dollars.

official request to liberate themselves from Spanish rule. The letter of request was signed on November 10, 1821, inside what is now the **Museo de la Nacionalidad** (© **966-8192;** Tues–Sun 9am–4pm; admission $1 adults, 75¢ students, 25¢ kids 11 and under). Located on the northwest side of Parque Simon Bolívar, the lovely building it is housed in features lofty ceilings and handmade ceramic floors. The curators have set up the room to show how it would have looked during the signing of the declaration.

More worthwhile is a visit to the most beautiful church in the Azuero Peninsula, **Iglesia de San Atanacio,** also located on the Bolívar plaza. This statuesque baroque church was declared a national monument for its interior decorative work, which has remained intact from the year it opened, 1782. Some features of the church are even older—the church was built in stages beginning with the *retablo* (the structure forming the back of the altar) in 1721, and the ornamented archway in 1733. The altar and archway are simply gorgeous, intricately carved with cherubs and flowers that are almost completely covered with gold leaf and decorative paint. There is also a wooden, full-scale sculpture of Christ, as well as plaques designating the names of priests buried here.

WHERE TO STAY & DINE

Hotel La Villa ★   Open since 1980, this inexpensive midsize hotel is a good alternative for those not tied to Chitré. Rooms open up to exterior walkways like a motel, and the hotel has a surprisingly great pool, surrounded by palm trees, that makes for a great break from the stifling heat. Rooms are a mixed bag, though, a timeline of renovations from one to the next. Most have odd, multicolored mosaic-tile display on the walls, though with regional handicrafts used as decorations and a decent air-conditioning system, you can't complain too much.

La Villa de los Santos. © **966-8201.** 38 units. $55–$99 doubles. **Amenities:** Restaurant; outdoor pool; free Wi-Fi.

Kiosco El Ciruelo ★ PANAMANIAN   A few minutes outside of town, this rustic roadside cantina, a truck stop really, is worth planning your day around. Everything here is cooked over a wood fire. There are tempting barbecued meats, but the spicy pork tamales wrapped in a plantain leaf are the house specialty.

La Villa de los Santos. 3km (1¾ miles) southeast of town. No phone. Main courses $2–$6. No credit cards. Days and hours vary, although typically Fri–Sun 6am–9pm.

Las Tablas

Las Tablas is the provincial capital of Los Santos, known as the "cradle of national folklore," chiefly for its famous **Carnaval** festivities (see "Party On! Carnaval in the Azuero Peninsula," below). The spruce town is comprised of adobe colonial homes with iron balustrades and terra-cotta roofs, interspersed with more modern, utilitarian architecture and service-oriented businesses. It's a quiet place without much to see or do, except wander the streets and relax in the plaza with an ice-cream cone. Most tourists visit Las Tablas only for Carnaval or on their way south to Pedasí.

The town's sole museum, **Museo de Belisario Porras** (© **994-6326;** Tues–Sat 9am–4pm; admission 50¢ adults, 25¢ kids), located on the south side of the plaza, pays homage to Panama's national hero and three-term president Dr. Belisario Porras, who died in 1942. The museum is inside Porras's old home and features military decorations, stamps with his likeness, and documents pertaining to his time spent as a national leader. But you can easily skip this museum altogether.

GETTING THERE & DEPARTING

BY BUS OR TAXI The bus terminal is located about 5 blocks north of the plaza on the Carretera Nacional and Avenida Dr. Emilio Castro. Buses to Las Tablas from Panama City leave every hour from 6am to 7pm. Buses to Panama City generally leave every hour from 6am until about 5:30pm. Hours change frequently, so it's a good idea to pop in and buy your ticket and check schedules; the fare is $10 for buses with air-conditioning. To Pedasí, buses run every 45 minutes from 6am to 7pm and cost $3. Taxis are plentiful in Las Tablas; they can be found at the bus terminal and also at the taxi stand at Calle 2 and the Carretera Nacional next to the Banco Nacional. A taxi to Pedasí costs about $25 to $30.

PARTY ON! carnaval IN THE AZUERO PENINSULA

Some say the only thing that Panamanians take seriously is Carnaval, and here in the Azuero, especially in **Las Tablas,** it's celebrated with a fervor unseen elsewhere in Panama. For old-timers who lament that Carnaval has marched toward vulgarity in Panama City, the festival in the Azuero has maintained its folkloric traditions. It begins the Saturday before Ash Wednesday and continues for 4 days with dancing, heavy drinking, music, and parades. The atmosphere is enlivened by the famous rivalry between Calle Arriba and Calle Abajo (High St. and Low St., respectively), whereby the town is divided into two groups that try to outdo each other with the fanciest costumes and floats and even their own queens, who are specially chosen for the event. Other highlights include the parade of the polleras. Be forewarned that *mojaderos,* guys who

spray passersby with water from pistols, garden hoses, buckets, and even fire hoses, are out before noon, so be prepared to get drenched.

Carnaval is a tremendously enjoyable cultural and party event, but keep in mind that in Las Tablas it is also a raucous and sometimes disorderly event that might be too much for some people. For this reason, many tourists opt to lodge elsewhere and visit Las Tablas for the day. Or, for a low-key version of Carnaval, head to a quieter town such as Pedasí or La Villa de los Santos. *Note:* Hotels in Las Tablas and Chitré, and many others around the Azuero, sell 4- and 5-night Carnaval packages at prices that are about double the standard rate. You will need reservations at least a month in advance, and most hotels expect you to pay 100% upfront.

BY CAR   Las Tablas is 282km (175 miles) from Panama City, and 32km (20 miles) from Chitré. The Carretera Nacional funnels into town and passes the main plaza; if continuing on, you'll need to hang a left at the end of the plaza (Calle Belisario Porras) to keep following the Carretera Nacional out of town.

WHERE TO STAY

Hotel Piamonte y Restaurante ★   Las Tablas lacks good accommodations, and this budget hotel has very little going for it, other than a decent restaurant on the ground floor that stays open late and a coat of cheerful yellow paint. The rooms are dingy and lack light, and suites are only slightly better. The location is good, though, and during Carnaval it puts you a short walk from the festivities. Note that the hotel sells only 5-night packages during Carnaval, for upwards of $450, lodging only.

Av. Belisario Porras. ℂ **923-1603.** 16 units. $45 double; $60 junior suite. **Amenities:** Restaurant; no phone in rooms.

Villa Pelicano ★   With options in Las Tablas so poor, commuting from this much more agreeable, Belgian-owned hotel on Playa Uverito, about 10km (6¼ miles) away, makes a lot of sense. Instead of a sad, cramped room in town, your airy, bright room opens on to a balcony looking out over the pool and an okay beach. During Carnaval, reservations cost $1,000 for a 4-day package.

Playa Uverito. www.villapelicano.com. ℂ **6870-8178.** 5 units. $130–$160 double. Rates include breakfast. No credit cards. **Amenities:** Pool.

Pedasí ★

Arguably the region's prettiest town, this is without a doubt the choice destination in the region, and I hesitate to say that because it is one of those special places you want to remain a secret. Pedasí is the kind of small town where no passing visitor goes ungreeted—locals camped out on their front porch give a pleasant wave to any stranger passing by. It's a place where you might glimpse a drunk man passed out on a horse that is walking back home on its own. The autochthonous architecture is well preserved, and residents have recently painted and spiffed up most of the facades of residential buildings. The town is one long main street called Avenida Central, with a tidy plaza 2 blocks from the main road. The paved and signed streets and other well-tended civic structures exist because the former president Mireya Moscoso is from here—you'll see her bust in the plaza.

A little farther south in the village of **Los Destiladores,** you'll find luxury lodging; and to the southwest in **Playa Venado,** there's high-end beachfront lodging. The region is known for its beaches, surfing, fishing, and Isla Laguna Wildlife refuge. There is even a scuba-diving operation.

GETTING THERE & DEPARTING

BY PLANE   Several weekly commercial flights travel between Panama City and Pedasí during the high season, though they can be nonexistent during the rest of the year. **Air Panama** (www.airpanamaonline.com; ℂ **316-9043**) can also organize a charter flight for you; however, this option is expensive and not really worth it unless you're traveling with a large group.

BY CAR   To continue through Las Tablas to Pedasí, follow the Carretera Nacional until it dead-ends at Avenida Belisario Porras. Turn left, and drive until the road turns back into the Carretera Nacional. The road from Las Tablas to Pedasí is straightforward.

BY BUS & TAXI   Buses from Panama City or Chitré change in Las Tablas. Buses from Panama City to Las Tablas are $10; from Las Tablas to Pedasí, it is $3. A taxi from Chitré to Pedasí costs around $30 to $35.

GETTING AROUND
BY TAXI   Taxis do not cruise the streets frequently, but if you wait long enough on a corner, one will eventually pass by. If not, ask your hotel to call for you.

FUN IN THE OCEAN
Beaches
This region offers a lot of fine beaches, though unfortunately few are well cared for. **Playa Arenal,** about a mile from the main street in Pedasí, is a prime example, and visitors might only want to stop here briefly before carrying on to the Isla Laguna Wildlife Refuge, which is reached by boat from here—take the road past the scuba shop near the ATP office. **Playa del Toro** has good swimming conditions, but its murky waters are not very inviting. The best beach here is in **Los Destiladores,** another 10km (6¼ miles) south of Pedasí. The waves pound, but the beach is cleaner and altogether more beautiful. Also, see "Playa Venado," below. Like most beaches on the Pacific, the beaches of the Azuero Peninsula aren't the most attractive in Panama, but the availability of comfortable lodging makes them a good choice for those who don't want to go as far as Bocas del Toro or don't want to rough it in Kuna Yala.

Isla Iguana Wildlife Refuge
This 55-hectare (136-acre) island refuge, about 3km (1¾ miles) from shore, is reached by boat from Playa Arenal. Isla Iguana is surrounded by an extensive coral reef that attracts thousands of colorful fish—the blue sea here is ideal for snorkeling. The island was once used as target practice by the U.S. military, and it's said that unexploded bombs are still occasionally found here, so be careful and stick to the main beaches and trails.

The island is home to green iguanas and, if you're lucky enough to be here from June to November, humpback whales breed in the area and are commonly seen by boat. The refuge can be reached by hiring a local boatman at Playa Arenal or you can book a trip with **Pacific Paradise Dive Shop** (see below)—you'll need to rent snorkel gear from them anyway, so you might as well plan your trip here. The cost is about $60 for a half-day, and boats run from 8am to 6pm. The boat ride out is smoothest from April to December; if you've come between January and March, strong winds may prevent you from reaching the island.

Snorkeling, Diving & Fishing

Pacific Paradise Dive Shop (www.pacificparadisepedasi.com; © **6788-4572**) offers activities that include snorkel tours to Isla Iguana, Professional Association of Diving Instructors (PADI) diver training, and certification courses, plus dives to Isla Iguana, Frailes North, and Frailes South.

WHERE TO STAY

Casa de Campo ★★   Despite its prime location right in the heart of town, this cheerful compound feels secluded. The rooms are set back from the road, across stone walkways under coconut palms within small buildings with clay-tile roofs. Most open up to a pleasant pool area surrounded by lounge chairs, and several shady nooks and patios provide seating and hammocks where you can escape the heat. The rooms are spacious, with polished concrete or tile floors and high-beamed ceilings with lots of dark woodwork throughout, not to mention oversized bathrooms with walk-in showers and stylish concrete bathrooms.

Av. Central in the center of town. www.casacampopedasi.com. © **6780-5280.** 7 units. $88–$99 double. Rates include breakfast. **Amenities:** Restaurant; bar; pool; free Wi-Fi.

Casa Margarita ★   Low-key Casa Margarita is a step up from most other Pedasí B&Bs. The rooms feature wood floors and earthy tones and have handmade teak closets and clean, modern bathrooms. Two guest rooms are on the ground level and three are on the third level. The casa offers a handful of extra services that can come in handy, such as the kitchen cooking up your fishing catch, snorkel and surfboard rentals, and sack lunches you can take with you.

End of Av. Central. www.pedasihotel.com. © **995-2898.** $89–$99 double. Buffet breakfast included in rates. **Amenities:** Bar; honor bar; free Wi-Fi.

WHERE TO DINE

Aside from the dining options listed below, **Pasta e Vino** (on the road to Playa el Toro) offers tasty and affordable Italian dishes.

Bienvenidush ★ MIDDLE EASTERN   This quirky, adorable cafe and wine bar in front of the Pedasito hotel serves Mediterranean small plates amid a mostly white decor. The menu is comprised of traditional Middle Eastern dishes, like *labane* (yogurt cheese) and *shakshuka* (eggs poached in a tomato sauce), and a list of $3 tapas. A great back pastora terrace has live music on occasional weekends. Note that weekday hours tend to be sporadic.

Across from Pedasito Boutique Hotel. www.bienvenidush.com. © **6426-3105.** Main courses $7–$12. No credit cards. Tues–Sat noon–8:30pm.

La Huerta de Manolo Caracol ★★★ PANAMANIAN   You cannot get much more farm-to-table than this restaurant from Manuel Madueño, the owner of Manolo Caracol in Panama City. He relocated here to Pedasí to concentrate on farming one of several *fincas* he owns in the region. Heirloom rice and dozens of other ingredients grow only a few steps from the dozen or so rustic tables on a covered patio. The menu changes based on what's fresh at the farm and whatever seafood is pulled in by local fisherman that morning.

To get here, follow the road to the airport from the main drag and after a few twists and turns it will be on the right.

Calle del Colegio. www.manolocaracol.net. ℂ **995-2205.** Main courses $15–$20. No credit cards. Thurs–Sun 5:30–9pm.

LUXURY LODGING IN LOS DESTILADORES

A tiny hamlet about a 5-minute drive from Pedasí, Los Destiladores has two fine resorts offering travelers the most upscale accommodations on the Azuero Peninsula (one is reviewed below). The beach here is also the best in the area—with the exception of Playa Venado, which has its own deluxe B&B (see below). A taxi to town from here costs $5.

Posada Los Destiladores ★★   There are no TVs, no phones, and no kids at Posada Los Destiladores. Secluded among 8.1 hectares (20 acres) of tropical plants and teak trees fronting 250 meters (820 ft.) of private beach, this collection of eclectic, artsy bungalows is one of Panama's most original oceanfront properties. French-expat owners Philippe and Jean Francois, one a restaurateur and the other a furniture maker, have created their own village of sorts using a combination of cobblestone floors, palm-thatched walls, and custom-made furniture crafted of local materials. A main building with a restaurant, sundecks, and a small pool anchors the property.

Los Destiladores. www.panamabambu.net. ℂ **995-2771** or 6673-9262. 17 units. $150–$300 double bungalow. Rates include breakfast. **Amenities:** Restaurant; outdoor pool; horse rental; tours; no phone in rooms.

Playa Venado

Playa Venado (often called "Venao") is an up-and-coming destination, notable for its surfing and half-moon sandy beach. The surf here is legendary, though the destruction of the mangroves and a sand bank for new hotels has changed the course of the waves.

There's no sign to Playa Venado, so keep your eyes open for the turnoff. If you don't have a vehicle, you'll need a taxi, which will charge around $20 to $25. Like most of the beaches in this area, currents bring in trash—also, during high tide the sand fills with crabs, making swimming unpleasant. Low tide brings better swimming conditions.

The coastline of the Azuero Peninsula is rich with marine life and pelagic fish like tuna—so much so that it is often called the "tuna coast." Here at Playa Venado, the Inter-American Tropical Tuna Commission (IATTC), which monitors tuna fishing to prevent its depletion, has a research facility, **Achotines Laboratory** ★ (www.iattc.org; ℂ **995-8166**), which offers educational tours. It sounds dry, but it's actually fascinating to see the various stages of tuna reproduction (among other fish like sea bass and snapper), and especially to witness the frenzy that occurs when the staff feed huge broodstock yellowfin tuna. Visiting hours are Monday through Friday from 8:30am to noon and from 1 to 4:30pm. You must make advance arrangements.

About 11km (7 miles) from Playa Venado is the **Refugio de Vida Silvestre Isla de Cañas,** an island village that receives more nesting turtles than any other location on the Pacific Coast. From April to October, hundreds of thousands of Pacific green, olive ridley, leatherback, loggerhead, and hawksbill turtles arrive here to lay eggs, but there is no surefire date that guarantees you'll see any. The view of Isla de Cañas, a barrier island reached by boat, is worth seeing even if you do not visit the island itself. Getting here can be difficult; only one local boat can take you from the mainland (it leaves from the end of the road). If you show up, it may or may not be there.

WHERE TO STAY & DINE

El Sitio ★   This tasteful hotel right on the beach is a favorite among visiting surfers for having its own surf shop, reasonably priced rooms, and easy access to the breaks. Each room is decorated with handcrafted furniture and polished concrete floors; some have private oceanview balconies. Casa Billabong, on the second level over the surf shop, has a kitchenette and two bedrooms, making it ideal for families or groups of surfers. A thatched-roof beachside restaurant with a bar is open year-round.

Playa Venado. www.elsitiohotel.com. ℂ **832-1010.** 14 units. $90–$175 double. **Amenities:** Restaurant; bar; surfboard and snorkel rental; free Wi-Fi.

Selina Playa Venao ★   This is not your typical backpacker dive. Crafty and cool, the Selina features a mix of bright, clean private rooms and 6- to 12-person dorms set in two rows of colorful buildings just off the beach. Recycled and reclaimed furnishings decorate the property, which includes a beachside restaurant, outdoor pool, and surf school. Summer weekend nights may have too much of a party atmosphere for some guests to handle.

Playa Venado. www.selinahostels.com. ℂ **996-6551.** 10 units. $45 double w/shared bathroom; $70 double w/private bathroom; $18 per person for dorms. **Amenities:** Restaurant; bar; outdoor pool; beach volleyball; surfboard rental; tours; free Wi-Fi.

Villa Marina ★★   Villa Marina feels like one giant, tropical-chic beach house. The setting—89 hectares (220 acres) of private coastal land—is the best in Playa Venado. Filled with bright, vibrant color, the hacienda-style inn with terra-cotta-tiled roof is fresh and breezy, thanks to countless outdoor spaces to hang out and an abundance of hammocks tied beneath the shade of tall palms. The rooms feature French windows and are adorned with antique furnishings, though never feel anything less than cozy. The staff offers a variety of tours, including fishing, surfing, horseback riding, and stand-up paddleboarding (SUP). Plans call for another 40 rooms to be added to the property.

Playa Venado. www.villamarinalodge.com. ℂ **211-2277** or 646/383-7486 in the U.S. 10 units. $165–$225 double. **Amenities:** Outdoor pool; putting green; free surfboards and snorkel gear; horseback riding; fishing trips; free Wi-Fi.

THE WESTERN HIGHLANDS & THE GULF OF CHIRIQUÍ

Western Panama is home to the cool highlands of the Chiriquí Province, a tropical mountain paradise brimming with lush rainforest and trout-filled streams, and dotted with storybook villages nestled on the verdant slopes of the region's dominant peak, the 3,478m (11,410-ft.) Barú Volcano. Given the region's fertile soil and ideal year-round temperatures, the Chiriquí area is Panama's agricultural breadbasket, and many of the mountain's valleys and hillsides are blanketed with a colorful patchwork of fruit trees, vegetable fields, and coffee plantations—one of the country's signature products. The air is fresh and sweet here, and the roads that wind through the peaks and valleys overflow with pretty pink and white impatiens and exotic blooms.

The Chiriquí Highlands region is a mecca for adventure, and travelers can participate in activities such as white-water rafting and kayaking Class II to Class V rivers, canopy rides, or hiking through primeval forest dripping with vines and bromeliads and interlaced with creeks. Laidback activities include scenic drives and tours of coffee plantations or orchid farms. The Chiriquí region is well known as a hot spot for **bird-watching,** and hundreds of species have been recorded in the area, including showcase birds such as the resplendent quetzal, blue cotinga, trogons, and toucans. The region is a corridor for migratory species that pass through from November to April.

The eastern side of the Barú Volcano is home to **Boquete,** an enchanting valley town that has received a lot of press lately as a top retirement area. Indeed, it's not uncommon to see a number of foreigners here. On the volcano's western side are picturesque agricultural communities such as **Cerro Punta.** Both towns are linked by the Los Quetzales Trail, which winds through the gorgeous forests of **Parque Nacional Volcán Barú.** Additionally, the western side offers access to one of the most important parks in Central

The Western Highlands & the Gulf of Chiriquí

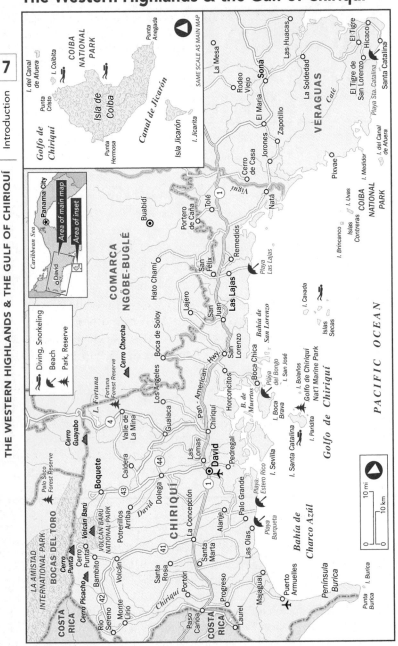

America, **Parque Internacional La Amistad,** which Panama shares with Costa Rica.

The Highlands are accessed from the province's capital **David,** a service-oriented city located on the hot and humid lowlands. A little farther south is the Gulf of Chiriquí, Panama's up-and-coming travel destination that offers outstanding scuba diving, snorkeling, and sport fishing in the crystalline waters around such revered sites as **Isla Coiba,** and the islands in and around **Parque Nacional Golfo Marino.** This chapter covers the extensive region that includes the Highlands, the Gulf, and even the remote village of Santa Catalina, for its epic surfing and direct access to Isla Coiba.

The Chiriquí Highlands have microclimates that produce cloud forests and phenomena such as the misting rain *bajareque,* so it is important that you bring clothing that is waterproof if you plan to spend time outdoors. Also, be sure to pack for temperatures that are decidedly cooler than in the rest of Panama.

DAVID

440km (273 miles) W of Panama City; 40km (25 miles) south of Boquete

David, Panama's third-largest city, with a population of about 145,000, has an economy based around commercial services and Chiriquí Province's thriving farming industry. At just 45 minutes from the Costa Rica border, the city has the ambience of a frontier town, with little here to offer travelers other than a transportation hub and services. David's location on a coastal plain means the heat and humidity here can be suffocating—another reason many use it as a jumping-off point to the beach or the highlands.

Essentials
GETTING THERE & DEPARTING
BY PLANE The **Aeropuerto Enrique Malek** (DAV) is about 4.8km (3 miles) from the city center and is serviced by **Air Panama** (www.fly airpanama.com; ✆ 316-9000), with flights to and from Panama City, Bocas del Toro, and even San José, Costa Rica. There are three daily round-trip flights from **Panama City.** The cost is from $80 to 200 round-trip, including taxes. Flights from **Bocas del Toro** to David travel on Monday, Wednesday, and Friday. Flights from **San José** are on Monday, Wednesday, and Friday at 10am with the return trip from David leaving at 9:30am.

There is a **Tourism of Authority of Panama (ATP) visitor center booth** at the airport (no phone; daily 7am–3pm), manned by a helpful and friendly representative who has a limited number of brochures and maps. A taxi into town costs $3 to $4 per person.

BY BUS The **Terminal de Transportes** is located on Avenida Estudiante. Daily service to and from Panama City is offered by the bus line **Terminal David–Panama** (✆ 775-2974), with regular service leaving every hour daily from 6am to 8pm, and express service leaving daily at 10:45pm, midnight, and 3am. I recommend buying your tickets a day in advance for overnight

The Feria Internacional de David

The **Feria Internacional de David (FIDA)** is the largest commercial, industrial, agricultural, ranching, and folkloric festival in Panama, taking place every year around the middle of March. The weeklong event draws 300,000 people, most of whom come to visit the booths of international companies and catch up on the newest technology, but folklore, culture, and handicrafts play a large role, delighting tourists, too. Check the website **www.feriadedavid.com** for exact dates.

trips. **Padafront** (© 775-8853) has approximately 10 regular bus services daily, and express buses leave at 10:45pm and midnight. Both companies charge $16 for regular service (7 hr.), and $20 for express service (5½ hr.). Call ahead to confirm departure times.

Volcán–Cerro Punta–Guadalupe buses from David leave every 35 minutes from 5am to 7pm ($4–$5); buses to **Boquete** leave every 15 minutes from 4:15am to 9pm ($2). Buses to Costa Rica via the Paso Canoa border are available from several small companies, usually traveling in the afternoon. Costa Rica company **Tracopa** (www.tracopacr.com; © 775-0585) has two daily services to San José, Costa Rica, for $22 (8-hr. trip).

BY CAR David is reached from Panama City via the Interamericana Highway (Pan American Highway), which skirts the edge of town and continues on to the Paso Canoa border with Costa Rica. If you are heading on to Boquete or Volcán, see "Getting There & Departing," later in this chapter. Personally, I find renting a car to be the best option, because it allows you to explore the Boquete/Cerro Punta region.

GETTING AROUND

BY TAXI Taxis are plentiful in David. The fare for a taxi from the airport to the city center is $4 per person; to Boquete, it's $35; to Volcán, it's $50; and to Guadalupe, it's $60. Around town, fares cost $2 to $4.

BY CAR Rental vehicles are available at the David airport, including **Alamo** (www.alamopanama.com; © 236-5777); **Budget** (www.budgetpanama.com; © 263-8777); **Ancon** (www.anconrentcar.com; © 730-9229); and **National** (www.nationalpanama.com; © 721-0974). If you plan to visit the surrounding Chiriquí Highlands, you'll need a four-wheel-drive (4WD) for difficult, unpaved roads if exploring off the beaten track.

FAST FACTS

You'll find banks with ATMs on the streets around the plaza; **Banco Nacional** is at Calle B Norte and Avenida 3 Este/Bolívar on the plaza; and **HSBC** is at Avenida 1era Oeste and Calle D Norte. There's an excellent hospital here, the **Mae Lewis Hospital** (www.hospitalmaelewis.com; © 775-4616). For the **police,** dial © 771-4231. The **post office** can be found 1 block northeast of the plaza on Avenida 4 Este and Calle C Norte; it's open Monday through Saturday from 7am to 5:30pm.

What to See & Do in & Around David

Despite the fact that David is one of Panama's largest cities, it has surprisingly few attractions to keep a tourist occupied. The historic **Parque Miguel de Cervantes** plaza is one of the rare areas in David that offers shade trees and a respite from the oppressive heat; vendors there sell ice cream, fresh coconut juice, and cold beverages. Take a stroll down to **Barrio Bolívar** by following Calle A Norte west of the plaza to Avenida 8 Este. This is the city's "old town," where a couple of blocks boast the last vestiges of colonial architecture from David's early days.

Residents of David escape the heat by heading to **Playa Barqueta,** about a 30-minute drive from town. This long, black-sand beach is often breezy, and the ocean can be too choppy for swimming (beware of riptides here). Also located here is a nature preserve that's a turtle-nesting site from about August to October; it's an excellent spot to view wildlife and birds year-round. **Las Olas Resort** is also here (see "Where to Stay," below); you can dine at its restaurant or bring a picnic lunch. **Las Lajas,** 70km (43 miles) east of David, is a 10km (6-mile) stretch of tan sand that is also popular. The current is not strong, making swimming conditions better here than at many other Pacific Coast beaches. Along the beach you'll find simple B&Bs, thatched *bohio* picnic sites, and a couple of cheap restaurants—but it's all a bit weather-beaten and half-open unless it is a summer weekend. To get here, head east from David on the Pan-American Highway and turn at the signed road at Las Cruces. Continue for 13km (8 miles), passing through the village Las Lajas, until you reach the beach.

Where to Stay

Hotels and B&Bs in the Chiriquí Highlands and the Boca Chica region offer much more ambience and character, but if you absolutely need to spend a night in David, the hotels below are your best bet. If you're just looking for a cheap place to stay, head to the **Purple House Hostel** (www.purplehouse hostel.com; ✆ **774-4059**). It's a mostly backpacker crowd, but rooms are clean and comfortable enough and you can get a double with A/C for around $30 a night.

Gran Hotel Nacional ★ Opened in 1949, this grand hotel with a mock-colonial façade has lost much of its original luster, though it still has some redeeming qualities. With a 24-hour casino, a six-theater cinema, an outdoor swimming pool, and three restaurants, the Gran Nacional is a social center for the entire town and receives many day visitors. The rooms have something of a quirky Branson, Missouri, vibe, and some of the hallways feel almost institutional, but there's still more atmosphere here than anywhere else in David. Businessmen and travelers making a stop on the drive to Costa Rica or Bocas del Toro are more typical guests than straight-up leisure travelers.

Av. Central. www.hotelnacionalpanama.com. ✆ **775-2222.** 119 units. $95 double; $135 junior suite; $150 pool suite. Rates include breakfast. **Amenities:** 3 restaurants; bar; outdoor pool; cinema; casino; room service; free Wi-Fi.

Hotel Ciudad de David ★ Cool, modern, and clean is the best way to describe this chain-like business hotel. It's right in the heart of town and a 15-minute ride to the airport. All guest rooms have wood floors, standard chain decor and furnishings, and modern amenities such as flatscreen TVs. The suites are the best rooms in David, though pricey. The decent restaurant, lounge, and cafe are more than sufficient for a late-night meal or drink, plus there's a large outdoor pool and sauna.

Calle D Norte at Av. 2da Este. www.hotelciudaddedavid.com. ☎ **774-3333.** 103 units. $99 double; $295 suite. Rates include breakfast. **Amenities:** Restaurant/bar; cafe, pool; fitness center; sauna; room service; free Wi-Fi.

A BEACH RESORT OUTSIDE OF DAVID

Las Olas Resort ★ Open in some capacity since 2001, Las Olas is the only moderately upscale lodging option along Playa Barqueta, the lengthy, undeveloped black-sand beach near David. It offers lots of amenities, from tennis courts and spa to a pool and gym, making it an ideal quick weekend escape from David or Boquete. The smallish guest rooms feature white, blue, and turquoise aquatic decorations over tile floors and oceanview terraces. Common areas are tidy and well kept. A small spa offers massages and facials, while the restaurant emphasizes sourcing locally, including grass-fed beef from a neighboring ranch. The resort sells all-inclusive packages that include lodging, meals, drinks, and use of the facilities, or you can book for the night and order meals a la carte, but the latter is more expensive.

Playa Barqueta. www.lasolasresort.com. ☎ **831/920-4866** in the U.S. or 772-3000. 90 units. $86–$108 double; $128–$238 suite. **Amenities:** 2 restaurants; bar; outdoor pool; tennis courts; horseback riding; gym; sauna; spa; bike rentals; room service; free Wi-Fi.

A REMOTE SURF CAMP

Morro Negrito Surf Camp ★ This chilled-out surf camp is on Isla Ensenada 3.2km (2 miles) off the coast of the Chiriquí Gulf, about halfway between Santiago and David. The tiled rooms, all with shared bathrooms, are very rustic, with mosquito nets and electricity the only luxuries. The pleasant common areas include a yoga deck and a few nooks with hanging hammocks, though the focus here is on surfing. There are 10 different breaks, averaging between 1.2 and 2.4m (4–8 ft.), for beginners to advanced surfers. Rates include a daily boat trip to the best waves and three daily meals.

Isla Ensenada. www.morronegrito.travel. ☎ **760/332-8105** in the U.S. or 6561-6206. 10 units. $120 per day all-inclusive. No credit cards accepted at camp. **Amenities:** Restaurant; bar; surf lessons and surfboard rental; yoga; boat rides; horseback riding; media room with TV/DVDs; free Wi-Fi.

Where to Dine

Restaurante Cuatro ★★★ PANAMANIAN Although top restaurants in Panama City tend to highlight the country's cultural influences, Luis Mendizábal, a Culinary Institute of America in New York graduate, is more product driven, focusing on the ingredients in surrounding Chiriquí. This is one of the most biodiverse regions of the country, and Mendizábal uses that to his advantage, applying techniques such as making emulsions from *ají criollo* (spicy salsa) or fashioning gnocchi from the root vegetable otoe. The restaurant itself is quite relaxed, but for the quality Mendizábal puts out, his a la carte menu and six-course tasting menu are possibly the best restaurant value in all of Panama.

6176 Calle Estudiante at Av. Obaldía. www.restaurantecuatro.com. ✆ **730-5638.** Main courses $14–$20; tasting menu $50. Mon–Sat noon–3pm and 6:30–10:30pm.

VOLCÁN

33km (21 miles) N of David

The road from La Concepción to Volcán slowly winds 34km (21 miles) up from the humid lowlands and into a cooler climate with a landscape characterized by a patchwork of *fincas*, or dairy and cattle ranching farms. Eventually, the road opens up to a wide plateau and the village of Volcán, the highlands center for services such as banks, pharmacies, grocery stores, and just about everything else.

Although Volcán isn't as picturesque as Cerro Punta or Guadalupe, the fresh mountain air and open views of rugged landscape give Volcán a decidedly alpine atmosphere, part of the reason so many European immigrants chose to settle around here in the early 1900s. The town sits at the skirt of the Barú Volcano and offers grand views of that peak, although it is commonly shrouded with a layer of clouds and hidden from view.

Considering Volcán's location at the axis of the roads to Guadalupe and Río Sereno, near the Costa Rica–Panama border, the town is a convenient base from which to explore the western highlands area. Volcán is centered around a blink-and-you-miss-it main street, Avenida Central, which forks in the center. Head right to continue on to Guadalupe and Cerro Punta, and straight ahead for the road to Río Sereno and the Costa Rica.

Like Boquete, its neighbor to the west, Volcán and the surrounding mountain communities are being discovered by foreigners, which is evident in the new, foreign-owned restaurants that seem to be popping up all over the place.

Attractions are not within walking distance, and using a taxi will cost you just as much (or more) as renting a car. A 4WD vehicle will give you more freedom to visit some of the region's more remote and difficult-to-reach attractions.

Blackberry Wine: ¡Salud!

For more than 10 years, Abelardo Coba has been producing delicious organic blackberry wine, which he claims acts as a treatment for and prevention against circulatory problems. His wine is also rich in vitamin C and antioxidants, so you can feel good about drinking it. The blackberries are fermented for 20 days and matured in a barrel for 3 months. Pick up a bottle at his small facility, just before Volcán, located on the right side of the road. (You'll see a sign for VIÑA DON COBA).

Essentials

GETTING THERE & DEPARTING

BY BUS & TAXI   Buses to **Volcán, Cerro Punta,** and **Guadalupe** leave from the Terminal de Transportes in David every 35 minutes from 5am to 7pm ($2–$3). If traveling from Costa Rica, Panama City, or elsewhere, you'll need to transfer in David. A taxi from David to Volcán is $50, and to Guadalupe it is $60.

BY CAR   From the David airport, turn left and drive 3.4km (2 miles); then turn left again onto Calle Miguel Brenes (also called Calle F Sur). Continue for 1.8km (1 mile) until you reach the Interamericana Highway. Turn left and continue to Concepción, 21km (13 miles) after passing the Chiriquí Mall; then turn onto the road to Volcán and Cerro Punta. The drive from Concepción to Volcán is 34km (21 miles).

FAST FACTS

There is an ATM at **Banco Nacional** (⌀ **771-4282**), located on the main street in front of the police station, after the road forks, and another is located at HSBC Bank, diagonal to **Farmacia Volcán** (⌀ **771-4651**), open Sunday through Thursday 7:30am to 10pm; Friday 7:30am to 6pm; and Saturday 6 to 10pm. The **post office** can be found on the right-hand side of the road to Guadalupe, just after turning on the fork. It's open every day, except Sunday, from 7am to noon and 2 to 6pm.

TOUR OUTFITTERS

Check with your hotel regarding outdoor excursions, such as hiking in La Amistad and Volcán Barú parks, canoeing in Lagunas de Volcán, horseback riding, or bird-watching; otherwise, contact one of the tour operators based in Boquete.

Considering that the renowned Chiriquí Viejo River is on this side of the volcano, travelers can take part in absolutely thrilling white-water rafting offered by the Boquete-based company **Chiriquí River Rafting.**

What to Do & See Around Volcán

For information about Volcán Barú and La Amistad parks, see "Bambito, Cerro Punta & Guadalupe," p. 159.

Sitio Barriles ★   This is perhaps the most famous archaeological site in Panama. It's on the private land of the Landau family, whose grandfather discovered hundreds of artifacts when excavating to build a coffee plantation. The artifacts are from the Barriles culture, an indigenous population that lived in the area from 600 B.C. to 300 B.C. before being forced to evacuate after the eruption of Volcán Barú. It's a curious attraction because hardly anything is known about the culture, and accordingly little interpretive information is available to visitors. Artifacts include a burial tomb with funeral urns, pottery, and tools made of basalt. The Landau family offers guided tours in English and Spanish and also sells fresh cheese and homemade jams.

5.5km (3½ miles) SW of Volcán. Follow the Río Sereno road west out of Volcán; the turnoff is on the left. ⌀ **6607-5438.** $6 donation. Daily 7am–5pm.

Lagunas de Volcán ★ Along a rough, poorly maintained road sit the highest wetlands in Panama: Lagunas de Volcán. The wetlands comprise two lakes surrounded by exuberant forest, with dramatic views of Volcán Barú rising in the distance. It's a lovely spot to visit, but it especially draws bird-watchers who come to see northern jacanas, tanagers, collared trogons, emerald toucanets, masked ducks, and the rose-throated becard, among others. *Note:* You'll need a 4WD vehicle to get here. Considering that the Lagunas are close to the Janson coffee farm (see below), you might want to tie in a visit to both.

A 15-minute drive from Volcán. Turn left off the main road at the sign for Vía Aeropuerto at the Agroquímicas Volcán building, and follow the signs for Lagunas de Volcán. No admission fee.

Janson Coffee Farm ★★ The Janson Family produces extraordinary coffee, and a visit to their estate gives connoisseurs a chance to learn how coffee is processed (and, of course, to sample and buy coffee at the on-site shop). The splendid views of Volcán Barú and the Janson's lovely farm are worth the visit alone. The Jansons pride themselves on environmental protection, producing shade-grown, organic beans that are handpicked and roasted in small batches, and then packed up and shipped overseas to the U.S. and Europe. The farm tour is in Spanish and English and lasts about an hour; tours include a visit to the production facility, followed by a coffee tasting. Tours are operated by **Lagunas Adventures** (www.lagunasadventures.com; ℂ **6569-7494**). You can skip a tour if you like and visit the coffee shop for free.

Head west on the main road and turn left at the sign for the Vía Aeropuerto at the Agroquímicas Volcán building; continue until you see the sign for Janson Family Coffee, turn right, and continue to the airport strip, where you'll turn right and follow the signs. Tours range from $10 for a 1-hour tasting to $35 for a 3.5-hour Geisha VIP tour.

A NATURE SANCTUARY & COFFEE FARM

Part of the allure of a visit to **Finca Hartmann** ★★★ (ℂ **6450-1853**), west of Volcán, is the twisting road there, full of hairpin turns through beautiful dense forest, which surely ranks among the **top-five scenic drives in Panama.** The boutique coffee farm produces shade-grown, high-quality beans typically sold to small specialty distributors. What's fascinating about the tours is the care that goes into producing such flavorful beans and the Hartmann family's devotion and passion for the natural environment that surrounds them. More than anything else, the *finca* (farm) is known for is its position in the north–south corridor of migrating birds, thus ranking it as one of Panama's **bird-watching hot spots,** and many specialty bird-watching tours include this as part of their itinerary. Finca Hartman sits on the edge of La Amistad Parque Internacional; though they are not "official," hiking trails do exist and can be walked if reservations are made in advance. The only people you will see around the *finca* and along the trails—if you see anyone at all—are Ngöbe-Buglé Indians.

A wooden *rancho* has an attractive coffee-tasting area and a small museum containing extensive bug collections and indigenous artifacts collected in the century that the Hartmanns have lived here. Coffee tours cost $15 per person, but a better bet is to plan a **walking-and-coffee tour** that includes lunch—contact Finca Hartmann for prices (each full-day tour is organized and priced individually). The Hartmanns also have two rustic cabins tucked away in a small cloud forest at the end of a very rough road. Finca Hartmann is located in the tiny community of Santa Clara, on the road to Río Sereno. The turnoff is 27km (17 miles) from Volcán. Turn at the signed road and drive 1km (½ mile) until you reach the *finca.*

SHOPPING FOR HANDICRAFTS

Just before entering Volcán, on your left-hand side is **Arte Cruz ★★★** (www.artecruzpanama.com; *①* **6622-1502**), a shop that showcases the exquisite woodworking and glasswork crafted by the talented José de la Cruz, who studied his craft in Italy. He's usually there between 8am and noon and 1:30 and 5pm, but call ahead to make sure he's around. You can watch him work for as long as you like. José has many ready-made items for sale, but given a few days he'll also custom-carve anything from signs to furniture to doors, which can be shipped to you or picked up later—so stop here on your way into the area, rather than on your way out.

Where to Stay & Dine

Restaurants close very early in Volcán, usually at 9pm (or earlier when tourism's low).

Cerro Brujo Gourmet ★★ CONTEMPORARY PANAMANIAN   This small farm-to-table restaurant, using herbs and vegetables from the chef's own organic garden, is the best dining option in Panama west of Volcán Barú. The restaurant offers a fixed-price menu that changes daily according to what's fresh and usually includes just a few appetizers and entrees with chicken, beef, fish or vegetarian. Chef Patricia Miranda does wonders with local ingredients such as the tropical fruit, pixbae, otherwise known as *chontadura,* which she prepares in a traditional stew.

Brisas del Norte. *①* **6669-9196.** Reservations recommended for lunch and dinner. Fixed-price menu $15–$20 per person. Daily noon–3pm and 6–9pm. (Call to verify open days during low season.)

Hotel Dos Ríos ★   On the outskirts of town, Volcán's best lodging has been around in some form since 1970, though it was completely rebuilt in 2001. There's nothing of an old-timey feel here. The big, bright log-cabin–like lobby and towering stone entryway feel rather modern, a vibe that extends into the wood-floor guest rooms, which feature stenciled wall paintings. Suites, on the end of the two-level structure, add a sofa bed. The hotel's moderately priced on-site restaurant, **Estrella Volcanera Restaurant,** serves decent international fare, mostly meats, pasta, and fish, and has a pizzeria (daily 7am–10pm). The staff can put together tours for guests.

Vía Río Sereno, west end of town. www.dosrios.com.pa. *①* **771-5555** or 771-4271. 18 units. $77 double; $99 junior suite; $150 suite. **Amenities:** Restaurant; bar; kids' play area; room service; Internet access.

BAMBITO, CERRO PUNTA & GUADALUPE ★★★

Bambito is 18km (11 miles) N of Volcán; Cerro Punta is 7km (4¼ miles) from Bambito; Guadalupe is 2.5km (1½ miles) from Cerro Punta

Bambito, Cerro Punta, and Guadalupe are three of a dozen or so tiny farming communities nestled in a bucolic, alpine paradise. The area is characterized by rugged hills and peaks cloaked in thick emerald forest speckled with flowers and interspersed with a patchwork of colorful fields. Bambito is just a sprinkling of homes and services along the road. Cerro Punta is located in the crater of an extinct volcano and is the epicenter of agricultural production. Cerro Punta sits at 1,800m (5,900 ft.), looking out over a fertile valley and craggy peaks beyond, and provides for a quick scenic drive past strawberry and flower farms. Guadalupe, too, has flower-filled streets and is flanked by quilt-like farms that slope up the surrounding hills. From here, the roads branch out to La Amistad International Park and Volcán Barú National Park. This is truly the loveliest alpine region in Panama.

What to See & Do in the Northwestern Highlands

For information about hiking in **Volcán Barú National Park,** see "What to See & Do," in the Boquete section, below. Hikers on this side of the park are usually headed to Boquete along the stunning **Quetzal Trail.** The trail from this side of the volcano to Boquete is mostly downhill, and it's recommended that hikers walk the trail in this direction unless they're looking for a strenuous workout. If you don't plan on hiking this trail in its entirety, it's worth walking a portion of it and then heading back when you've had enough. The Respingo ranger station can be reached by walking 45 minutes up a rutted road from the main road near Bajo Grande, or by driving a 4WD to the station, where you'll find a high-altitude picnic site with views.

HIKING IN PARQUE INTERNACIONAL LA AMISTAD ★★★

La Amistad Park, popularly known by the Spanish acronym PILA, is "international" in that half the park is located in Costa Rica. It was formed in 1988 by the Panamanian and Costa Rican governments to protect the virgin forests and fragile ecosystems of the rugged Talamanca Range and its surrounding lowland buffer zones, as well as to protect one of the most biodiverse areas in the Americas. UNESCO designated the park a World Heritage Site in 1990, and for the most part the park is totally untouched, creating a home for an extraordinary array of more than 100 mammal species, including endangered tapirs, jaguars, ocelots, pumas, and howler monkeys. There are also more than 400 species of birds, including resplendent quetzals, crested eagles, harpy eagles, three-wattled bellbirds, and a rare umbrellabird. The Panama side of the park encompasses 207,000 hectares (511,500 acres), the majority of which is part of the Bocas del Toro Province—but it is here at the administration area near Cerro Punta where hikers can access the primeval rainforest that is this park's characteristic feature. This is one of the wettest regions in Panama, so come prepared with waterproof clothing and shoes.

Four trails leave from the ranger station. **Sendero Puma Verde** is the easiest walk here and can be completed in 15 minutes. **Sendero El Retoño** is 2.1km (1.3 miles) and an easy 1-hour loop trail that is mostly flat. The trail is simply gorgeous, taking hikers through a dense jungle and a bamboo tunnel and across babbling brooks. Signs along the way identify trees and other plants. **Sendero La Cascada** is 3.5km (2 miles) and about a 2-hour round-trip hike to a series of lookout points with mountain and valley views and a crashing 49m (160-ft.) waterfall. Along the way is a detour to a lookout point that, on a very clear day, offers a view that stretches to the Caribbean. Taking this detour will add an extra 1½ hours to your trip; take a left at the fork at the Mirador Barranco. About half of this hike is uphill, so it's moderately strenuous.

Lastly, **Sendero Cerro Picacho** takes gung-ho hikers along a narrow and poorly marked trail through primary forest up to a peak at 2,937m (9,636 ft.), where you can see from the Pacific to the Caribbean—and you can even spend the night here in a rustic hut. This trail is uphill, about 4km (2.5 miles), and a strenuous slog that should not be attempted without a guide. If you're not already booked with a guide, call the co-op near the ranger station (see below for the number) and they can arrange one. It takes about 3½ hours each way for this trail.

La Autoridad Nacional del Ambiente de Panamá (ANAM) charges $5 per person to enter the park. Hours are daily from 8am to 4pm. You can visit the **Asociación Agroecoturística La Amistad (ASAELA;** ✆ **771-2620;** daily 8am–4pm) co-op near the station, which has a small cafe with breakfast and daily specials such as stewed chicken, beans, and rice. It also sells locally produced preserves and other goodies. There are also rustic bunks and camping available for a small fee.

FINCA DRACULA ★★

Despite the spooky name, this *finca* is revered as one of the most important orchid farms in Central America, displaying more than 2,200 species that are cloned to produce 250,000 plants yearly. The farm claims to have Latin America's most complete collection of rare Central and Latin American orchid species, some of which no longer exist in their natural habitat. It's owned by master orchid horticulturist Andres Maduro, who bought the property in 1969 and has allowed the former cattle ranch to reforest and return to its natural, exuberantly tropical state. The name of the *finca* refers to the Dracula orchid, an elegant purple flower that hides itself during daylight. Peak months are from April to June, but on any day you're bound to see dozens of orchids in full bloom. Tours are $10 per person and include a visit through the facilities and laboratory. Finca Dracula (www.fincadracula.com; ✆ **771-2070**) is open Monday through Friday from 8 to 11:30am and 1 to 5pm.

Where to Stay & Dine

In contrast to Volcán, the lodging options below are nestled in forested areas that put travelers closer to natural surroundings (with the exception of Hotel

Cerro Punta) and the two parks. Aside from the options included below, **Cabañas Kucikas** (www.kucikas.com; ℘ **771-4245**) offers 18 stand-alone units for $80 to $200, but you'll need to bring your own soap and toilet paper.

Casa Grande ★   This 121-hectare (300-acre) forested property, bordered by river and dense forest, is in a location as beautiful as they come. It is criss-crossed with trails and dirt roads, perfect for quiet hikes with staff guides and bike rides, and there's an artificial lagoon with trout fishing and a zipline canopy ride as well. Guest rooms boast handsome teak and pine paneling and polished wood floors. The **spa** here is very complete, reasonably priced, and open to the public with advance notice. The **restaurant** serves tasty international fare with main courses ranging from $7 to $18; hours are 7am to 10pm.

Bambito. www.casagrandebambito.com. ℘ **201-5555** or 771-5126. 20 units. $123–$196 suites. **Amenities:** Restaurant; bar; outdoor adult and children's pools; full-service spa; bike rentals; children's play area; room service.

Cielito Sur ★★   In Nueva Suiza, between Volcán and Cerro Punta, this family-run mountain estate dates to 1948, though it was expanded in 2000. The property oozes country tableaus, from the large parlor with a fieldstone fireplace to the porch overlooking a stream stocked with rainbow trout. Rooms, named after Panamanian indigenous groups, have a laidback rustic feel and are decorated with native artwork. In the house there's a comfy living room with reclining chairs and a well-stocked library, while outside a short trail winds through the property and a thatched *bohio* hut is lined with hammocks. There is a 2-night minimum stay during the high season.

Nueva Suiza. www.cielitosur.com. ℘ **771-2038.** 5 units. $105–$125 double. Rates include breakfast. Closed Oct. Children 11 and under not accepted. **Amenities:** Whirlpool; bike rentals; free Wi-Fi.

Los Quetzales Ecolodge & Spa ★   Set beside a river in the village of Guadalupe, on a 400-hectare (988-acre) reserve, Los Quetzales' backcountry cabins appeal to hikers, nature lovers, and bird-watchers alike. Although the standard rooms are rather cramped, the suites are a bit better with wood-paneled walls, kitchenettes, and fireplaces. The real find here are the rustic cabins with patio terraces that are submerged in the cloud forest of Volcán Barú National Park, surrounded by wildlife and close to trail heads for hiking.

Guadalupe. www.losquetzales.com. ℘ **771-2182.** 22 units, 6 cabins. $85–$95 double; $135–$165 suite; $120–$240 cabin; $18 per-person dorm. **Amenities:** Restaurant; bar; horseback riding; volleyball; spa; bike rentals; tours; free Wi-Fi.

WEST OF VOLCÁN BARÚ: BOQUETE ★★★

40km (25 miles) from David; 473km (294 miles) from Panama City

This is the destination of choice for most tourists visiting the Chiriquí Highlands, and with a sizable chunk of the population hailing from the United States, Canada, or Europe, it feels somewhat like a tropical colony—you'll find plenty of foreign-owned, international restaurants here, and you'll get along just fine even if you don't speak a word of Spanish.

Boquete is located in a steep-walled, green, and flower-filled valley on the flank of the Barú Volcano and at the shore of the Caldera River. Despite its utilitarian downtown made of cheap, concrete-poured buildings, the town on the whole is charming and offers a bounty of activities for travelers. With so many foreigners living in the area, mostly in large-scale gated communities on the outskirts, Boquete has indeed taken on a more international feel than its counterpart Cerro Punta on the other side of the volcano. But given the bounty of services, tours, attractions, gourmet restaurants, and wide scale of lodging options, Boquete makes an ideal base for exploring the Chiriquí Highlands. Travelers who are keen to hike the Quetzal Trail would do well to visit Cerro Punta on the western side of the volcano first and then walk to Boquete, sending their luggage around by vehicle.

Essentials
GETTING THERE & DEPARTING
Most hotels either provide transportation from the David airport or can arrange for you to be picked up by an independent taxi driver for the 45-minute drive to Boquete.

BY BUS & TAXI Buses for Boquete leave from the David bus terminal every 25 minutes, take approximately 1 hour, and cost $2 one-way. You can catch a bus from Boquete to David from the north side of the main plaza. If you're coming from Bocas del Toro or from Panama City, you'll need to transfer in David. It takes 7 hours by bus from Panama City and costs $15 to $20. A taxi from David to Boquete costs approximately $25 to $30 one-way.

BY CAR If you're driving from Panama City, you'll turn right on the signed turnoff for Boquete before entering David. From the airport in David, turn right onto the main road, drive until you arrive at the intersection with the Shell station, and then turn left. Drive until you reach a stop sign at the four-lane highway, turn right, and continue until you reach the intersection at the supermarket. Turn left and continue onward to Boquete.

The road to Boquete is well paved; two side roads provide shortcuts if you're driving from the Bocas del Toro area.

GETTING AROUND
I strongly recommend **renting a car** in Boquete—it's the best way to explore the countryside at your own pace. It's a good idea to rent your car from the David airport (p. 151); alternatively, some hotels will arrange for a rental car to be delivered to you in Boquete.

Taxis around town cost $2 to $4. Unless your hotel is located in the town center, you'll need one to get back and forth. Have your hotel call for a taxi or flag one down on the main strett.

RESTAURANTS ◆
Art Café 11
Deli Barú 10
Machu Picchu 16
Morton's Bakehouse 18
The Panamonte 5
The Rock 2
Sabrosón 9

ATTRACTIONS ●
Boquete Bees 3
Boquete Mountain
  Safari Tours 13
Boquete Outdoor
  Adventures 15
Boquete Tree Trek 4
Chiriquí River Rafting 14

HOTELS ■
The Coffee Estate Inn 6
Finca Lérida 8
Hotel Oasis 17
Hotel Panamonte 5
Hotel Villa Marita 1
Isla Verde Hotel 12
Los Establos 7

ARCO IRIS

ALTO LINO

PALO ALTO

Río Palo Alto

HORQUETA

LOS NARANJOS

BAJO LINO

Río Caldera

To Sendero
Los Quetzales

To Volcán
Barú (peak)

LOS CABEZOS

Quebrada La Zumbona

JARAMILLO ARRIBA

Quebrada Grande

Volcán Barú
3,475 m
(11,400 ft)

See inset map

BOQUETE

JARAMILLO CENTRO

VOLCANCITO

APT
Visitor's Center

JARAMILLO ABAJO

Río Caldera

Iglesia
San Juan
Bautista

Feria de
las Flores

Calle Central

Av. A Oeste

Av. A Este

Av. B Este

Calle 1 Sur

Av. A Este

Av. B Oeste

Avenida Central

Calle 2 Sur

Parque
D. Médica

Calle
4 Sur

Calle

Police

Río Caldera

Calle 5 Sur

Av. A Este

Av. B Porras

Gas Station

ALTO BOQUETE

To La Estrella

Caribbean
Sea

Colón

Panama City

Boquete

P A N A M A

Golfo de
Panamá

43

0   50 mi
0   50 km

0   1/2 mi
0   500 m

VISITOR INFORMATION

Pick up tourist information and maps at the **Centro de Interpretación y Facilidades Tursíticas (CEFATI) visitor center** (✆ **720-4060;** daily 9am–4:30pm; part of ATP), the large building on your right just before you enter town. With its location high above the Río Caldera, the visitor center provides sweeping views of town. You'll find **Café Kotowa** here, too, with a small shop. On the center's second floor is an interpretive display (in Spanish) of the history and anthropology of the region. Ask for a representative here to give you a quick tour and translate the displays.

ORIENTATION

The main street, Avenida Central, runs the length of town from north to south, and businesses and transportation services are clustered around the main plaza on streets that run east–west. From downtown, a series of paved and gravel roads climb the hilly terrain surrounding Boquete.

FAST FACTS

BANKS/ATMS   Twenty-four-hour ATMs can be found up and down the main drag. Among them, **Banco Nacional** and **Global Bank** lie across from each other at Calle 5 Sur.

EMERGENCY   For the **police,** dial ✆ **104;** for the **fire department,** dial ✆ **720-1224.**

MEDICAL   The **Centro Médico San Juan Bautista** (www.cmsanjuan bautista.com; ✆ **503/2301-1850**), located on Avenida Central, 2 blocks up the road past the Hotel Panamonte, has English-speaking doctors; for serious health problems, you'll need to head to the hospital in David.

POST OFFICE   The **post office** is located on the plaza. It's open Monday to Friday 8am to 5:45pm and Saturday 8am to 4:45pm.

What to See & Do

There's no shortage of things to see and do in Boquete, from adrenaline-pumping outdoor adventures to quiet forays in the rainforest seeking the elusive quetzal to walks among perfume-scented flowers at public gardens. You can learn about ultra-premium Geisha coffee or the local Ngöbe-Buglé tribe . . . and the list goes on. As mentioned earlier, a lot of visitors opt to rent a car—the area offers so many beautiful scenic drives.

The **Bajo Mono Loop** takes you high above the town along an asphalted road for panoramic vistas and beautiful forest scenery. This is a good drive

A Mist So Soft It Caresses the Face: The *Bajareque*

The *bajareque* is a unique weather phenomenon that occurs from December to March, when a fine misting rain is pushed over from the Atlantic and into the highlands. The mist is so soft it "caresses the face," as locals like to say. The combination of sun, wind, and *bajareque* provides endless rainbows.

from which to get your bearings and see why everyone's gone wild about living in Boquete. To get here, follow the main road past the church and head left at the fork, staying left until you see the sign for BAJO MONO. Just as pretty is the **Volcancito Loop**—to get here, follow the main road out of town and when you see the CEFATI visitor center, turn right and follow the loop until you arrive back at town. You can bike these loops as well. (See "Biking," below.)

One of the most beautiful drives in Panama heads to **Finca Suiza** (p. 177) on the main road to the Atlantic Coast in the Bocas del Toro Province. The scenic drive winds through mountain forests and open fields with sweeping views, and farther down to the lush lowlands and rainforest of Bocas Province. Take the left turn to Caldera 16km (10 miles) south of Boquete and continue along paved and gravel roads until you hit the major road to Bocas.

Boquete Mountain Safari Tours (http://boquetesafari.com; ☎ **6627-8829** or 6742-6614) offers bilingual, open-air yellow jeep tours. They offer wildlife tours ($35), as well as half-day tours to the Caldera Hot Springs ($35) and jeep trips to the summit of the volcano ($125), among others. The ATV coffee tour travels through the lush cloud forest and mountainsides to visit various boutique coffee estates for tastings ($65). Boquete Mountain Safari Tours is a professional operation, and all tour guides speak English. Check the website for a full listing of full- and half-day excursions.

HIKING & BIRD-WATCHING OUTFITTERS/GUIDES

The following tour outfitters and local guides offer hiking, bird-watching, and other general excursions to destinations and attractions listed below in this section. With its new office in Boquete, the reputable Panama City–based adventure company **Ecocircuitos** recently closed its Boquete office, but the company's Boquete representative can be reached at **6617-6566**. Ecocircuitos is a one-stop shop for short adventures in the Chiriquí area; it offers kayaking, hiking, family adventures, and bird-watching day trips and focuses on green tourism that promotes local communities.

Coffee Adventures (www.coffeeadventures.net; ☎ **720-3852**), offers guided excursions around Boquete, and their bird-watching tours are particularly good. Coffee Adventures offers cultural excursions to a Ngöbe-Buglé community near the Caribbean Coast, guided hikes on Los Quetzales Trail from Boquete to Cerro Punta (or vice versa), and low-key excursions like bird-watching and trips to the Caldera Hot Springs. For more on Coffee Adventures, see "Coffee Tours," below.

Boquete Tree Trek (www.boquetetreetrek.com; ☎ **720-1635**) and **Boquete Outdoor Adventures** (www.boqueteoutdooradventures.com; ☎ **720-2284** or 6630-1453) also offer hiking and bird-watching tours of Boquete, the surrounding area, and the Chiriquí lowlands. For more on Boquete Tree Trek, see "River Rafting & Kayaking," below. For more on Boquete Outdoor Adventures, see "Other Outdoor Activities in the Area," below.

SPAS

The best spa in town is the **Haven** (www.boquetespa.com; ☎ **730-9345**), located just left of the Accel gas station. Boquete's best gym is also here, and you can take part in exercise and aquatic classes, use their whirlpool and infrared sauna, or enjoy a hot stone or traditional massage. Most of the staff speaks English. There is also a small boutique hotel on-site if you want to focus your visit to Boquete on the Haven. The spa offers day passes for $25 and week passes for $50, which allow guests to use the pool, gym, sauna, and whirlpool. There are also spas at **Valle Escondido** and **Isla Verde** (www. boquetemassage.com; © **6948-6664**).

EXPLORING EL PARQUE NACIONAL VOLCÁN BARÚ

As the name states, this national park is centered around the 3,475m (11,400-ft.) extinct **Barú Volcano,** the highest point in the country and the beloved center of adventurous outdoor pursuits for bird-watchers, hikers, rafters, and nature lovers. The park is situated on the Pacific-facing side of the Talamanca Mountain Range, encompassing 14,000 hectares (34,600 acres) of rugged topography cloaked in primary and secondary rainforest. This rainforest provides a home to nearly 250 species of birds, the most notable of which is the **resplendent quetzal,** whose extraordinary beauty puts the bird in the number-one spot on many a bird-watching list. Other rare birds here include the silky flycatcher, the three-wattled bellbird, and the hairy woodpecker. Thanks to the volcano's height and isolation, this area is considered a "bioclimatic island." Its forest is home to unique species of orchids and uncommon flora such as magnolia and giant oak trees, some of which are between 600 and 900 years old. You'll also see wild bamboo gardens and gigantic, gnarled trees dripping with vines and sprouting prehistoric-looking bromeliads from their trunks. In higher reaches, an intermittent cloud forest provokes an eerie ambience. It's a wonderful place to hike and immerse yourself in wild beauty, but come prepared with waterproof outerwear and shoes and a dry change of clothes. In this national park, temperatures average 50° to 60°F (10°–16°C).

Natural beauty aside, the park is economically important because it protects the headwaters that provide irrigation to the country's prime agricultural region, concentrated in the fertile areas of the volcano's skirt. These rivers are also revered by rafters and kayakers for their Class III to V rapids, which provide thrills and a sense of remote solitude.

Volcán Barú National Park is administered by ANAM, which has ranger stations at the Los Quetzales trail heads in both Boquete (Alto Chiquero) and Cerro Punta (El Respingo) and charges a $5-per-person entrance fee. Both ranger stations have a handful of truly rustic bunks with shared bathrooms. There's not much ambience at the Boquete station to encourage even the hardiest of nature lovers to lodge there, however. A taxi to the ranger station, about 8km (5 miles) from Boquete, costs around $5.

HIKING By any measure, the most popular trail is **Sendero Los Quetzales** ★★★, a superb, short-haul day hike—regarded as the best in Panama by most visitors to the country. The rainforest here is thick, lush, and dazzling with its array of colorful birds, panoramic lookout points, and crystalline streams rushing across velvety moss-covered rocks. Most important, and most unique, is the fact that the trail connects Cerro Punta (and Guadalupe) with Boquete, allowing hikers to have their baggage sent from one town to the other, and to arrive by foot at their next destination. If you're physically up to it, the entire trek is one of the region's highlights—but there are *a few things to consider* before setting out. First, Cerro Punta's altitude is 1,981m (6,500 ft.), while Boquete's is 975m (3,200 ft.)—so the trail is mostly downhill from Cerro Punta. Going in reverse from Boquete is tough, so unless you are looking for a workout, it's best to start with the western region of the volcano first and then Boquete.

For those who want to just get out and hike around a little, you'll be okay because the first couple of kilometers from the Boquete ranger station are relatively flat, offer outstanding opportunities to see birds (especially the quetzal), and put you in the middle of a stream-lined forest. You can walk as little or as much as you like and then turn around and head back.

The Quetzales Trail from Boquete begins with a 45-minute walk from the ranger station on a semi-paved road. After the sign for the trail head, the trail continues for about 2 hours before heading up into a steep ascent. Midway up the ascent is a picnic area with tables. Farther up, about halfway along the trail, is a sweeping lookout point, with a roofed eating area and a couple of campsites.

From the Cerro Punta ranger station, a rutted road requiring a 4WD heads downhill for almost 3km (1¾ miles) until it reaches the paved road to Cerro Punta. Tour operators and taxis with 4WD traction can make it up and down this road, but few seem willing—so prepare yourself to walk this portion. The total number of trail miles is anyone's guess, as park signs, rangers, and tour guides all disagree on the distance; it's estimated that the trail is about 9.7km (6 miles). From station to station, plan on 6 to 7 hours if walking uphill, and 4½ hours if walking downhill, plus another 45 minutes to 1 hour for the last leg of the Cerro Punta ranger station to the road.

Keen adventurers might be interested in the trail to the **volcano's summit,** a very arduous climb that puts visitors at the highest point in Panama and offers electrifying views from the Caribbean Sea to the Pacific Ocean. Although this trail can be reached from the Cerro Punta side, the trail from the Boquete side is far easier and better marked. You don't want to get lost on the volcano and spend the night freezing in the wet rainforest. This is but one of the serious considerations you must make when attempting to summit the volcano. The trail, an old service road, is ragged and rough, and even the most agile hikers often slip and fall on the slick downhill trip. Second, the trail is confusing in some areas, so it's highly recommended that you hire a guide. Lastly, the peak is shrouded in thick clouds with such frequency that the chances of seeing the view are not particularly good, but even on good-weather days you'll want to begin the hike at the crack of dawn to increase your chances of clear skies. The trail takes between 5 and 6 hours to climb, and about 4 to 5 hours to descend.

RIVER RAFTING & KAYAKING

The translucent rivers that pour down the Talamanca Mountain Range in the Chiriquí Highlands provide for thrilling Class III to V white-water kayaking and rafting, plus gentler floats for the whole family. What's special about the Chiriquí area is that relatively few paddlers have discovered it, so rafters and kayakers will have the crystalline river and pristine, tropical mountain scenery—replete with birds and wild animals—all to themselves. Also, the variety and number of rivers in this area provide fanatics with a week of rafting or kayaking.

Technical rides that are 2 to 5 hours in duration with Class III to V conditions are principally on the **Chiriquí River** east of Volcán Barú and close to Boquete, and the **Chiriquí Viejo River** west of the volcano, near the Costa Rica border. The Chiriquí Viejo River is revered by rafters for its challenging rapids and exuberant scenery, but it is a full-day trip that requires a scenic drive to the other side of the volcano. (Visitors to Volcán or Cerro Punta are closer to the put-in site for this river.) There are tamer floats, too, such as the **Esti River,** a Class II that is perfect for young rafters, families, and beginners; and the **Gariche River,** with Class II and III rapids that are suitable for beginners but a bit more technical and adrenaline-charged than an easy float. Many rivers can be rafted year-round, but others, like the Chiriquí and the Gariche, are rafted from July to November when the rivers are full.

Two reputable rafting companies in Boquete have years of experience and expert knowledge of the region. **Chiriquí River Rafting,** on Avenida Central (www.panama-rafting.com; ✆ **720-1505** or 6618-0846), is run by Héctor Sanchez, a rafting pioneer in the Chiriquí Highlands, with more than 2 decades of experience and an excellent safety record. Héctor and his guides are fluent in English. Depending on the river and logistics, rafting trips cost between $60 and $90 and require a minimum of four guests (a few trips require only three guests); trips include all gear, transportation, and lunch. Héctor can also plan multiple-day packages that include rafting, hiking, fishing, and more. Note that Chiriquí River Rafting offers accommodations at **El Bajareque Lodge,** a hostel-like spot with dynamite views, simple bunks, and communal meals; Héctor also offers more upscale rooms in his private home.

Boquete Outdoor Adventures (www.boqueteoutdooradventures.com; ✆ **720-2284** or 6630-1453) is run by the friendly and enthusiastic Jim Omer and specializes in white-water kayaking trips, offering a number of different excursions in the Chiriquí Highlands as well as the Boca Chica Region. Some of its sea-kayak excursions include Boca Brava and the 1-day white-water kayak sampler, which serves as an introduction to white-water kayaking. There are motorboat excursions to the Laguna de Chiriquí and the Golfo de Chiriquí, as well as excellent excursions to Isla Coiba. Trips range from $65 to $90 per person.

OTHER OUTDOOR ACTIVITIES IN THE AREA

BIKING   Boquete provides visitors with kilometer upon kilometer of picturesque, winding roads; moderate terrain; and pastoral views. Bicyclists on main paved roads will need to keep an eye open for speeding motorists, however, as there are lots of blind curves and virtually no shoulders. For bike rentals, check out **Boquete Tree Trek** (see "Canopy Tours," below). The cost to rent is $4 per hour.

CANOPY TOURS   Canopy tours, the adventure fad of zipping through the treetops suspended by a harness attached to a cable, are available through **Boquete Tree Trek** at Avenida Central (www.boquetetreetrek.com; ✆ 720-1635). This exhilarating ride is appropriate for kids as young as 3, and the weight limit for each rider is 113 kilograms (250 lb.) for men and 77 kilograms (170 lb.) for women. The zipline is 3km (1¾ miles) long, with a drop of 351m (1,150 ft.), and is located in the upper reaches of the Palo Alto valley, about 45 minutes from town. A 2½- to 3-hour canopy adventure costs $65.

HORSEBACK RIDING   **Franklin Rovetto** (✆ 6588-5054), a local guide from Caldera that speaks English and Spanish, runs 2½-hour backcountry horseback riding tours for $35. Also contact **Ecocircuitos** (see "Hiking & Bird-Watching Outfitters/Guides," above) and **Boquete Mountain Safari** (see "What to See & Do," above) for horseback rides around town and to coffee farms.

COFFEE TOURS

Did you know that Panama produces some of the most flavorful coffee in the world? A relatively new player on the gourmet-coffee market, the country produces traditional shade-grown-coffee varieties that are generally considered to be more complex and distinctive than those produced by its more famous neighbor, Costa Rica. In particular, Geisha, a varietal that was brought here from Ethiopia and then mutated, has made the region famous among coffee aficionados. Most coffee plantations in Panama are centered around Boquete—the region boasts fertile volcanic soil and the high altitude required for prime coffee growing.

Coffee tours are available and highly recommended. Even coffee snobs will glean insight not only into the meticulous growing process, but the economics of the local Ngöbe-Buglé indigenous labor and culture, as well as the "shade-grown" theory in protecting the environment and growing a better bean (see "Shade-grown Coffee, Songbirds & the Environment," below). Tours are capped off with a "cupping," which, much like a wine tasting, lets you sample different flavors, strengths, and roasts. In addition to the following companies, see Finca Lérida under "Attractions in & Around Town," below.

Casa Ruiz, S.A. ★ (www.caferuiz-boquete.com; ✆ 730-9570), is one of the oldest coffee producers in the country and the largest coffee-roasting organization. A guided tour entails a three-stop visit: to the plantation, the processing plant, and the roasting-and-packaging facility. This is an ideal tour for those interested in seeing large-scale production that includes boutique operation and quality traceability. Visits, led by a bilingual local Ngöbe-Buglé guide, are offered Monday through Saturday from 9am to noon or 1:30 to 4:30pm; the cost is $30 per person. Alternatively, you can visit the roasting facility for a 90-minute general information session on high-end quality coffee; the cost is $15 per person.

Café Kotowa ★ (www.kotowacoffee.com; ℂ **720-1430**) is a boutique coffee farm founded nearly a century ago by a Scottish immigrant, and it's still run by the same family. Kotowa, the indigenous word for "mountain," has earned a reputation for producing award-winning coffee beans, and though they've since moved on to modern production means, the farm's antique, water-powered mill still exists and is part of the tour. Visits to Kotowa are one-stop—first you amble through the coffee plantation behind the mill, then you tour the production-and-roasting facility, and finally you have a cupping in the old mill. The tour is led by **Coffee Adventures** (www.coffeeadventures. net; ℂ **720-3852**), which pioneered coffee tours in Boquete and whose guides are animated and amusing. Tours are Monday through Saturday at 2pm and cost $35 per person, which includes transportation from Boquete to the farm in Palo Alto. Children must be 10 or older, unless they're part of a private tour.

Nuare Tours (www.gnuaretours.com; ℂ **6225-4433**), runs trips to the quirky **Finca La Milagrosa ★**, a wild and untamed plot of land where the owner has created his own roasting equipment from old car parts. Tours are at 9am and 2pm and last 2 to 3 hours, costing $35 per person.

Finca Lérida ★★★ (see below) also offers coffee tours.

SPANISH-LANGUAGE PROGRAMS

Habla Ya Spanish School, located on Plaza Los Establos (www.hablaya panama.com; ℂ **730-8344**), offers intensive "survival" Spanish courses, as

SHADE-GROWN COFFEE, songbirds & THE ENVIRONMENT

Although modern coffee plantations tend to be destructive to the surrounding flora and fauna, shade-grown coffee offers an alternative. The practice, which is common at coffee farms in the Boquete area, is actually a more traditional method of growing coffee beans. Most coffee plants are intolerant of direct sunlight, so hybrid varieties were developed in the 1970s that do not require shade trees. Production has increased, and these hybrids are often dependent on chemicals and cause soil erosion, leading to the clearing of more rainforest so more coffee can be planted. Coffee grown in the shade, on the other hand, is much more eco-friendly—it requires no chemical fertilizers, pesticides, or herbicides. The shade provided from the trees filters carbon dioxide, while their fallen leaves help retain moisture in the soil and minimize erosion. The variety of trees that provide the shade provide additional habitat for songbirds, whose populations have been on the decline since large-scale coffee plantations were introduced. There's yet another benefit: Not only is shade-grown coffee better for the environment, it *tastes* better. Shade-grown beans mature more slowly, allowing for more natural sugars and enhanced flavors, resulting in better-tasting coffee.

well as more advanced conversational and fluency courses. Beginner survival courses are ideal for the traveling monolinguals with little time in Boquete but who'd love to speak enough to get around; weekly group classes cost $725 for 20 hours; weekly private courses cost $225 for 10 hours and $395 for 20 hours.

ATTRACTIONS IN & AROUND TOWN

One of the more intriguing attractions here is **Boquete Bees** (http://boquete bees.com; ℂ 720-2929), located beyond Café Ruiz in Los Naranjos. A honey plant and coffee plantation, Boquete Bees offers 2-hour tours of their Casita de Miel, honey facilities, and coffee farm for $30 per person, which includes a tasting of different rare and gourmet honeys from native pollinators, showcasing the region's biodiversity.

Finca Lérida ★★★   This lovely 324-hectare (800-acre) coffee plantation, nature reserve, and ecolodge is located 10 minutes from Boquete in the lofty alpine setting of Alto Quiel. The *finca* is a hot spot for seeing the resplendent quetzal and is widely regarded as one of the most important bird-watching sites in Panama. It has three nature trails (one easy, two moderate) that offer a chance to put yourself in the middle of pristine primary and secondary forest. Independent visitors are charged $20 per person for access to the marked trails, but no maps or interpretive information are available. The *finca* works with the best local birding and naturalist guides, if you need one (it's highly recommended if you come to bird-watch); the cost is an additional $35. Or you can book a 2-hour coffee tour for $35 per person, and take to the trails after the tour.

Alto Quiel. www.fincalerida.com. ℂ **720-2285.** Access to trails: $20 per person; 2-hour coffee tour: $35 per person. Daily sunrise–sunset.

SHOPPING

Coffee is the local product you won't want to leave Boquete without, and bagged beans are sold all around town in cafes and grocery stores. **Café Kotowa,** at the visitor center just before town, sells top-rated blends along with souvenir and gift packs. No stores in the Tocuman International Airport sell coffee, though **Café Unido** branches in Panama City have access to the best *fincas* and have better roasting equipment than anywhere in Boquete. **Souvenir El Cacique,** on Avenida Central at the plaza, has handicrafts made by the Ngöbe-Buglé, Kuna, and Emberá indigenous groups, as well as handicrafts from indigenous groups all around Central America.

Where to Stay

Travelers can stay in town and be close to services and restaurants, or opt for lodging outside of the town center in a more forested setting. No hotel mentioned here is farther than a 10-minute drive from town.

Air-conditioning is available at some hotels, though really not necessary given the elevation here. Breakfast is included in the price unless otherwise specified.

Note that some hotels sell out for the Flower and Coffee Festival in January, so you'll need to plan ahead.

STOP & smell THE FLOWERS: FESTIVALS IN BOQUETE

Boquete's largest annual festival is the **Feria de las Flores y del Café (Flowers and Coffee Festival),** which coincides with the coffee-harvesting season and takes place at the local fairgrounds in mid-January. The festival is one of the grandest celebrations of flowers in the world, drawing thousands of people to Boquete, clogging roads, and filling up hotels (book well ahead of time). During the 10-day festival, the fairgrounds fill with lushly landscaped and intricately designed flower displays that stretch the length of the facilities. Local residents follow suit and spruce up their gardens too, giving Boquete the feel of a horticultural Xanadu. Coffee plays a big role, with tastings of local java and sales of coffee by the bag and by the cup. There are other festival-oriented attractions like food stands, live music, amusement rides, handicrafts booths, and more—these activities take place only during the festival, but from January to April the flower exhibits are on display daily; entrance fee is $1.

Later, in mid-April, Boquete holds the same kind of festival but on a reduced scale, the 4-day **Feria de Orquídeas (Orchid Festival),** when local orchid growers showcase thousands of varieties of these delicate flowers for public viewing (many orchids bloom in Apr). Other large-scale festivals in Boquete are celebrated nationally; however, considering Boquete's charm and desirable ambience, many Panamanians head here for a few days of respite. Book your hotel well ahead of time during these dates: Carnaval (Feb), Semana Santa (Holy Week before Easter), and Independence celebrations (weekends of Nov 3, 10, and 28).

EXPENSIVE

The Coffee Estate Inn ★ On a very steep slope overlooking a lush valley and the Volcán Barú, this quaint coffee estate has some of the most in-demand accommodations in the Boquete area. The three two-person bungalows each come equipped with a kitchen, living area, and outdoor terrace and are submerged in native forests brimming with flowers and wildlife, despite being just 2.5km (1½ miles) from downtown Boquete. You'll want a car if you're staying here, and owners can help you snag a good rate if you turn up without one. A continental breakfast of homemade breads, estate-grown fresh-roasted coffee, and fruit is delivered daily to guest bungalows, and one of the owners leads an on-site coffee tour. There is a 2-night minimum stay.

Jaramillo Arriba. www.coffeeestateinn.com. ✆ **720-2211.** 3 units. $180–$195 bungalow. Rates include continental breakfast. Children 14 and under not accepted. **Amenities:** Optional daily dinner service; library; free Wi-Fi.

Finca Lérida ★★★ This attractive ecolodge has quickly become Boquete's most emblematic hotel. It's set on one of the region's oldest and most historic coffee estates and a preeminent bird-watching destination. With their private porches and hammocks, the elegant guest rooms are outfitted with polished woods, flowered bedspreads, and tufted headboards (suites add a Jacuzzi tub and fireplace). Even more atmospheric are the cabins, particularly the two-level historic suite that dates to 1908 and has an old stone hearth and library. **La Brulerie** restaurant, with its sweeping terrace and international menu, paired with a **hotel coffee shop** that comes complete with hip brewing methods, gives Lerida top culinary credibility. Hiking tours around the property and farm, coffee tastings, and bird-watching excursions can be arranged for an additional fee.

Palo Alto. www.fincalerida.com. ✆ **720-1111.** 21 units. $205 doubles; $280 cabins. Rates include breakfast. **Amenities:** Restaurant; bar; café; tours; free Wi-Fi.

Hotel Panamonte ★   Dating to 1914, just 3 years after Boquete was founded, the Panamonte is tied to the history of the town. The landmark country-style inn, with its sky-blue paint, manicured gardens, and white picket fence, has maintained its sense of place maybe more than any other hotel in the area. The rooms are in a mix of older and newer buildings, some lovelier than others, like the spacious superior rooms in the original hotel or the terrace suite set in the back gardens. The hotel's fine restaurant, bar, and culinary program, headed by the great chef Charlie Collins, includes cooking classes for an additional fee. It's right in the center of town, making this one of the few hotels in Boquete where renting a car isn't necessary.

Av. Central (take a right at the fork). http://panamonte.com. ✆ **720-1324.** 31 units. $65 standard double; $132 cabin. **Amenities:** Restaurant; bar; full-service spa w/sauna and steam room; cooking school; free Wi-Fi.

Los Establos ★★   High on a grassy slope above Boquete amid 6.5 hectares (16 acres) of coffee plants, with spectacular views of the valley and Volcán Barú, Los Establos is one of the region's best full-service hotels. The ranch-style theme runs deep, with a terra-cotta–tiled roof, heavy iron chandeliers, and cowhide rugs, not to mention lots of dark woods and country decor. The rooms are all spacious, though if you want a view ask for one of the two suites, which have a glass-enclosed seating area and four-poster bed, or one of the stand-alone coffee cottages.

Jaramillo Arriba. www.losestablos.net. ✆ **720-2685.** 9 units. $180–$235 double and coffee cottages; $260–$330 suite. Extra person $35. Additional child 12 and under $25. Rates include full made-to-order breakfast and complimentary afternoon coffee and wine. **Amenities:** Bar; billiards; tours; free Wi-Fi (in main house and business center only).

MODERATE

Hotel Villa Marita ★   The views alone, from high atop the El Santuario plateau, 3.5km (2 miles) above town, are worth the very reasonable prices of these casual rooms and cottages. The standard rooms in the mustard-colored main building are rather plain with tile floors and clunky furnishings, though the ones in a detached newer wing open up to sweeping vistas of the mountains. Cottages add a lounge, plus a kitchen or a private terrace. A family unit that sleeps six to eight guests has a kitchen but lacks a view.

Alto Lino. http://villamaritaboquete.com. ✆ **720-2165.** 10 units. $77–$85 double; $120 cottage; $180 family cottage. Rates include continental breakfast. **Amenities:** Restaurant; lounge; billiards; free Wi-Fi.

Isla Verde Hotel ★ German-owned Isla Verde lies in a residential area a short walk from downtown Boquete. In addition to seven suites in the main building, the hotel has six cheery "roundhouses," round cabins based on native architecture, each of which sleeps four to six guests and has a kitchen and living area with a loft bed; the larger units add another bed on the ground level. The roundhouses are well designed and get lots of light, opening on to balconies and porches surrounded by lush greenery. The suites in the main building offer similar amenities, though some, like the Sark and Mariposa suites, are better than others. The hotel has a new onsite restaurant, **Mango,** which serves lunch and dinner.

Calle 2 Sur Bajo Boquete. www.islaverdepanama.com. ℂ **720-2533** or 6677-4009. 13 units. Prices based on double occupancy: $130 big roundhouse; $110 small round-house; $110–$160 suite. Extra person $20; children 5–8 $10; children 4 and under stay free in parent's room. **Amenities:** Restaurant; spa; laundry service; free Wi-Fi.

INEXPENSIVE

Hotel Oasis ★ Cheap and simple, this family-run hotel on the riverfront is more than reliable in a pinch. Things like bedspreads and curtains could get a facelift, but otherwise this place has good bones. It has the same tile floors and tidy bathrooms as pricier options, plus views of the volcano from rooms 1, 2, 4, 5, 11, and 12. The included breakfast is served on an outdoor patio, and a common area has a coffeemaker and microwave. The location is close to the fairgrounds, making it particularly convenient during the Flower Festival in mid-January.

Av. Buenos Aires, across the bridge. www.oasisboquete.com. ℂ **720-1586.** 17 units. $80–$108 double; $120–$180 suites. **Amenities:** Restaurant; free Wi-Fi.

Where to Dine

Given that many of Boquete's residents are retired folk who tend to dine in or not stay out too late, the restaurants mentioned below can unexpectedly close early or for the night during the low season from May to November. In addition to the places reviewed below, several kiosks and cafes offer quick meals and are worth considering.

Worth a stop is the locally famous **Fresas Mary** (ℂ **720-3394;** daily 9:30am–7pm), which you'll find on the left side of the road to Volcancito, reached by turning onto the road opposite the CEFATI visitor center. The specialties here are *batidos,* or fresh fruit drinks, made with strawberries and local fruit such as *guanábana* (soursop); they also make fresh yogurt and *duros,* or frozen fruit sherbet. Sandwiches and hamburgers go for $2.

The **Deli Barú** (ℂ **720-2619;** Tues–Sun 8am–10pm) is a gourmet deli with sandwiches, soups, and salads, and a market with an excellent selection of cheeses, cold cuts, wine, fresh bread, and specialty goodies. **Olga's** (ℂ **720-2123;** daily 7am–noon), located on Calle 6A S, near Avenida Belisario Porras, is *the* spot for breakfast. Have your omelets, fruit pancakes, and fresh coffee on their pleasant outdoor patio. **Restaurante Lourdes,** Avenida Central (ℂ **720-1031**), serves typical Panamanian fare at low prices. Centrally located

Sugar & Spice, Avenida Central (www.sugarandspiceboquete.com; ℰ **730-9376;** Thurs–Sat 8am–6pm and Sun 8am–4pm), is a bakery with cookies, fresh baked breads, and other tasty baked goods, as well as a great breakfast with killer burritos.

MODERATE

Art Café ★ MEDITERRANEAN   Run by a Panamanian and his New Yorker singer partner (who occasionally performs here), Art Café has a jovial, welcoming atmosphere. The place is always full of life, featuring colorful European-poster artwork decorating yellow and red walls. The menu has standouts like the almond-crusted trout and vegetarian lasagna, though the more simple options like the *croque monsieur* and burger are reliable too. The fresh baked bread is always superb, particularly paired with the lentil soup.

Calle Principal, next to Zanzibar. ℰ **6769-6090.** Main courses $7–$15. No credit cards. Tues–Sun 10am–9pm.

Machu Picchu ★ PERUVIAN   Homey, hearty Peruvian food suits the mountain atmosphere here. With the Gulf of Chiriquí still rather close, Peruvian chef Aristóteles pulls off a seafood-heavy menu of dishes like ceviches and grilled sea bass, though classic Peruvian criollo dishes like *lomo saltado* (stir-fried beef and potatoes) are good too. Weekday fixed-priced lunches are one of the best dining values in Boquete. The decor—yellow and blue walls accented with Peruvian art—makes it feel a bit like a strip-mall Mexican restaurant in an American suburb, though in a weird way it's comforting.

Av. Belisario Porras. ℰ **264-9308.** Main courses $7–$16. Daily 11am–3pm and 6–11pm.

The Panamonte ★★★ INTERNATIONAL   Due to his experience with the products of the region and his decades in the kitchen, Panamanian Charlie Collins is one of the most recognizable chefs in the country. Whether it's trout caught from the Caldera River, wild boar hunted on the mountain, or seafood pulled from the waters off Chiriquí, not to mention herbs and fruit from the on-site gardens, Collins cooks with an international perspective. The Panamonte has a 1940s-style formal dining area, with its floral motif, though the laidback bar area with a roaring fire is more pleasant. A separate bar menu has lighter fare and casual meals like burgers, empanadas, and chicken brochettes, as well as an excellent wine list.

Hotel Panamonte, Av. Central. ℰ **720-1324** or 720-1327. Reservations recommended for main dining area. Main courses $9–$18. Daily 7–10am, noon–2:30pm, and 6–10pm. Bar daily noon–11pm.

The Rock ★★ INTERNATIONAL   This laidback bistro with a wide deck overlooking the Palo Alto River is one of Boquete's most popular dining options. The comforting dishes, sourced from local producers, include lots of fried snacks like corvine wafers with a sweet chile dip or creative share plates like beef tartare with bits of green apple. Larger courses include Angus burgers and baby-back ribs in a sugarcane and papaya barbecue sauce. The airy dining area has a Mediterranean style, with brick floors, glass walls, and a zinc roof strung with iron chandeliers. The wine list is mostly Spanish, with a few Chilean varieties, though more interesting are the craft beers, including some made specially for the house.

Road to Palo Alto. www.therockboquete.com. ℂ **720-1076.** Reservations recommended. Main courses $7–$16. Daily noon–9pm.

INEXPENSIVE

Morton's Bakehouse ★★ BAKERY/DELI   This artisan bakery and deli in a small strip mall is about as good as they come. Morton, nicknamed "the rye guy," is a retired attorney from Cincinnati who is keen on doing everything himself, which extends beyond baking fresh bread every morning to smoking his own salmon. Morton is famous for its Jewish rye bread, though things like rugelach and sticky buns, along with traditional Reuben sandwiches (Wed and Sat only), are also hits. Morton's occasionally holds bread-making classes on Saturday afternoons; call in advance to reserve a space.

3 Plaza San Francisco, Av. Central. www.mortonsbakehouse.com. ℂ **730-8499.** Breads and sandwiches $2–$7. Daily 9am–5pm.

Sabrosón ★ PANAMANIAN   This no-frills cafeteria-style eatery is a good option for cheap, local Panamanian fare. Stand in line and point to the roasted chicken, trout, or empanadas with a side of *patacones* (fried plantains) or rice and beans, and they'll heap it onto a plate for you to take into the barebones dining area.

Av. Central, near the church. ℂ **720-2147.** Main courses $3–$5. No credit cards. Mon–Thurs 6:30am–10pm; Fri–Sun 6:30am–11pm.

Boquete After Dark

Most Boquete residents are tucked into bed by 11pm, but there are a couple of places where you can get a nightcap or enjoy a night out. **Boquete Brewing Company** (www.boquetebrewingcompany.com; ℂ **6494-4992**) on Avenida Central has a beer-garden–like atmosphere with a chalkboard list of small-batch coffee porters, IPAs, brown ales, and a few ciders, though it is only open from 4 to 10pm. The fireside bar at the **Panamonte** is always a good option until 11pm, though for something later, with cocktails and loud

> ### Guayamí Indian Handicrafts
>
> Ngöbe-Buglé (Guayamí) Indians sell copies of their traditional, flouncy dresses, beaded jewelry, and other handicrafts at stalls along the roadside in **Tolé.** If you're driving from David, stop 97km (60 miles) east of David.

music, try **Zanzíbar,** located on Avenida Central on the right side past the church. Decorated with African odds and ends, it's the closest thing Boquete has to a club, though it's only open to midnight on weekends.

A Nature Lodge with Hiking Trails

The simple, Swiss-owned **Finca La Suiza** ★★ (www.fincalasuizapanama.com; ℂ **6615-3774**) is one of the best lodges in Panama to spend the night or visit for the day if you're an avid hiker. The trails are well maintained and marked (probably better than any others in the country), and the scenery and views along the trails are dazzling. Also, you don't need a guide.

Located on 81 hectares (200 acres) of land about 56km (35 miles) north of David, on the road to Chiriquí Grande, **Finca Suiza** is truly a find. With its clapboard walls and wooden shutters, the lodge looks out toward the Pacific with sweeping, sunset-facing views framed by blooming bougainvillea. Each of the two spotless guest rooms comes with two twin beds and a private bathroom. The rooms lean more toward comfort than rusticity, but this lodge will appeal more to easygoing nature lovers. There is a cozy living/dining area with a fireplace where meals are served (breakfast $5; dinner $12). The food is tasty and healthy, made with organic ingredients from the *finca*'s garden. Bring snacks and picnic lunch items with you, as well as alcohol, as none of these items are available. Rates for a minimum of 2 nights are $58 per night. Note that the lodge and the trails are closed in June, September, and October.

From the lodge there are three moderate loop trails through dense emerald tropical forest to lookout points, waterfalls, and through cloud forest. The **Small Circuit** takes 3½ hours or you can continue on and complete the **Large Circuit** for a total of 6½ hours, with the option of walking an extra hour to the Mirador Alta Vista lookout point. Hikers walking the Large Circuit and the **Cloud Forest Circuit** must be in good physical shape. July and August, when everything is green, are the best months to come; March and April are drier months with less foliage. For a day hike you'll have to arrive and start hiking between 7 and 10am, and be out of the *finca* by 4pm during the dry season (mid-Apr to Nov) or by 2pm during the rainy season. Admission is $8 per person, paid to the Ngöbe-Buglé woman at the entrance to the *finca*; you'll need to park your vehicle here and walk up the road until you reach the trail head. *Note:* Children 11 and under are not allowed on the trails.

PARQUE NACIONAL MARINO GOLFO DE CHIRIQUÍ & ISLAS SECAS ★★★

The Chiriquí Gulf National Marine Park is one of Panama's best-kept secrets—but not for long, given its proximity to Boquete and the wave of retirees and expats moving to the region every year. At **Boca Chica,** the closest town to the park, there are no high-rises, golf courses, or gated communities, just a couple of lodges and a tiny fishing community—and a lot of thick vegetation and crystalline water. The Marine Park was founded in 1994 to protect 14,730 hectares (36,400 acres) of extensive coral reef, mangrove swamps, and marine meadows—the park's most salient characteristics. Dozens of picturesque rocky outcrops are sprinkled across the gulf, as well as idyllic islands carpeted in forest and lined with slender coconut palms. Several of these islands boast tropical-paradise white-sand beaches lapped by turquoise waters (unlike the Pacific Coast beaches on the mainland), especially **Isla Gámez** and **Isla Bolaños.** The air is fresh and balmy, unlike the humid lowlands in the interior.

The sea is rich in marine life, providing **scuba divers** and **snorkelers** with the opportunity to see huge schools of colorful tropical fish, as well as large pelagic fish like white-tipped sharks. Scuba divers and snorkelers will need to book a boat tour to get to the offshore islands, where visibility is better than it is near shore (expect up to 15m/50 ft. offshore). The shore near Boca Chica and the pier is shrouded in mangrove and the water is cloudy, making it unsuitable for underwater sports.

As with Coiba, the **sport fishing** in the Chiriquí Gulf beyond the national park is legendary, especially around **Islas Ladrones, Islas Secas,** and **Islas Contreras.** Islas Secas is a cluster of 16 private islands that were once part of a now-closed luxury ecolodge.

Boca Chica fronts a large island called **Boca Brava;** here two lodges and a restaurant share space with howler monkeys, agoutis, raccoons, and other wildlife, and there are walking trails through the forest. You can reach the island via a $1 water-taxi ride from shore.

Essentials

GETTING THERE & DEPARTING

BY PLANE The closest airport to Boca Chica is in David (see "Getting There & Departing" under "David," earlier in this chapter).

BY BUS There is frequent bus service from David to the town of Horconcitos, but bus service from there to Boca Chica is spotty, so many hotels arrange transportation.

BY CAR Heading east from David, drive 38km (23 miles) and turn right on the turnoff for Horconcitos. Drive about 4.8km (3 miles) to Horconcitos, when the road forks; stay right and turn at the sign for Boca Chica. The road continues from here for 16km (10 miles) to Boca Chica.

Fun in & on the Water

FISHING, SNORKELING & SCUBA DIVING

Private overnight fishing and scuba-diving charters that operate around Isla Coiba are described below (under "Isla Coiba"); these charters normally leave from the Pedregal pier near David, or from Puerto Mutis southwest of Santiago. Your lodge or hotel will be able to arrange kayaking, snorkeling, and fishing excursions for you. For lodges in Boca Chica that specialize in fishing, see below.

Boca Brava Divers (www.bocabravadivers.com; ② **775-5185**) is a locally based scuba-diving operation run by a friendly English-speaking Colombian named Carlos, a Professional Association of Diving Instructors (PADI) dive master who has lived and dived in the Marine Park region for years. Boca Brava offers a full-day diving trip that can go as far as Islas Secas or Isla Ladrones, leaving at 7am and returning at 4pm; the cost is $180 per person, with a four-person minimum. Boca Brava's boat, a 14m (46-ft.) converted commercial-fishing vessel, has live-aboard accommodations for five guests for multiday scuba-diving trips around the Gulf of Chiriquí, including to Isla Coiba.

Where to Stay & Dine

Bocas del Mar ★★   Draping a lush hillside overlooking the gulf, Belgian-owned Bocas del Mar is an all-around great hotel, yet a little less focused on fishing or being eco than some of the neighboring properties. It has a proper resort-style pool area beside the bar and restaurant, and although there isn't much beach to speak of, the resort's 8m-long (26-ft) excursion boat runs trips to remote sandy coves daily; it also does whale-watching trips and excursions to explore the mangroves. The airy, contemporary bungalows run up the hill from the pool to the parking lot, all with ocean views. There is a minimum two-night stay. Low-season offers online can drop the price in half.

Boca Chica. www.bocasdelmar.com. ℂ **6395-8757.** $189–$500 bungalows. Rates include breakfast. **Amenities:** Restaurant; bar; pool; fishing; spa; kayaks; whale-watching; free Wi-Fi.

Cala Mia ★★   On a small island across from Boca Chica, eco-friendly resort Cala Mia fronts two mangrove- and rainforest-lined coves. It's secluded from other properties, making it feel as if you are much farther from civilization than you actually are. The resort was completely renovated in 2014 by its New Zealander owner, who added air-conditioning and modernized the facilities throughout. The tropical-chic, solar-powered bungalows feature hand-carved woodwork and indigenous art. Each has an open-air, thatched-roof rancho with hammocks and couches with waterproof woven reed cushions. Local Ngöble-Buglé are employed at the resort and can also give tours of their villages elsewhere on the island, though a variety of other tours are offered as well. The hotel offers free pickup and drop-off before 8pm. Local boatmen can also get you to the hotel for about $25 to $30.

Isla Brava. www.boutiquehotelcalamia.com. ℂ **851-0059** or 6747-0111. $360 bungalow suite; $680 double bungalow suite. Rates include breakfast. **Amenities:** Restaurant; bar; pool; spa; kayaks; surfing and snorkeling equipment; no phone in room.

Isla Palenque ★★   *Lord of the Flies* meets glamping. Semi-attached to Isla Boca Brava, the 160-hectare (400-acre) Isla Palenque is home to miles of volcanic beaches, lagoons, mangroves, and coconut groves. The master plan at this eco resort is to build some 220 homes, 80 hotel rooms, and a marina, which will take up just 5% of the island, though right now there's just a handful of luxury tents and estate rooms. The tents are modeled after luxe African safari tents, featuring wood floors, canvas walls, and outdoor showers. They lack air-conditioning but catch the breeze off of Punta Rocas below. The more polished estate rooms do have air-conditioning, as well as floor-to-ceiling windows and outdoor showers seemingly suspended into the jungle; close by is an infinity pool that drips into a 12-foor waterfall. Well-marked trails allow you to hike on your own around the island, though more intense guided treks

Parque Nacional Marino Golfo de Chiriquí & Islas Secas

and other activities put you in touch with more extreme locations. The boat transport from Boca Chica to Isla Palenque costs $15.

Isla Palenque. www.amble.com/IslaPalenque. ℭ **777-9260.** $179–$299 tent suite; $229–$299 estate room; $499–$649 suite. Rates include breakfast. **Amenities:** Restaurant; bar; pool; spa; kayaks; surfing and snorkeling equipment; tours; free Wi-Fi.

7 **Panama Big Game Sportfishing Club** ★★ On a hilltop on Boca Brava Island, looking out over the gulf, this fishing resort is legendary among sport fishermen worldwide for the prolific fishing grounds found off nearby Hannibal Bank and Isla Montuosa. It's just a couple of minutes from Boca Chica by boat, and the facilities have been updated considerably over the years, adding an infinity pool and top-of-the-line electronics in the roomy (56 sq. m/600 sq. ft.) cabins. The lodge has four fishing boats to accommodate all guests. Prices are all-inclusive, including transportation from the David airport, lodging, fishing, meals, and beverages. Three-day packages start on Monday and Thursday, and 5-day packages start on Monday. If you aren't a fisherman, there are better hotels in the area for you.

Boca Brava Island. www.panama-sportfishing.com. ℭ **866/281-1225** in the U.S. 4 units. 3-day packages $4,475 per person, based on 2 anglers; $3,163 per person, based on 4 anglers; 5-day packages $6,875 per person, based on 2 anglers; and $4,637 per person, based on 4 anglers. **Amenities:** Restaurant; bar; pool; fishing excursions; business center; free Wi-Fi.

ISLA COIBA ★★★

SE Gulf of Chiriquí

Once the haunt of pirates, and in recent times feared by convicted criminals who were sent here, **Isla Coiba** (www.coibanationalpark.com; ℭ **998-4271** or 998-0615) is now a treasured national park, UNESCO World Heritage Site, and nature lover's, fisherman's, and scuba-diver's dream destination. Given Isla Coiba's astounding natural diversity, rich sea life, and rare species, it is frequently referred to as the Galápagos of Central America. It's the largest island in Panama, but the national park spreads beyond the main island, encompassing 38 islands, islets, and marine waters for a total of 270,128 hectares (667,500 acres). The area is home to the second-largest coral reef in the eastern Pacific, at **Bahía Damas,** and its waters teem with huge schools of colorful fish, hammerhead and nurse sharks, dolphins, manta rays, tuna, turtles, whales, and other gigantic marine species. Onshore, there are 36 species of mammals and 39 species of reptiles, including saltwater crocodiles. Beyond these impressive numbers, Coiba is one of the last places on Earth where it is possible to see a scarlet macaw in the wild. Indeed, few places in the Americas are as wild, remote, and full of life as Isla Coiba National Park.

   The island and its surrounding waters owe their pristine state to a notorious penal colony that existed on the island from 1919 to 2004 and kept tourists and developers at bay. It was there that Panama sent its most hardened criminals, who considered the isolated penal colony the most punishing sentence the government could hand down. The majority of visitors now are "temporary" travelers who descend en masse from small to midsize cruise ships to spend a couple of hours snorkeling around **Granito de Oro** or take a quick walk through the island's jungle trails. Granito de Oro is a tiny island whose waters offer outstanding snorkeling and a picture-postcard white-sand beach, but the waters surrounding Coiba are still virgin territory, and snorkeling and diving outfits have yet to discover all of Coiba's treasures.

The park is administered by ANAM, which has a ranger station (✆ **998-0615**) and the only lodging on the island, consisting of two basic air-conditioned cabins on a glorious white-sand and turquoise-water beach. The cost to visit Coiba National Park is $20 per person. The cabins are used by fishing, diving, and snorkeling tour outfitters (or by those with a private boat). Day visits to Coiba go through operators in Santa Catalina. A landing strip is on Coiba, but for charter flights only.

Outdoor Adventures in Coiba

HIKING

Two short trails at the ANAM station lead to lookout points, but each is less than .4km (.25-mile) long. **Sendero de los Monos (Trail of the Monkeys)** is located on the shore in front of Granito de Oro Island. You must walk this trail very early to see monkeys; otherwise, it's just an easy, 45-minute walk through dense forest that starts and ends at different points—you'll need a boat to get there and be picked up. Skip it if you've only got a day here.

FISHING

The fishing around Coiba and the Gulf of Chiriquí is legendary, but keep in mind that ANAM only allows catch-and-release fishing within 1.6km (1 mile) of the boundary of the national park–protected area. ANAM only recently began enforcing fishing laws, and after a few misunderstandings, charter boat captains are now aware of restrictions and adhere by them. Fishermen consider this area special because of the size and variety of fish, and the sheer number of fishing sites that could not be covered even in a week. By far, the most renowned sport-fishing areas near Coiba are Hannibal Bank, which is something like an underwater mountain, and Isla Montuosa, but plenty of other sites have underwater mountains and deep ledges that attract black marlin, roosterfish, cubera snapper, bluefin trevally, and other very big fish.

Coiba Adventure (www.coibadventure.com; ✆ **800/800-0907** in the U.S.) is operated by American Tom Yust, who is considered Panama's most renowned sport-fishing captain and has been sport fishing the Coiba area since 1991. Coiba Adventure has two boats, the *Joker,* a 9.4m (31-ft.) Bertram, and a 6.7m (22-ft.) Mako. Guests are flown to the Coiba landing strip on a chartered plane from Panama City, and lodging is on the island in the ANAM air-conditioned cabins (a generator is used for backup). Five-night all-inclusive packages vary by time of year.

Pesca Panama (www.pescapanama.com; ✆ **844/264-2246** in the U.S.) is a U.S.–based company that offers inshore and offshore sport fishing in the Gulf of Chiriquí around Coiba and Hannibal Bank. Pesca guests stay aboard their floating lodge, a 21-by-9.1m (70-by-30-ft.) barge with a maximum capacity of 16 guests (4 beds per room) and take day fishing trips aboard Pesca's five 8.2m (27-ft.) Ocean Master fishing boats. The weekly 6-day trips are for 1 to 16 anglers. Rates depend on the season and the number of people.

SCUBA DIVING & SNORKELING

Isla Coiba is not only the best place to scuba dive and snorkel in the area; it's the best place to dive and snorkel in all of Panama. Day excursions to this island and its surrounding waters are available only from local operations based out of Santa Catalina. It's not cheap, and it takes nearly 1½ hours to get there. (Both outfitters mentioned below can organize this.) Local boat operators will do the round-trip to Isla Coiba for about $300 to $350, but that's without rental equipment, and drivers are not schooled in even rudimentary first aid, nor do they carry radios or much safety equipment. It's a long, bumpy ride over open water, so it pays to play it safe. Closer to Santa Catalina is **Isla Cebaco,** which offers excellent diving and snorkeling around an extensive coral reef; it only takes about a half-hour to get here, and the fare is less.

Coiba Dive Center (www.coibadivecenter.com; ✆ **6774-0808**) is owned and operated by two Americans who are fully certified and boast years of diving experience. The company offers day trips to Coiba with two-tank dives for $140 per diver and 3-day trips for $650 per diver. It also has five onsite PADI instructors for travelers spending 4 or 5 days in the area. You can rent snorkel gear and other marine-related goodies from the dive center or from **Scuba-Charters,** Coiba Dive Center's sister company (www.scuba-charters.com).

Scuba Coiba (www.scubacoiba.com; ✆ **6575-0122** or 6429-3560) offers scuba diving, snorkeling, and eco-tours to Isla Coiba. Using local *panga* boats to get to the island, Scuba Coiba will give you a by-the-seat-of-your-pants traveling experience. The 2- and 3-night packages on Isla Coiba include eco-tours to the interior of the island. Two-day all-inclusive packages with stays on Coiba (six dives total) are $460 per person, while 3-day packages are $675 per person.

BOCAS DEL TORO ARCHIPELAGO

The Bocas del Toro Archipelago is a scattering of seven islands and more than 200 islets off the northwestern coast of Panama, near the border with Costa Rica. The region has all the trappings of a Caribbean fantasy: dreamy beaches, thatched-roofed huts, aquamarine sea, thick rainforest, and soft ocean breezes. Add to that a funky, carefree ambience and a large English-speaking population, and it's easy to see why Bocas del Toro has emerged as an ecotourism hot spot faster than any other part of Panama.

But scratch the surface and you will find an island destination that is as much a paradox as it is paradise. Backpackers and surfers first discovered Bocas, lured by big waves, an underwater playground, and cheap accommodations. Midrange hotels and restaurants moved in, and retirees and expats with disposable income followed, snapping up beachfront properties and building their own tropical Xanadu. Considering that Bocas consists mostly of Ngöbe-Buglé and Teribe Indians plying the waters in dugout canoes, as well as Afro-Caribbeans who go about living much as they have for nearly a century, the contrast between the mix of ethnicities and nationalities here is striking.

The principal island in the region is **Isla Colón,** 62 sq. km (24 sq. miles) and home to **Bocas Town,** the regional capital and the center of activity in the archipelago. A smaller island called **Isla Carenero** neighbors Isla Colón and is a quieter location with a few hotels and restaurants just a minute or two away from Bocas Town by water taxi. **Isla Bastimentos** and **Isla Cristóbal** offer accommodations and amenities and are better choices than Bocas Town for travelers seeking a more intimate, castaway-like experience in wild, natural surroundings. Visitors to island lodges also benefit from in-house tours planned by proprietors with local knowledge, but Bocas Town has plenty of tour operators to fill your days if you choose to stay closer to shopping, restaurants, and nightlife.

Bocas can hold its own against nearby Costa Rica when it comes to adventure travel in the Caribbean. The diving and snorkeling are outstanding in this region—Bocas is home to some of the

Bocas del Toro

best-preserved hard and soft coral on the planet—but make sure your tour operator is willing to take you to the finest examples instead of "typical" tourist spots with bleached-out coral. There are sailing tours, boat tours to deserted islands, visits to Indian communities, hikes through luxuriant rainforest in Isla Bastimentos Park, and wave riding in what is largely considered the surfing epicenter of the southwest Caribbean.

Historically, there has always been a rough, end-of-the-line feel to Bocas del Toro. Weathered plantation-style homes—many of which look as if a good sneeze would level them—line dirt streets; Jimmy Buffett types hold court at waterfront dive bars; and residents and foreign visitors languidly stroll from one point to another, or kill entire afternoons on a park bench in the town's central plaza, which is choked with overgrown tropical foliage. But much of this authentic charm is gradually fading away as multimillion-dollar hotels, gated residential communities, and waterfront condominiums are finding their way here. Happily, the laid-back friendliness that characterizes Bocas del Toro endures.

WATER, water EVERYWHERE

The major drawback to Bocas del Toro as a destination is its climate. Although the rest of Panama enjoys a generally predictable dry season from December to April, Bocas can experience cloudy skies and **downpours** any time of year. The most trustworthy months for sunshine are late August to mid-October and February and March.

Tourists with sensitive digestive tracts should stick to **bottled water** when in Bocas Town. Tap water is treated but not to the same standards as it is in the rest of Panama. Hotels on outlying islands generally use filtered rainwater that is okay to drink—but you still might want to play it safe and drink bottled water only.

Visitors should be extremely careful when swimming in the ocean because of the strong **riptides.** A riptide can be the scariest moment of your life and can be a challenge to anyone regardless of his or her abilities as a swimmer. At a beach, look for a section of the water that isn't being churned up by scanning for clear, not sandy, waves. If you're caught in a riptide, don't panic or struggle against the current; if you can touch bottom, you might be able to anchor yourself against the rip. Swim parallel to the shore until you feel yourself released from the current; then head back to shore. To play it safe, stick close to the shore at beaches with strong waves and riptides.

ISLA COLÓN: BOCAS TOWN ★

30 min. by boat from Almirante; 1 hr. by boat from Changuinola; 1 hr. by plane from Panama City

Christopher Columbus arrived at what is now known as Bocas del Toro in October 1502 on his fourth and final voyage to the New World. It is said that he repaired his ships at Isla Carenero (thus the moniker "Careening Cay") before continuing on to present-day Portobelo and back to the Veraguas coast in the never-ending quest for gold and riches for the Spanish crown. Columbus never found the fabled gold mines of the highlands backing Bocas del Toro; therefore, the area piqued little interest in the region for the Spanish. By the 17th century, the archipelago became the haunt of renegade pirates and buccaneers.

The United Fruit Company first settled Isla Colón in the early 1900s for large-scale banana production, designating **Bocas Town** as headquarters and regional capital. A wave of immigrants from Jamaica, as well as from San Andrés and Providencia, Colombia, followed, so that by the 1920s, Bocas Town had more than 20,000 residents. It ranked as one of the most prosperous regions in Panama, but when banana blight forced the company to shut down in the 1930s and move operations to the mainland, Bocas Town retreated into a state of relative anonymity.

Fast forward to the 21st century and tourism, though nascent, is alive on Main Street, and developers have their eye on the waterfront. Yet there is still little in the way of upscale accommodations and services here. Finicky travelers will be happiest visiting Bocas Town only as a jumping-off point to a lodge away from the hustle and bustle.

Essentials

GETTING THERE & DEPARTING

You can get to Bocas del Toro one of two ways: via a **land/sea combination** or by **air.** Considering the short flight (1 hr. from Panama City), most travelers opt to fly. If crossing into Bocas del Toro from Costa Rica by land, travelers head to Changuinola, where they can grab a boat shuttle to Bocas (1 hr.) or hop over on a small plane from Changuinola (10 min.).

Tip: If traveling from Costa Rica, remember that Costa Rica is **1 hour ahead** of Panama.

BY PLANE   The basic but spruce **Bocas International Airport** (*©* **757-9208**) is serviced by daily flights from Panama City, Changuinola, and Costa Rica. Flights average about $220 (including taxes) for a round-trip ticket from Panama City to Bocas Town, but prices can fluctuate from season to season.

Air Panama (www.flyairpanama.com; *©* **316-9000**) has service to Bocas del Toro from Panama City, Changuinola, and San José, Costa Rica (for Costa Rica flights, see "From Costa Rica by Plane," below). From **Panama City,** three daily flights leave between 6:30am and 3:30pm from Albrook Airport, though flights are added when demand is high. Return flights from Bocas to Panama City leave daily between 7:30am and 5pm, but call ahead to confirm.

BY BOAT   **Taxi 25** (*©* **757-9028**) operates between Almirante and Bocas, leaving every half-hour from 6am to 6:30pm. Trips run $6 per person, one-way, and leave from the Almirante dock. Taxi 25 can be found next to the ATP office. Also offering water-taxi service is **Bocas Marine & Tours** (*©* **757-9033**), on Main Street in Bocas. *Note:* Boats operate with a minimum of six passengers; this means that when business is slow they might not leave on schedule. To get to the Almirante bus station for the 4-hour bus ride to David, take a $1 taxi that waits at the port.

If you have a vehicle, you can park for $3 a day at the lot at the Almirante boat dock. **Transportes Marinos** (*©* **757-9028**) has a daily car ferry service between Almirante and Bocas Town, departing at 7am from Almirante, returning at 3pm. The price is only $2 for passengers, though the trip takes an hour. Rates for transferring autos begin at $25 per car and $10 per motorcycle.

Being Grounded

Air Panama occasionally **cancels flights** when there are not enough passengers to make the flight profitable or for any other unforeseen problem. It is a frustrating aspect of local air travel in Panama, especially when flights are canceled at short notice. If traveling to Boquete or David from Bocas, your second option is to take a boat to Almirante and negotiate a fee with a local taxi driver at the dock (around $100 one-way). It is about the same price as a one-way flight for two and takes around 3 hours. Don't hesitate to negotiate the price, and be certain to settle on a fee beforehand.

Bocas Town

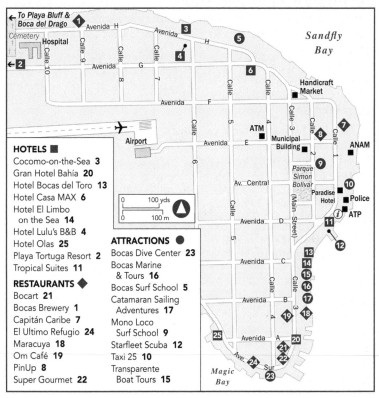

To Playa Bluff &
Boca del Drago **1**

Cemetery

Hospital

Avenida H

Avenida **3**

Sandfly
Bay

5

4

Avenida G

6

Handicraft
Market

Avenida F

Airport

ATM

Municipal
Building

7

8

ANAM

HOTELS ■
Cocomo-on-the-Sea **3**
Gran Hotel Bahía **20**
Hotel Bocas del Toro **13**
Hotel Casa MAX **6**
Hotel El Limbo
  on the Sea **14**
Hotel Lulu's B&B **4**
Hotel Olas **25**
Playa Tortuga Resort **2**
Tropical Suites **11**

RESTAURANTS ◆
Bocart **21**
Bocas Brewery **1**
Capitán Caribe **7**
El Ultimo Refugio **24**
Maracuya **18**
Om Café **19**
PinUp **8**
Super Gourmet **22**

Avenida E

Parque
Simon
Bolivar

9

Av. Central

Paradise
Hotel

10

Police

ATP

Avenida D

11

12

13

14

15

16

17

ATTRACTIONS ●
Bocas Dive Center **23**
Bocas Marine
  & Tours **16**
Bocas Surf School **5**
Catamaran Sailing
  Adventures **17**
Mono Loco
  Surf School **9**
Starfleet Scuba **12**
Taxi 25 **10**
Transparente
  Boat Tours **15**

0   100 yds
0   100 m

Avenida C

Avenida B

19

18

25

Avenida A

20

21

22

Ave. Sur

24

23

Magic
Bay

FROM COSTA RICA BY PLANE   **Nature Air,** a Costa Rican airline (www.natureair.com; ℚ **506/2299-6000** in Costa Rica, or 800/235-9272 in the U.S. and Canada), has daily flights to Bocas from San José (with connections from Quepos, Liberia, and Puerto Jiménez) at either 8am or 1pm; the return trip to San José leaves at 9:30am and 2:30pm. The flight costs $175 to $200 one-way, $350 to $400 round-trip.

FROM COSTA RICA BY ROAD   Travelers entering Panama from Costa Rica by road at the Sixaola–Guabito border can take a taxi (about $18–$20) to **Changuinola,** and then a boat to Bocas del Toro with **Taxi 25** (see above). Have your taxi driver take you to the dock at Finca 60, just outside of Changuinola. The boat journey passes through the San San Pond Sak wetlands and an old banana plantation canal, and is so scenic it could be considered a low-price tour. From Changuinola, boats leave daily at 8am, 9:30am, 11am, 12:30pm, 2pm, 3:30pm, and 5pm. From Bocas Town to Changuinola, boats leave at 7am, 8am, 9:30am, 11am, 12:30pm, 2pm, 3:30pm, and 4:30pm. The cost is $7 per person one-way. Remember, if you're crossing into Panama from Costa Rica, you'll have to go through immigration. This can take a long time on a 50-passenger bus, so be prepared for a 1- to 2-hour process. If you're arriving by car, immigration should only take 15 to 20 minutes.

GETTING AROUND

Everything in Bocas Town is within walking distance, but collective taxis are plentiful if you need one. If arriving by boat, find out where your hotel is in relation to the dock—you may already be close enough to walk. Most hotels arrange pickup and drop-off for guests arriving by air, but taxis are also waiting for every arrival at the airport, and they cost between $1 and $2. There are two principal roads on the island: One runs along the coast and ends at Playa Bluff; the other crosses the island to Boca del Drago.

Money Matters

Many hotels and restaurants in Bocas del Toro do not accept credit cards, and of those that do, it's mostly **Visa** and **MasterCard** only. Some hotels will request that you pay your deposit via PayPal or a bank deposit in your home country, and then pay cash or traveler's checks for the remaining balance. A 24-hour ATM is located at Banco Nacional de Panamá, located at the corner of Calle 4 and Avenida E, and an ATM is in the Taxi 25 building—but bring extra cash in case both are down, which can happen here, especially during high season.

You'll find **bicycle** rentals on Main Street across from the plaza; rentals run about $1 an hour, or $7 to $10 a day. Informal **water taxis** are available at the dock next to the ATP office, with service to neighboring Isla Carenero ($2 one-way) and Isla Bastimentos ($6). Hours are irregular, with service generally running from 7am to 9pm. Most people visit Isla Bastimentos as part of a day tour; resorts on that island include round-trip transportation in the price and an extra charge for additional trips.

For beaches outside of Bocas Town, see "What to See & Do," below.

VISITOR INFORMATION

A **Tourism Authority of Panama (ATP) visitor center** (www.visitpanama. com; ⓒ **757-9642;** Mon–Fri 9am–12:45pm and 1:45–4pm) is in a barn-size yellow building on the waterfront at Calle 1, near the police station. It appears that ATP blew its budget on this sparkling new office, because English-speaking, trained information officers, maps, and brochures are all in short supply. Around lunchtime, you'll be lucky to find anyone staffing the desk, though the office does have public bathrooms, and the second floor has a display on the natural history of Bocas. For additional information about Bocas, try the Web portal **www.bocasdeltoro.travel**, which has links to hotels, tourism services, transportation information, and more.

Note: Though Bocas is not dangerous by any means, keep an eye on your personal belongings as you would anywhere else; you are highly unlikely to be violently assaulted, but if you're careless with your wallet or camera you may not find it where you left it.

ORIENTATION

Bocas is the only town on Isla Colón, centered around a bustling (though far from picturesque) Main Street (Calle 3) and Simon Bolívar Plaza. Bocas has fewer than two dozen streets, and most are unpaved. The airport is just a couple of blocks away from the main plaza, meaning you could walk to your hotel if you felt like it. Calles 1 through 10 run west–east, and Avenidas A to H run north–south. Bocas has no "downtown" per se, but most hotels and restaurants are concentrated on the south end where Calle 1 meets Main Street. You'll find Internet cafes and shops along Main Street between Avenidas E and D.

LOCAL EVENTS

The **Feria del Mar (Festival of the Sea),** which takes place around the second week of September, is a 5-day event featuring handicrafts booths, food stands serving local cuisine, and exhibits by the Smithsonian Institute and ANAM (the park service), with displays of animals and natural-history information. Nightly events include folkloric presentations and dances, all culminating with the crowning of the Sea Fair Queen. Contact the ATP office for exact dates. The **Fundación de la Provincia de Bocas del Toro (Founding Day of Bocas del Toro)** takes place on November 16 and is celebrated with parades and other events; on November 23, residents of Isla Bastimentos celebrate **Bastimentos Day** with parades and live music. There is a maypole dance in Bocas and on Isla Bastimentos for **Palo de Mayo,** which takes place on May 1. Lastly, on July 16 is the **Día de la Virgen del Carmen,** which honors the patron saint of Bocas with a parade; the following Sunday hundreds make the pilgrimage across the island to visit the shrine of the virgin at La Gruta.

[Fast FACTS] BOCAS TOWN

Bookstore   A small bookstore (☎ **6452-5905**) sells used and new books with a decent selection of English-language titles; it's located on the corner of Calle 2 and Avenida E.

Emergency   For an ambulance, call ☎ **757-9814;** for fire, dial ☎ **103;** for the police, dial ☎ **104** or 757-9217.

Hospital   Bocas has a basic **hospital clinic** with a 24-hour emergency room.

It's located at Calle 10 and Avenida G (☎ **757-9201**). Service is limited, however, and those with more serious health problems will need to seek medical care in Panama City or David.

Internet Access   Multiple Internet cafes are located on Bocas's main street, and most hotels and restaurants also offer free Wi-Fi.

Laundry   Bubbles, on Avenida C at Main Street

(☎ **6591-3814;** Mon–Sat 8am–6pm), has coin-operated machines and drop-off laundry services, including pickup and delivery.

Post Office   The post office is located at Calle A and Avenida 2; no phone. It's open Monday through Friday from 8am to noon and 2 to 4pm (some days 3–4pm "when I feel like taking a long lunch") and Saturday 8am to noon.

What to See & Do

Despite its location in the warm, cerulean Caribbean Sea, the Bocas del Toro Archipelago is not your quintessential beach destination. That's not to say that there are no beaches here; in fact, a handful of idyllic beaches appear straight from the pages of a travel magazine—it just takes a little effort to reach them. Also, most beaches in Bocas offer poor swimming conditions because of strong riptides. (See "Water, Water Everywhere," above.) For this reason, those traveling with small children may want to consider another beach destination, or stick to **Boca del Drago** and **Starfish Beach,** both of which have calm waters and excellent swimming conditions.

The closest decent beach to Bocas Town, **Bluff Beach** is an 8km (5-mile) bike or taxi ride away, and the beaches on Isla Bastimentos can only be reached by boat, followed by a short to medium-long walk. During the calm-water months (early Sept to early Nov), it's possible to arrive directly by boat to the beaches of Isla Bastimentos.

If you don't have an all-inclusive package with your hotel, or if your hotel simply does not offer trips, plenty of tour agencies can fulfill your excursion needs. Bocas Town is a good base for exploring the archipelago—nearly every kind of excursion and destination can be reached from there, including spots for watersports and cultural visits. Trips to Isla Bastimentos and the Zapatilla Cays are better with fast boats that offer flexible itineraries. If you have a group or can afford a private-boat rental, do so because it offers you the freedom to plan your own itinerary.

Tip: The old cliché "You get what you pay for" rings true in Bocas. Plenty of agencies pitch the same day tour to the masses, usually for dirt-cheap prices. These companies cut corners by hiring semi-qualified guides with little concern for the environment; others try to save on gas by not taking clients far enough out to the best snorkeling and diving sites—providing less-than-memorable experiences and the dreaded cattle-herd sensation. To avoid disappointments, when booking, ask detailed questions about destinations, snorkeling and diving sites, safety precautions, and schedules.

BEACHES & OTHER NATURAL ATTRACTIONS
Boca del Drago Beach, Starfish Beach & Swan's Cay ★★

Boca del Drago is the best beach on Isla Colón for swimming, and when the sea is calm visitors can snorkel from the shore. Often there isn't much beach to speak of—just a couple of feet or so for throwing down a towel or beach chair, but it's a lovely spot. The beach is on the north shore of Isla Colón. Tour companies include Boca del Drago as part of their standard day tours and include a visit to nearby **Swan's Cay,** a picturesque rocky outcrop and bird sanctuary that attracts nesting boobies, frigates, and the magnificent red-billed tropicbird. There is no coral reef at Swan's Cay, but the sea-battered rocks are an interesting place to snorkel. Do not disturb nesting birds by going ashore. You can also get to Boca del Drago from Bocas Town by taxi, which costs $25 to $30 round-trip and takes 30 minutes, or you can take a $3 bus that stops in front of the park. **Starfish Beach,** located right next to Boca del Drago Beach, is one of my favorite beaches for its calm, crystal-clear waters and the hundreds of starfish that dot the bottom of the ocean floor. To get here, simply keep walking after you pass Boca del Drago beach. There's not much of a beach at **Starfish Beach** either, but swimming conditions are perfect. Both beaches are home to schools of colorful fish and make for good informal snorkeling time. *Note:* You'll have to bring your own snorkeling gear.

Bluff Beach ★

This golden-sand beach would be perfect if it weren't for a light sprinkling of trash. It's still the prettiest beach close to town for catching some rays—but don't plan on getting more than your feet wet here because the ocean is fraught with riptides. The beach is about 8km (5 miles) from the city center and can be reached by taxi for $15 one-way. Some drivers are willing to hang around if you plan on staying an hour or two; if not, you'll need to arrange for pickup later. In this case, negotiate to pay when the driver returns (to make sure that he comes back). You can also rent a bicycle and pedal here, which is quite a pleasant ride if you're up to peddling the 8km (5 miles). Rain can wreak havoc on the road, so be prepared for lots of puddles. (Incidentally, taxi drivers often inflate their price when the road calls for a four-wheel-drive.) On the way out of town you'll pass by the less-scenic **Punch Beach,** which is popular with surfers. Punch is known for its right and left breaks, reef bottom, and swells that average 1.5 to 1.6m (5–5¼ ft.).

San San Pond Sak Wetlands ★★★

The San San Pond Sak Wetlands, covering nearly 16,187 hectares (40,000 acres), are located on the coast about 4.8km (3 miles) north of Changuinola. The wetlands are home to sloths, white-faced capuchin monkeys, and caimans, but more important, San San is the natural habitat of the manatee, an elephant-like aquatic mammal that weighs between 363 and 544kg (800 and 1,200 lb.). **Banana Republica Tours** (http://bananarepublicatours.com; ✆ **6632-1762**) offers a full-day excursion (7am–5pm) that provides for an out-of-the-ordinary experience. Because there is so little human traffic in this region, your chances of spotting a manatee are very good, but please note that manatees are protected animals. Do not chase, pet, or harass these magnificent, gentle creatures—and report anyone who does. The $30 per-person fee (minimum of five people) includes a full lunch, park entrance fees, guides, and transportation.

The Soposo Rainforest ★★

The Soposo Rainforest is home to the Naso culture, the only culture in the Americas still governed by a king. Though the Naso number only about 4,000, they are a proud people hoping to hold on to their traditions by promoting sustainable tourism in their native lands and sharing their culture and traditions with visitors. The rainforest on the Bocas del Toro mainland sees few visitors, so like the San San Pond Sak Wetlands above, the likelihood of spotting wildlife is high here. **Soposo Rainforest Adventures** (www.soposo.com;

© **6631-2222**) offers day trips as well as weeklong adventures. Day trips cost $90 per person for two or more people, 1-night/2-day trips cost $140 per person, and 2-night/3-day trips cost $275 per person. Expect to see sloths, frogs, monkeys, and other wildlife. The highlight of the trip, however, is the opportunity to interact with and experience the Naso culture.

WATER SPORTS
Boating & Sailing
For catamaran tours, see **Catamaran Sailing Adventures,** under "Scuba Diving & Snorkeling," below. **Boteros Bocatoreños** (© **757-9760;** boteros bocas@yahoo.com) is a group of local boatmen who have banded together in the face of encroaching competition—they can provide custom tours at slightly lower prices than outfitters. Most speak at least some English and have local knowledge, and they can be found on the Via Principal by the ATP office. **Boteros Nuestra Senora del Carmen** (© **757-9039**) is another group of local operators. They require a minimum of five people and tours usually cost $5 to $25 per person, though Cayos Zapatilla costs $35 per person. You can find them at Calle 3 next to Catamaran Tours. They have snorkeling equipment. Another good source for local boatmen is **Ancon Expeditions** (www.anconexpeditions.com).

Kayaking & Stand-Up Paddleboarding (SUP)
Gran Kahuna hostal (www.grankahunabocas.com; © **757-9551**) on Isla Carenero rents two-person kayaks and SUPs that cost $5 per hour, or $15 half-day. During bad-weather days, you'll only be able to navigate around mangrove swamps and the coast. Other providers along the waterfront in Bocas Town also offer watersports, some for a lower price, but be sure to ask a lot of questions.

Scuba Diving & Snorkeling
Scuba diving and snorkeling are among the most popular activities in Bocas del Toro, thanks to well-preserved displays of hard and soft coral, mangrove swamps, volcanic-rock walls, and underwater caves—not to mention balmy water temperatures that average around 86°F (30°C). Beyond tropical reef fish, divers are privy to larger species such as nurse sharks, spotted eagle rays and southern rays, turtles, and more unusual species such as batfish and toadfish. You might also see colorful sponges, and there is even an underwater landing craft that was sunk to create an artificial reef. Snorkeling and diving sites that are recommended are **Crawl Cay** (or Coral Cay), with shallow waters and some of the best coral formations in the area; **Hospital Point,** just a 10-minute boat ride from Bocas and easy to reach by water taxi; **Polo Beach,** a shallow system of caves suitable for snorkelers but reachable only 6 months of the year; **Swan's Cay,** with interesting rock formations created by battering waves and also a migratory-bird site; and **Cayos Zapatilla,** two delicate islands with white-sand beaches surrounded by an extensive reef system that attracts lots of tropical fish—note, however, that Zapatilla also has currents and is for strong swimmers only. Divers also head to **Buoy Line** near Isla Solarte, which is a deepwater channel where pelagic and larger

marine species can be seen; the same is true of **Tiger Rock,** an offshore site and rocky outcrop whose long distance from Bocas Town keeps the crowds away. Adventurous divers and snorkelers really looking to get away from other travelers might consider visiting **Isla Escudo de Veraguas,** which is a full-day trip and a fairly ambitious undertaking (available usually only Sept–Oct). The beaches there are generally considered to be the loveliest in the entire region.

The principal shortcoming of Bocas del Toro as a diving and snorkeling destination is the **unpredictability of the weather,** with spontaneous downpours and wind gusts that can churn up the sea and cloud visibility. If the focus of your trip is diving and snorkeling, come from September to early November, when the sea is tranquil and flat. Other months with better visibility are March and April, but rain and wind can occur at any time during these months. Dive sites with deeper water and larger species (mostly offshore sites such as Tiger Rock) can be visited only during these more tranquil months.

Bocas Dive Center, at Calles 6a and 4ta (www.bocasdivecenter.com; Ⓒ **757-9737**), a PADI five-star dive center that opened in 2012, is perhaps the most advanced dive center in Bocas. It offers two tank dives for $85, plus a full range of certification classes, including advanced Emergency First Response and Dive Master courses.

Starfleet Scuba, at Calle 1A (www.starfleetscuba.com; Ⓒ **757-9630**), has a spotless record and a British owner who last ran diving operations in Indonesia. Starfleet has three boats plus an 80kmph (50-mph) inflatable Zodiac boat that gives the company the edge in terms of more quickly getting to remote destinations like Tiger Rock ($145 for a two-tank dive). Two-tank dives cost $70, a one-tank dive $40.

Several companies offer snorkeling and diving trips in addition to the two companies mentioned above. Day trips include equipment; lunch is extra so bring cash for a local restaurant, or bring your own food. Among the numerous operators along the waterfront, **Transparente Boat Tours** (http://transparente tours.bocas.com; Ⓒ **757-7326**) offers trips to all the islands, but they're garden variety. Tours cost $20 to $25 per person and suffer from a get-em-in and get-em-out mentality. However, Transparente is the company to call for charterboat rentals, which start at $275 for a full day, not including lunch.

Odin Sailing (www.odinsailingpanama.com; Ⓒ **6795-5123**) offers day tours ($45 per person; departing at 9:30am, returning at 4:30pm) to area destinations like Bahía Honda, Playa Estrella, and Coral Cay from their cushy 60-foot trimaran equipped with below-deck cabins and a kitchen. Odin also runs a 3-hour sunset cruise ($25 per person) and multi-day excursions.

Catamaran Sailing Adventures at Main Street (www.bocassailing.com; Ⓒ **757-9710** or 6637-9064) has a 12m (40-ft.) catamaran for laid-back and enjoyable full-day snorkeling trips to Bocas del Drago or around Isla Bastimentos for $45 per person (four-person minimum, 18 maximum), including a sack lunch. Charter rentals cost $450 a day. The catamaran has little protection from the sun, so bring sunscreen and a hat.

NEXT VACATION: PICK UP A skill

Take advantage of your trip to Bocas del Toro to learn a new skill. Scuba courses taught in swimming pools may earn you the basic dive certification you need, but they don't give you much practical experience in open water. Starfleet Scuba and Bocas Water Sports (see "Scuba Diving & Snorkeling," above) offer well-respected **scuba training academies** for everyone from absolute beginners to divers seeking to brush up—and even for those who want to be certified as instructors. The Discover Scuba course is a half-day introduction to scuba diving for $65 to $85 per person; the Scuba Diver course is 1½ to 2 days for a partial certification program that allows you to dive up to 12m (39 ft.) with a certified dive master, and costs $185 per person; the open-water course, the standard certification program for worldwide independent diving, takes 3 to 4 days and costs $210 to $235 per person. Contact the companies for more information about Rescue Diver and Instructor programs. Bocas Water Sports also offers an advanced open-water class and dive master class.

Stop blaming your rusty Spanish for misunderstandings with locals, and start doing something about it. **Spanish-by-the-Sea language classes,** Calle 4, behind Hotel Bahía (www.spanishatlocations.com; © **757-9518**), has inexpensive classes that are as long or intensive as you want them to be. Weekly programs (5 days only) include group lessons at $225 to $300 per week (20 hr.); private customized courses are also available. Spanish-by-the-Sea also has packages that include lodging in its comfortable hostel (catering to younger adults), as well as $250 open-water dive excursions and volunteering at a retirement home. Homestays can also be arranged.

Tip: Ask a lot of questions before embarking on the standard, full-day snorkeling tour that starts in Dolphin Bay and ends at Hospital Point. Boat drivers and guides on these tours practice poor environmental management by racing around a dolphin breeding site, and then dumping guests at an expensive restaurant where they are left to "snorkel" around dead coral and bits of trash.

Surfing

Bocas experiences the largest and most consistent swells from December to March, and during June and July, with reef point breaks, beach breaks, and huge, challenging waves recommended only for experienced surfers. The waves in Bocas are more suitable for shortboarding and bodyboarding; if you're bringing your own board, check with your airline about requirements because some smaller planes may not accept a long board. **Mono Loco Surf School** (www.monolocosurfschool.com; © **6612-6886**) offers surf lessons, board rentals, and surf shuttles to places like Paki Point ($10 per person). Additionally, they offer guided surf tours and surfaris to many of the best surf spots in the archipelago, ranging from 3 hours to a full day (from $50-$210). **Bocas Surf School** (www.bocassurfschool.com; © **6852-5291** or 757-9057) has been a Bocas mainstay since 2006 and offers beginner through advanced surfing courses and surf camp packages.

8

BOCAS DEL TORO ARCHIPELAGO | Isla Colón: Bocas Town

194

SPAS & YOGA

If you're winding down from a day of activity (and a hammock isn't doing the trick), try **L'il Spa Shop** (www.spashopbythesea.com; ℭ **6591-3814**) on Avenida H and Calle 7, for deep-tissue massages, ginger-mint scrubs, and reflexology, as well as an assortment of beauty services such as haircuts and facials. **Danuta's Holistic Therapy** (www.danutashealing.com; ℭ **757-9308**) has Zen Shiatsu massage, Reiki, and Thai foot massages.

For yoga, contact Laura Kay of **Bocas Yoga,** Casa Morada, 4th Street (www.bocasyoga.com; ℭ **658-1355**). Drop-ins at regularly scheduled classes are available for $5.50 plus a 50¢ mat fee, or you can set up a private session for $35. They also offer massages.

Where to Stay

Although most hotels on Isla Colon are concentrated in Bocas Town, luxury accommodations have opened up in recent years on more remote spots, such as **Playa Tortuga Hotel & Beach Resort** and **Punta Caracol Acqua-Lodge,** with over-the-water bungalows (both reviewed below). Others may be happier at a lodge such as **Tranquilo Bay** on Isla Bastimentos (see later in this chapter). Easygoing travelers enjoy the laid-back Caribbean vibe in Bocas Town, and its proximity to restaurants, bars, and shopping, not to mention people-watching and cultural encounters. But loud music and other street noise is a factor, and travelers seeking peaceful isolation will do better lodging elsewhere. Neighboring Isla Carenero is close enough that you can occasionally hear music on particularly loud party nights in Bocas, but it still gives travelers an option for being near Bocas without actually staying in it.

Nearly every hotel sits over the water, so try to snag a view if you can. The north shore of town is usually breezier, which is a definite plus in the Bocas heat. If a price range is shown, it indicates that a hotel applies high- and low-season rates. Low season is generally mid-April to December. Lodging in Bocas tends to be more expensive for what you get compared with other destinations in Panama, although most hotels drop their prices during low season. Be sure to make reservations at least a few weeks in advance from mid-April to November, as hotels here fill up quickly then.

IN & AROUND BOCAS TOWN
Expensive

Playa Tortuga Hotel & Beach Resort ★   One of the more family-friendly Bocas resorts, the easily accessible hotel—it's a 3.2km (2 miles) free shuttle ride from Bocas town—Playa Tortuga doesn't sacrifice modern comforts like some of the more remote resorts. It's flush with amenities like an oversize pool area with a pool bar and a separate children's pool, plus access to a tranquil beach, a sand volleyball court, and banquet facilities. There are no thatched roofs or rickety fans here: Guest rooms come equipped with air-conditioning and cable TV, plus private balconies with hammocks and ocean views in most. An excursions desk can arrange fishing, snorkeling, and wildlife trips around the archipelago. It won't blow you away, but if time is limited or you need to stick close to town, there's nothing better.

Playa Big Creek. www.hotelplayatortuga.com. © **302-5424.** 118 units. $174 double; $200 1-bedroom suite; $350 grand master suite; $600 Almirante suite. Rates include breakfast. **Amenities:** Restaurant; 2 bars; room service; free Wi-Fi.

Tropical Suites ★ This over-the-water wooden building is one of the more reliable properties in the center of Bocas Town. A total renovation in 2012 gave the guest rooms a cookie-cutter feel with tile floors and clunky wooden furniture that isn't particularly interesting—though if clean and functional is what you are after more than character you will be satisfied. Other additions include Jacuzzi tubs, LCD TVs, and pillowtop mattresses. Each room has a good-size terrace, though the ocean-facing ones are well worth the extra cash. Breakfast is served at **Lili's Waterside Café** next door. The hotel offers big discounts during the off-season and for early booking.

Calle 1. www.tropical-suites.com. © **757-9081.** 16 units. $129 island-view double; $189 sea-view double. Rates include breakfast. **Amenities:** Watersports equipment, tour desk; laundry service, free Wi-Fi.

Moderate

Cocomo on the Sea Bed & Breakfast ★ This American-owned B&B, in a white clapboard house perched behind a turquoise and purple picket fence, is full of Bocas charm. Set over the waterfront just a few minutes outside of the town center, Cocomo has only four rooms, but they're airy and get lots of light, and all come with private bathrooms. Most activity is on the back porch, which is partially covered and gets a steady breeze to make that hammock all the more inviting. Free breakfast served on the veranda and the use of kayaks are an added bonus.

Av. Norte at 6A St. http://cocomoonthesea.com. ©/fax **757-9259.** 4 units. $85 double. Rates include breakfast. No children 8 and under. **Amenities:** Bar; kayaks, laundry service; library; no phone in room.

Gran Hotel Bahía ★ Set in a historic 1905 wooden building that was once the local headquarters of the United Fruit Company, the Gran Hotel Bahía has more history than any other hotel in Bocas Town. Check out the giant safe in the lobby, which has been there as long as the building and was once used to store cash to pay banana farmers. Renovations have given the rooms new wood floors, rather sterile wood furniture, and tacky tropical artwork, losing some of the atmosphere they once had. The shady, second-floor veranda is a pleasant place to bring a book, while the **Bocas Barna Q** restaurant has the widest selection of grilled meats in town. Steep discounts are available in low season.

South end of Main St. http://ghbahia.com. © **757-9626.** 18 units. $77 double; $115.50 "deluxe plus" double. Rates include "continental plus" buffet breakfast and airport transfers. **Amenities:** Restaurant; free Wi-Fi.

Hotel Bocas del Toro ★★ One of the best-maintained hotels on Isla Colon, Hotel Bocas del Toro has a prime waterfront location right in the heart of town. The airy rooms, many with slanted ceilings, feature handcrafted wood furnishings, high-thread-count linens, and nautical decorations. The premium rooms add balconies with either town or ocean views, with the third-floor luxury room giving the best views. The hotel has a full-service restaurant and bar, plus a nice dock area with a variety of lounge chairs.

Calle 1 at Main St. www.hotelbocasdeltoro.com. ℂ **757-9018** or 757-9771. 11 units. $129–$142 standard double; $162–$219 premium room; $299 luxury room. **Amenities:** Restaurant; bar; in-room massage; kayak rentals; free Wi-Fi.

Hotel El Limbo on the Sea ★

Sitting directly beside Hotel Bocas del Toro (see above), El Limbo is nearly the same hotel. Both are over-the-water buildings with a relaxing dock area and full-service restaurant. Both have a mix of nautically themed rooms with polished wood floors, some with balconies. However, El Limbo's service is just a bit slower and a bit less attentive, though price drops have made it competitive.

Calle 1 at Main St. www.ellimbo.com. ℂ **757-9062.** 15 units. $75 double standard; $90 double with balcony and street view; $135 double with balcony and sea view. Rates include breakfast. **Amenities:** Restaurant; bar; concierge; room service; free Wi-Fi.

Hotel Olas ★

Las Olas is on the quieter, less touristy side of town near the end of the peninsula in a colorful overwater wooden building. For the price, you won't find anything nearly as good, particularly in the off-season when rates drop dramatically. The rooms are spacious and have nice views of the water and other houses, though none (other than the suite) have balconies. Second-floor rooms are more cheerful and receive more light, while the ground-floor rooms with floor-to-ceiling wood can feel somewhat dingy.

Calle 6a and Av. Sur. ℂ **6914-4556.** 24 units. $90 double; $100–$120 suite. Rates include breakfast. **Amenities:** free Wi-Fi.

Inexpensive

Hotel Casa MAX ★

This Caribbean-style, two-story turquoise wooden building has some of the most budget-friendly rates in town. The rooms are more functional than fabulous, though they're big and clean and all of the ones on the first floor have a private balcony. If you can live with just a fan, the price drops considerably. The cafe/restaurant, **Rum Runners,** is a favorite among expats, and breakfast can be taken there until noon.

Av. G. ℂ **757-9120.** www.hotelcasamax.com. 20 units. $45 double with fan; $75 double with A/C. **Amenities:** free Wi-Fi.

Hotel Lula's Bed & Breakfast ★

On the north side of the waterfront, a 5-minute walk to town, this quaint B&B sees lots of repeat visitors. The rooms are smallish, divided into either doubles or triples, and feature polished wood floors and wood paneling. The covered balcony is a nice place to catch a cool breeze. Lots of little extras include an honor bar and book exchange, plus the **Bocas Surf School** (see above) operates out of the house. Ask about discounts for longer stays. The owner grew up in Bocas and can provide in-depth information and excursion-planning information about the area.

Av. H at Calle 6. www.lulabb.com. ℂ **757-9057.** 8 units. $77 double; $88 triple. Rates include breakfast. **Amenities:** Shared full kitchen; free Wi-Fi.

AROUND ISLA COLON

Punta Caracol Acqua-Lodge ★★   These colorful, tropical-chic thatched-roof bungalows sit directly over a beautiful stretch of clear Caribbean waters and are connected by a single wooden walkway that curves the length of the property, allowing for a dramatic image that's worth the price of staying here alone. Your only contact with land after leaving the dock in Bocas Town for the 25-minute boat ride to the property will likely be when kayaking near the mangroves, which are a short paddle from this aquatic retreat. Each of the nine bungalows, painted a very Bocas-y lime green, are decorated with eclectic wood furnishings and French doors that open on to large verandas where you can catch the occasional spotted eagle ray glide right beneath your feet. Each comes equipped with a couple of chaise lounges and a hammock. If you have the desire to interact with other humans, you just walk over to the restaurant or hop in a kayak.

15 min. by boat from town. www.puntacaracol.com.pa. ℭ **757-9410.** 9 units. $350–$450 double. Extra person $90. Rates include breakfast and dinner. **Amenities:** Restaurant; bar; kayaks; snorkeling equipment; free Wi-Fi; no phone in room.

Where to Dine in & Around Bocas Town

Believe it or not, tiny Bocas is home to one of the few gourmet supermarkets in the region, **Super Gourmet** (ℭ **757-9357;** Mon–Sat 9am–7pm), with imported foods, vegetarian and organic products, and very expensive produce. Super Gourmet, which has a full-service delicatessen, is located next to the Hotel Bahía on the south end of Main Street by the ATP office. You'll find good coffee drinks at **Déjà Brew Cafe** (ℭ **6158-9144;** Thurs–Tues 8am–3pm) on Av. E in front of the Banco Nacional. Street carts are found all over town, selling everything from hot dogs to falafel to fried chicken. I recommend **Kiosco Nani,** a turquoise wooden cart on Main Street that serves local items like *hojaldre* (a fried bread that you can slather in their homemade hot sauce), empanadas, and *patacones*. Also, try **Bocas Blended** (ℭ **6158-9144;** Mon–Sat 8am–6pm), in a refurbished Thomas school bus on Av. North between 5th and 6th, with wraps and smoothies.

Keep in mind that many restaurants do not accept credit cards, so make sure you have plenty of cash.

MODERATE

Bocart ★★ MEDITERRANEAN   Thinking beyond the typical expat grub and local dives, Bocart brings a touch of gourmet to a town severely lacking it. The menu leans Mediterranean, though there are Asian and Peruvian influences throughout, and most of the ingredients are sourced locally. Start with the tuna *tiradito* (a sort of ceviche) with a ginger-infused ponzu sauce before moving on to a ribeye steak slathered with melted brie. Or just snack on tapas and cheese over a bottle of wine. The space is quite plain, just a concrete and corrugated-metal-roof canvas that allows the food to be the decoration.

Calle Tercera, beside the ferry. www.bocartrestaurant.com. ℭ **757-7040.** Reservations required. Main courses $8–$16. Wed–Mon 6pm–midnight.

Bocas Brewery ★★ BREWPUB   Near Saigon Bay, this beachside brew-pub has quickly become a favorite eating and drinking option among locals, expats, and tourists. Eight beers are on rotation, including a Bocas-brewed amber ale and less-standard brews like a Grapefruit IPA. The food is designed to pair with the suds, so we're talking fried pickles, beer-battered coconut shrimp, and pulled pork sandwiches. The brewery also has Wednesday wing nights and corn hole in the sand.

Calle Carretera, Las Cabanas. http://bocasbrewery.com. ℐ **6347-5279.** Main courses $7–$10. Mon–Sat noon–8pm.

El Ultimo Refugio ★ CARIBBEAN/INTERNATIONAL   The epitome of a Bocas expat restaurant and bar, El Ultimo Refugio is that funky, divey waterfront eatery where Christmas lights, bamboo, and tiki drinks feel effort-lessly placed amid the weathered wood walls and floorboards. The menu relies heavily on the day's catch, which makes its way into things like tuna tartar, shrimp and grits, and miso-crusted grouper filet. It's a favorite spot among locals and tourists.

100m (109 yds.) past the ferry dock on the water. www.ultimorefugio.com. ℐ **6726-9851.** Main courses $7–$15. No credit cards. Mon–Fri 6–10pm.

Maracuya ★ INTERNATIONAL   This colorful little wooden house on the main drag, from the owner of OM Café, is the most eclectic restaurant in Bocas Town. It's a little bit Indian, a little bit Thai, a little bit Mediterranean, though every plate is driven by what's fresh. You might find lobster skewers in a green curry mango sauce or pork souvlaki. Breakfast goes beyond the standard with plates like Indian French toast and homemade granola. Occa-sionally, there's live music.

Calle 3a. www.maracuyabocas.com. No phone. Main courses $11.50–$13.50. Mon–Fri 8am–noon and 4–10pm.

OM Café ★ INDIAN   An Indian restaurant might seem like a surprising choice for one of the most beloved restaurants in Bocas Town, but that's exactly what OM Café is, having been around since 2002. The open-air dining area sits on the second floor with a street-facing balcony and has a chilled-out vibe that feels more Bocas than Mumbai. The menu is comprised of Indian standards like tandoori chicken, samosas, and several vegetarian dishes. The cocktail menu is one of the most inventive in town, and locals and tourists alike flock to the bar for the 4pm to 6:30pm happy hour. OM no longer serves breakfast since it's offered at its sister restaurant, Maracuya, across the street.

Av. E at Calle 2. www.omcafebocas.com. ℐ **6127-0671.** Main courses $5–$9. Mon–Sat 4–10pm.

INEXPENSIVE

Capitán Caribe ★ PANAMANIAN   Capitán Caribe is proof that even fast food can be made with love. This yellow wooden cart fronting a gravel lot with tables serves some of the most interesting local food in Bocas Town. Here burritos are stuffed with coconut rice, curried chicken, and pineapple chutney. It also makes a spectacular fish burger and much-hyped-about ceviches. Wash everything down with a fresh fruit smoothie.

Calle 1, beside Selina's Hostel. No phone. Main courses $5–$8. No credit cards. Tues–Sun 4–11pm.

PinUp ★ CAFE   In an old wooden building above a bookstore, this quirky cafe has a sort of thrown-together feel with its red-and-white-striped wall and clunky wooden tables. The menu is equally as random, with an emphasis on Italian, like homemade pastas (pumpkin gnocchi), and artisanal ice creams. But then there are classic island dishes like garlic shrimp and breakfast johnnycakes. Nothing is amazing, but PinUp is generally consistent.

Calle 2 at Av. E. ℂ **6700-4941.** Main courses $3–$10. No credit cards. Daily 8am–9pm.

Shopping

Funky design boutique **Black Cat,** Calle 1ra (ℂ **6139-5437;** Mon–Sat 10am–7pm), specializes in unique items like handpainted T-shirts and original artwork with a Bocas theme. A varied and ultra-cool selection of beachwear, flip-flops, and surf gear can be found at **Reggaeland** (daily 9am–9pm) on Main Street. You'll find a good selection of handicrafts, including Kuna Indian-made *molas,* at the compact **open-air market** at the end of Main Street and Avenida H.

Nightlife

Bocas Town is Party Central for the archipelago, but there are plenty of low-key venues for a quiet drink, and the town's laid-back, friendly atmosphere creates an environment that encourages meeting fellow travelers and locals. Nearly every bar and restaurant offers happy hour for about 4 hours, generally sometime between 4 and 8pm, with beer priced as low as 50¢. **La Iguana Surf Bar,** on Calle 3ra, is a good all-around bar, with a cool surfer theme and a wood-hewn, comfy ambience that's good for conversation and suitable for all ages, though late in the evening the party can pick up. The open-air waterfront bar **Barco Hundido (Shipwreck Bar),** on Calle 1, is the all-out party zone with late nights and dancing. The bar often has live DJs or bands with a cover charge. On Friday nights everyone takes a $1 water taxi ride to Isla Caranero to **Aqua Lounge** (www.bocasaqualounge.info), which has a dance floor, a large deck, and a swimming area that sees more than one person thrown in per night.

ISLA CARENERO (CAREENING CAY)

Isla Carenero practically adjoins Isla Colón, just a 2-minute water-taxi ride away. It is a more tranquil location to spend the night than Bocas, meaning you can be close to the action but get away from it when you choose. Water-taxi service only runs regularly until about 9pm, unless you arrange transportation ahead of time (and even then, taxis aren't enthusiastic about providing service past 10:30pm or so) or if it's a Friday and partygoers from Isla Colón are flocking to Isla Carenero's **Aqua Lounge** (www.bocasaqualounge.info) until the early morning. It is technically possible to walk around Isla Carenero, though the island has no roads, and the narrow beach disappears at points, making a meandering stroll more of a hike across rocks and up and down a few muddy slopes. The island has a sprinkling of hotels and restaurants, but most of the structures are the very modest homes of local Bocatorinos. Everything on the island is located on the waterfront, but only the hotels on the island's east side face a strip of beach (which, little by little, is disappearing). *Chitras,* those no-see-ums that bite like mad, are common on the island, so come armed with insect repellent.

Where to Stay on Isla Carenero

Casa Acuario ★ With the bright blue skies above and turquoise seas directly below, the blue-hued facade of this stilted guesthouse almost blends right into the horizon. The rooms are spacious, with lots of wood paneling and brightly colored Caribbean flair in the form of painted benches, rugs, and bedspreads. A huge wooden veranda, right outside your door, is laden with hammocks. You can loll about in a hammock or jump right off into the crystalline water. There's no formal restaurant on-site, but guests are able to use the kitchen to fix breakfast and light meals. Full breakfasts are available for an additional charge.

Isla Carenero. www.casaacuario.com. (✆) **757-9565.** 5 units. $88–$100 suite. No credit cards. **Amenities:** Shared kitchen; free Wi-Fi; no phone in room.

Tierra Verde ★ This family-run B&B fronting a small but pleasant beach, hidden behind swaying palm trees, is one of the better options on Isla Carenero for those looking for a sense of Bocas seclusion and not a lot of time. It's on the more tranquil eastern side of the island, isolated from the noise of Isla Colón, though close enough for a semi-quick water taxi ride to anywhere. The rooms are smallish and wood paneled but lack great views, aside from the two-bedroom suite, which has a private terrace. The owners are surfers and can arrange surf trips, as well as general tours, to almost anywhere in Bocas.

Isla Carenero. www.hoteltierraverde.com. (✆) **757-9903.** 7 units. $65–$75 double; $150 suite. Rates include breakfast. No credit cards. **Amenities:** Beverage bar; Internet station; no phone in room.

Where to Dine on Isla Carenero

Receta Michilá ★★★ PANAMANIAN When Chef Joseph Archibold was offered to open a restaurant in Panama City after years working in some of Paris's best kitchens, he turned it down, surprising everyone instead by opening in Bocas. Not only did Archibold and his French wife open a restaurant on Isla Carenero, but it is in the very same kitchen his parents once ran and where he learned to cook. Despite a laid-back setting beside a surf hostal on an island with no roads, and barefoot waitresses, Archibold's five-course tasting menus are by far the best thing to eat in Bocas del Toro, if not all of Panama. Sourced entirely from the region, Archibold's food revives traditional recipes, like the frothy banana coconut porridge called Michilá. On some nights the kitchen breaks from the more formal menu and serves things like Southern barbecue and Caribbean-style fish and chips.

Beside Gran Kahuna hostal. © **6368-5251.** Tasting menu $30. No credit cards. Reservations required. Tues–Sat 8–10am and 7:30–11pm.

ISLA BASTIMENTOS

Isla Bastimentos is the second-largest island in the archipelago and one of the region's most popular destinations for outstanding snorkeling and diving. It is also home to **Isla Bastimentos National Marine Park,** a boomerang-shaped park that protects a species-rich tropical jungle, pristine coral formations, and two tiny Robinson Crusoe–style islands ringed with powdery white sand. The island also has a few highly recommended lodges that put travelers far away from the hustle and bustle of Bocas Town, and closer to the aforementioned attractions.

Taking the island as a whole, Isla Bastimentos is a curious microcosm of ethnicities and income levels, of pristine landscapes and overdeveloped hamlets. There is one town here, the second largest in the Bocas Archipelago, called **Bastimentos Town.** Locals often refer to the town as Old Bank, and it can be found on the western tip of the island, about a 15-minute boat ride from Bocas Town. The community of 200 is principally Afro-Caribbean descendants (many prefer to be called *Creole*) from the banana plantation days. It's a little like Jamaica in the 1950s, and the poverty here can be equally heartbreaking and frightening: a collapsed pier, piles of garbage, women playing cards, men drinking beer or lurking about.

The official industry here is tourism, but you'd have to be an adventurous soul to brave spending a night here or even visiting the town's restaurant **Roots** (© **6662-1442**) for its popular "Blue Mondays" night with cold beer and reggae music. Still, Bocas residents consider Roots *the* local restaurant in the area, for its Caribbean vibe and inexpensive Creole food, arguably the best Creole food in the Bocas area. **Wizard Beach,** also called First Beach, is a popular surf spot for beginners for its smaller waves and absence of rocks; it can be reached by landing in Bastimentos Town and following a short path, but beware of youths who skulk at the path's entrance, demanding bribes to pass. The beach can also be reached by walking west from **Playa Segunda,** or Second Beach, home of the **Red Frog Beach Club** (www.redfrogbeach. com; © **757-4559**), a luxury resort development with two-bedroom homes and condos. Both Playa Segunda and Wizard Beach can be reached by walking from Red Frog Beach.

Beyond Afro-Caribbeans and wealthy foreigners, the island is also home to the Ngöbe-Buglé indigenous group, who live in two tiny communities in **Bahía Honda** and **Salt Creek Village,** the latter located on the southeastern shore and consisting of a cluster of thatched-roof huts, a small school, and a store.

What to See & Do

PARQUE NACIONAL MARINO ISLA BASTIMENTOS

A do-not-miss highlight in Bocas del Toro, this national park is an irregularly shaped swath of virgin tropical forest, pristine coral reef, and two white-sand islands called **Cayos Zapatilla,** or "Little Shoes Cays" (so-named for their resemblance to two footprints). There is no development here, save a small park-service hut and a ranger who may or may not charge the $10 per-person entry fee to walk on the islands. The more westerly island has an easy nature path called the "forest behind the reef."

The national park covers 12,950 hectares (32,000 acres), more than ¾ of which is marine park with a complex and diverse array of underwater life that makes an outstanding site for snorkeling and diving. Expect to see healthy brain, lettuce, and Elkhorn coral; tropical reef fish such as parrotfish and angelfish; and, in deeper water, spotted eagle rays. The wealth of coral species, fish, and marine invertebrates makes this one of the most extraordinary national parks in Panama. The park is also home to the largest concentration of mangrove swamp on the Caribbean coast. *Note:* When the sea is choppy, swimming and snorkeling here require extra work, and visibility is poor.

On land, the national park protects a portion of the island's dense tropical rainforest and endangered and threatened reptile species such as the Jurassic-era leatherback turtles and hawksbill turtles, which nest along with three other turtle species on **Playa Larga ★★,** a 5.6km-long (3½-mile) beach on the northern shore. The trail to this beach is one of the unsung excursions in Bocas del Toro, starting in the indigenous village of Salt Creek (see below), at Old Point, continuing through thick, steamy jungle, and ending on a beach with (usually) no one else around. Along the way you might see sloths or white-faced capuchin monkeys, not to mention many of the island's 68 species of birds. The trail is moderate, with undulations that can be difficult in some areas, requiring hands and shoes sturdier than sandals. Most tour operators offer this trek in conjunction with a visit to Salt Creek (the village can also be visited in conjunction with Zapatilla Cays). Contact **Ancon Expeditions** (www.anconexpeditions.com; © **269-9415**) for details on their Bocas excursions.

Quebrada de Sal, or **Salt Creek,** is a village community of Ngöbe-Buglé Indians who no longer practice many of their traditions—even the women here no longer wear the billowy, colorful dresses they are known for. Apart from a few cement buildings, a collection of thatched-roof huts, and a tiny souvenir shop, there isn't much to see here—but combined with the enjoyable boat ride and hike to Playa Larga, this is a pleasant full-day trip if coming from Bocas Town. Visitors are charged $1 to enter. A round-trip boat ride from Bocas town to Cayos Zapatilla will cost you at least $90.

BEACHES

The loveliest beaches in Bocas del Toro can be found here at Isla Bastimentos and at the Cayos Zapatilla on the eastern tip (part of the national park; see above). Island beaches here play a critical role as nesting sites for four of

Panama's five species of marine turtles. From late August to October, when calmer weather prevails, visitors can get to Isla Bastimentos's beaches by taking a boat directly at the shore; the rest of the year you'll have to walk. The easiest beach to reach is **Red Frog Beach,** a heavenly stretch of white sand, arching palms, and turquoise water—but be aware that riptides are treacherous here. The beach gets its name from a strawberry-colored poison frog that inhabits the surrounding forest. The frog is the size of a fingernail and can be difficult to spot; focus your search near trees and around loose leaves and you'll find one. Standard tours include Red Frog Beach as part of their day tour, but a water taxi can get you there for about $10 (20 min. from Bocas Town). Visitors get off in Magic Bay, pay a $1 entrance fee, and continue along an easy path for 5 minutes. The beach has a rustic bar with soft drinks, beer, and snacks. Continue west along the shore (if you can) to arrive at **Wizard Beach,** sometimes referred to as First Beach. A trail leads from Wizard Beach to Bastimentos Town.

CRAWL CAY

Alternatively called Coral Cay or Kraal Cay, Crawl Cay is located on the southern tip of Isla Bastimentos, about 30 minutes from Bocas Town. The area is known for shallow, translucent waters and an enormous garden of soft and hard coral, with excellent snorkeling and diving. There are two traditional restaurants here too, making this one of the most popular excursions in Bocas del Toro. The restaurants, a collection of thatched huts over water, serve Panamanian-style seafood, including crab, snapper, and shrimp ($8–$15 for a main course). Orders must be placed a full 1 to 2 hours ahead of time, so don't come hungry, or at least bring a snack to tide you over. Some unscrupulous tour companies save on gas by dumping guests here to snorkel around the restaurant. Insist that they take you out to the actual reef and then back for lunch.

BAHÍA HONDA COMMUNITY & NIVIDA BAT CAVES ★★

A visit to the Nivida Bat Cave in the Bahía Honda ranks as one of the most enjoyable—even spooky, but in a fun way—half-day tours in Bocas. After a 20-minute ride to Bahía Honda, visitors travel by motorized boat up a jungle-shrouded channel that provides excellent opportunities to see sloths hanging from tree branches and the occasional caiman silently resting in shallow water. Visitors walk through an old cacao farm, then don hard hats and rubber boots, and enter a subterranean river cave home to hundreds of tiny fruit bats. The journey is an impressive, Indiana Jones–style adventure, though not for the ultra-squeamish; tours normally end with a visit to the Bahía Honda Ngöbe-Buglé indigenous community for a typical—and quite delicious—lunch. The community comprises 20 indigenous families living in homesteads around the bay, with a small "village" center located on the lee side of Bastimentos Island. Here Ngöbe-Buglé women demonstrate their process of weaving traditional bags and have many on hand for sale. Spanish-speaking **Rutilio Milton** (© **6669-6269**) offers tours, or try **Oscar's Bat Cave Tours** (© **6515-9276**). Tours cost about $25 per person, and you'll need to make a reservation at least a day in advance for lunch.

Where to Stay & Dine

If you're the kind of traveler who'd rather get away from it all, consider basing yourself on Isla Bastimentos. Some of the region's best lodges are concentrated here, and a few (such as Casa Cayuco) front the tranquil waters of the island's eastern shores, providing good swimming conditions year-round and a safe environment for families with kids. *Note:* Because of the distance from Bocas Town, meals and snacks are generally included as part of any resort package on Isla Bastimentos, but be sure to inquire about what's *not* included, in most cases alcoholic beverages, gratuities, and guided excursions.

It can take from 45 minutes to an hour by boat to reach lodges here on Bastimentos. There are no stores here, so bring along any necessities.

Casa Cayuco ★ Planted right on a chilled-out Bastimentos beach, Casa Cayuco is popular with weddings and corporate retreats, thanks to PG jungle fun like a well-marked forest trail and lots of watersports activities. Thatched roofs adorn the open-air cabins, all of which have covered porches and beds fitted with gel-top memory-foam mattresses made for tropical environments. The three-story, treehouse-like main lodge has high ceilings supported by Nispero log beams native to Panama. The property has three boats, which allow for several different guided excursions (requiring an additional fee), such as snorkeling in the Zapatilla marine park or visiting a chocolate farm in Dolphin Bay. Because of its remote location, the resort has a 3-night minimum stay.

Isla Bastimentos. www.casacayuco.com. ℂ **509/996-4178.** Cabins $270–$345 for two; main lodge $300–$325 for two; single guest rate $205–$235. Rates include all meals, snacks, and roundtrip boat transfers. Discounts offered for groups of 10 or more. Closed Nov. No children 5 and under. **Amenities:** Restaurant; bar; watersports equipment (extensive); tours; free Wi-Fi.

La Loma Jungle Lodge ★ Part jungle resort, part cacao farm, La Loma's 23 hectares (57 acres) stretch from the mangrove-lined shoreline of Bahía Honda up the forested hillsides to one of the highest points on Bastimentos. The four thatched-roof ranchos have solar lighting and are primarily open-air (get inside that mosquito net at night!), giving a sense of closeness to the elements. Cabin nos. 2 and 3, a bit higher up the hill, have better views and increase your chances of glimpsing troops of monkeys swinging through the forest canopy. Idyllic beaches are found a 5-minute boat ride away within the marine park that borders the property. The property works closely with the 30 indigenous Ngöbe-Buglé families that live in Bahía Honda, using them as guides and buying organic produce from their farms. There is a 2-night minimum stay.

Isla Bastimentos. www.thejunglelodge.com. ℂ **6619-5364** or 6592-5162. $90–$125 per person based on double occupancy. Rates include all meals, roundtrip boat transfers, tours of the cacao farm and food gardens, and trips to Red Frog Beach. No children 5 and under. **Amenities:** Restaurant; kayaks and dugout canoe; watersports rentals; no phone in room.

Popa Paradise Beach Resort ★★ "Barefoot luxury" is the theme of this adults-only, all-inclusive resort on the tip of Isla Popa in the outer archipelago. Two white sandy beaches meet guests on arrival after a 35-minute boat ride from Bocas Town, but the fun is just getting started. The property also includes an infinity pool, a 464 sq.-m (5,000 sq.-ft.) clubhouse, and an on-site restaurant that uses fruits, vegetables, and herbs grown on the property. The 10 casitas feature Balinese furnishings and large, shaded verandas, while the five lodge rooms are quite plain. A two-bedroom luxury suite adds a full kitchen, living areas, and a wraparound balcony.

Isla Bastimentos. www.popaparadisebeachresort.com. © **832-1498** or 6550-2505. 16 units. $310–$465 economic rooms; $365–$625 casitas; $495–$745 junior suite; $575–$845 luxury suite. Rates include all meals, beverages, and roundtrip boat transfers. **Amenities:** Restaurant; bar; infinity pool; watersports equipment (extensive); free Wi-Fi.

Tranquilo Bay ★★★ Tranquilo Bay is the all-around top luxury hotel in the Bocas Archipelago and one of the island's most family-friendly lodgings—kids of all ages are welcome. For those adventurous travelers looking to be submerged in the region's stunning natural surroundings, from lush jungle to thick mangroves, without giving up hot showers and Wi-Fi, this is the place to be. The deluxe cabins are air-conditioned and feature local hardwoods throughout, as well as granite countertops in the bathroom and large decks looking out towards the ocean. A canopy tower gives spectacular views of the 200-forested acres of land, including monkeys and more than 180 species of birds found here. Although Tranquilo Bay lacks a beach, excursions to the Zapatilla Cays rectify this. On most of the included adventures you won't see other tourists, since the snorkel trips, jungle hikes, and river kayaking tend to be where no one else will go.

Isla Bastimentos. www.tranquilobay.com. © **620-4179.** 6 units (cabanas). Packages $275–$411 per person per night, based on double occupancy. Rates include roundtrip boat transfers (Wed and Sat only; all other days $100); all meals and snacks; many guided activities and tours; and nonalcoholic beverages, Panamanian beer, South American house wine, and Panamanian rum. **Amenities:** Restaurant; bar; lounge; watersports equipment (extensive); free Wi-Fi; no phone in room.

ISLA SOLARTE

2km (1¼ miles) E of Isla Colón

Isla Solarte, also known as **Nancy's Cay,** is a 1.3-sq.-km (½-sq.-mile) island known for **Hospital Point,** one of the best areas for snorkeling and close to Isla Colón. Hospital Point is named for an old hospital built by the United Fruit Company to treat plantation workers suffering from yellow fever and malaria. Today a gated, upscale residential community is spreading across the island, protected by security services and attracting foreigners seeking a slice of paradise.

ISLA CRISTÓBAL & LAGUNA BOCATORITO

10km (6¼ miles) S of Isla Colón

Isla Cristóbal is a 37-sq.-km (14-sq.-mile), mostly deforested island south of Isla Colón. The island and a peninsula that juts from the mainland form a nearly enclosed bay called **Laguna Bocatorito,** or Dolphin Bay—so-called for the bottlenose-dolphin breeding site found here. Dolphins swim up close to visiting boats and prance about, making this one of the region's most enjoyable attractions. The best time to come is from June to September, when dozens of dolphins meet in the bay to create a wild version of Sea World. For the rest of the year, here's a tip: Try to visit the bay after the morning tour boats do their thing (which amounts to speeding around in circles in an effort to stir things up and draw the dolphins to the surface but ends up disturbing the dolphins instead), and find a tour or book a custom trip going at a quieter pace. More dolphins show themselves when the bay isn't being churned up. For tours, see "What to See & Do" under "Isla Colón: Bocas Town," earlier in this chapter.

COMARCA KUNA YALA

With more than 350 picture-postcard islands and islets ringed by powdery white sand, a coral reef, and piercing turquoise water, the Comarca Kuna Yala is a fascinating and primitive region that fulfills every tourist's, yachter's, and cruiser's island fantasy. Given the pristine beauty of the region—most islands are populated with no more than a cluster of coconut palms—it is *the* premier beach destination in Panama. But what really sets it apart is that it provides you with the opportunity to spend time with the Kuna indigenous group that lives here.

The region formerly known as the San Blas Archipelago is now officially known as the Comarca Kuna Yala (although many Panamanians continue to use its former moniker). The "Kuna Yala" means "Land of the Kuna," and a *comarca* is a semiautonomous province governed by three tribal chiefs, or *caciques,* with the input of dozens of regional representatives. As a semiautonomous province, the Kuna have maintained their cultural identity and integrity, and have complete control over economic matters such as tourism. (For example, it is considered improper to travel with an "outside" tour company that has not requested permission from tribal chiefs.) Since the colonial period, the Kuna have successfully resisted invasions by pirates, colonists, missionaries, adventurers, and developers.

An estimated 50,000 Kuna are spread across 49 communities in the region and are scattered in areas as far away as Panama City and farther east in the Darién. Of the seven indigenous tribes in Panama, the Kuna Yala are the most visible, not only for their ubiquity, but for the kaleidoscopic-colored costumes worn by the women in the tribe. Men wear western clothing, but Kuna women wear skirts and *mola*-appliquéd shirts in yellows and reds, head scarves, a gold ring in their septum, and usually a single black line drawn down the crest of their nose; their arms and legs are bound with tiny beads. The Kuna's livelihood depends on coconut harvesting, fishing, and subsistence farming, and, on a very small scale, tourism.

The comarca extends well beyond the island region, incorporating the coastal forest on the northern slope of the San Blas mountain range. Because it has been allowed to remain untouched, the virgin forest is home to a species diversity not found anywhere else

Area of detail

El Porvenir

Panama City

Caribbean Sea

PANAMA

Golfo de Panamá

10 mi
10 km

Diving, Snorkeling

50 mi
0 50 km

CARIBBEAN SEA

COMARCA KUNA YALA (SAN BLAS)

COMARCA KUNA DE WARGANDÍ

COMARCA KUNA DE MADUNGANDÍ

PANAMÁ

COLÓN

Achutupo
Mamitupo
Ailigandí
Ogobgandí
San Ignacio de Tupile
Playón Chico
Sábalo

Chepo
Piriá
Cañazas

Ipetí Kuna
Ipetí Colono
Ipetí
Piriatí

Pan-American Highway

Ticantiquí
Tigre
Niatupo
Corazón de Jesus
Narganá
Río Azúcar

Cayos Ordupuquip

Diablo
Río Diablo
Chepo
Pirtegua

Icantí
Icantí
Pintupo

Akua Yala (El Puente)
Lago Bayano
Majé

Cayos Holandéses

Cayos Los Grullos

Kuanidup
Río Sidra
Soledad
Carti Suitipo

Jenené
Cañita

Majecito

Wichiyupo Grande
Isla Perro
Ogobsibu
El Porvenir

Golfo de San Blas

Wichubwala

Naranjos Grandes

Nusagandí
Carti Gde

Aswa
Carti Chico

Cañita

El Llano

Jesus María
Trapiche
Seis Reales

Paja

Chepo

Chepo

Mamoni

9

COMARCA KUNA YALA | Introduction

in Panama; if visiting the mainland jungle interests you, you'll need a local guide (your lodge can provide you with one), or you can book a trip with a company such as Xtrop. (See "Adventure-Tour Outfitters & Activities," below.)

LODGING IN THE SAN BLAS ARCHIPELAGO   There are no megar-esorts or five-star hotels in the Kuna Yala Islands. Do not expect to find satellite TV, Internet, widespread telephone service, 24-hour electricity, or even laundry service at lodges and hostels here. This is Panama unplugged, although two simple lodges in the eastern side of the comarca provide a few creature comforts to satisfy travelers who don't relish roughing it. If you're a particularly fussy traveler, you'll want to book with one of the luxury sailboats that can be chartered here, or you might want to consider just coming for the day or a different beach destination in Panama. Some hostels and lodges mentioned in this chapter now have an e-mail address, and some even have websites. E-mails are checked within 2 days; however, you might find it far more convenient to have a travel agency or tour operator book your stay, since most lodge owners speak little or no English. Also, because credit cards are not accepted in the region, you can charge your stay if booking with a tour operator or agency. It is highly recommended that you book ahead of time to secure a room or *cabaña,* and also to verify that a boat will be waiting at the airport dock to get you there. Spontaneous travelers who just show up will have better luck finding lodging in the El Porvenir area. All prices shown are per person, per night, and are **all-inclusive,** meaning three meals a day and local tours and transportation are included. Most hostels have Spanish-only guides, or you can go with a tour operator who will provide a bilingual guide during your trip.

One of the things that makes the Kuna Islands unique compared with other regions of Panama is that the Kuna Indians have not allowed foreign (or even Panamanian) investments on their lands, which accounts for the lack of resorts and high-end hotels favored by foreign investors. Although some argue that this strictly enforced Kuna law has slowed possible economic development on the comarca, others believe it is the main reason the Kuna's culture has been able to survive and flourish. There is always talk of possibly changing this law in the future, but as of now, all hotels and lodging options must be Kuna owned and run. Although this might mean there isn't going to be a Four Seasons San Blas anytime soon, the Kuna's determination to keep their land autonomous and free of foreign investments is what makes it so special; unlike Boquete, the Pacific Coast, and Bocas del Toro, which feel somewhat like tropical American/Canadian colonies, the San Blas Islands feel refreshingly free of overdevelopment and foreign encroachment. As the islands become more and more popular with visitors, the tourism infrastructure will likely slowly catch up.

EL PORVENIR & WESTERN COMARCA KUNA YALA

El Porvenir is the governmental seat of the Comarca Kuna Yala and the principal gateway for most travelers. There isn't much marine life in the immediate area for snorkeling; what you come for here is to swing in a hammock, swim, and get some sun. With this in mind, 2 or 3 nights is about the maximum travelers stay here. There is one hotel on El Porvenir Island, but most travelers head straight to the dock for the short boat ride to hostels on the islands of Wichubwala, Nalunega, Ukutupu, and Ogobsibudsup. The cheapest lodging in San Blas can be found in this area, making it a popular destination with backpackers. Porvenir is a service-based island—but that isn't saying much, since all you'll find is an administrative center for governmental offices, a police station, a tiny museum that's usually closed, and public telephones. For a **map** of the region, stop at the police station to buy the "Mapa de Comunidades, Recursos Turísticos y Servicios del Golfo de Kuna Yala" ($5).

Essentials

GETTING THERE & DEPARTING

BY PLANE   **Air Panama** (www.flyairpanama.com; ✆ **316-9000**) has semi-regular flights and charters to El Porvenir, Achutupo, Corazón de Jesús, Mulatupo, Ogobsucum, Playón Chico, and Puerto Obaldia (check the website for schedule information). With many travelers now arriving via the road from Los Llanos to Cartí, the frequency of flights has slowed, and many previously regularly scheduled flights must now be chartered. The 20-minute flight to El Porvenir from Panama City costs about $50 to $120 each way, taxes included. The worst aspect of traveling to the comarca is that flights leave at the crack of dawn (6am), although large groups may charter a flight at a later hour. Return flights leave at 7am. *Tip:* If you do not have a return ticket or are unsure of your departure date, the Hotel El Porvenir sells plane tickets for Air Panama. For **charter flights,** contact Air Panama (✆ **315-0439;** charter@flyairpanama.com). Be sure to call ahead to confirm flight times—these are subject to changes by season.

BY ROAD & BOAT   There is no public ground transportation to the comarca, meaning most travelers arrive by boat or plane. The road to the Comarca Kuna Yala is mostly paved all the way to Cartí, though it can still be rather rough, with frequent landslides and fallen branches, not to mention steep inclines and winding stretches. Do not attempt this road with a regular car—you *will* get stuck if you try. Also, note that you'll sometimes have to cross a small river, so road travel to the comarca during rainy season is complicated at best and out of the question at worst, depending on the rainfall. That said, the El Llano–Cartí road offers great mountain and rainforest scenery that, in my opinion, makes the rough ride worth it. However, it's important to note that this road is best for adventurous types who aren't daunted by an

SPECIAL considerations IN THE SAN BLAS COMMUNITY

All islands here are owned by Kuna families, no matter how isolated or even if they're totally uninhabited. Therefore, it is not permitted to **camp** overnight on an uninhabited island without an owner's permission. Though you will not receive anything as serious as jail time or a fine, it is considered by the Kuna to be a tremendous breach of respect. The **cost to visit an island** is anywhere from $1 to $20 per person; you'll be expected to pay for every island you visit, no matter how close they are to each other. Of course, if an island is uninhabited, the owner might or might not show up to charge you.

Although **scuba diving is prohibited** within the Comarca Kuna Yala, **snorkeling** is not. If you are interested in diving just outside the San Blas, you'll need to contact **Panama Divers** (www.panamadivers.com; ✆ **448-2293**).

Kuna people are extremely **sensitive to having their pictures taken.** *Always* ask permission before taking a photo of a Kuna Indian, especially if it is a Kuna chief (recognizable by a felt hat and short jacket). Most Kunas, especially those in areas frequented by tourists, will charge $1 to $3 to have their photo taken.

Movistar cellular phones do not have coverage in the comarca, but others do, though there is only service in the Cartí-Río Sidra sector. There are **public telephones** on the islands of El Porvenir, Wichubwala, and Gardi Sugdup, and the Sapibenega Kuna Lodge has telephones. Many hostels and lodges on islands have cellphones for emergencies. There are also satellite phones in areas where there's no cellphone coverage.

Basic **medical facilities** are located in Gardi Sugdup and Río Sidra; for more serious medical issues, you'll need to fly to Panama City.

There is only one **bank** in the entire region, in the Nargana community, so come with enough cash plus a little extra just in case. Also, bring enough small bills for purchases.

The **food** served in the comarca is almost always fish and shellfish—usually cooked the same way every day. If you are allergic to fish, are a vegetarian, or simply do not fancy dining on seafood day in and day out, advise your hosts well ahead of time so that they can be prepared when you arrive, or simply bring your own food. Bringing your own snacks and sunscreen is essential because there are no stores.

extremely bumpy ride, the possibility of getting stuck in mudholes, and crossing a (possibly) high river.

Note that a flight from Panama City to El Porvenir takes about 20 minutes, while the last 45km (28 miles) of the El Llano–Cartí road alone can take upwards of 1.5 hours. From Panama City, you can usually make the trip in about 2.5 to 3 hours each way. If you'd like to go by road but find driving a bit overwhelming, most travel agencies in Panama City can arrange 4x4 jeeps that can drive and pick you up from the Port of Cartí for about $40 to $60 each way. You're required to pay a $20 tax per car at a control point along the road.

From Cartí, *cayucos,* which are large dugout canoes with outboard motors, transport travelers to the islands in the insular region. Boat transportation from the Port of Cartí costs about $15 to $40 each way, depending on your destination.

BY CRUISE SHIP   The Comarca Kuna Yala is a popular cruise-ship destination for its shimmering white-sand beaches. Ships dock and tender guests usually to Ikodue, which has bathrooms. Depending on the circumstances, it can, unfortunately, be an uncomfortable experience, since some cruises are approached by poor Kuna women in *cayucos* begging for coins. Kuna women will also cart over their handicrafts to sell.

GETTING AROUND

Transportation around the islands is by motorboat (sometimes called a *panga*), or a *cayuco*. All lodging options listed in this chapter provide boat transportation as part of their all-inclusive price; day excursions by boat are included except for faraway destinations such as the Cayos Holandéses. Travel to and from the western comarca's gulf to the east (to the Dolphin Lodge or the Sapibenega Lodge) by boat is nearly impossible, thanks to choppy sea conditions, time (up to 4 hr.), and reluctance by boat owners to undergo the distance. The only air service between the two regions is a thrice-weekly flight from El Porvenir to Corazón de Jesús. You can also hire a *cayuco* to get you around the different islands if you're camping or you want to see the region on your own. Because gas is expensive on the Kuna Islands, boat transportation can get expensive fast. However, island hopping and searching for the perfect, secluded beach among 350-plus islands is part of the fun, and if you have a big enough group and can split the cost, this option is well worth it.

What to See & Do

BEACHES & SNORKELING   Local tours are included in the price of lodging, but to neighboring islands and attractions only. The beaches at **Isla Hierba** are the closest to El Porvenir, and visitors to lodges near that island normally head there when they want to loll in the sun. A popular snorkeling site nearby is **Isla Perro ★★**, which has a sunken ship just off the coast. A stone's throw away is the **Isla Pelicano ★**, with fine white-sand beaches.

For the best snorkeling, you'll need to head out to **Cayos Holandéses ★★★**, a chain of utterly perfect islands ringed by blue water and coral, and home to more marine life than you'd find closer to the overfished area around El Porvenir, but no tourism facilities. There is also a wreck reef that has sunk many drug-running boats from Colombia. Private sailboats and yachts like to hang out around the Cayos; getting here requires extra time (2–3 hr. round-trip by boat from El Porvenir) and extra money ($250–$300), depending on the price of gas and number of people. The Cayos are roughly equidistant from El Porvenir and Río Sidra, about 20km (12½ miles).

From Cartí, many head to **Isla Naidup** or **Isla Iguana ★**. Both can easily be reached on a day trip, but the dining and lodging facilities there are basic. The water is still crystal clear, though the reef is better farther away from the mainland.

KUNA VILLAGES   Visits to Kuna communities can be custom-arranged with your lodge. Arranging visits is not complicated; however, a few villages

ADVENTURE-TOUR OUTFITTERS & activities

Before embarking on a tour to Kuna Yala, be sure that your outfitter is actually permitted to give tours in the comarca; Kuna Yala is an autonomous region of Panama, and tourism rules and regulations are set by the Kuna Council.

KAYAKING No outfitter has more experience operating in the comarca or is more dedicated to preserving the Kuna Yala culture than **Xtrop ★★★** (www.xtrop.com; ✆ **317-1279**), short for **Expediciones Tropicales.** The Panama City–based company is highly respected, specializing in sea-kayak tours with an emphasis on nature and culture, and employing only local Kuna guides. Xtrop, which works with companies like Mountain Travel Sobek in the U.S., has received permission from Kuna chiefs to operate in some of the areas that are richest in marine life (they call them "aquatic trails"), and they have access to areas no one else can go, including forested coastal areas. Best of all, Xtrop is very active in developing programs in the region for sustainable tourism, so you can feel good about how your money is spent. Xtrop has approximately 20 years of experience in the comarca and is one of the few companies officially allowed to take tours and excursions to Kuna Yala. Trips are from 3 nights to a week long, and lodging is in tents or huts. Xtrop can also book just lodging for you, if that's the only service you need.

HIKING & GENERAL TOURS Ecocircuitos ★★ (http://ecocircuitos.com; ✆ **314-0068** or 800/830-71142 in the U.S.) has guided walks through PEMASKY (Project for the Study and Management of Wilderness Areas of Kuna Yala), a protected coastal jungle in the comarca around the road to Cartí Suitupo, ranked as one of the best trails in the world for spotting birds and diverse flora. Ecocircuitos also offers multiday trips around Panama that include a couple of days visiting islands in the comarca.

For a truly custom tour of the Kuna Yala Islands (or for that matter anywhere in Panama) contact freelance guide **Gilberto Alemancia,** who oversees the Indigenous and Local Communities Department at the ATP (✆ **6948-0525**; gilbert04@yahoo.com). Gilberto has coordinated expeditions for *National Geographic*, Photo Safari, PhotoAdventure, Discovery Channel Adventure, and the BBC, and is the go-to guy for all things Kuna. Fully bilingual and U.S.–educated, Gilberto is himself a Kuna and extremely knowledgeable about that culture's history and customs. With advance notice, he can organize specialized tours, set up boat transportation and camping trips, or even accompany visitors to the different islands, which can include a stay at a traditional Kuna hut.

The outfitter **Adventures in Panama** (www.adventuresinpanama.com; ✆ **877/726-6222** in the U.S.) can also book lodges for travelers having a hard time booking one on their own.

SAILING San Blas Sailing ★ (www.sanblassailing.com; ✆ **314-1800**) is a French-owned company with a fleet of monohull and multihull sailboats; the largest boat can hold eight passengers. San Blas Sailing has been based in the comarca since 1997 and knows the area intimately. Trips, which run from 3 to 14 nights and include meals, drinks, tours, and onboard accommodations, involve sailing around the islands, snorkeling, kayaking, and visiting Kuna villages. If you are looking for fine accommodations in the comarca, this is your best bet, but of course you'll spend all your nights on board.

are more conservative than others and have not embraced the idea of tourism. Check your options with your tour/boat guide. The most common village, and one that's really worth a visit because it seems like a metropolis when compared with the surrounding island villages, is **Gardi Sugdup.** This island is part of the community of **Cartí,** which consists of several island villages and a stretch of coastline. It's a heavily populated island with a warren of passageways that fan out spiderlike around squashed-together wooden huts and cement public buildings and stores. There's a lot of trash floating around the place, but once you get past the dock, you'll find that putting yourself in the middle of this thriving Kuna community is a truly fascinating experience. In terms of tourism, this is probably the most visited Kuna village in the comarca, and it has a landing strip, a store, and a **museum** (daily 8am–4pm; admission $3). It's a humble museum, located in a thatched-roof hut, but there's enough here to keep a visitor's interest. You'll see displays of Kuna culture and rituals, and often a "docent" is available who speaks enough English to convey the meaning behind the artifacts on display.

Where to Stay & Dine

Aside from the lodging options listed below, another option in the Kuna Islands is camping or sleeping in a hammock under a couple of palm trees. Despite its tropical location, the islands have few mosquitoes or other biting insects, and nights are breezy and cool, making for comfortable sleeping conditions; in fact, you may even want to pack a light sweater or blanket. Just ask your boatman to take you to an empty island, and you'll have your own private tropical paradise. You can arrange to have your meals brought to you by boat for an additional price. Remember, however, that you'll be without electricity or bathrooms, so this option is best for just 1 or 2 nights. *Note:* Be sure to get permission from the island's owner before your stay. The most popular islands for camping are **Icotupu** (✆ **299-9074**); **Isla Pelicano** (✆ **299-9000**); **Isla Achutupu** (✆ **299-9000**); and **Isla Porvenir** (✆ **299-9056**). Camping can also be set up through your hotel. All hotel options below include three meals a day.

AROUND EL PORVENIR

Cabañas Narasgandup ★ On the tiny island of Narasgandup, or Naranjo Chico, the friendly Del Valle family runs this small, simple complex. It's a mix of sandy-floor oceanfront huts with shared bathrooms and wood-floor overwater huts with private bathrooms. All units have electricity from 6 to 10pm. Rates also include snorkeling, boat trips, and visits to local communities, as well as transportation from either the El Porvenir airstrip or Cartí. Note that checkout is at 8am.

Isla Narasgandup Bipi. www.sanblaskunayala.com. ✆ **6687-7437.** 6 units. Oceanfront double $220; overwater double $170. No credit cards. **Amenities:** Restaurant; bar.

THE KUNA revolution

The Kuna are the only indigenous group in Panama to gain their autonomy through violent rebellion. After Panama gained its independence from Colombia, the Kuna felt that the new Panamanian state was attempting to suppress their culture, customs, and lands. A determined people, they believed the only way they could protect their culture and guarantee their survival was through violence.

On February 21, 1925, the Kuna took advantage of the February Carnavales and attacked the national Panamanian police. The police had been drinking heavily, and the Kuna caught them off guard. An armed battle ensued through February 27, resulting in 27 casualties between the two sides.

On March 4, 1925, a peace act was signed between the Kuna and the Panamanian government that resulted in the creation of the Autonomous Kuna Comarca, encompassing the Caribbean coastal region and over 350 islands near the Colombian border. The government also promised to respect the customs of the Kuna, to establish schools on their lands, and to guarantee them the same rights and privileges enjoyed by other Panamanians. In return, the Kunas agreed to disarm, renounce their call for independence, and obey Panamanian law.

Today the Comarca Kuna Yala is, for the most part, autonomous from the Panamanian government, and they consider themselves their own country. The Kuna continue to abide by their own rules and laws, and in fact, the only time the National Police are allowed to make decisions in the Comarca is when narco-trafficking is involved; otherwise, police only enter the comarca if they are called upon to do so by the *caciques* (policy-makers) of the comarca.

Every year, on February 25, the Kuna reenact the events that lead to their autonomy. This is an interesting time to visit the islands, as you'll have the opportunity to see reenactments and enjoy the accompanying festivities.

Hotel El Porvenir ★   Directly beside the airstrip, the Porvenir is the closest thing San Blas has to a proper hotel; it makes a good base for exploring the surrounding islands. The rooms, encircling a common courtyard, are quite basic, with tile floors and semi-orthopedic beds, though they do have private bathrooms, and a generator provides electricity for a few hours each day, a real luxury here. The very average restaurant and bar are a hangout for passing travelers. A small strip of beach has lounge chairs, but most guests plan day trips to better beaches on nearby islands. Ask about discounts for longer stays.

Isla El Porvenir. www.hotelporvenir.com. © **6718-2826.** 14 units. $110 per person. No credit cards. **Amenities:** Restaurant; bar; pool table.

AROUND RÍO SIDRA

Kuanidup Island Lodge ★   This stunning little island, surrounded by crystalline waters and ringed with palm trees, is one of the most idyllic in the western side of the comarca. Although it is remote and the rustic sand-floor bungalows are clustered tightly together, many travelers appreciate the authenticity of the experience. A foam mattress and a shared bathroom are the extent of the creature comforts you get with the accommodations. The island

THE KUNA society

The Kuna are a tightly knit indigenous group who live much as they have for centuries. Although three male *caciques* reign as policy deciders, it is a matriarchal society in which inheritance is passed down through women. Women are also the primary breadwinners, considering the income they earn from selling *mola* panels and other handicrafts to tourists. Still, such modern delving into economics is new for the Kuna, who not very long ago had no word for money and used coconuts as a "monetary" unit. (As proof of the effects of tourism on society, Kunas use the word "money" instead of *dinero*.)

When a Kuna girl is born, she is given a nickname but does not receive her official Kuna name until she reaches puberty. Of course, the nickname is what everyone goes back to calling her soon after her traditional puberty ceremony. During this ceremony, a girl is expected to cut her hair short and keep it this way her entire adult life. Kuna women, with their colorful dress, gold jewelry, and *mola*-making talent, are guardians of Kuna culture. Men, on the other hand, wear Western clothing and rely on coconut-collecting and fishing to make a living. Kunas are monogamous and consider adultery a crime.

Squat with broad shoulders and disproportionately large heads, the Kuna are the second-smallest people in the world (African pygmies are the smallest). Although scientists still have no idea why, the rate of albinism here is the highest in the world. Albinos are called "Moon Children" and are considered to hold special powers and possess a high intelligence.

Molas are brightly colored reverse-appliqué panels and the principal artistic expression of the Kuna. *Molas* are made by sewing together layers of fabric and cutting down through the layers to form imaginative designs and figures. Kuna women wear *molas* sewn onto their blouses, and *molas* average $25 per panel but often the price can be negotiated, especially when buying several.

features a volleyball net and minimal solar power, though the bar is well stocked to help make up for the lack of amenities. This is one of the few lodges to provide ground transportation from Panama City, besides three daily meals (beverages extra) and a daily shared tour. ***Another plus:*** Payments can also be made by credit card in advance.

Isla Kuanidup. www.kuanidup.com. © **6656-4673.** 12 units. $199 per person the first night and $107 each additional night. Rates includes three daily meals, shared daily tour, and roundtrip ground transportation from Panama City. Children 18 and under get a 20% discount when traveling with 2 adults. **Amenities:** Restaurant; bar.

EASTERN COMARCA KUNA YALA

The eastern region of the comarca is visited less frequently by tourists than the El Porvenir area. Travelers can expect to find a higher level of biodiversity and wilder natural surroundings here; according to Smithsonian scientists, the islands that dot the coast feature the highest diversity of coral species in

Panama. Yet this region, too, has suffered from overfishing. If you're lucky, you might see dolphins, manta rays, and manatees. Kuna villages in this region, especially **Corazón de Jesús,** are significantly more Westernized, and the people who live here reside in modern buildings, don less traditional clothing, and participate in modern pastimes like watching TV. If you'd like to visit a traditional village in this region, your best bet is the tidy **Isla Tigre,** which was the site of the violent overthrow of Panamanian forces in 1925 when the Kuna first asserted their independent authority over the region. Isla Tigre is a little less than 5km (3 miles) east of Corazón de Jesús. This village, along with Playón Chico and Mamitupo, has landing strips with flights from Panama City.

You'll find the Comarca Kuna Yala's most **deluxe lodging** in this region, at Yandup and the Dolphin Lodge, or you can tour the region in kayaks with the outfitter Xtrop (p. 214), which has a special license to visit the area's pristine regions. Lodges mentioned in this section include tours of the immediate area in the price; note that Corazón de Jesús has no accommodations.

Essentials

GETTING HERE & DEPARTING

BY PLANE   Air Panama (www.flyairpanama.com; *©* **316-9000**) offers regular connecting flights from Panama City to Achutupu, Corazón de Jesús, and Playón Chico, costing about $100 to $140 roundtrip. Call the airline to verify the days when flights leave for Corazón de Jesús, Playón Chico, and Mamitupu, since this information is subject to change.

Where to Stay

The Dolphin Lodge ★★   Sometimes called Uaguinega Ecoresort, this above-average Kuna-run lodge has been around since 1992. There's no village to speak of on the island, just a thin strip of beach. The cabins have been continually updated or rebuilt over the years, leaving a mishmash of differing styles. Most of the stylish bungalows have hardwood floors, ocean views, bamboo-thatched walls, and terraces; a few simpler rooms come with cement floors and wood walls. All have private bathrooms and solar-powered electricity. The daily tours are a highlight here and include visits to the museum on Alligandi, handicraft making on Mamitupu, hiking along the Sangandi River, and snorkeling at Akwanasad or Cainora. The only way to get here is to fly to Achutupu, a 15-minute boat ride away.

Isla Uaguitupu. www.dolphinlodgesanblas.com. *©* **394-4805.** 11 units. $200 double; $255 triple. **Amenities:** Restaurant; bar.

Yandup Island Lodge ★★   This family-owned lodge is on a small private island not far from the airstrip at Playón Chico in the far east of the comarca. Though rustic, the thatched-roof oceanfront and overwater cabins are some of the better-designed and most complete accommodations in San

Blas, with wood floors, hand-carved wooden furniture, and terraces. Pillows have *mola* covers, and each unit comes with a private bathroom and a fan. Electricity is generated from solar panels 24 hours a day. Packages include meals, airport transfers, and two daily tours to uninhabited islands and a hike to a waterfall. See "Special Considerations in the San Blas Community," earlier in the chapter, for details on community fees to visit the islands.

Isla Yandup. www.yandupisland.com. © **203-7762.** 7 units. $250 oceanfront double; $277 overwater double. No credit cards. **Amenities:** Restaurant; bar.

THE DARIÉN PROVINCE

10

The Darién Province, a remote, sparsely populated expanse of tropical rainforest and swampland along Panama's eastern boundary with Colombia, is considered Central America's last grand, untamed wilderness. Home to nearly .8 million hectares (2 million acres) of protected land, the Darién includes **La Reserva Natural Privada Punta Patiño** and the **Parque Nacional del Darién,** Panama's largest protected area and a UNESCO Biosphere Reserve. This entire wilderness is commonly called the "Darién Gap," which refers to the roadless swath of forest that is the "missing link" in the Pan American Highway from Alaska to Chile. Colombia would like to extend the road, but Panamanians fear widespread environmental destruction and an increase in drug trafficking. For now at least, a road seems unlikely.

Given the Darién's inaccessibility, there are few places a traveler can actually visit within the boundaries of the province. The national park measures a staggering 860,000 hectares (2.1 million acres), yet only the **Pirre** and **Cana** stations offer trails and basic services. On the southern coast at Piñas Bay is the famous Tropic Star Lodge, and there are trails and dugout canoe trips on rivers around Punta Patiño.

Travelers can drive to the end of the Pan American Highway to Yaviza on their own, but it's unlikely that you'd want to. The road is flanked by mostly deforested land with nothing of interest except for a few blink-and-you-miss-it hamlets providing truly grim lodging and mediocre services. The road is mostly unpaved and requires a four-wheel-drive (4WD) during the rainy season. Some tours use the Pan American Highway to reach their final destination in the Darién.

The Darién is just not developed for do-it-yourself travelers, and tales abound of travelers getting lost for days in the jungle or having run-ins with terrorist groups along the northern Colombia border. Let someone else do the planning for you. Destinations such as the Cana Field Station actually require booking a tour that includes a charter flight to get there. Considering the lack of roads and the

inexpensive flights aboard small planes that exist, most travelers fly here any-way, which can be an adventure in itself, soaring above the treetops, viewing Emberá villages below, and holding on tight for a landing on a dirt or grassy landing strip. If booking a tour, you will be put on a charter flight organized by your outfitter, or at the very least they will be able to book you on a regularly scheduled flight.

WESTERN DARIÉN ★

The Pan American Highway from Panama City is a relatively featureless road that is paved until Lago Bayano; from here, it's a rocky ride to the endpoint at Yaviza. Given the poor condition of the road, it can take nearly a full day to drive this stretch—and when you're done, the only thing to do is turn around and head back. The exception is the turnoff to Metetí, which leads to Puerto Quimbo and to boats to La Palma, near the Punta Patiño reserve. **Ancon Expeditions** (www.anconexpeditions.com; © **888/760-3426** in the U.S. and

Travelers to the Darién should not be cavalier. The jungle is dense and can easily disorient hikers, and any kind of walking trip here should always be undertaken with a guide. In the Darién, you'll find a lot more creepy-crawlies than you would in the rest of Panama; snakes, some of them poisonous, will surprise you if you're not scanning the trail ahead. Hikers should also protect themselves from ticks and skin-burrowing chiggers; tuck your pants into your socks and bring lots of repellent with DEET. The May-to-December rainy season is wetter than in most parts of Panama, shrouding your vision and turning trails and roads into slick and gloppy mudpaths. Unless you're fishing at the Tropic Star Lodge, it is not recommended that you visit the Darién during the rainy season. Also, if you're heading to higher altitudes like the Cerro Pirre, bring a jacket. Although danger levels have been exaggerated greatly, the border with Colombia near the Caribbean Sea is unsafe due to narco-terrorist activity that spills over into Panama. The destinations mentioned in this chapter, however, are perfectly safe.

Canada, or 269-9415) offers custom itineraries to the upper tributaries of the Sambú River in the southwestern Darién, where you can explore deep rainforest seldom visited and stay in indigenous villages still practicing their traditional way of life. Contact Ancon for more information. **Ecocircuitos** (www.ecocircuitos.com; ☏ **314-0068** or 314-0698) also offers 4-day ethnic expeditions of the Darién.

An hour before the end of the Pan American Highway, near the town of Metetí, **Canopy Camp Darién** (www.canopytower.com/canopy-camp; ☏ **264-5720**) is a tent camp from the owners of the very bird-focused Canopy Tower and Canopy Lodge, bordering the eastern side of the 26,000-hectare (65,000-acre) Serrania Filo del Tallo Hydrological Reserve. Each of the eight 16- to 23-sq.-m. (179- to 249-sq.-ft.) safari tents, sitting on raised platforms, has teak wood floors and private outdoor bathrooms. Despite the low-impact model, it's not exactly roughing it in the jungle. High-season rates—including all meals, wine, lodging, taxes, and tours—are $3,339 per person for a 7-night package. Last-minute deals can sometimes be had.

PUNTA PATIÑO ★★★

Punta Patiño was the first private nature preserve to be established in Panama, and at 30,351 hectares (75,000 acres) it is the country's largest. The preserve is bordered by the Gulf of San Miguel and is characterized by a coastal web of mangrove swamps and the mighty Tiura River, which ribbons through undulating and endangered dry tropical forest. The preserve is also home to Emberá Indian communities and a concentration of harpy eagles, Panama's national bird. Owned and managed by the nonprofit Asociación Nacional Para la Conservación de la Naturaleza (ANCON), the preserve is tangible proof of the ability of nature to recover from human intervention, considering that a large swath of land here was once a cattle ranch and small farming community and now is a thriving forest. Punta Patiño can be reached by road and boat, or by small plane and boat.

The region gives visitors a chance not only to explore dense primary and secondary forest that's home to peccaries, coatimundis, and capybaras that feed near the shore, but it also provides for an adventurous ride aboard a *piragua,* or motorized dugout canoe, up the Tiura River. Along this river's shores, three species of ancient mangroves thrive and provide refuge for bottlenose dolphins and marine birds such as kingfishers, herons, spoonbills, and ibises. For bird-watchers, the prize sighting here is the harpy eagle, one of the largest raptors in the world. Harpy eagles like this region for its concentration of trees like the Quipo, whose chubby trunk and height make for ideal nesting conditions. Another reason to visit Punta Patiño is the **Mogue Emberá Indian community,** which gives travelers a cultural introduction to native peoples and their traditional arts, such as tagua carvings and basket-making. Through tourism, the Emberá tribes in this area have found a way to make a living based on protecting wildlife—instead of killing it—to draw more tourism dollars.

Adventure Tours & Where to Stay

Visits to the Punta Patiño preserve must be planned as part of an expedition. Two companies currently offer trips to Punta Patiño (which can be as short as 2 nights) that are part of a longer itinerary covering other destinations in the Darién.

Ancon Expeditions (see "Western Darién," above), affiliated with ANCON, is the Darién's foremost tour operator and manages **Punta Patiño Lodge.** On a high bluff overlooking the Pacific Ocean, the simple, two-story building has 10 air-conditioned cabins with private bathrooms. Ancon Expeditions uses this lodge as a base for all three of its expeditions to Punta Patiño. Quick, in-and-out tours include the 3-night/4-day "Coastal Darién Explorer" (from $850), which includes light hiking through the forest and a day visit by canoe to an Emberá village. Ancon also offers the "Realm of the Harpy Eagle" (from $895), focused on searching for the elusive bird and visiting a nest.

Ecocircuitos (http://ecocircuitos.com; 🕿 **800/830-7142** in the U.S., or 314-1586) is another excellent tour operator offering a Punta Patiño expedition. The major difference between this tour and Ancon's is that with Ecocircuitos Punta Patiño is reached by road along the Pan American Highway to Puerto Quimba, where travelers board a dugout canoe to travel to the Mogue Emberá Indian community. Base camp is established there, with lodging in tents, giving visitors more exposure to the Emberá (the reason why they've dubbed their tour the "Darién Ethnic Expedition"). The trip lasts 3 nights/4 days, and includes transportation, guided excursions, meals, and lodging for $945 per person, based on four travelers.

DARIÉN NATIONAL PARK & CANA FIELD STATION ★★★

The .6-million-hectare (1.5-million-acre) Darién National Park is not only the largest park in Panama—it is the largest in Central America. The park extends along 90% of the entire length of the border with Colombia, incorporating a dazzling rainforest rich in biodiversity, coastal lagoons, mangrove swamps, serrated peaks, and toffee-colored rivers that snake down to the Pacific Ocean. The vast size and pristine state of the park mean that populations of endemic and endangered species—jaguars, tapirs, ocelots, and pumas—are allowed to flourish. But what visitors see most, and with surprising frequency, are spider, howler, and white-faced capuchin monkeys, as well as sloths. The Darién is considered one of the last pristine wildernesses in the Americas, and it therefore has been designated a UNESCO Biosphere Site. It is an extraordinary, *Jurassic Park*–like wilderness, ideal for adventurous travelers who seek absolutely primeval surroundings and the sense of being far from civilization and the modern world.

What visitors also come to see here are **birds,** and indeed the Darién forest has been rated as one of the top 10 bird-watching sites in the world. Even non-birders can't help getting caught up in the excitement of so many colorful "showcase" species like macaws and toucans fluttering about. Dozens of tanager species in a kaleidoscopic range of colors are here, too, not to mention rare and endemic species such as red-throated caracaras, peregrine falcons, golden-headed quetzals, and the Pirre warbler. There are so many birds and in such abundance that sighting them doesn't take much effort—while swinging in a hammock, for example, you can eye parrots and macaws zipping through the air.

But as vast as the Darién National Park is, the majority of it is largely inaccessible. The only two access points are the ANAM park ranger's **Pirre Station** on the north side of the Cerro Pirre peak, and Ancon Expedition's **Cana Field Station** on the southeast side of the peak (reached by small plane). Cana is owned and operated by **Ancon Expeditions** (www.anconexpeditions.com; © **888/760-3426** in the U.S. and Canada, or 269-9415), and trips here must be booked as a tour through that company. Tours are infrequent and usually custom, so contact Ancon for more information.

The Darién is one of the few places in Panama where it is recommended that you **do not travel independently or without a guide.** The reasons are plentiful: Hardly a soul here speaks English, getting lost on any trail is a considerable risk, and you're exposing yourself to a variety of potential pitfalls such as a twisted ankle or snakebites—and the nearest medical clinic is hundreds of miles away. Also, with such a diversity of flora and fauna, a guide who can provide interpretive information, historical background, and cultural insight into the Emberá and Wounaan communities will only enhance your experience.

The **ranger station at Pirre** (© **299-6965**) offers basic shelter with bunk-style beds, a kitchen, and shared bathrooms. There is no electricity, and you must bring all supplies with you (food, water or a water purifier, flashlights, towels, and so forth). The cost to spend the night is $15, with a park entrance fee of $15, which should be paid in advance in Panama City at SENAFRONT. Several trails, from easy to difficult, lead from the ranger station, but as stated earlier, it is unwise to walk these trails without a guide.

The Pirre Station is about a 3-hour walk during the dry season from the village of El Real, or you can get there in 2 hours in a dugout canoe from El Real, followed by a 1-hour hike to the station.

BAHÍA PIÑAS ★★★

Visitors to Bahía Piñas come for the legendary sport fishing. Beyond the Tropic Star Lodge are two villages near Bahía Piñas, but both hold little interest to travelers. If the cost of the Tropic Star is too rich for your blood, you'd be better off setting up a fishing trip elsewhere along the Pacific Coast rather than eking out a local tour in Jacqué. Call **Air Panama** (www.flyairpanama. com; ✆ **315-0439**) for information about flights between Panama City and Bahía Piñas.

Where to Stay & Dine

Tropic Star Lodge ★★★   The Tropic Star is Panama's premier fishing lodge, attracting elite sportfishermen from around the world who come for the record-breaking sailfish, black marlin, and other billfish. The fishing is done no farther than 20km (12 miles) off Zane Grey Reef in the lodge's dozen or so 9.4m (31-ft.) Bertram boats. More than 200 fishing records have been broken here, which is why rooms can be booked more than a year in advance. The lodge was founded in 1961 as a private fishing retreat by a Texas oil tycoon but has been operated by an American family, the Kittredges, since 1976. Despite the reputation for attracting the rich and famous, the retro-1960s design lodge itself, fronting Piñas Bay and backed by endless jungle, is quite down to earth and family friendly. The individual air-conditioned cabins sprawl across a hilly slope and feature outdoor decks looking onto the bay. Rates include fishing excursions, lodging, four-course meals, and all drinks except cocktails. Beyond fishing there are additional excursions to go diving, kayaking the Río Piñas, hiking the lodge's wilderness trail, which connects to the white-sand Playa Blanca beach, or taking a cruise upriver to visit a Wounaan village. To get here, you take a regularly scheduled flight or a small charter plane from Panama City (see above) to Piñas Bay, where they'll pick you up for the 10-minute boat ride to the lodge.

Piñas Bay. ✆ **800/682-3424.** www.tropicstar.com. 16 units. Packages per person, based on double occupancy: 7 nights $4,250–$5,600; 4 nights $3,095–$5,995. Rates include fishing excursions, lodging, 4-course meals, and all drinks except cocktails. **Amenities:** Restaurant; bar; outdoor pool; sport-fishing excursions; cultural excursions; kayaks; limited cellphone service; Wi-Fi (free but limited; on veranda, dining room, and business center only).

PLANNING YOUR TRIP TO PANAMA

P anama is just starting to take off as a major tourist destination, and many areas remain deliciously free of
crowds while offering the same pristine wilderness and
action-packed adventure as its more popular neighbor,
Costa Rica. Panama is but a thin squiggle of a country, but it
has a wealth of diversity packed within its borders, from lush
rainforests to sultry beaches to craggy mountain peaks—all
of which can be reached by a short drive or flight. The Caribbean Sea and Pacific Ocean are so close to each other that
you can swim in both in 1 day. If you're a nature lover, consider that Panama is a land bridge between North and South
America, and hundreds of wildlife species—more than 900
species of birds alone—meet here at the isthmus, providing
a rich environment for eco-travel.

Panama is a safe country, too, and Panamanians are some of the
friendliest people in Latin America. So many residents speak English that it could almost be called Panama's second language. And
in comparison to Costa Rica's, Panama's infrastructure and capital
city are decidedly more modern, and travel budgeting is easier considering that the country's national monetary unit is the U.S.
dollar.

So now the question isn't whether you should go, but when?
What is the best time to visit, and which destinations should you
visit? How can you preplan a trip and find cheap deals and other
tantalizing offers? These are just a few of the questions that this
chapter answers to help you plan an unforgettable vacation.

For additional help in planning your trip and for more on-the-
ground resources in Panama, please see "Fast Facts: Panama" on
p. 245.

ENTRY REQUIREMENTS

Passports

U.S. citizens traveling to Panama are required to present a valid passport. For an up-to-date, country-by-country listing of passport requirements around the world, go to the U.S. State Department's website at **http://travel.state.gov**. Click on "U.S. Passports & International Travel" and then choose "Country Information."

Important: When entering the country, travelers must be able to demonstrate proof of sufficient funds if requested, and they must present an onward or return ticket. However, it's rare that an official will ask for this.

In an effort to prevent international child abduction, many governments require a parent or legal guardian (or someone other than the parent) traveling alone with a child to provide documentary evidence of relationship and travel permission. Having such documentation on hand can facilitate entry/departure if immigration requests it, although it is not always required. Inquire when booking your airline ticket about updated entry/departure procedures for children.

Visas

Citizens of the United States, Canada, Great Britain, and most European nations may visit Panama for a maximum of 180 consecutive days. No visa is necessary. If transiting the Panama Canal as vessel passengers, there is no need to even show a passport if not disembarking. A passport must be valid for at least 3 months from arrival in the country.

Carry your passport with you at all times. Panamanian police will sometimes ask for your documents, particularly on long bus rides on routine checks. The last thing you want is be detained by police for hours on your way somewhere, so be sure to have your passport with you. If you absolutely refuse to carry your passport, make a copy of your ID page and your Customs arrival stamp. Even in Panama City, police are known to take advantage of "gringos" without documents, threatening jail time or demanding a payment of whatever you have on you. (If you don't have enough on you, they'll be happy to drive you to the nearest ATM.) This little trick is most likely to happen to men walking around at night after a few too many drinks, but the bottom line is to *always* carry your passport or a copy of your ID and entry page.

Medical Requirements

There are no vaccination requirements when entering Panama. However, if you'll be traveling to the tropical lowlands or to the jungle, it's wise to get vaccinated for typhoid, yellow fever, and hepatitis A. All travelers should also be up-to-date on their tetanus immunizations. Occasionally, spikes in dengue fever occur, so travelers will want to be especially careful during the rainy season. If you're going to the Darién, you may also want to take malaria pills, which should be prescribed by your doctor at least 10 days before your departure. However, if you're traveling during the dry season or won't be exploring the tropical lowlands or rainforests too much, your risk of tropical disease is relatively low.

Customs
WHAT YOU CAN BRING INTO PANAMA
Visitors to Panama may bring with them personal items, such as jewelry, and professional equipment, including cameras, computers, and electronics, as well as fishing and diving gear for personal use—all of which are permitted duty-free. Visitors may bring in up to 200 cigarettes and 3 bottles of liquor tax-free. Customs officials in Panama seldom check arriving tourists' luggage.

WHAT YOU CAN TAKE HOME FROM PANAMA
For information on what you're allowed to bring home, contact one of the following agencies:

U.S. Citizens: U.S. Customs & Border Protection (CBP), 1300 Pennsylvania Ave. NW, Washington, DC 20229 (www.cbp.gov; ✆ 877/287-8667).

Canadian Citizens: Canada Border Services Agency, Ottawa, Ontario, K1A 0L8 (www.cbsa-asfc.gc.ca; ✆ 800/461-9999 in Canada, or 204/983-3500).

U.K. Citizens: HM Customs & Excise, Crownhill Court, Tailor Road, Plymouth, PL6 5BZ (www.hmce.gov.uk; ✆ 0845/010-9000; from outside the U.K., 020/8929-0152).

Australian Citizens: Australian Customs Service, Customs House, 5 Constitution Ave., Canberra City, ACT 2601 (www.customs.gov.au; ✆ 1300/363-263; from outside Australia, 61/2-6275-6666).

New Zealand Citizens: New Zealand Customs, The Customhouse, 17–21 Whitmore St., Box 2218, Wellington, 6140 (www.customs.govt.nz; ✆ 04/473-6099 or 0800/428-786).

GETTING THERE
By Plane
Almost all international flights land at **Tocumen International Airport** (PTY; http://tocumenpanama.aero; ✆ 238-2700), located 21km (13 miles) from Panama City. Flights from Costa Rica to Panama City with the country's domestic carrier, **Air Panama** (www.flyairpanama.com; ✆ 316-9000), land at the **Marcos A. Gelabert Airport** (PAC), more commonly referred to as **Albrook Airport.** There is also direct service from San José, Costa Rica, to the David and Bocas del Toro airports (see chapters 7 and 8, respectively). In addition, **Avianca Airlines** (see below) has service from Costa Rica, arriving at Tocumen.

The following airlines serve Panama City from the United States, using the gateway cities listed. **American Airlines** (www.aa.com; ✆ 800/433-7300 in the U.S., or 269-6022 in Panama) has two daily flights from Miami. Avianca (© 800/284-2622 in the U.S., or 206-8222 in Panama; www.avianca.com) has flights from many major U.S. hubs, but most include a stopover in Bogotá, El Salvador, or Costa Rica. Copa Airlines (www.copaair.com; © 800/359-2672 in the U.S., or 227-0116 in Panama) has the most flights in and out of Panama City, with daily or weekly flights from Miami, Orlando, New Orleans, New York, Las Vegas, Los Angeles, and Washington, D.C., as well as destinations from around Latin America and the Caribbean.

Delta Airlines (www.delta.com; © 800/241-4141 in the U.S., or 214-8118 in Panama) offers one daily flight from Atlanta. **United Airlines** (www. united.com; © 800/044-0001 in the U.S., or 265-0040 in Panama) offers flights between Panama and Chicago, Houston, Miami, New Orleans, New York, Orlando, Tampa Bay, and several regional cities.

From Europe, Iberia (www.iberia.com; © **0870/609-0500** in the U.K., or 227-3966 in Panama) has daily flights to Panama City that connect in either Madrid or Amsterdam. **American Airlines** (see above) and **British Airways** (www.britishairways.com; © **800/246-9297** in the U.S.) have daily flights that connect in Miami.

From Australia, Qantas (www.qantas.com; © **9691-3636**) has daily flights in conjunction with Copa Air from Sydney, connecting in Los Angeles; Air New Zealand (www.airnewzealand.com; © **507-264-8756** in NZ) also works in conjunction with Copa Air with one daily flight from Auckland, connecting in Los Angeles.

For details on getting into Panama City from the airport, see chapter 4.

By Bus

Comfortable, air-conditioned international bus routes from Panama run to neighboring Costa Rica with **Tica Bus** (www.ticabus.com; © **314-6385** in Panama), departing from Albrook station. There are three daily departures for the approximately 16-hour drive.

By Boat

Several major international cruise lines have itineraries that include the Panama Canal, often continuing on to various Caribbean or Latin American ports. **Carnival, Celebrity, Holland America, Norwegian,** and **Princess** ships travel through the 64km (40-mile) canal, rising and falling with the locks, from one ocean to the other.

Yachts also travel frequently between Portobelo and Cartagena, Colombia, on the Caribbean Coast. These are less formal and are usually arranged directly with the boat owners at marinas in either destination.

GETTING AROUND

Getting around Panama is relatively easy compared with other Latin American countries, and major roads are well maintained and delightfully free of potholes, making it a good place to rent a car to get from destination to destination. In Panama City, taxis, including Uber, are the best way to get around: They're cheap, and you don't have to deal with the stress of chaotic city driving. You can also get around by bus or Central America's first subway line, though these can be confusing for the passing tourist, not to mention dangerous. Panama City (except for the Casco Viejo neighborhood) isn't the best place to explore on foot, since most major tourist attractions aren't within walking distance from each other.

If you're traveling between cities or destinations, you can do so by bus, plane, or car. If you're driving, most destinations will be off the paved and well-maintained Pan American Highway. Once you leave the highway, however, some secondary roads can be a bit rough. To enter or leave Panama City, you'll take the Puente de Las Americas or the newer Puente Centenario.

By Plane

Air Panama (www.flyairpanama.com; ✆ **316-9000**) is Panama's main local carrier, servicing most destinations in the country. Air travel is safe, quick, and relatively inexpensive. Check the website for schedules and fares.

By Car

Driving in Panama allows you the most flexibility and is the best way to see the country. It's not the cheapest option, however: Renting a car costs about as much as it does in the U.S., and gas is a little more expensive. But self-driving allows you to enjoy the scenery, adhere to your own schedule, make pit stops, and visit destinations away from your hotel. Generally speaking, speed limits in Panama are about 60 to 80kmph (35–50 mph) on major roadways and slower on secondary roads. You'll want to stick to this limit, as police speed traps are common, and you don't want a speeding ticket to put a damper on your trip.

Car-rental kiosks are located at both the Tocumen and Albrook airports (car-rental agencies at Tocumen are open 24 hrs.; Albrook rental agencies are open 8am–6:30pm), and each agency has a few locations in town. The Tocumen Airport car-rental agency contact information is as follows: **Alamo** (www.alamopanama.com; ✆ 236-5777), **Avis** (www.avis.com; ✆ 238-4037), **Budget** (www.budgetpanama.com; ✆ 263-8777), **Dollar** (www.dollarpanama.com; ✆ 270-0355), **Hertz** (www.hertzpanama.com.pa; ✆ 301-2611), and **National** (www.nationalpanama.com; ✆ 275-7222).

When renting a car in Panama, you must purchase two basic insurances. The agency will also offer a variety of other full-coverage options, but generally, your credit card rental insurance should cover you, and you really only need the obligatory insurances.

Keep in mind that, depending on your destination, it's sometimes better to get a four-wheel-drive (4WD) vehicle, because some of Panama's roads are unpaved and rocky. If you're staying close to Panama City or all your planned destinations are right off the Pan American Highway, you should be fine with a two-wheel-drive.

Although most Panamanians drive stick-shift vehicles, automatics are readily available at all car-rental agencies, though you should expect to pay a bit more. Generally speaking, renting a car in Panama can cost you between $20 and $80 a day, depending on the kind of car and how you reserve. For the best deals, book through an online agency, such as Expedia, Hotels.com, or Kayak. com. You can also book directly through the car-rental agency's websites, since booking ahead of time generally gets you a better rate. The agency will provide a road map upon car rental.

Some distances are as follows:

Panama City to Colón: 1 hour
Panama City to Gamboa: 25 minutes
Panama City to Portobello: 1½ hours
Panama City to Cartí: 3 hours
Panama City to Boquete: 7 hours
Panama City to the Azuero Peninsula: 7 hours

There are also car-rental agencies in David, Colón, and other popular tourist destinations.

By Bus

Bus routes between major and minor destinations in Panama are frequent and relatively inexpensive. Expect to pay about $3 to $5 per hour, depending on your destination. Bus travel between cities is relatively cheap but slower than driving. Nearly all buses from Panama City to other destinations depart from the bus terminal (© **303-3030**) near Albrook Airport and adjacent to the Albrook Mall. It's not necessary to reserve your tickets ahead of time unless you are traveling on a holiday weekend or during December or Easter week. Be sure to arrive at the terminal at least 45 minutes ahead of time. You'll need a nickel to get on the bus, so make sure you have change. Long-distance buses are air-conditioned and comfortable, have an onboard bathroom, and usually show several movies. Shorter routes tend to use smaller, less comfortable buses, but are usually air-conditioned. If your route is 4 or more hours, the driver will make a pit stop about halfway through for lunch or dinner.

SPECIAL-INTEREST TRIPS & TOURS

This section is divided by activity, with listings of the prime destinations in Panama for doing each one as well as the tour operators and outfitters who tailor trips to the specific activities. Tour operators have local knowledge and, more important, they provide guides and, in most cases, equipment. If you are planning to focus your trip to Panama around one sport or activity, these tour operators and outfitters are your best bet.

Adventure travel carries risks, and travelers should be well aware of the dangers before participating in any tour. The operators mentioned in this chapter have been chosen for their safety records and reputations, but ask questions on your own. For example, if your adventure involves boating, what kind of vessel will be used? Dugout canoes known as *pangas* are common and a colorful way to get around, but for long journeys they're uncomfortable, wet, and dangerous in choppy water; also, few local boat drivers carry radios or safety equipment. Check individual chapters for smaller regional tour operators.

Adventure & Wellness Trips

BIKING

Mountain biking is relatively new in Panama. Few places are suitable for riding, other than well-established paved and dirt roads, but many of these roads can be dangerous if vehicular traffic is heavy. Roads in Panama are curvy, often with hairpin turns, and do not have bike lanes or a proper road shoulder, so keep alert for speeding vehicles coming around a bend. If you just feel like getting out and pedaling around town, you'll find bicycle rentals in more touristy areas that rent for an average of $10 to $20 a day, and bicycle rental shops are listed in regional chapters in this book. No tour companies offer multiday packages that focus entirely on biking entirely in Panama (yet); however, the operators listed below can custom-build a trip for you.

In **Panama City,** the most popular and safest bike-riding area is the Amador Causeway, which is flat and has bike lanes—and a pretty spectacular view to boot. Outside the city, the Gamboa Resort rents bicycles for touring around; from here, it's a couple of kilometers to the Pipeline Road Trail, a dirt-and-mud road that is flanked by tropical jungle. **El Valle de Anton** was made for bike riding: Vehicle traffic is light, roads are flat and paved, and a few steep, technical dirt roads offer a good workout. **Boquete,** too, has picturesque, winding roads that provide moderate terrain and pastoral views. Note that rental bicycles around Panama are *not* top-of-the-line models and usually lack shocks and other deluxe features.

Adventures in Panama (www.adventuresinpanama.com; ☎ **315/849-5144** in the U.S., or 260-0044) offers two bike day trips around Panama City. Its day excursion to the Pipeline Road Trail gives cyclists a chance to get (a little) dirty and ride through jungle at one of the best bird-watching sites in Panama. Across the isthmus, Adventures in Panama offers a day tour that begins with a bike ride across the Gatún Locks, connecting with a 6.4km (4-mile) dirt road to Fort San Lorenzo, a road known for birds and wildlife. The Toronto-based company **Bike Hike Adventures** (www.bikehike.com; ☎ **888/805-0061**) combines biking on the Amador Causeway and near Fort San Lorenzo as part of its multisport package trips.

BIRD-WATCHING

Panama ranks as one of the world's top bird-watching sites, with some 980 registered species of resident and migrant birds—more than the U.S. and Canada combined. Because Panama is a land bridge connecting two continents, birders are privy to viewing species from both North and South America. Many of the birds found here are "showcase" birds such as toucans, macaws, and the resplendent quetzal, which delight even non-birders. Keen birders often return home having seen dozens of "life birds," or their first sighting of a bird species. If you head out with a qualified birding guide, expect to see upwards of 100 or more in a single day.

Lodges with the best bird-watching include **Canopy Tower** (p. 102) in Soberanía National Park and its sister property **Canopy Lodge** (p. 132) in El Valle de Antón; **Cana Field Station** (p. 224) in Darién National Park; **Punta Patiño Lodge** (p. 223) in Darién Province near the Gulf of San Miguel; and **Los Quetzales Ecolodge & Spa** (p. 161) on the edge of International Amistad and Volcán Barú national parks. Note that these lodges provide professional bird-watching guides either as part of an all-inclusive package or ordered a la carte. Tour operators listed below center their trips around these all-inclusive lodges, so really what you're getting is a 24-hour professional who is both problem-solver and educational guide.

Bird-watching hot spots include the following locations:

o **Darién Highlands** for macaws, large toucans, colorful tanagers, and endemics such as Pirre warblers.
o The **Darién Lowlands,** especially known for harpy eagles.
o The **Nusagandi** region for speckled antshrikes and sapayoas.
o **Soberanía National Park** and Pipeline Road, home to more than 525 species, including trogons, antbirds, blue cotingas, and other canopy dwellers.
o **Achiote Road,** near Fort San Lorenzo and Colón, for diurnal raptors and spot-crowned barbets, oropendolas, and pied puffbirds.
o **El Valle** for North American breeding warblers and black-crowned antpittas.
o The neighboring national parks **International Amistad** and **Volcán Barú** (Chiriquí Highlands) for the resplendent quetzal, three-wattled bellbirds, trogons, long-tailed silky flycatchers, tapaculos, and Andean pygmy owls. Two popular birding areas here include **Finca Hartmann** and **Finca Lérida,** both coffee plantations with endemic and migratory species.
o **Isla Iguana** in the Azuero for Seabirds such as magnificent frigate birds nest; they also nest on **Swan's Cay** in Bocas, where you'll also find brown boobies and red-billed tropic birds.

U.S.–based Tour Operators
Field Guides (www.fieldguides.com; © **800/728-4953** or 512/263-7295) is a specialty bird-watching travel operator, with highly esteemed and friendly guides. It offers five all-inclusive programs from December to March. The "Lowland Darién" visits Canopy Camp and the "Western Panama" tour focuses on the Chiriquí Highlands and Bocas del Toro. There are also tours to the Canopy Lodge and the Canopy Tower. Tours cost an average of $2,850 to $3,875. Group size is limited to eight people.

Victor Emanuel Nature Tours (www.ventbird.com; ✆ **800/328-8368** or 512/328-5221) is a well-respected tour operator and the largest company in the world specializing in bird tours. VENT offers not just December-to-March tours, but tours year-round either with one of its own guides or a local guide (or combination). Group limit is 10 people; tours average 7 nights and are based around one destination (mostly the Canopy Tower) with optional add-on trips. Prices start at about $3,140.

Wings (www.wingsbirds.com; ✆ **866/547-9868** or 320-9868) offers fall and spring tours based around the Canopy Tower, with options for extensions. Call for prices.

Panamanian Birding Companies

For local independent guides, see the regional chapters in this book. These tour operators provide travelers with multiple-day journeys, but more importantly they are the companies to contact for shorter day excursions, especially around Panama City.

Ancon Expeditions (www.anconexpeditions.com; ✆ 888/760-3426 in the U.S. or Canada, or **269-9415**)) has the largest staff of professional birding guides, many of whom are contracted by international companies, and they own and run both the Cana Field Station and the Punta Patiño Lodge in the Darién.

Advantage Tours (www.advantagepanama.com; ✆ **6676-2466**), which runs the Soberanía Research Lodge in Gamboa, is the travel organizer and outfitter for the international Audubon Society. Their secret asset is Guido Berguido, a degreed bird-watching guide who is one of the friendliest and enthusiastic guides anywhere. Their year-round "Birdwatchers Paradise" tour combines Soberanía and Achiote Road with Volcán Barú.

Birding Panama (www.birdingpanama.com; ✆ **392-5663**) offers day tours ($90-170) to Pipeline Road and other birding hot spots, as well as 4- to 10-day trips to destinations around Panama.

DIVING & SNORKELING

Isla Coiba, in the Chiriquí Gulf of the Pacific Ocean, is simply *the* best diving site in Panama, often described as a cross between the Cocos Islands in Costa Rica and the Galápagos Islands of Ecuador. Until 2005, Isla Coiba was the site of a notorious penitentiary that kept visitors away, and therefore the surrounding waters are untouched. The snorkeling here is outstanding, too—Coiba is surrounded by one of the largest coral reefs on the Pacific Coast of the Americas—but diving puts you close to pelagics such as white-tipped sharks, sailfish, manta rays, and dolphins. Other islands such as **Islas Secas** and the islands within the **National Marine Park** in the Chiriquí Gulf also provide outstanding diving.

On the Caribbean Coast, **Bocas del Toro** is where you'll want to go to view some of the best and most colorful hard and soft coral in the world. In the Caribbean, visibility is best from March to May and during September and

October. The reef at **Baja Escribano,** between the San Blas and Colón, is the new talked-about dive site for its clear waters and colorful sponges.

Some of the best snorkeling in all of Panama is in the waters surrounding the **Pearl Islands,** due to the abundance of marine life found there. Expect multitudinous schools of tropical fish and large pelagics such as white-tipped sharks. Bocas is billed as a top snorkeling site, but you'll need to get away from the standard tours to find the good stuff. **Isla Iguanas,** off the coast of Pedasí in the Pacific Ocean, is excellent for snorkeling, too.

The outfitters listed below offer diving trips around Panama, including multidestination trips. For local dive operations, check the listings in regional chapters. The resort **Islas Secas** in the Chiriquí Gulf and the **Coral Lodge** in the Caribbean are two lodges with on-site dive shops and personalized tours for guests only. For diving in Bocas del Toro, see chapter 8.

Panama Divers (www.panamadivers.com; ☏ **448-2293,** 314-0817, or 6613-4405) is the premier dive operation in Panama, based in Panama City and Portobelo. It also offers dives around Las Perlas and Kuna Yala. Panama Divers, which is fully insured, has decades of experience and a Professional Association of Diving Instructors (PADI) facility.

Panama Dive Center (www.panamadivecenter.com; ☏ **6665-7879**) is based in Santa Catalina on the Azuero Peninsula, focusing on Isla Coiba, though it also offers specialized trips around the region. PADI certification is available as well.

Scuba Panama (www.scubapanama.com; ☏ **261-3841**) has a bicoastal dive that starts in the Caribbean Sea—visiting a sunken B-45 plane—and then goes to the Pacific Ocean for a dive there. It also offers a unique (and spooky) dive in the Panama Canal, as well as dives around Portobelo and Isla Grande.

Bocas Dive Center (www.bocasdivecenter.com; ☏ **757-9737**) is a five-star PADI dive center with beginning through expert training and dives around Bocas del Toro.

FISHING

Panama is a world-class fishing destination known for its fast and furious reeling-in of monster species such as blue, black, and striped marlin; yellowfin tuna; wahoo; and swordfish. Marlin and tuna are most abundant from January to April, but fishing takes place year-round. The Pacific Ocean is where the best fishing is—there's also fishing in the Caribbean, but the infrastructure (marinas and such) isn't well developed. Anglers looking for a sure bet can't beat Lake Gatún for peacock bass—throw your line in and in minutes you'll snag one.

Fishing charters are available for day and multiday excursions, either as part of a trip organized by a competent operator or by simply hiring a local boatman to take you out on the water. Custom sport-fishing tours head to the Pearl Islands, the Gulf of Chiriquí (around Coiba Island), and Piñas Bay—the latter is home to the **Tropic Star Lodge** (see below), and when they're sold out, a fishing charter is a good second option. Charters typically include transportation, meals, fishing gear, and bilingual or native-English-speaking guides.

Fishing Charters

Pesca Panama (www.pescapanama.com; ℗ 844/264-2246 in the U.S.) is a U.S.–based company that offers inshore and offshore sport-fishing in the Gulf of Chiriquí around Coiba and Hannibal Bank. Pesca guests fish from a fleet of five Ocean Masters, a 17-foot *panga*, and four ocean kayaks. Prices vary considerably between itineraries.

Panama Fishing & Catching (www.panamafishingandcatching.com; ℗ 6622-0212) has custom charters with prices that vary according to group size and desires. It offers multiday offshore fishing charters (prices run from bare-bones to all-inclusive), as well as day trips in central Panama.

Fishing Lodges

Tropic Star Lodge (Bahía Piña, Darién; www.tropicstar.com; ℗ 800/682-3424 in the U.S.) is considered the best saltwater fishing resort in the world for its monster black and blue marlin, sailfish, and more. American-run, the prestigious lodge has been around since the early 1960s and is located on the remote shore of Piñas Bay in the Darién Province. The lodge draws famous VIPs but is homey enough for families with kids. See p. 225 for a complete review.

Gone Fishing Panama Resort (Boca Chica; www.gonefishingpanama.com; ℗ 6573-0151) is a fishing lodge with friendly American owners and comfortable, ranch-style accommodations on the shores of Boca Chica. The focus is on fishing around the Gulf of Chiriquí, aboard one of the lodge's two 9.4m (31-ft.) open boats, but there are also activities for nonfishing guests.

Panama Big Game Sportfishing Club (Boca Chica; www.panama-sportfishing.com; ℗ 866/281-1225 in the U.S.), like the aforementioned lodges, is American owned, in this case by two retired charter-boat skippers from Miami. The club is located near the Gone Fishing Lodge in Boca Chica and has four upscale teak cabins perched high on a hill, offering lovely views. The lodge has four fishing boats to accommodate all guests. See p. 180 for a complete review.

GOLF

Panama isn't known for its spectacular golf courses, but that is quickly changing as more and more resorts build private courses. Panama provides golfers with a variety of championship courses, some of which are open for public day use, others as part of an all-inclusive resort. Close to Panama City, **Summit Golf & Resort** (www.summitgolfpanama.com; ℗ 232-4653) is the ideal venue for those staying in the capital; it's located on the east bank of the Panama Canal on the Gaillard Highway and is accessible by taxi from the city for about $20 one-way.

The **Radisson Summit Hotel** (www.radisson.com; ℗ 232-3200) is here too, as well as a restaurant and a pro shop. Designed by noted architect Jeffery

Myers, the course is spread across rolling hills, with sweeping views of the Gaillard Cut of the Panama Canal. It's very classy, and there is a traditional 18-hole course as well as a 6-hole course for juniors and beginners. The course is open every day from 6am to 6pm; call ahead to book a tee time.

Buenaventura Golf Club (www.buenaventuragolfclub.com; ℭ **908-3333**), an 18-hole, Jack Nicklaus–designed golf course on the Pacific Coast, is perhaps the top course in the country. The par-72 championship course and state-of-the-art club are mostly for members and guests of the JW Marriott Panama, though eight rounds a day are offered to the public.

The **Bluebay Coronado Golf & Beach Resort** (www.bluebayresorts.com; ℭ **240-4444**) is a premier golf resort located on the Pacific Coast, about an hour from Panama City. Designed by Tom Fazio, this is one of the only seaside 18-hole courses in the country; players can come for the day from Panama City, but the resort specializes in packages with lodging included. For more information, see "Pacific Beaches" in chapter 6.

Costa Blanca Golf & Villas (www.costablanca.com.pa; ℭ **986-1915**) is located next to the Decameron Resort on the Pacific Coast, about 1½ hours from Panama City. It has an 18-hole course that is lighted, so you can play both day and night. The cost is closer to a bargain than other resorts: Monday through Friday, it's $30 per person, with an additional $22 for a cart; weekends cost $72 per person (including cart). The course is within a residential development and has a clubhouse and restaurant.

HORSEBACK RIDING

Horseback-riding outfits are sparsely distributed throughout the country. On Bocas del Toro, **Panama Horseback** (www.panamahorseback.com; ℭ **6905-9659**) offers half- and full-day tours for $50 to $75 per rider. In **Boquete,** horses can be rented from **Eduardo Cano** (ℭ **720-1750** or 6628-0814) for $10 an hour for tours around the surrounding countryside. Horseback riding here takes place along mountain paths that provide riders with sweeping vistas of the Boquete valley. Eduardo speaks Spanish only, so depending on your own facility with *el español,* have your hotel make arrangements. Many higher-end hotels on the Pacific and the interior also rent horses.

KAYAKING & WHITE-WATER RAFTING

Panama has some of the most thrilling white-water rafting and kayaking in the Americas. The translucent rivers that pour down the Talamanca mountain range in the Chiriquí Highlands provide wild Class III and IV kayaking and rafting, principally on the **Chiriquí River** east of Volcán Barú, and the **Chiriquí Viejo River** west of the volcano, near the border with Costa Rica. Unfortunately, the Chiriquí Viejo is being threatened by a series of dams for a hydroelectric project, but for now it's a pristine river and a lot of fun to ride. There are tamer floats, too, such as the **Esti River,** a Class II, that are perfect for younger rafters, families, and beginners. What's special about the Chiriquí area is that relatively few paddlers have discovered it, so rafters and kayakers have the river and enveloping lush mountain scenery full of birds and wildlife all to themselves. There are two local rafting companies in Boquete with years of experience and expert knowledge of the region (see contact details below); an option is to book with a tour operator that can put together multiday, multidestination, or instructional trips.

On the other side of the Talamanca, the Guarumo River has family-friendly Class I and II rapids that descend into the Caribbean Sea at Bocas del Toro; only two lodges offer this excursion: **Tranquilo Bay** (p. 206) and **Casa Cayuco** (p. 205).

Closer to Panama City, you can go rafting on the Class II and Class III **Chagres River** with **Aventuras Panama** (see below), a 5-hour float through rainforest and past Emberá Indian villages (p. 100).

You'll find kayaks at many hotels and resorts that are located near the ocean, but multiday sea kayak trips have yet to take off in Panama except in the San Blas Archipelago (Kuna Yala), and even there it is a nascent industry, considering that any company that operates here must be granted permission by Kuna Indian chiefs.

Chiriquí River Rafting (www.panama-rafting.com; ℂ **6879-4382**) is owned and operated by Hector Sánchez, who has been rafting this region for more than 3 decades. Hector and his professional crew offer year-round half- and full-day rafting excursions around the Chiriquí, both for die-hards and families seeking an easy, fun float. Packages include lodging at the El Bajareque coffee plantation.

Boquete Outdoor Adventures (www.boqueteoutdooradventures.com; ℂ **720-2284**) is a young, American-owned company offering rafting and kayaking on the many rivers in the Chiriquí Islands, as well as excursions to Isla Coiba and Boca Brava. The crew is professional and enthusiastic, and many day trips are family- and kid-friendly.

Aventuras Panama (www.aventuraspanama.com; ℂ **6679-4404** or 800/614-7214 in the U.S.) is one of Panama's top rafting and kayaking tour

---

Se Habla Espanõl: Language Classes

Brush up on your high-school Spanish or sign up for extended lessons as part of a long-term stay with a language class in Panama. **Spanish Panama** (www.spanishpanama.com; ℂ **213-3121**), in Panama City, is Canadian directed with certified bilingual professors and offers a range of private and group classes, as well as month-long programs. Spanish Panama can set up homestays with local families as well. Classes begin at $260 per week. **Spanish Abroad, Inc.** (www.spanishabroad.com; ℂ **888/722-7623**) and **EPA!** (www.studyspanishinpanama.com; ℂ **391-4044**), both in Panama City, offer a range of classes and month-long programs, some of which include homestays. **Spanish-by-the-Sea** (www.spanishatlocations.com; ℂ **757-9518**) has inexpensive group classes in Bocas del Toro that run from $150 to $300 per week (20 hr.); private customized courses are also available. Spanish-by-the-Sea can also pair classes with open-water dive certification.

companies, offering rafting trips close to Panama City on the Chagres River and the Mamoni River (Class II–Class IV), as well as multiday trips to the Chiriquí Highlands and 5-day sea kayaking trips in the San Blas.

MOTORCYCLING

Motorcyclists with their own bikes should know that the lion's share of Panama roads are twisty-curvy, with the exception of the Pan American Highway. Also, most roads off this highway are peppered with potholes, and it is common to see farm animals blocking or sharing the road. The company **Moto Tour Panama** (www.mototourpanama.com; © 264-8515) offers 1-, 2-, 5-, and 8-day Panama motorcycle tours on BMW bikes. Tours are offered year-round and include stays at four-star (and up) hotels and cost $150 to $2,200 (rider) and $150 to $1,260 (passenger).

SPAS

Panama has no "destination" spas, but most resorts and a couple of upscale hotels have top-of-the-line spas, or at the very least provide services such as massages, a gym, a sauna, and sometimes a steam room. I don't foresee a huge boom in this market, in spite of its rapid growth worldwide, but a few hotel owners are slowly catching on to this hot trend.

The **InterContinental Playa Bonita Resort & Spa** (www.ichotelsgroup. com; © 211-8600) is located on the Pacific, just a 30-minute drive from Panama City. This plush beach resort has a sybaritic spa facility with all the trimmings; services are booked individually or as part of a package that combines fruit- and chocolate-infused skin treatments, massage, aromatherapy, and body wraps.

Decapolis Radisson (www.radisson.com; © 215-5000), a sleek, trendy hotel, has the **Aqua Spa,** one of the top spas in Panama City in terms of service and hip decor, and you don't have to be a guest to book an appointment. It offers a full range of treatments and a stylish beauty parlor for one-stop makeovers.

Veneto Hotel & Casino (www.venetocasino.com; © 340-8888) has a building facade that screams Las Vegas, but inside it's as elegant as can be, and the **Veneto Spa** is a calm oasis that opens out onto a rooftop swimming pool. This is the spa with the widest range of treatments (Vichy-style), including hot stone massage, mud baths, aromatherapy, hydrotherapy, and facials.

Gamboa Rainforest Resort (www.gamboaresort.com; © 314-9000) is the best-known spa in Panama. The topnotch service, along with the recently renovated premises, make this one of the best spas in Panama. Expect traditional massages, body scrubs, and facials. If you're not staying at the resort, you can visit the spa anyway and combine it with a bike ride and lunch.

Los Quetzales Ecolodge & Spa (www.losquetzales.com; © 771-2291) is a slight misnomer—there is a "spa" building here, but it is small and services are not up to snuff. Massage rooms are shared, for example, unless you throw down extra cash for a private room. There is a sauna, and the spa center is backed by forest and a rushing river, but the center is more a lodge amenity than a spa destination.

Los Mandarinos Boutique Spa and Hotel (www.losmandarinos.com; ✆ **983-6645**) offers one of the nicer spas in Panama. Though the spa area is small, it offers a range of facials, massages, and body treatments, in addition to a thermal circuit including a sauna, Turkish bath, bio-thermal shower, and Jacuzzi. The spa is open to nonguests by appointment. **Yogini Spa** (www.yoguini.com/en/spa; ✆ **832-2430**) also offers full spa services in a more casual, laidback setting.

Haven Spa (www.boquetespa.com; ✆ **730-9345**) is a sprawling, recently opened Boquete spa offering every service you can imagine, from a high-tech sauna and Turkish bath to relaxing massages. Plus, there are exercise classes, a pool, and half a dozen guest rooms for those looking for a relaxing few days. Haven Spa is definitely one of the nicest spas in Panama.

The **JW Marriott Panama** (www.marriott.com/hotels/travel/ptyjw-jw-marriott-panama-golf-and-beach-resort; ✆ **507/908-3333**) in the Buenaventura complex on the Pacific Coast has a high-end spa with massage rooms, a Turkish bath, a sauna, and more. This elegant spa is one of the better hotel spas in Panama, and the staff is particularly warm and inviting.

SURFING

The powerful swells and hollow reef breaks off the Pacific and Caribbean coasts make Panama *the* destination for a surfin' safari. The water's warm, the waves are uncrowded, and surfing here is consistent year-round, with the largest swells between April and October in the Pacific, and December to March in the Caribbean. If you're a beginner or need tips on technique, a couple of camps specialize in surfing instruction.

Bocas del Toro is often compared to Tahiti or Hawaii for its huge swells— from December to March, and June and July—and monster waves such as **Dumpers** and **Silverbacks,** the latter a right-hand, reef-bottom point break comparable to the Backdoor Pipeline in Oahu. Waves in Bocas range between 1.2 and 7.6m (4–25 ft.), and can be powerful beach breaks, big waves, reef point breaks, and spitting tubes. **Isla Grande** has powerful reef breaks and is a good bet if you want to surf the Caribbean but don't want to go as far as Bocas.

In the Chiriquí Gulf, the surf meccas are at **Morro Negrito** (see below), and **Santa Catalina,** internationally renowned among surfers and located straight across the bay from Isla Coiba in the Pacific. Santa Catalina is a scruffy town, but the surfing is epic, with a consistent easy-to-line-up, rock-bottom point break that averages 1.5 to 6.1m (5–20 ft.). Farther east on the Azuero Peninsula are **Cambutal, Punta Negra, Dinosaurios,** and **Horcones,** other reliable spots for consistent breaks, including beach, point, and reef-bottom breaks that are sometimes even better than at Santa Catalina and less crowded. The up-and-coming **Playa Venado,** near Pedasí, is a long beach break with lefts and rights and swells that can be as little as 1.5m (5 ft.) or as high as 4.6m (15 ft.), though resort developments there have altered the breaks somewhat. The Pacific beaches that lie between 1 and 2 hours from Panama City are beach breaks and point breaks.

If you just don't want to waste time planning your surf trip, or if you want a local's insider information on the best breaks, check **Panama Surf Tours** (www.panamasurftours.com; ✆ **6671-7777**), a respected company with flexible 1- and 5- to 8-day tours that run from economical to luxury. Be sure to check out the smaller, regional surf schools and tours in the Central Panama and Bocas del Toro chapters.

Morro Negrito Surf Camp (www.morronegrito.travel; ✆ **760/632-8014** in the U.S.) is located in an out-of-the-way region of the Chiriquí Gulf, about halfway between Santiago and David on an island 3.2km (2 miles) off the coast. Guests are limited to 25, and with 10 different breaks (averaging 1.2–2.4m/ 4–8 ft.), you've pretty much got the whole wave to yourself here. Accommodations are one step above camping—the focus here is on waves, not luxury lodging. The camp has surf guides and lessons.

Río Mar Surf Camp (www.riomarsurf.com; ✆ **345-4010** or 6516-5031) is just 1½ hours from Panama City, near San Carlos on the Pacific Coast. The camp has simple rooms (most with A/C) that can accommodate three guests, and surf lessons can be booked on an hourly basis. It's a good spot in which to brush up on your technique when you don't have much time in Panama.

Bocas Surf School (www.bocassurfschool.com; ✆ **757-9057**) offers a variety of beginner, intermediate, and advanced surfing courses. The school operates out of an over-the-water hostel, where participants can stay in dorm beds or a private room.

YACHTING & SAILING

Panama Yacht Adventures (www.panamayachtadventures.com; ✆ **263-2673**) specializes in luxury yacht charters. The company has more than a dozen boats of different sizes and also offers other activities such as parasailing, diving, sports fishing, and canal transits.

San Blas Sailing (www.sanblassailing.com; ✆ **314-1800**), a French company, has a fleet of sailboats based in the San Blas Archipelago, offering 4- to 14-night all-inclusive adventures sailing around the islands, snorkeling, kayaking, and visiting Kuna villages.

Panama Sailing Tours (www.panamasailingtours.com; ✆ **831-1626**) offers guests a variety of multiple-day sailing classes, plus day trips to the Pearl Islands or Taboga. The company operates from the Amador Causeway in Panama City and also charters yachts for those who'd rather let someone else do the steering.

Colombia Panama Sailing (www.colombiapanamasailing.com; ✆ **310/ 521-8709**) organizes passengers on sailboats and catamarans sailing between San Blas, Panama, and Cartagena, Colombia.

YOGA

Sansara Surf & Yoga Retreat (www.sansararesort.com; ℰ 6243-5705) in Cambutal on the Azuero Peninsula offers yoga with additional options for surf lessons and spa treatments. Retreats can run for a few days to a full week and often fill up well in advance. **Sailing Yoga** (www.sailingyoga.com; ℰ 6144-3632) is a program in the San Blas Islands aboard the *Carpe Diem,* a 13m (42-ft.) yacht. Although the boat can be chartered privately, weeklong yoga retreats are held about once per month, with classes mostly held on remote islands in the archipelago.

Panama Canal Trips

Visiting the Panama Canal doesn't mean you are limited to the visitor center at the Miraflores Locks. Dozens of tour operators offer a variety of activities centered on the canal, from full and partial transits to fishing on Gatún Lake and wildlife-watching in the surrounding jungle:

o **Ancon Expeditions** (www.anconexpeditions.com; ℰ 269-9415): Ancon offers full and partial transits of the canal from the Port of Balboa, where it has a passenger ferry. Ancon also offers rainforest boat trips on Gatún Lake, Embera village visits, and hikes and bird-watching trips along Pipeline Road.

o **Canal & Bay Tours** (www.canalandbaytours.com; ℰ 209-2009 or 209-2010): One of the original canal boat operators, Canal & Bay have two boats, the refurbished wooden *Isla Morada,* with a capacity for 100, or the steel *Fantasía del Mar,* with room for 500 passengers.

o **Jungle Land Explorers** (www.junglelandpanama.com; ℰ 209-5657): Offering a motorboat tour of Gatún Lake and a stop at their anchored, double-decker floating lodge, this tour group also leads kayaking trips across the canal and even *Survivor*-style corporate retreats.

o **Panama Canal Fishing** (www.panamacanalfishing.com; ℰ 315-1905): Run by Panamanian–American Richard Cahill, Panama Canal Fishing has a 5.5m (18-ft.) boat with a 115-horsepower motor for trips to Gatún Lake as well as the Bayano River to fish for peacock bass.

o The **Panama Canal Railway** (www.panarail.com; ℰ 317-6070): The railway runs between Panama City and Colón, flanking the canal. It's a good alternative to driving between the two cities, giving you a chance to view the canal from a different angle.

o **Panama Marine Adventures** (www.pmatours.net; ℰ 226-8917): For those looking to spend some time on the water, Panama Marine Adventures offers a partial canal transit with a shuttle leaving from the Flamenco Resort and Marina on the Amador Causeway at 10am and going to its boat, *Pacific Queen,* docked at Gamboa.

o **Panama Pete Adventures** (www.panamapeteadventures.com; ℰ 888/726-6222): This long-running, reliable operator offers standard Panama Canal and nature tours, including combination boat and bus tours along the canal, as well as bird-watching, hiking, and Emberá village day tours.

RESPONSIBLE TOURISM

Responsible tourism is conscientious travel. It means taking care to maintain the preservation of the environments you explore and respecting the communities you visit. In a place like Panama, with such extremely high levels of natural and cultural diversity, this is particularly important.

Ecotourism

In 2015, the Panamanian government launched a strategy to develop sustainable ecotourism, which included an application for smartphones that directs tourists entering protected forest areas throughout the country. The program, known as the **Iniciativa Turismo Verde (Green Tourism Initiative),** is a joint venture of the Ministry of Environment, the Tourism Authority of Panama (ATP) and the National Institute of Culture (INAC). Known as **Ecotur Panama** (www.ecotour.gob.pa), the app works with Android and Apple-powered cell phones to provide comprehensive information about the country's protected wildlife areas, including maps and trail information. It also features an alert system that can be engaged in the event someone finds themselves lost in the woods.

The **International Ecotourism Society** (TIES; www.ecotourism.org) defines ecotourism as "responsible travel to natural areas that conserves the environment, sustains the well-being of the local people, and involves interpretation and education." TIES suggests that ecotourists follow these principles:

- Minimize environmental impact.
- Build environmental and cultural awareness and respect.
- Provide positive experiences for both visitors and hosts.
- Provide direct financial benefits for conservation and for local people.
- Raise sensitivity to host countries' political, environmental, and social climates.
- Support international human rights and labor agreements.

You can find tips for responsible travelers under "Get Involved" at the **TIES** website.

Ethical Tourism

Although much of the focus of ecotourism is about reducing impacts on the natural environment, ethical tourism concentrates on ways to preserve and enhance local economies and communities, regardless of location. You can embrace ethical tourism by staying at a locally owned hotel or shopping at a store that employs local workers and sells locally produced goods.

GENERAL RESOURCES FOR green TRAVEL

In addition to the resources listed above, the following websites provide valuable wide-ranging information on sustainable travel:

o **Carbonfund** (www.carbonfund. org), **TerraPass** (www.terrapass. org), and **Cool Climate** (http://coolclimate.berkeley.edu) provide info on "carbon offsetting," or offsetting the greenhouse gas emitted during flights.

o **Greenhotels** (www.greenhotels. com) recommends green-rated member hotels around the world that fulfill the company's stringent environmental requirements. **Environmentally Friendly Hotels** (www.environmentally friendlyhotels.com) offers more green accommodations ratings.

o For information on animal-friendly issues throughout the world, visit **Tread Lightly** (www.treadlightly. org). For information about the ethics of whale-watching, visit **Whale and Dolphin Conservation** (http://us.whales.org).

Responsible Travel (www.responsibletravel.com) is a great source of sustainable travel ideas; the site is run by a spokesperson for ethical tourism in the travel industry. **Sustainable Travel International** (www.sustainable travel.org) promotes ethical tourism practices and manages an extensive directory of sustainable properties and tour operators around the world.

In the U.K., **Tourism Concern** (www.tourismconcern.org.uk) works to reduce social and environmental problems connected to tourism. The **Association of Independent Tour Operators** (**AITO;** www.aito.com) is a group of specialist operators leading the field in making holidays sustainable.

Volunteer Travel

Volunteer travel has become increasingly popular among those who want to venture beyond the standard group-tour experience to learn languages, interact with locals, and make a positive difference while on vacation. Volunteer travel usually doesn't require special skills—just a willingness to work hard—and programs vary in length from days to weeks. Committing a day or two of volunteer work while you're on vacation is another popular option: On Bocas del Toro, for example, the **Red Frog Beach Resort** and the **Red Frog Foundation** (http://redfrogbeach.com/volunteer-in-panama) offer a number of short-term volunteer programs you can join during your vacation, including food distribution, sea turtle conservation, or beach cleanup.

Before you commit to a volunteer program, it's important to make sure any money you're giving is truly going back to the local community. **International Volunteer Programs Association** (**IVPA;** www.volunteerinternational.org) has a helpful list of IVPA-accredited programs and member organizations, as well as questions to ask to determine the intentions and the nature of a volunteer program.

ATMs ATMs, called *cajeros automáticos,* are widely available in banks and supermarkets, and are identifiable by a red SISTEMA CLAVE sign with a white key. Although ATMs are found primarily in larger towns, you can increasingly find them in of-the-way destinations. Still, if you are visiting remote destinations such as an offshore island, plan to bring extra cash. Remember that you can usually only take up to $500 a day out of an ATM in Panama, so if you need a larger sum of money, start withdrawing a few days in advance.

Business Hours Hours for service-oriented businesses in Panama are generally 8am to 1pm and 2 to 5pm on weekdays, and 8am to noon on Saturdays. Businesses in Panama City usually don't close for lunch. Shops open at 9 or 10am and close at 6 or 7pm; shopping malls close around 8pm. Many grocery stores are open 24 hours or from 8am to 8pm.

Car Rentals See "Getting Around," p. 229.

Drinking Laws Panama's legal drinking age is 18, though it is rarely enforced. Beer, wine, and liquor can be purchased at any supermarket or liquor store, although only until 11pm. If you're in Panama during an election, liquor sales are prohibited for a 72-hour period until voting is over.

Electricity Electrical plugs are the same as in the U.S., as is Panama's voltage, 110 AC.

Embassies & Consulates The **United States Embassy** is located in Panama City on Demetrio Basilio Lakas Avenue in Clayton (☎ **317-5000**). The **Canadian Embassy** is at Torres de las Americas Tower A, 11th floor, in Punta Pacifica (☎ **294-2500**). The **British Embassy** is at Calle 53 Este and Nicanor de Obarrio in Panama City, in the fourth floor of the Humboldt Tower (☎ **297-6550**). **Australia** and **New Zealand** do not have embassies or consulates in Panama; however, the British Embassy can provide consular assistance to citizens of those countries.

Emergencies For fire or an ambulance, dial ☎ **103;** for police, dial ☎ **104.**

Etiquette & Customs Panama City professionals dress well in spite of the heat, meaning no flip-flops, shorts, or tank tops—so bring at least one nice outfit with you. Many better restaurants will not serve patrons in shorts, women included. In resort or beach areas, and in smaller towns with a large expat presence such as Boquete, casual wear is okay.

Panamanians usually greet each other with a light kiss on the right cheek, but they are accustomed to North American habits and most likely will greet you with a handshake if they know you're a gringo or if you are in a business environment. Punctuality is appreciated in business settings, but don't be surprised if your Panamanian guest shows up 30 or 45 minutes late for a dinner party. Many Panamanians do not like to be bothered on Sunday, so reconsider if calling on this day. In business settings, always begin a conversation with light talk before getting to the point. In contrast to North America, the do-it-yourself spirit is not very esteemed in Panama; rather, your ability to hire help to do it for you is what people value. Live-in and daily maids are very common in Panama, meaning as a guest you are not expected to make your bed or help out around the house. When entering a room, you are expected to greet everyone either individually or as a group.

In the San Blas Islands, Kuna Indians frequently request money to have their photo taken.

Gasoline (Petrol) Because Panama has no petroleum distilleries, gas is usually slightly more expensive than in the U.S. In more remote locations, such as Bocas del Toro and the Kuna Yala islands, gas can cost almost twice as much. Taxes are already included in the printed price. One Panama gallon equals 3.8 liters or .83 imperial gallons.

Health Travelers in Panama should have no problem staying healthy—standards of hygiene are high, and tap water is safe to drink in most areas. The most likely ailment you'll face in Panama is traveler's diarrhea from unfamiliar foods or drinks. Even though the water in Panama is perfectly safe to drink almost everywhere, travelers with very delicate stomachs may want to stick to bottled water. Also, those with delicate stomachs may want to stick to moderate and high-end restaurants, and avoid raw vegetables and peeled fruit.

Aside from sunburn, the most common health problems that affect travelers in Panama are mosquito bites. If you're traveling to the tropical lowlands or jungle areas, be sure to pack plenty of bug repellent with a high percentage of DEET, especially if you'll be hiking or spending most of your time outdoors. Dengue fever is the last thing you want to ruin your trip. Also, if you're traveling in the Darién or other heavily forested area, bring light, long-sleeved clothing to avoid bug bites.

Insurance For travel overseas, most U.S. health plans (including Medicare and Medicaid) do not provide coverage, and the ones that do often require you to pay for services upfront and reimburse you only after you return home. As a safety net, you may want to buy travel medical insurance, particularly if you're visiting a remote or high-risk area where emergency evacuation might be necessary.

Internet Access Internet access is plentiful in Panama, except in more remote areas. Nearly every hotel in the country now has Wi-Fi and at least one computer with Internet access (usually in the hotel lobby or business center). Cafes and restaurants usually have a signal too. Internet cafes charge between $2 and $3 per hour, though as Wi-Fi becomes more common, these are disappearing fast.

Language Spanish is the official language in Panama, though English is widely spoken in the tourism industry, and many hotel owners are native English-speakers themselves. Panama's seven indigenous groups speak their own languages in their communities, and in some isolated areas indigenous groups do not speak Spanish fluently. On the Caribbean Coast, Creoles speak a patois called Guari-Guari or Wari-Wari, a mix of English, Spanish, and Ngöbe-Buglé.

LGBT Travelers Panama is far less conservative than most other Latin American countries. Panama City has a vibrant gay scene, and the influx of different nationalities around the country has generally moved local populations in the direction of wider acceptance. Still, pockets of discrimination still exist, even in places as cosmopolitan as Panama City. It's *unlikely* as a tourist that a gay couple would be openly harassed, though it's always a possibility.

Mail Panama has no stamp vending machines or post boxes, so you'll have to head to the post office to send a postcard, or ask your hotel if they can do it for you. A letter sent regular mail to the U.S. will arrive in 5 to 10 days; the cost, at press time, is 35¢ for a letter and 25¢ for a postcard. For quick service, send a package via a courier; see "Fast Facts: Panama City," in chapter 4, for the location of the main post office and details on express-mail services.

Money The unit of currency in Panama is the U.S. dollar, but the Panamanian balboa, which is pegged to the dollar at a 1:1 ratio, also circulates in denominations of 5¢, 10¢, 25¢, and 50¢ coins. (U.S. coins are in circulation as well.) Balboa coins are sized similarly to their U.S. counterparts, and travelers will have no trouble identifying their value. Travelers with pounds or euros may exchange money at Banco Nacional, which has branches in the airport and across the nation. To save time, you may want to convert your money into dollars before arriving at Panama.

Pharmacies There are numerous reliable pharmacies in Panama, one of the largest chains being Farmacias Arrocha, found in most large cities; check the website (www.arrocha.com) for the nearest location. Headache, anti-diarrheal, and other common over-the-counter (OTC) medications are readily available at all pharmacies. Many prescription-only drugs in the U.S. are sold OTC in pharmacies.

Police For police, dial ✆ **104.**

Safety Panama is one of the safest countries in Latin America. That said, there are always general precautions to take. In large urban areas, such as Panama City or Colón, use common sense, especially in neighborhoods off the tourist path. Don't flash expensive cameras and jewelry, and don't keep your wallet in your back pocket. Avoid taking money out of ATMs at night, especially in dark areas. As anywhere, there might be the occasional purse or cellphone snatching, but it's not frequent.

While hiking, keep an eye out for snakes, such as boa constrictors and fer-de-lances, though on the whole, snakebites are rare. If you encounter a snake, don't panic or make any sudden movements, and don't try to handle the snake. Also, avoid swimming in rivers unless you know it is safe or are with a guide who can vouch for the river's safety. Caimans and crocodiles hide along shorelines, especially in mangrove swamps and river mouths.

Panama law requires that foreigners carry their passport with them at all times,

though it's rarely asked for unless you are pulled over in a car. If you don't want to risk losing it, carry a photocopy of only the opening pages and entrance stamp or tourist card.

Senior Travel Panama is one of the hottest retirement destinations in the world, and most Panama hotels and businesses offer discounts of up to 40% for seniors 60 and older (age varies from business to business). Some claim the discount is for Panamanian seniors and foreigners with a residential visa only; nevertheless, it doesn't hurt to request senior rates or discounts when booking.

Smoking In 2008, a countryside smoking ban made it illegal to smoke in offices, restaurants, bars, and dance clubs, so smokers will have to take it outside. Smoking isn't even allowed within outdoor dining areas or balconies.

Taxes All hotels charge 10% tax. Restaurants charge 5% on the total cost of the bill and often sneak in an automatic 10% for service.

Telephones Panama has a seven-digit phone numbering system, and no city or area codes. The country code for Panama is 507, which you use only when dialing from outside the country. Cellphones are prefixed by 6; in this book, telephone numbers include this prefix because most businesses' published phone numbers include the prefix. If you need operator

assistance when making a call, dial ✆ **106.**

If you have Web access while traveling, consider a broadband-based telephone service (in technical terms, **Voice-Over Internet Protocol,** or **VoIP**), such as Skype (www.skype.com), which allows you to make free or inexpensive international calls from your laptop or in a cybercafe.

Time Zone Panama is 5 hours behind Greenwich Mean Time (GMT) and 1 hour ahead of Costa Rica. Panama does not observe daylight saving, so from the first Sunday in November to the second Sunday in March, the time in Panama is the same as that in the U.S. Eastern Time Zone (New York, Miami, and others); from mid-March to early November, it's the same as that in the U.S. Central Time Zone (Chicago, Houston, and others).

Tipping Tipping in Panama at restaurants is 10%, and restaurants will often sneak in an automatic 10% for service—so check your bill carefully to avoid overtipping. Taxi drivers do not expect tips, but you might consider it if you've rented a taxi for the day. Porters and bellhops should be tipped $2 to $5 depending on the caliber of the hotel.

Toilets Most bathrooms in Panama have a standard Western toilet, although in some remote rural areas you might find the occasional outhouse. Outside of some large hotels, you are expected to throw the paper in a small trash bin beside the toilet, rather than flushing.

Useful Phone Numbers
U.S. Dept. of State Travel Advisory: ☎ 202/647-5225 (staffed 24 hr.); **U.S. Passport Agency:**

☎ 202/647-0518; **U.S. Centers for Disease Control International Traveler's Hot Line:** ☎ 404/332-4559.

Visas/Passports See "Entry Requirements," earlier in this chapter.

Water The water in most of Panama's major cities and

tourist destinations is safe to drink, except in Bocas del Toro. Many travelers' stomachs react adversely to water in foreign countries, however, so it might be a good idea to drink bottled water outside of major hotels and restaurants.

GLOSSARY OF SPANISH TERMS & PHRASES

The official language of Panama is Spanish. However, with so many new hotel owners hailing from the U.S. and Canada, English is widely spoken in the tour industry. But this doesn't get you off the hook—taxi drivers, waiters, local tour guides, and everyday Panamanians speak little or no English. Arm yourself with basic words and phrases in Spanish and your trip won't be a constant battle to make yourself understood. Panamanians appreciate the effort, and really, part of the fun of traveling is learning the local lingo. Due to the long U.S. presence in Panama, you'll hear a few expressions that have been adapted from English, such as "parkear," meaning to park, or "watchiman," for security guard (watchman).

Panamanians speak at a relatively relaxed speed, and they have a more neutral accent when compared with their Latin American neighbors. Panamanians speaking in a slangy manner have a tendency to drop the "d" from words that end in -*ido* or -*ado,* as in *pelao,* instead of *pelado.* Like most Latin Americans, Panamanians are more conscious of salutations. Before launching into conversation or asking a question, do not forget a greeting such as "Buenos días" or "Buenas tardes," or as most Panamanians say, simply "Buenas."

BASIC WORDS & PHRASES

English	Spanish	Pronunciation
Hello	Buenos días	**bweh-nohss dee-ahss**
How are you?	¿Cómo está usted?	**koh-moh ehss-tah oo-stehd**
Very well	Muy bien	**mwee byehn**
Thank you	Gracias	**grah-syahss**
Good-bye	Adiós	**ad-dyohss**
Please	Por favor	**pohr fah-vohr**
Yes	Sí	**see**
No	No	**noh**
Excuse me (to get by someone)	Perdóneme	**pehr-doh-neh-meh**

English	Spanish	Pronunciation
Excuse me (to begin a question)	Disculpe	dees-*kool*-peh
Give me	Deme	*deh*-meh
Where is . . . ?	¿Dónde está . . . ?	*dohn*-deh ehss-*tah*
the station	la estación	la ehss-*tah*-syohn
the bus stop	la parada	la pah-*rah*-dah
a hotel	un hotel	oon oh-*tehl*
a restaurant	un restaurante	oon res-tow-*rahn*-teh
the toilet	el baño	el *bah*-nyo
To the right	A la derecha	ah lah deh-*reh*-chah
To the left	A la izquierda	ah lah ees-*kyehr*-dah
Straight ahead	Adelante	ah-deh-*lahn*-teh
I would like . . .	Quiero . . .	*kyeh*-roh
to eat	comer	ko-*mehr*
a room	una habitación	oo-nah ah-bee-tah-*syohn*
How much is it?	¿Cuánto?	*kwahn*-toh
The check	La cuenta	la *kwen*-tah
When?	¿Cuándo?	*kwan*-doh
What?	¿Qué?	keh
Yesterday	Ayer	ah-*yehr*
Today	Hoy	oy
Tomorrow	Mañana	mah-*nyah*-nah
Breakfast	Desayuno	deh-sah-*yoo*-noh
Lunch	Comida	coh-*mee*-dah
Dinner	Cena	*seh*-nah
Do you speak English?	¿Habla usted inglés?	*ah*-blah oo-*stehd* een-*glehss*
I don't understand Spanish very well.	No (lo) entiendo muy bien el español.	noh (loh) ehn-*tyehn*-do mwee byehn el ehss-pah-*nyohl*

NUMBERS

1	**Uno**	*oo*-noh
2	**Dos**	dohss
3	**Tres**	trehss
4	**Cuatro**	*kwah*-troh
5	**Cinco**	*seen*-koh
6	**Seis**	sayss
7	**Siete**	*syeh*-teh
8	**Ocho**	*oh*-choh
9	**Nueve**	*nweh*-beh
10	**Diez**	dyehss

Monday	**Lunes**	*loo*-nehss
Tuesday	**Martes**	*mahr*-tehss
Wednesday	**Miércoles**	*myehr*-koh-lehss
Thursday	**Jueves**	*wheh*-behss
Friday	**Viernes**	*byehr*-nehss
Saturday	**Sábado**	*sah*-bah-doh
Sunday	**Domingo**	doh-*meen*-goh

SOME TYPICAL PANAMANIAN WORDS & PHRASES

A la orden   You're welcome.

Bien cuidado   A homeless person or beggar. Means "well taken care of," and refers to what such a person says when seeking a tip for having watched a parked car.

Blanco   Cigarette.

Bomba   Gas station.

Buay   Boy, adapted from English.

Buco   A lot, from the French "beaucoup."

Buenón/buenote   A handsome man.

Casa bruja   A cheap home made of scraps and usually built illegally on taken land.

Chinito   Corner store or small market, so-called because they are usually owned by Chinese descendants.

Cholo   Villager or country bumpkin.

¡Chuleta!   Interjection, akin to "Oh my God!" or "Shoot!"

Con mucho gusto   With pleasure.

Diablo Rojo   Red Devil, name for the old school buses used for public transportation.

Fría   Slang for beer.

Fulo/a   Blonde.

Gallo   Distasteful, tacky, awful.

Goma   Hangover.

Guaro   Hard alcohol.

Guial   Girl, adapted from English.

Ir por fuera   To leave. "*Voy por fuera*" means "I'm leaving."

La "U"   University.

Maleante   Gang member or low-class male.

Mami/Papi   Commonly used to address a stranger with friendly affection, or used to describe an attractive woman or man.

Palo   One dollar or one balboa, as in "It costs 10 *palos*."

Pebre   Food.

Pelado   Young boy, usually pronounced *pelao*.

Policia muerto   Speed bump, means "dead policeman."

Push-button   A pay-by-the-hour motel, adapted from motels that attracted U.S. military personnel and had signs saying "Push the button to shut the door."

Priti   Pretty, but can also be used to describe something nice.

Rabiblanco/a   Term for a member of the elite, usually Caucasian. Translated, the term means "white tailed."

Racataca   A low-class, tacky woman.

Refresco   Soft drink.

Tongo   Slang for police officer.

Vaina   Thing or object.

Washington   A dollar.

Yeye   Wealthy show-off.

MENU TERMS

FISH

Almejas   Clams

Atún   Tuna

Bacalao   Cod

Calamares   Squid

Camarones   Shrimp

Cangrejo   Crab

Ceviche   Marinated seafood salad

Corvina   Sea bass

Dorado   Dolphin or mahimahi

Langosta   Lobster

Langostina   Jumbo shrimp

Lenguado   Sole

Ostras   Oysters

Pargo   Red Snapper

Pulpo   Octopus

Trucha   Trout

MEATS

Bistec   Beefsteak

Cordero   Lamb

Costillas   Ribs

Jamón   Ham

Pavo   Turkey

Pollo   Chicken

Puerco   Pork

Tasajo   Gooey smoked beef

VEGETABLES

Aceitunas   Olives

Ensalada   Salad

Lechuga   Lettuce

Ñamé   Starchy root vegetable

Papa   Potato

Tomate   Tomato

Yuca   Cassava or manioc

FRUIT

Fresa   Strawberry

Guayaba   Guava

Manzana   Apple

Maracuyá   Passionfruit

Marañyón   Cashew nut fruit

Naranja   Orange

Piña   Pineapple

Plátano   Plantain

Sandía   Watermelon

BASICS

Aceite   Oil

Ajo   Garlic

Azúcar   Sugar

Bollos   Corn patties filled with chicken or coconut

Chicha   Fruit juice

Chicheme   Sweet and hearty corn drink

Empanada   Crunchy cornmeal pastry filled with meat

Emparedado   Sandwich

Frito   Fried

Gallo   Corn tortilla topped with meat or chicken

Gallo pinto   Rice and bean soup

Hielo   Ice

Limón   Lemon

Mantequilla   Butter

Miel   Honey

Mostaza   Mustard

Pan   Bread

Patacones   Pounded and fried green plantains

Pimienta   Pepper

Queso   Cheese

Sal   Salt

Sancocho   Chicken stew

Tamale   Filled cornmeal pastry

Tortilla   Flat corn pancake

Index

Restaurants

Photo Credits

ISBN 978-1-62887-254-5 (paper), 978-1-62887-255-2 (ebk)

Editorial Director: Pauline Frommer
Editor: Alexis Lipsitz Flippin
Production Editor: Michael Brumitt
Cartographer: Liz Puhl
Photo Editor: Helen Stallion
Cover Design: Howard Grossman

For information on our other products or services, see www.frommers.com.

FrommerMedia LLC also publishes its books in a variety of electronic formats. Some content that appears in print may not be available in electronic formats.

Manufactured in the United States of America

5 4 3 2 1

ABOUT THE AUTHOR

Food and travel writer **Nicholas Gill** lives in Lima, Peru, and Brooklyn, New York. His work appears in the *New York Times*, *Wall Street Journal*, *Fool*, *New York Magazine*, and *Roads & Kingdoms*, among others. He is the co-founder of Newworlder.com, a website dedicated to exploring food and travel in the Americas.

ABOUT THE FROMMER TRAVEL GUIDES

For most of the past 50 years, Frommer's has been the leading series of travel guides in North America, accounting for as many as 24% of all guidebooks sold. I think I know why.

Though we hope our books are entertaining, we nevertheless deal with travel in a serious fashion. Our guidebooks have never looked on such journeys as a mere recreation, but as a far more important human function, a time of learning and introspection, an essential part of a civilized life. We stress the culture, lifestyle, history, and beliefs of the destinations we cover, and urge our readers to seek out people and new ideas as the chief rewards of travel.

We have never shied from controversy. We have, from the beginning, encouraged our authors to be intensely judgmental, critical—both pro and con—in their comments, and wholly independent. Our only clients are our readers, and we have triggered the ire of countless prominent sorts, from a tourist newspaper we called "practically worthless" (it unsuccessfully sued us) to the many rip-offs we've condemned.

And because we believe that travel should be available to everyone regardless of their incomes, we have always been cost-conscious at every level of expenditure. Though we have broadened our recommendations beyond the budget category, we insist that every lodging we include be sensibly priced. We use every form of media to assist our readers, and are particularly proud of our feisty daily website, the award-winning Frommers.com.

I have high hopes for the future of Frommer's. May these guidebooks, in all the years ahead, continue to reflect the joy of travel and the freedom that travel represents. May they always pursue a cost-conscious path, so that people of all incomes can enjoy the rewards of travel. And may they create, for both the traveler and the persons among whom we travel, a community of friends, where all human beings live in harmony and peace.

Arthur Frommer